KING ARTHUR

KING
ARTHUR

NORMA LORRE
GOODRICH

PERENNIAL LIBRARY

Harper & Row, Publishers, New York
Grand Rapids, Philadelphia, St. Louis, San Francisco
London, Singapore, Sydney, Tokyo, Toronto

First PERENNIAL LIBRARY edition published 1989.

LIBRARY OF CONGRESS CATALOG CARD NUMBER: 85-22558

ISBN: 0-06-097182-7

94 95   RRD   20 19 18 17 16 15 14 13 12

CONTENTS

Illustrative Material

To John Hereford Howard

whose knowledge of air, land, and sea, of armies, battles,
and aerial reconnaissance, of ships, bridges, and harbors
proved invaluable, and who drove the roads, walked
the walls, and climbed the hill forts, checking each site,
seeking indefatigably to know.

ACKNOWLEDGMENTS

The author wishes to thank the many libraries in Britain, France, and the United States that have extended their facilities over the past years, but especially those which have lent rare books and permitted microfilming: the Butler Library of Columbia University, the British Museum, the Bibliothèque Nationale, the Catholic University of America, the University of Pennsylvania, and the Cleveland Public Library. Particular thanks are offered here to the librarians of the Denison and Honnold Libraries of the Claremont Colleges, for their many services and advice, searches, and generous acquisitions of medieval materials for my use.

The author wishes to thank correspondents at Edinburgh, Penrith, Carlisle, and Glastonbury, at the Bodleian, and at the Universities of Cardiff, Glasgow, Cambridge, and North Wales. Warm thanks go to colleagues, the historian James W. Gould, and the Professors Emeriti Neal H. Brogden and Ralph Ross. Special debts are owed fellow teachers in medieval humanities: Professor Bradford B. Blaine for his lectures on medieval history, for his gifts of books and maps, and for his kind counsel; and also Professor of Art History Arthur D. Stevens and Professor of Medieval Music William Chris Lengefeld.

The author wishes to remember four early teachers and sponsors at the University of Vermont: Professors of English Frederick J. Tupper and George Lyman Kittredge and Professors of French Arthur B. Meyrick and the Reverend Jean De Forest.

Private thanks are offered to a childhood teacher, Aunt Alma Elsana Falby, for my first copy of *Idylls of the King*.

Many thanks to my typists, to my friend and student Dr. Joan Milliman, to Mrs. Carole Deane Gledhill, to Jo Corbett, and to my agent, Harold Schmidt.

I also wish to thank my editor, Elizabeth R. Hock, for her instant appreciation of *King Arthur*, for her calm authority during its preparation, and now for her friendship.

"If King Arthur did not live, he should have."

SIR WINSTON CHURCHILL

INTRODUCTION

ILLE ARTURUS: THE (GREAT) KING ARTHUR

1

The Lost King

Some fifteen years ago, on a Christmas Eve remarkable for its quiet, I made a discovery in an Old French text that set me inexorably upon my course: to answer the challenge thrown down to us by the writers and scholars of the Middle Ages and confront the mysteries surrounding King Arthur and his kingdom—and to solve them. Primary among my intentions was to offer the first historical proof of the existence of King Arthur.

Who was he? A manly man, a son, a brother, a husband, a father, an uncle? A sponsor of youths and a renowned warrior? A righter of wrongs and the ultimate authority in times of danger? An ideal leader who personified justice, law, order, and harmony? The defender of the Celtic realm and the savior of his country? The greatest and best of kings?

Or was he the stuff of literature and legend, the mythic native son with a magical kingdom who nevertheless suffered a queen turned adulterous and a great vassal become traitorous? Certainly no other hero of the Dark Ages figures so preeminently in such a vast body of world literature as does King Arthur. Who does not thrill to Sir Thomas Malory's account of the rise and fall of King Arthur's ancient Celtic realm? And who fails to be moved by Alfred Lord Tennyson's "coming" and "passing" of Arthur? From Germany and Scandinavia to Switzerland and France, from England and Wales to Scotland and Ireland, masters of Western literature have, with genius and ardor, claimed King Arthur for some corner of Britain or France.

Whatever King Arthur may have been, today he is considered largely a myth, a hazy shadow wrapped, as the Welsh bards put it, in the gray veil of concealment, staring out over the kingdom from the westward-facing cliff of Camelot.

Yet the mystery concerning King Arthur and his kingdom, the conse-
quent arcana of the discordant Lancelot, and the problem of the strange
Queen Guinevere linger to this day as the most vexing questions. Who was
King Arthur? Guinevere? Lancelot? Where were Camelot, Avalon, and the
Round Table? What was the Holy Grail?

The scholars of the Middle Ages were confronted by the same questions as
we are today. Having few resources and virtually no access to colleagues
and their work, however, they failed to reply convincingly to them. Given
their scanty libraries (more often, none at all); the lack of such disciplines
as history, anthropology, archaeology, and linguistics; and the paucity of
means of travel, one might well ask how they could possibly unwind any
thread that led all the way back to King Arthur's day. That day had been
swallowed up along with the Dark Ages. Many of them simply gave up and
in so doing let King Arthur and his world slip deeper and deeper into the
realm of mythology.

And yet, without benefit of a dictionary, these writers and scholars
hand copied, deciphered, pondered, and translated as best they could an
inordinately large number of manuscripts dealing with King Arthur, his kingdom, and his court. They were every bit as interested and as passionately
involved in their endeavor as we are in ours, and not a few of them devoted
their lives to it.

Today their mysteries are our mysteries. To solve them logically, it is
necessary to start with the earliest records and track them from century to
century and from text to text. It is time to clean house in Camelot.

Who was King Arthur, or Arturus? Why has this king of Britain not been
found? Where was his kingdom? Was there such a place as Camelot? Could
Lancelot and Guinevere have looked down from its height and seen the
funeral barge of the maiden floating past?

Avalon, the disappearing island in the stormiest waters of all Britain,
rises out of the texts too real and too beautiful. It seems a foregone conclusion that some medieval writers knew its location. One of them, a Cyprian
clerk, had in his possession a lost manuscript that had come to him from
the city of Carlisle in Britain. Though he was by then too old to undertake
a journey, no such limitations impede us. And there are other texts containing directions from Arthur's castle at Carlisle to the Grail Castle. Has no
one ever followed them? Carlisle, now on the M6 Freeway, is a big enough
target not to be missed—by the scholars of the Middle Ages, by the ancient

folk balladeers, or by us. The directions are clear, if intentionally incomplete. What king would provide detailed directions to his treasure house? And we know, from a reliable encyclopedist on the continent, that it was that: a "palace" magnificent, an enormous treasure in gold and a treasury, a king's ransom in art—set amidst a landscape of brooks and exotic tropical plants. Yet only one precious piece, his sword Excalibur, has turned up in the intervening centuries.

Some time ago, a distinguished linguist in Scotland figured out, by etymology alone, where King Arthur anchored or beached his fleet of ships. For centuries Arthur had been labeled a cavalryman—as if a king or anybody else could defend Britain with cavalry. Here as elsewhere, the science of linguistics comes to our aid as we try to make sense of the medieval texts and the medieval authors' attempts to translate medieval and Dark Age texts.

As for the Holy Grail, there is new evidence that makes it possible to draw some conclusions as to whether or not King Arthur was pagan. Because no one has known for sure what or where the Grail was, most scholars until now have argued that the Grail itself was imaginary. The manuscripts that bear on this have only recently been edited and are hard to come by, so few scholars have scrutinized them. Charges and countercharges have filled the air whenever the subject of the Grail was entertained. Thus I pose my question: Is it possible King Arthur was, as the earliest sources claimed, a Christian king? Here it will be necessary to consider the account of one of his religious services recently discovered in Germany and published in Scotland and then to compare it to the same service, with King Arthur as worshiper, in an Arthurian manuscript written during the High Middle Ages at Glastonbury Abbey in England. Also, that the Grail existed independently of King Arthur can now be proved.

And what about Guinevere, Arthur's gorgeous but supposedly immoral queen? Among the medieval writers there were misogynists who also happened to thrive on scandal and so branded Guinevere an adulteress. So busy were they tarring the royal couple and the warrior vassal Lancelot with their accusations that they never bothered to look at Guinevere's background, education, and rank. Surely all of these were unusual, since no one has known how to spell her name, not even the learned Geoffrey of Monmouth. And no one gave her credit for being a brave queen of ancient Britain.

Lancelot did not fare much better. Not only has no one learned to spell his name—the French translation is what we've been handed—but his parentage (painstakingly given in the texts), the place of his coronation, and his kingdom and its whereabouts were virtually ignored in favor of the allegations of adultery. Why are the conclusions concerning him, after such an illustrious career under King Arthur, so distressing? Further, if Lancelot were an epic hero, his story would have ended in his funeral celebration. How *did* he meet his end? And how did such an important person disappear from the texts or fade away in disgrace?

We no longer need to credit the nasty stories automatically. It is important to note that each author probably worked in solitude in a monastery or scriptorium, with only one text at his disposal (and that probably borrowed for a short time only). It can also be assumed that he or she—Marie de France is included here—was working under some instruction from the patron and purchaser of the material.

Furthermore, the medieval author who wrote six and more centuries after their deaths was not asked to subscribe to any affection for the Arthurian personages or for their world. Nor were the authors exclusively British or even working in Britain as they wrote. One was our intellectual ("clerc") in Cyprus, where he had been employed for 40 years. He is among the best of our sources, even though he was a tired 105 years old, as he confides to his readers, when his patroness, the Lady of Baruch, commissioned him.

Not much of the Arthurian literature that has come down to us spoke from a point of view favorable to King Arthur, his queen, or Lancelot. It seems likely that when Arthur passed on to his secure refuge, his fastness on the island of Avalon, he left the field to his foes. Lancelot and Gawain must already have been dead. Such conjectures have already been made but have not been developed.

Who told the tales, then? Those who survived. Those who inherited Arthur's kingdom: his foes at Camlan, that last great sorry battle in the west.

If those who survived the Battle of Camlan told the tales then did they also destroy the archives of King Arthur's reign? In fact, the lost archives were said to have surfaced in the twelfth century at Oxford, England, but there is reason to suspect that fragments also turned up at roughly the same time in the city of Troyes in France. Supposedly the earliest account of King Arthur stemmed from these fragmentary archives of his reign.

There are texts that say that Queen Guinevere had King Arthur's records under her care and in her keeping. It has become clear that the earliest versions of the Arthurian story are not fiction. Too many precisions as to geography, history, events, politics, customs, usages, places, roads, fords, and times are evident. Also, the early texts, written in the Middle Ages, are too annalistic in character to be fiction.

Other texts considered unusually reliable assure us that it was Merlin who acted as scribe and recorder of King Arthur's reign. Certainly the artistic representations of Merlin show him with a rolled scroll in one hand. But where are the annals? Were they suppressed and then, presumably, destroyed?

There have been documented cases of intentional concealment and cases of lost knowledge over the length of historical time, of course. The

stories of high dignitaries who have plotted to conceal and managed to ob-
literate even written evidence are legion.

We are sure of one thing: among the ancient kings of Britain, only
King Arthur is still popularly acclaimed with an affection bordering on veneration. And among ancient heroes, only he is loudly hailed far and wide as
a native son—from Brittany in France, to England, and then southwest into
Cornwall. But inherent in these claims is a major problem: they are not
based precisely upon history, but upon later literature that is clearly comical
and fictional.

The more intelligent authors employed in their treatments all the resources proper to great literature. But what does that mean to us? When
authors observed, for instance, that King Arthur's birth, pedigree, and childhood were shrouded in mystery, they were not daunted. They simply borrowed a page or two from the begetting and birthing of Hercules. What
more appropriate solution? As we know, they thought that Arthur had been
born in Tintagel Castle. They also knew, as did anyone who had studied
Ptolemy's original map of Britain in the ancient world, that Tintagel Castle
lies just south of Hartland Point on the coast of Cornwall, where in the days
of the Roman legions Hercules was worshiped. If these authors read, without questioning it, that Arthur as a "kid conqueror" in his teens drew the
sword from the stone, they let the same exploit of the youthful Theseus in
ancient Athens underlie their treatment. When they read that Arthur declared himself a Roman patrician on his father's side, they let him observe
the Roman taboo against death—by stepping down from his life, as the
Romans did, in his case passing away in order to "come again." When we
read such highly imaginative prose, infused with the learning of the great
schools of mythology of the Middle Ages, we understand all over again that
most great literature is doubled with mythology.

One contemporary of King Arthur, fortunately, provided corroboration and a date for the king: the year 500. He also gave King Arthur's career
and military rank and mentioned his twelve victories, especially that of Mount
Badon, which this witness knew because it was his own birthplace. He excoriated the kings of Britain who had in some way survived Camlan, and
who followed Arthur. Furthermore, an epic poem composed near Edinburgh
only a few decades after the death of Arthur saluted King Arthur's outstanding military prowess. A subsequent chronicler listed the twelve battles, particularly the great victory in the last one, which freed Britain from Saxon
incursions for some twenty years. Thus, it will behoove us to consult the
military historians of Britain.

Welsh scholars finally consented to release the principal part of the
ancient, secret bardic knowledge concerning the Welsh people and their
forebears in the north of ancient Britain, and twentieth-century scholarship

has benefited tremendously from the recent publication of these *Annals of Wales*. The yield is incomparable—ample and precise verification for the historical King Arthur.

Starting from a solid base in history, I have, for a number of precisions, turned to Roman maps, which are excellent and from which can be learned the names and emplacements of Roman roads and forts along their length. I wanted to determine, for example, how many days it took the smaller horses of Arthur's day to cross the country and from what centers each route began. From such calculations it will be possible to see how Lancelot arrived in the far north from his meeting with the sentries at what a French author called "the stony passage" and to follow the elusive Percival from one sponsor of his new manhood to the next—all way stations along the route to the Grail.

My real thrust is toward the Grail Castle, which cannot remain *terra incognita* as long as the islands of Britain remain on the Ordnance Survey maps.

A very close look at Percival will reveal the secret of the wounded Arthur's escape from the battlefield to his secluded fortress on Avalon. The identity of the queens who bore him away will become clear—most especially in the case of the Widow Lady of Camelot. No victor at the Battle of Camlan would have dared refuse or offend her. From a consideration of the relationships that bore on all of this can be deduced the reasons for action.

Until recently, much scholarship has been devoted to mythology for an identification for Arthur. Sir John Rhys and Sir Edmund K. Chambers, two of Britain's greatest Arthurian scholars, have thought of King Arthur as a native god, perhaps of the harvest. Whatever historical truth was held about Arthur seems to have slipped with him into the fog bank enveloping Avalon.

Little was heard of Arthur after 542, so presumably this is the date of his death. Historians in France, as early as the eighteenth century (the learned Turgot and Vérémond) have taught that King Arthur died during the reign of Justinian (483–565). In the absence of the Welsh annals, there were few— and scattered—references by historians. Significantly, however, youths of noble and royal birth began to bear the name *Arthur* after the year 542. A strange name, it has not been found prior to King Arthur, and its Latin version, *Arturus*, has never been found anywhere else. Thus, the name *Arthur* probably is derived from the lost king of the Dark Ages, or of prehistoric Britain.

Then without warning, in the year 1136 the best writers of the twelfth century apparently happened upon written materials containing mention of this ancient lost king, his queen, and his commander Lancelot. It has always been assumed that the first French writer of renown, Chrétien de Troyes, differed in his account from the first English writer (although he wrote in Latin), Geoffrey of Monmouth. We shall see that, in fact, each was using an annalistic source and that their sources did *not* differ, as was once thought.

Rivaling each other, writers by the score began hashing over the life of King Arthur, pro and con, certainly without agreeing whether or not Arthur was real (as Geoffrey of Monmouth had demonstrated). His followers at home and abroad cared little whether Arthur was dead or alive, real or mythical, good or evil, a once or future king. That he was good subject matter sufficed.

Almost at once the curtain of mystery descended around King Arthur again as piercing accusations of perjury were hurled at Geoffrey of Monmouth and charges of false witness and hack writing were flung back and forth by generations of monks and poets, abbots and courtiers, historians and bishops. The quarrels rang out to the far corners of medieval Europe, even causing riots in foreign streets. With attention focused on the disputes, the invaluable treasures—their written sources—disappeared. Kings and princes lost them at gaming tables, traded them during the Crusades, used them to pay their ransom, lost them on Cyprus, or gave them away, unmindful of their worth. Until now their loss has been considered irreparable. But the tools of modern scholarship enable us to work with what we have—the Arthurian corpus, perhaps the single largest body of literature in the world—and to glean from the second- and thirdhand texts written, for the most part, during the twelfth and thirteenth centuries, the archives we have lacked.

The lure of King Arthur began drawing tourists into Britain by the middle of the twelfth century. Monks and friars from every monastery on the continent, it would seem, swarmed over the terrain, particularly that of Cornwall. Everywhere in Britain sites bear the name of King Arthur; he is a point of national pride for the British. Yet some of these sites date from the second millennium B.C.! I, too, have loved clambering over the headlands at Tintagel, counting off the monoliths at Stonehenge, and peering out to sea from Merlin's Cave. I have tramped the farmer's pasture above the Golden Valley of Wales, even though the site called Arthur's Grave is plainly labeled neolithic, or New Stone Age. I have walked through the ruins at Glastonbury Abbey and gazed up at the Tor wondering whether Lancelot could have ridden his horse up its steep sides to pray at Guinevere's tomb. And I have come away from all of this with one response: not likely.

Much of it is simply ridiculous. Arthur was not a figure of the Middle Ages or of the Age of Chivalry, when knighthood was in flower. His 150 or so warriors were not gallant knights gaily bedight. He was not born at Tintagel Castle, which was not built until the age of stone castles, in the twelfth and thirteenth centuries. (In Arthur's day the site of Tintagel Castle may have been occupied by a Celtic monastery for hermits, however.) And the rest of the above-mentioned geography will have to go by the board, including Glastonbury (though it is an ancient and holy site), Bath, Dover, South Cadbury, Winchester, Salisbury, London, York, the Cornwall sites, and Brittany.

The legend has not been easy to counter; it has had centuries to swell and be embellished upon. In the hands of Sir Thomas Malory, who recounted the collapse of his own fifteenth century under the guise of a rise and fall of King Arthur's ancient Celtic realm, and Alfred Lord Tennyson, among others, Arthur's real life and deeds have been swept aloft into high tragedy.

Romances and modern comedies have served further to obscure the real Arthur from view; that he may have lived on this earth and reigned is, for many, not even a question. What a fate for someone who was for so long a renowned warrior, a defender of the Celtic realm, the greatest and best of kings. He was said to have been brave and powerful, valiant and resourceful, honorable and beloved—an ideal, just ruler. Historians used to think that he once ruled all Britain. Now they are more careful with their superlatives.

Historians still tell us that King Arthur successfully defended all Britain from invasion by sea. They had it on excellent authority that he halted the Saxon invaders for a considerable period of time and won all his engagements except the last one, in which he was fatally wounded. Very few scholars still insist that he fought in Cornwall or that he was born there, for the simple reason that the Saxons were not invading Cornwall during Arthur's lifetime. The Welsh have never claimed that he was born and raised in what is now Wales—much less that he came from Brittany, in that part of the continent which has been Celtic since the fifteenth century. Historians have wandered far and wide in ascribing some English city as the site of the battle and great victory of Mount Badon. They used to say that Badon was Bath, which is not exactly a mountain. They also used to say that Avalon was Glastonbury, which is not exactly an island in the middle of the sea! They used to think that Arthur must have landed on the coast of southern England, near Portland Bill, where the ancient Romans came ashore sometimes. Or that, as Malory had it, he came ashore at Dover where the Romans left a lighthouse. They sometimes put his forest of Brocéliande in Scotland, where ancient Ptolemy had put a little picture of the Caledonian Forest on his map, and where Geoffrey of Monmouth had also put Arthur's forest, so named. The French are still hunting for the forest of Brocéliande somewhere inside Celtic Brittany, but so far they haven't found a trace of it. Their problem seems to be that they think *Brocéliande* is a French name and not, as I will demonstrate, actually a poor translation from the original Celtic and British place name. The word *Brocéliande* merely gives us a fairly simple problem in phonetics.

Historians of the Anglo-Saxons say that Arthur could not have won his battles in England, because they know from the several manuscripts of the *Anglo-Saxon Chronicle* that the Saxons conquered England in King Arthur's lifetime and that it has been English territory ever since. Therefore, if Arthur fought a battle in "Salisbury," near "Winchester," the possibility that he did not fight at the Salisbury in southern England or at *that* Winchester either must be considered. And Malory was wrong to write "Westminster," referring to the city on the Thames River in London, for what the French text had called King Arthur's fortress, or "Snowdon West Castle." Meanwhile a historian at Winchester has denied categorically any connection between that ancient city and King Arthur. Nor does Winchester claim that its relic of a wooden table is *the* Round Table of King Arthur.

Many English historians became discouraged with the myths and mystifications of the Arthurian literature. Only a specialist of medieval languages can read the manuscripts in the original anyway, a task compounded in difficulty by the fact that one must figure out each writer's idiosyncratic style and vocabulary. There were neither grammar texts for Old French nor dictionaries in the Middle Ages. One was free to write as one liked—which complicates the reader's task no end.

Confronted with swan knights, tyrants, giants, dragons, and sword bridges, and weary of imputations of incest, adultery, and treachery, many historians must have willingly handed both King Arthur and his supposed kingdom back to the Old French writers of romances.

A good knowledge of medieval French is essential to the understanding of the manuscripts from the twelfth and thirteenth centuries, when Old French was also the official language of Britain. It will prove to be the key that opens the doors to discovery, that allows us to pierce not only the upper level of the texts but their hidden, secret language.

Another key lies in the approach. I have positioned Arthur as living in prehistoric Britain, of which there are virtually no extant records or chronology or annals. Thus, when it comes time to seek his probable birthplace, the search will be not for the ruins of a medieval castle but for a barely discernible castle mound of piled earth—a construction characteristic of the Dark Ages. We will think of Arthur as not in those territories which he could not have conquered but in those which the Saxons failed to overrun. We will forgo looking for him in Cornwall, or in England for that matter, or modern Wales, where his name does not appear in the regnal lists.

It will be necessary to focus on time, for when the wounded Arthur left the coast of Britain in 542 to be ferried to his hidden island for surgery or ancient burial practices, he brought the Dark Ages to a close. In that sense he was a last Roman, as historians have frequently observed, a last king of the ancient world. Recorded history began with his death. Arthur fell as Rome itself was falling. Eastern England had already submitted to Saxon rule; there an admirable, efficient new race of Saxon kings—who never succeeded for long in conquering Arthur's kingdom before or after his death—rose to the fore. They soon subscribed even more ardently than the older Celtic kings to King Arthur's legend. They were pleased by the thought, however erroneous, that he was buried in Glastonbury, a Saxon town.

The aforementioned purpose of my search for King Arthur was to solve several of the problems handed down through the ages and in stripping the legend to thereby present a fully authenticated portrait of the king and his kingdom. At its most exciting the search yielded the day when I opened an Ordnance Survey map and moved my finger to the spot where so many centuries ago the Grail Castle stood; at its most enchanting it offered the day, a year later, when my husband and I stepped from the punt onto the little island and saw before us the soft-colored orange ruins of later fortresses. Within minutes the sun disappeared behind rosy clouds and a deluge of driving rain obscured even our hands before our faces—just as the medieval manuscripts said happened daily on the Isle of Avalon in the middle of those dangerous, dark blue western waters.

But behind the desire to bring a lost Golden Age to light, there lies my strongly held belief that such discoveries are infinitely enriching, that they amount to more than just setting the record straight. From King Arthur—from his bravery and daring action, his charisma and dynamism, his dignity and his honorable life—we can draw renewed hope.

The time has come for the legend to take a back seat to the historical King Arthur, a superior king of the ancient world.

2

King Arthur's World

King Arthur lived in an unsettled world. Most people from that day seem to have remained silent about this overturning of their world unless, of course, later powerful persons destroyed more records than we have supposed. Silhouetted against an otherwise undocumented Dark Age, he is the one man who successfully opposed floods of invasion all his life, if not forever.

King Arthur seems to demonstrate the heroic theory of history, which holds that an individual can permanently alter the course of events. Local historians of Britain have studied and counted the names on gravestones and concluded that a very large area of that land remained Celtic, never having been settled by Anglo-Saxon immigrants even during the turbulent days of King Arthur. In this sense and to this degree he altered the course of history.

While no Greek historian of the caliber of Plutarch wrote a biographical essay about King Arthur, and no Roman studied Arthur's successes and failures as Suetonius did for *The Twelve Caesars*, Geoffrey of Monmouth did include King Arthur among the old, lost kings of Britain. It was the British Saint Gildas, a contemporary of King Arthur, who first testified to the historicity of Arthur. Arthur himself, it seems, was no writer, for unlike Julius Caesar, who daily dictated the results of his engagements in Britain and Gaul and sputtered about the quartering of his men, he left no account of his conquests. The annals of Arthur, supposedly drawn up by Merlin have all disappeared.

But we *can* place Arthur against the real world in which he moved. Excellent records were being kept across the Channel in Gaul, which was in the process of being named France as it made way for its invaders from the east. It acquired a new race of kings even before the Saxons finished moving into Britain. (The Saxons had been held up by King Arthur.) And down in Rome and Ravenna the Ostrogoths, though new barbarians and new conquerors, were fast transforming themselves into "Roman" emperors.

While the Franks and the Ostrogoths proudly represent the new men, King Arthur, in his position of "duke" of the Britons, like Romulus Augustulus as the last "Roman" emperor in Rome, represents older peoples in the process of being removed from the centers of wealth and power. The clash in Britain must have been more pronounced than that in Gaul, where the incoming Franks accepted the Latin tongue of the conquered natives and their Roman, Christian religion. In Britain, the native peoples clung tenaciously to their own speech, as they had during five hundred years of Roman occupation. Similarly, they clung to their own history and were said to have refused to convert the Anglo-Saxons to their own mysterious Celtic Christianity. Theirs was not yet a Roman Christianity. Even today we see separation; books from these centuries are divided into histories of the Welsh, of the Anglo-Saxons, and of the Scots.

We know that the search for King Arthur takes us back to the most obscure centuries of the Dark Ages. His realm illustrates the idea of lost knowledge. The fifth and sixth centuries waited at that crossroads in historical time when the ancient world was drawing to a chaotic close and the Middle Ages were embarking on a course that would end in even more turbulence. Before Arthur was born, Rome had suddenly been forced to abandon the empire. The Roman Legions were very quickly recalled from distant Britain. The ports, bridges, roads, and lighthouses, built and maintained by the Roman administration stood untended. The milecastles along Hadrian's Wall for a while became British garrisons but eventually were taken over by the local farmers (some of them are used today as pastures and barnyards). After a five-hundred-year military occupation by very efficient Romans, Britain fell into an interregnum. Now the vast, deserted Roman capitals of Britain were toured by the ladies of the local strongmen who marveled at the architecture of Carlisle and at its fountains and baths run dry and abandoned. Arthurian literature paints such a picture: Lancelot riding through a huge, empty Roman fortress.

As the native Celtic peoples recovered and began to move again and fight over the ruins and the spoils, paying some obedience to those noble Romans who had nowhere else to go and who therefore had stayed in Britain, the Saxon invasions began in earnest. There was virtually no one to stop the Vikings, immigrants, and land-hungry farmers from Scandinavia and the continent. The largest bloc of Anglo-Saxon colonizers clashed heavily with the native Celtic peoples. All struggled for footholds, livings, farmlands, and real estate. The only person to make a name for himself in all this turmoil was King Arthur. For that reason his role and his case seem unique in the history of the world.

Arthur's equal on the continent was the powerful King Clovis of the Franks, who is considered to have founded France. In Scandinavia his equal was the largely mythical Beowulf of the Geats, that long-distance swimmer who fought some sort of dragon, hopefully not one of the British Pendragons of Arthurian literature. Written records of the Frankish church report the eventual sainthoods of Clovis and his queen, Clothilde, but only the pseudohistory of the epic recounts the dreadful contemporary adventures of Brunhilde, of Kriemhilde, and of Theodoric of the Ostrogoths. Of Hrothgar's Queen Wealtheow in the *Beowulf* we know principally that she passed the cup to the warriors in the mead hall.

The puzzle of King Arthur's birth and kinship is tantalizing. Nothing definitive has yet been said concerning the kin of the king: three sisters perhaps, two fathers perhaps, three wives of the same name perhaps. His mother's story is a case in point because her lovers, Zeus and Amphitryon, come from Greek mythology. We never know her name for sure either, for authors stray from "Ygerne" to the German anagram of "Arnive."

In the twentieth century we have arrived at an understanding of the world around Arthur that should help break the stalemate in the matter of his origins. Somewhere in the welter of legend, witticisms, hostility toward women, enmity, nasty jokes, and prejudice, a truth can be found. Rather than lifting the veils that separated them from the strange world of the Dark Ages, earlier scholars and writers turned away from difficulties, refusing to admit the possibility that behind the nonsense lay odd, strange truths. When Geoffrey of Monmouth could not find an account of Arthur's birth, he gave him that of Hercules, for he knew that Hercules was once worshipped near Tintagel Castle, then under construction. When the Loathly Damsel triumphantly paraded on horseback, bearing the severed head of her enemy, scholars who had not studied anthropology shrugged. Surely royal damsels, wearing peacock feathers, did not act in this way. But severed heads decorated the walls of English cities well into the fifteenth century, at least. This practice reminds us of ancient totemism.

Arthur was born into a savage world. His Britain had nonetheless been for some five hundred years Roman and for some time a province of the Roman Empire, garrisoned by Roman Legions, and governed by Roman administrators. Now, Rome no longer occupied Britain and no longer accepted responsibility for its former province. Yet Arthur claimed descent from Romans, specifically from a Constantine who may have been the Emperor Constantine. We now know that Arthur was British on his mother's side. After such a long occupation and such a close relationship between Britain and Rome, many people treasured connections with Rome or thought of them-

selves in terms of that great empire. Its upheaval and transfer of power to
the Ostrogoths in Ravenna could not overnight dissolve ties that were hundreds
of years old.

Thus, one series of indications in the Arthurian texts, which lends
them authenticity, has to do with the vestiges of Roman rule in Britain.
Geoffrey of Monmouth's life of Arthur is written in Latin, as are the earlier
references to Arthur in the chronicles. His name, Arturus, is given in Latin
in these three passages. His father Uther Pendragon suffered a massive defeat at the Roman fort of Trimontium in Scotland. Arthur beat with his
hammer upon the stone walls built by the Romans. Lancelot crossed Hadrian's Wall near Carlisle after having overcome the sentries in one of the
milecastles. Traveling south via the Great Northern Road of the Romans
(Berwick to Edinburgh), he passed through the silent, deserted Roman fort
at Camelon. This adventure, and this static description in the text, struck
such chords of realism in authors that it remained in the late French translation and was not deleted from this last text.

Until about two hundred years before Arthur's birth Rome had struggled to maintain order in its British province by garrisoning it with one-third
of the entire military force of the Roman Empire. Even so, this staggering
number of trained troops could not keep the small island of what is now
Scotland, England, and Wales safe from invasions.

In the north the Sixth Legion remained stationed permanently in the
city of York, to ward off the Caledonian warriors from southeastern Scotland, who time and again breached Hadrian's Wall and descended into the
Yorkshire downs. North of York the ancient tribe of the Brigantes, who
once under their battle queen Boudicca had beaten the entire force of Rome
on the island of Britain, stirred continuously, beaten but unsubdued.

Grave danger to the Romans was also posed by Ireland and the western tribesmen or clansmen who had obliged the Roman governors to quarter
two entire Legions, the Twentieth and the Second Augustan, at Chester and
at Isca (the modern Caerleon in Wales). Wealthy Roman landowners had
not developed estates and great villas in these dangerous border areas. The
more northern wall of fortification, the Antonine Wall, which ran near the
modern Glasgow-Edinburgh Freeway, served little real military purpose, so
often was it breached. When breaching was not feasible, the Picts from
north of the Firth of Forth crossed that stretch of stormy water and landed
upon the south shore of the Firth, east of Edinburgh, thus swarming up the
sandy shore, having circumnavigated the Romans.

By the time of Arthur's birth, when the Roman troops had finally withdrawn completely and left the island without governors, certain large areas
of Britain still spoke only Celtic tongues. This is noteworthy when one considers the alacrity with which the Gauls in what is now France adopted the
Latin of their Roman conquerors as their own language, rolling it frontward

in their mouths in such a peculiar, characteristic fashion that it became the new, modern language of French. Even today, populations in these same un-Romanized areas of Britain—Cornwall, Wales, and Strathclyde—persistently retain their native Celtic stance and character.

As in Arthur's day, the largest of these properly Celtic populations still resides in the area called Strathclyde, a border area of what is northwestern England and the lowlands of southern Scotland. It includes all the ancient battlefields adjacent to both the Antonine and Hadrianic Walls, going on the northeast from the Firth of Forth to the southwestern part, the Solway Firth and the Rhinns of Galloway, where western Scotland almost touches Ireland. Modern road maps refer to much of this area as military, especially Stirling Castle, the road from Stirling via the south shore of Loch Lomond to Dumbarton on the Clyde River, and the Kershope Forest, which extends roughly between Carlisle and Edinburgh. Strathclyde also includes the wilderness areas of Cumberland and the Lake District. The Roman road from York passed westward through it to the last Roman capital city of Carlisle, where Hadrian's Wall ended in the massive Roman fortifications of Bowness on the south shore of the Solway Firth. The other branch went due north, into the Eastern March of Scotland, passing Hadrian's Wall at the Roman fort of Camelon. The logic before evidence is introduced seems tenable: this is conspicuously the only large area unconquered by the Anglo-Saxons. The Saxons in Arthur's day did conquer the area from York north to Berwick on the North Sea, including the medieval Saxon fortress now called Bamborough.

It seems logical to expect that the Arthurian literature, if it is authentic and nonfictional, would acknowledge Strathclyde in detail and would lament the loss of the York-Berwick area. It ought to revolve around the areas of the ancient fortresses of Strathclyde: Dumbarton on the Clyde River, Stirling on the Firth of Forth, Carlisle on the Solway Firth, and the milecastles on Hadrian's Wall. The hub of this area would probably be Carlisle, where today seven railway lines meet at the center and fan out over the whole area, all the way from western to eastern seas.

If Arthur lost York, and if Lancelot's father lost Bamborough, which popular tradition insists was their property, then the king still had two vast forested areas into which to withdraw and reorganize: behind Hadrian's Wall and behind the Antonine Wall. The Romans themselves failed to occupy the far north, or the Highlands. There Arthur and Lancelot would have been as safe as Californians would be in the Sierra Nevada. From Stirling on the east coast, and Dumbarton on the west, Arthur could have launched raids by ship upon Ireland first, and then upon the lowlands of the continent of Europe: Friesland and Denmark, or even the coast of Saxony. In the case of Arthur, once we have examined the textual evidence, we may find ourselves face to face with one of the greatest military thinkers of all time.

SCOTLAND

THE HIGHLANDS

ANGUS

NORTH SEA

St. Andrews•

Dalriada

Loch Lomond

•Stirling

Camelon•

•Dumbarton

Glasgow•

Edinburgh•

Firth of Forth

•Dunpelder (Traprain Law)

Lothian•

LAMMERMUIR HILLS

•Berwick upon Tweed

Trimontium or Newstead (Eildon Hills)

Firth of Clyde

•Prestwick

•Ayr

THE BORDER COUNTRY

Bamborough•

•Ballantrae

Loch Ryan

THE RHINS OF GALLOWAY

Ruthwell•

•Caerlaverock

•Bowness

Carlisle•

•Newcastle upon Tyne

Solway Firth

•Old Carlisle

Whithorn (Candida Casa)

Penrith•

ISLE OR MAN

York•

IRISH SEA

ENGLAND

Roman roads

THE BORDER COUNTRY

In the case of Arthur we ought to think in terms of the geography of Britain. The medieval Welsh called Arthur *imperator* (translated as "emperor"), when it should probably have been appended to his name as a military title: commander in chief. The earliest historians of Arthur's time remind us he won twelve victories. Those recognizable among the twelve lie in the north, in Strathclyde. South of there, in any case, all the victories were Anglo-Saxon. It is now English territory. Geoffrey of Monmouth put Arthur in Strathclyde, in the fortress of Dumbarton Rock, at Loch Lomond (four miles away), and close to the ancient and modern military road which runs from Stirling (on the Firth of Forth) to Glasgow (on the Clyde River).

King Arthur lived in a world undergoing rapid change. During the fifth century, the Roman Empire of Julius Caesar and Augustus was vanishing, in an administrative as well as in a military sense. In Arthur's day Christianity was the new religion, intent upon holding the world together. Arthur was not to our knowledge represented, any more than Christ was represented, in Christian art of that time, for we have of Arthur no ancient depiction, no picture of him being christened or baptised as we have of King Clovis of the Franks.*

The Christian Emperor Justinian and the Empress Theodora are represented in the Ravenna mosaics standing with their nine or ten lavishly dressed courtiers. Of King Arthur not a single artistic representation or description from the Dark Ages has yet been located. Artists have therefore felt free to portray him as dark with an elegant pointed curly beard, as white haired, or as blond with a red tinge to his hair as became Irish royalty. The mendacious monks who were supposed to have exhumed Arthur and Guinevere at Glastonbury in the twelfth century said they saw the queen's golden hair dissolve as the air reached it. Queen Guinevere is not described in the texts, yet she is said to have been impressive physically, Romano-British, educated like Arthur, and a keeper of archives. Her name, affirmed Geoffrey of Monmouth, was perhaps Guanhumara but also Regina, and she was a crowned queen of Britain. Both Arthur and the queen worshipped at the Grail Castle. The Roman Emperor in the east was known to be Christian. Arthur said he was related to the eastern emperor Constantine. The massive head of Constantine the Great, sculpted in stone, was discovered in the city of York in Britain. If there was a family resemblance, then Arthur was almost terrifying in aspect, with great rolling eyes, high cheekbones, and an aggressive, powerful head. It is a fearsome countenance with its flared nostrils and brutish nose. This eastern emperor, son of a British mother, was a huge

---

*As the Frankish queen looks dutifully into an ornamented bathtub, her King Clovis stands waist deep in the water, naked but sporting a very pretty haircut. Or again he stands beside his queen, crowned in majesty. She wears her hair in the Roman fashion, parted in the middle, with waves along the side of her face, and her four braids wound in ribbons reach well below her knees.

man. Arthur also was the son of a British mother, and he was called the Bear and the Hammer.

Although the western Roman Empire had ceased to exist by 476, approximately the time of Arthur's birth, the Romans continued their building program in Rome, remodeling the emperor Constantine's Lateran Baptistery and building new churches: S. Sabina (422–32), S. Maria Maggiore (432–40), and S. Stefano Rotondo (468–83). It is instructive to note, since we shall want to see whether Arthur built structures in Britain—the texts claim that this was so—that the church of S. Maria Maggiore was dedicated to the Virgin Mary. Around the year 500 there was also a wall painting of the Virgin, crowned and enthroned, at the church of S. Maria Antiqua in Rome. Arthur is said to have honored the Virgin by bearing her image on his shield. Second, one detail of the construction of S. Maria Maggiore needs stressing: Its interior walls are built with an entablature instead of an arcade level. In other words, above the columns the builders placed a superstructure, called an entablature, which consisted of the architrave or molding resting closest to the columns, and a cornice. The church of S. Stefano Rotondo, built to honor that Christian martyr whose relics it housed, was a martyrium.

When a manuscript says that Arthur traveled to Jerusalem in order to bring home relics of a martyr, which he housed in (Old) Melrose Abbey south of Edinburgh, that remark ties him to Rome. The fashions of that early day required veneration of the Virgin and the building of martyria.

King Theodoric of the Ostrogoths, prominent in Arthur's day, continued in his capital at Ravenna another massive building program: S. Apollinare Nuovo, Sant' Apollinare in Classe, the Arian and Orthodox baptisteries, and Theodoric's mausoleum. Since the Arthurian texts contain mention of Lancelot's tomb, of Arthur's, of Gawain's, and of the tomb of Lancelot's grandfather, which was under the young hero's care, it is important to note that the building of tombs was a praiseworthy activity in the fifth century. King Theodoric's tomb still stands, a two-storied structure like those of imperial Rome, built of ashlar blocks instead of bricks and covered by a monolithic dome. Theodoric died in 526, a few years ahead of Arthur.

And in Ravenna the princess Galla Placidia, noble and Roman, and the sister of the emperor Honorius, built not only the church of S. Croce, or Holy Cross, in 425–50, but also a mausoleum for herself, her husband, and the emperor Honorius. This building still stands, a cross-shaped structure of bricks with a dome on pendentives. The interior is not plain but rich with mosaics and marble paneling. The texts tell us that Queen Guinevere had built and prepared a splendid tomb for King Arthur. If Lancelot also built tombs, he was, one supposes *a priori*, also a king.

If King Arthur made the grand tour of the sites in the Holy Land, then he might have been influenced to adopt the cult of the Virgin Mary from her cathedral at Ephesus. It would not have been anachronistic to venerate the Virgin in the Dark Ages. But perhaps Arthur's "Jerusalem" was the Grail Castle on its western island.

Nor was it unusual in the Dark Ages to journey by sea and land to the Holy Land, especially to Jerusalem, where Constantine's British mother had found a piece of the True Cross, and had founded the martyrium of Christ and Church of the Holy Sepulcher. Her name was Elen (Helen, Elaine), the same name as the mother and later of the wife of Lancelot, the mother of Galahad's name too. Both Perceval, who was the last of the Grail Kings, and Galahad, who also achieved the Holy Grail, died not in Britain but in the Holy Land itself.

Arthur presumably died at the Castle of the Holy Grail, near his tomb and his treasure. Three or four queens took him there in a craft or funeral barge. The Grail Castle was not on the mainland but on the Isle of Avalon, off the west shore of Britain, where in most ancient times the royal dead were ferried for burial. Similarly in Celtic Gaul the necropolis was at Aliscans (*Alise champs* = Elder [Alder] Fields, now *Champs Elysées*) on the Rhône River. This too was once an island (in the river), and here too the dead were placed on a barge, like that of the Lily Maid of Astolat, and ferried downstream.

Thus, the Grail Castle *must also have been designated as a holy spot within Britain*, just as the island of Iona is today universally respected as a holy place and focus of pilgrimage. Delphi in Greece was such a holy shrine, also called the navel of the earth. Lyons in France was called the head of Gaul, *caput Galliae*, or it was the "maidan" Castle, or place of assembly for the Gallic tribesmen. One will feel reassured that the Grail Castle is truly found if some such term or logograph indicating most ancient holiness comes associated with it.

During the Renaissance the great writer and "impenitent evangelist" François Rabelais wrote about the western isle of the dead, which he called the "isle of discession," from the Roman taboo against the word *dead*, replaced by the periphrase "to step down from one's life," *de vita discedere*. The ancient dead, he knew, were ferried for burial services on to a western island in the sea.

By Arthur's time Constantine the Great had been dead for one hundred fifty years, but the eastern emperor ruled the Balkan peninsula and Asia Minor, which were Christian. Thus, the Grail Castle as King Arthur knew it may also be presumed to have been Christian, for the texts say Arthur reconverted the people there to Christianity.

A certain broad-mindedness must be allowed here, for the Celtic peoples insist that Christianity was introduced at the earliest into Britain. They believe that it was introduced by Christ Himself, or by the Virgin Mary herself, and at least by their Saint Joseph of Arimathea, who took Christ from the Cross. Arthurian personages are said to be descended from Joseph of Arimathea or to have a holy and sainted pedigree, Perceval and Lancelot notably.

A second wave of Christianity was introduced by Papal Rome at the end of the sixth century when Saint Augustine of Canterbury arrived there to convert the Anglo-Saxons. For religious reasons, then, an expected undercurrent of tension exists in the Arthurian material: Lindisfarne and Durham, Canterbury and Saint Cuthbert, and Bede, lording it over Saint Joseph of Arimathea, Saint Kentigern of Scotland, and the Grail Castle. This unresolved conflict is later joined by the great Roman Catholic intellectuals of Glastonbury Abbey, by the historian Gerald of Wales, and by many others who took up the cudgels against Geoffrey of Monmouth.

In the age of Arthur, east of the North Sea and the Channel, the barbarians terrorized northern and northwestern Europe: Ostrogoths in Italy and on the Adriatic coast, Visigoths on the Iberian peninsula, Clovis and the Franks in what is now France and western Germany, and the Anglo-Saxons from the coastal lands between the Rhine and Elbe rivers pushed the Celtic peoples north.

By the time of Arthur's death, says the linguist and historian Kenneth Hurlstone Jackson, the Saxons held east of a line roughly south to north from the Isle of Wight to Edinburgh.

It is particularly when dealing with the end of Arthur's Celtic realm that the manuscripts drafted in Old French become troublesome, and also because Lancelot has never been found in Geoffrey of Monmouth's original *History of the Kings of Britain.* The other major figures of Arthur's world are all very much there. Although there is no physical description of Arthur anywhere in Geoffrey either, the French sources tell us about the two young princes Gawain and Lancelot, so graphically that we can visualize both. These were young colonels, both of whom served the queen before they served Arthur, and both of whom wielded Excalibur in Arthur's name. In Roman military terms, both bore his *imperium,* or held in the king's name the power, the right, and the authority of command. When Gawain grew weak from wounds, after a period of some years, Lancelot finally wore, as it were, the four stars of generalship. Arthur remained duke, king, and commander in chief.

As *dux bellorum,* or commander for the duration of the war, as duke with his ensign of the clawed hammer and as king afterward, Arthur must be recognizable in human terms. Like Constantine the Great, to whom he was related, at least in some way, and to whom Geoffrey of Monmouth equated him, Arthur was the son of a Roman on his father's side and the son of a Briton on his mother's side. The Welsh sources claim that she was the daughter of a Celtic commander in chief. Thus, Arthur's widowed sister, who was descended from Joseph of Arimathea, from whom Arthur is not said to be descended, must have been Arthur's half sister. She is Perceval's mother, called the Widow Lady of Camelot, who commanded so much respect from all. Knowing Arthur's antecedents and his prominence in his world, as the great military commander and as one of the most noted military men of all time, one should be able to suggest at least a characteristic profile.

Constantine had the face of a skull smasher, the physiognomy of a Scottish hammer thrower, and the physique of an athlete at the Highland games, where the contestant pivots and hurls a long stick with an iron ball fixed to its tip. Arthur not only carried one, but was called the "Hammer." He used a hammer in his coastal sieges of western Scotland, in Dalriada. He was the youth, when his country was *in extremis*, who was chosen by the united chieftains of the Britons to launch the defensive operation that was successful for so long. What kind of man is chosen for such a task?

Literature knows, if one looks at the best of authors, or those with the widest knowledge. In Plutarch's *Parallel Lives*, he tells of a similar situation in Rome, when the nation was paralyzed by the lightning attacks of the brilliant Hannibal. The government chose Fabius, later called the Great, or Maximus. Fabius was the only man to halt and to beat Hannibal, just as Arthur was the only possible choice in his time. As to his personality, he was mild and fair, sober and steady; he was slow of speech, considerate in every situation, able without collapsing, as Arthur was able, to bear the loss of his son in battle. Like Arthur, and even Malory agreed here with the English poem, the *Alliterative Morte Arthure*, Fabius looked with equanimity upon the mutability of Fortune. As Arthur said in Malory, her wheel was now up and now upso down. Fabius looked calmly upon death as the common father of us all, and sought an end no less honorable than his life had been. Both Fabius and Arthur were said to be a son of some great personage, and both were heroically born, like Hercules, of two fathers Fabius resembled a lion in temper, and Arthur a grizzly bear. Both were exceptionally stable, both big men, both free from passions, confident but also cautious. Both had undergone in youth the most rigorous training for war. Neither man could be ridiculed by derision. Neither could be turned from the course he'd taken. Neither one fell for tricks. Finally the brilliant Hannibal came to see that Fabius would sooner or later fall from the mountain upon him like a dark cloud. Arthur was said to be able to draw about him the same dark cloud, the *lengel*, the old Celtic veil of concealment belonging in the dawn of the west to the Old Irish sea god Manannan mac Llyr from the Isle of Man.

Consider the words of another of the world's finest authors and greatest hearts, Geoffrey Chaucer. In his prologue to *The Canterbury Tales* Chaucer speaks first of the warrior or knight, who from childhood loved truth, honor, freedom, and courtesy. He had in his career as a military man fought four major campaigns, surviving many sieges and fifteen pitched battles. In manner he was "meek as a maid," never uttering a villainous word in his whole life. He was loved for his gentle authority. No description is given, for his equipment was most ordinary. His enemies doubtless hated him for his hammer and sword. Chaucer's keen insight pierces appearances and seizes the essence of reality.

The tones of lofty condemnation of King Arthur regarding moral turpitude in personal relationships, the dreadful triangle of adultery, and the supposed war between Lancelot and Gawain that brought down the realm arise in the French sources. One outstanding dissenting opinion comes from the epic *Gododdin*, written in prototypical, old Western Celtic, or P-Celtic. Here the few words spoken concerning Arthur regret the loss of his great heroism and his mastery of the war; someone in Edinburgh praised Arthur, in the Dark Ages.

As the Romans conquered Britain, they recorded the names of the Celtic tribes, just as they had done in Gaul and Belgium. In the border area between what would become the Antonine and Hadrianic Walls, they noted the presence of a population divided into four major tribes, all speaking P-Celtic, which today is modern Welsh (as opposed to Irish and Manx, which are Q-Celtic). These tribes were the Votadini (the Edinburgh area of Lothian), the Selgovae (in the Tweed River valley), the Novantae (in the southwestern area), and the Damnonii (in the valley of the Clyde River, and Glasgow). The poem *Gododdin* takes its name from the Latin appellation of the Votadini (Gododdin). Thus, Arthur is praised not later than one hundred years after his death by an inhabitant of the Edinburgh area, dominated today by the volcanic peak called Arthur's Seat.

The essential point of the *Gododdin* allusion to Arthur is that he really lived and died somewhere in the area described by the unknown poet. Centuries later, after the Votadini had migrated into what is now Wales, their memory of Arthur became more poetic and fanciful. Thanks in part to the Welsh bardic tradition, as developed in stories like those in the *Mabinogion* and in Welsh poetry, Arthur's legend expanded until it eclipsed his history.

Until recently scholarship has concentrated upon the late legend, which contains beautiful, mythological views of Arthur. Medieval poets added the classical traditions of Greece and Rome, gods and goddesses, seasonal celebrations, and houses of the Zodiac to their epics and romances. Thus has King Arthur more or less been situated halfway between history and mythology. His world seems to have been equally divided.

The mythological view of Arthur occurs in one of the most haunting Welsh poems of the Middle Ages, the *Preiddeu Annwn* (Treasures of the Otherworld). Here King Arthur took twenty-seven champions in three ships on ocean raids upon eight castles of the sea, including the Castle of Glass ("Caer Wydr") and that of Middle Earth. In each case only seven heroes returned alive. It was a "glorious labor," beyond which point the "prowess of Arthur" was unknown, a plunge into the "mournful battle," with Arthur of "mournful memory." The poet may have intended to write twelve adventures to correspond to the twelve battles of Arthur ascribed to him early in his career. Gematria, the mystical use of numbers, alerts the reader, who has succumbed to magic, that there is a mystical orientation in the poem. Readers have theorized that the "seven score" may refer to the 140 stones of Stonehenge.

During the Middle Ages writers specializing in mythology took the circumstances of Arthur's life and enhanced them until his biography resembled various mythical plots and characters. The Anglo-Saxon Layamon thought of the king as "Alfadur," the great father of his country, as were Augustus Caesar and George Washington. The possible allusions to Stonehenge set imaginations working until Arthur came out as another Cyclopean builder, and himself a giant Cyclops, or Orion in the sky. Or Arthur became the constellation of the Great Bear Arktos, one of the more gallant but equally erroneous attempts to solve the etymology of the name *Arthur*.

Very early in the Middle Ages, the circumpolar constellations became identified with Arthur, for the Great Wain (our Big Dipper) makes the circle of the heavens around the Polestar once every twenty-four hours and bears down upon north Britain. Or Arthur's name may come from that of Arcturus, the orange star of first magnitude that crosses the summer sky and disappears below the eastern horizon on Hallowe'en. By extension Arthur became Sagittarius, the Archer, also a great teacher with many youthful protégés, including Gawain, Lancelot, and Perceval. As Sagittarius his festival fell upon or close to the ancient Celtic feast of autumn, Samhain, or again, upon Hallowe'en. Thus, Arthur made the circle back to his stance as great father of mankind, the god of the dead who opened the tombs at the fall equinox, as the sun crossed the equator.

If Arthur rode across the sky with his pointed hat upon his head, astride his magical horse, then Gawain could also become Aries, the Ram at the spring equinox, Perceval could become Pisces during the epigomenal days at the end of each calendar year (the twelve days of Christmas), and Lancelot, always associated with the Red Lion, could become Leo the Lion in the height of summer with the sun on the Tropic of Cancer. Very soon the other characters of Arthur's court fall into the other of the modern twelve houses of the Zodiac. This brings us back to Arthur's birth as Hercules, his twelve battles as twelve labors, and the Welsh poem *Preiddeu Annwn*. Hercules also harried Hell, wresting treasures from the earth which jealously guards them underground. From the god of Hell, says an Irish fairy tale, Arthur stole the horse and the dog, which he gave to Ireland alone for that land to domesticate.

Medieval authors easily transformed each Arthurian adventure into a fairy tale. That genre seems to have developed on parallel lines with the medieval romance. According to the structure of the fairy tale, Arthur becomes in each incident the first character, called the Dispatcher. It is he, in other words, who dispatches the young hero upon his dangerous and lonely quest. *Gawain and the Green Knight* serves as an excellent example, but in that poem reality almost breaks through at several points. In that case also the ending is missing, for in the fairy tale the young hero always weds the princess and becomes king.

When Arthur's legend became a political embarrassment, it was forcefully debunked. In the twelfth century Gervase of Tilbury and Walter Map held Arthur up to the most adroit ridicule. King Henry II could not endure the competition from a "once and future king" of the united Celtic peoples, a king who might rise and come again at any moment. Thus, courtiers trifled with the legend, transforming the ancient king into the Dwarf of the Antipodes, a near relative of the Loathly Damsel as she appears in ballads. Or Arthur was discovered sleeping in a cave in Sicily. Even this version powerfully responded to the old belief in a sleeping god, Cronos, or to the wounded and dying god of autumn lying alongside Hadrian's Wall, where Arthur is still held to have spent the night after his last and final battle, at Camlan. There he is said to have awaited the barge from the Isle of Avalon. The ruins of Sewingshields Castle in the Border Country are still pointed out as his final refuge on British soil. Throughout history the Welsh continued to mourn Arthur and to honor his veil, sometimes called "Llen," and classed among the Thirteen Treasures of Britain.

An ancient English ballad says that the Battle of Camlan occurred early on the morning of a Trinity Monday. And according to the balladeers Arthur met the Loathly Damsel just south of Carlisle, on the road from that city to Penrith. One of the ancient community dwellings lies at Penrith, which people there say might be the original "Round Table." Several other such traces of structures have been excavated on the Isle of Man, however, which indicates that no one of them is Arthur's Round Table.

According to another mythological view, King Arthur is said to ride across the sky at night, followed by the red and white hounds of Hell. This apparition in the Middle Ages was called the "household of Hell." Goethe's famous poem "Erl King" reproduces this legend.

King Arthur and his legend have been kept alive throughout the ages— a king feared and loved at the same time. Scholars have unearthed resemblances between his legend and those of other areas, particularly of Ireland and the Isle of Man. Arthur has been thought to resemble the sea gods of Britain. In this geographical area—the Irish Sea—he has seemed most at home, sailing these waters, or rowing over them and returning to his private hoard and incomparable Grail Castle.

Now, it is time to forgo the allure of the mythology in order to look closely at the evidence. Surely beneath the fog of legend and the veil of concealment lies the real Arthur.

3

The Nature
of the Evidence

The search for the historical king involved examining and reexamining objects from his ancient past: art objects, manuscripts, annals, documents, *itineraria,* maps, histories, romances, epic poems, saints' lives, regnal lists, chronologies, triadic lore from the Welsh bards, and all other tangible sources, including mentions of Arthur's name and career. Then came the hundreds of works by critics who over the centuries devoted studies to King Arthur.

Obviously, those who knew the king personally, such as Lancelot and Gawain, who were probably closest to him for the longest time, draw one's interest immediately. The ceremonies at which Arthur presided demand close scrutiny, for like all moments of high social importance, these were occasions when the powerful of the realm paraded in all their finery—and occasions that were recorded in minute detail. Arthur's deeds, both public and private, present problems that must be analyzed according to our knowledge of human actions in similar circumstances. Names of persons and places form a particular branch of study in which there are recognized and reliable specialists. Arthur's contemporaries across the Channel, in Ravenna, Rome, and even Constantinople, who knew him by reputation, inform about conditions in his day.

Most of the written evidence, which is my particular province, comes from the High Middle Ages, from persons known and unknown who lived six and seven hundred years after the death of King Arthur. What they wrote has to be viewed through two optics: their thinking about Arthur at *their* point in time, and our thinking about Arthur *and* about these intermediaries. Needless to say, they may have been exceptionally able, but it would be naive to assume that their accounts are free of prejudice and bias.

Such considerations are important and should be noted before embarking upon an examination of the evidence. Epistemology and the philosophy of history tell us how we know what we know, and what are the ways of knowing employed by historians.

Research implies another inquiry into what is known or thought to have been known. The ignorance of the present finally weighs too heavily, presses too hard. We may read forever, but no one text will ever enable us to know or understand what was really going on in King Arthur's realm.

The old questions nag: Did King Arthur live? Was Queen Guinevere abducted? Did the Grail Castle stand upon a western isle? What was the Round Table? What is meant by the mounted warriors of the king's court? Who was King Urien of Gorre? Was he indeed King Arthur's worst foe? Where is the Isle of Avalon now?

As stated earlier, the intervening centuries have not provided us with answers but have dealt with the questions by ascribing everything to the realm of the magical, or a kind of fairyland. Now the effort must be directed toward estimating what is probable, what is reasonable, and what is likely about the events of Arthur's day.

The best tool for wrestling with the literature is textual analysis, a discipline that was introduced during the Renaissance. Now that anthropology has begun to bring the cultures of the Dark Ages to light, it is time to examine all the old textual evidence closely. In addition to reexamination, reevaluation, and reinterpretation, I offer translations for some material hitherto considered incomprehensible and in so doing am able to correct, for example, the tangle into which Geoffrey of Monmouth's translator strayed when he decided that Arthur's forebears built Stonehenge.

Recent discoveries and new disciplines have fortunately not closed the doors to inquiry from the literary scholars; on the contrary, collaboration has been welcomed.

Twentieth-century art historians pointed up the difference between pagan and Christian sculpture to the extent of the subjects chosen by both. Jessie L. Weston confidently called the Grail Castle pagan. But today scholars are more careful about distinguishing between pagan and Christian objects; hence, the Grail Castle and its practices and ceremonies deserve a new look. Archaeology, particularly the research of Leslie Alcock at Cadbury Castle in England and at Dumbarton Rock outside Glasgow, has shown where King Arthur *cannot* be proven to have been. No physical evidence such as a pillar stone or a golden chalice has yet been found to validate Arthur's kingship and lordship over the Grail.

Prehistory, especially the work of Stuart Piggott, has suggested new directions for further scholarship and has established striking parallels between Arthurian society and that of archaic and Homeric Greece; the cruel warrior ethos of the one resembled closely that of the other, Piggott demonstrated. O. G. S. Crawford and I. A. Richmond walked the terrain between the two Roman walls, the Antonine and Hadrianic, plotting the Roman roads into the north and hunting for the battle site of Camlan, which Crawford felt sure he had found.

The brilliant work of the linguist M. K. Pope has unlocked the relationship between Latin and the medieval vernaculars (always unreliable languages, Dr. Johnson used to say). Each of these two new disciplines has demonstrated something that has inspired the renewal of inquiry: the past survives in the present.

The twentieth century has made it possible to appreciate at what great advantage we work. The interpreters of the twelfth and thirteenth centuries labored at tremendous disadvantage (history was not even taught in the medieval schools) under the watchful eyes of their superiors in monasteries and convents, dictated to rather than left alone to follow the truth wherever it led and at whatever consequence. One can see why a Chrétien de Troyes turned to high comedy and tossed Gawain, as it were, into the sea from his "water bridge."

Despite these disadvantages, the voices of the great authors and scholars, such as Geoffrey of Monmouth, ring across the centuries. Today we are able to watch Geoffrey wrestle again with the problems presented in his alleged source, wonder about its likelihood, and succumb to his inability to travel around Britain and see places for himself. We see him struggle with names of persons and places and manfully defend Queen Guinevere, deferring to the sanctity of a crowned sovereign. Putting other voices from the past into the witness box, we insist that they tell us again how they ascertained their facts. If they have spoken at any length, they have revealed themselves, as each one of us reveals himself, his education, and his mindset. In this witness box bigotry and prejudice will be exposed, and enthusiasm, courage, and love saluted. We shall watch for errors in judgment, alternatives in which the wrong choice was made, and we will note the abysmal lack of knowledge of elementary geography.

The medieval scholar walked between the same variables and invariables as we, assessing general sets of circumstances, continuity in situations large and small, behavior under threat of death, pomp and circumstance in ceremonies, characteristics of institutions, probable progression, and causes and results. Then as now the author depended upon his own experience before being able to judge that of others, upon his own observation about what led his subject to any decision taken. The work of his critic involves the same construction and, wherever necessary, reconstruction. This is a method proper to history—the movement from one's authorities to a critical weighing of evidence, and often to new constructions from the original givens of each proposition.

In the case of King Arthur we cannot at the moment put our hands upon such hard evidence as his sword or his helmet with his name upon it, and we have as yet no grave with his bones lying head to the foe. There is a place called Arthur's Head (Arthuret) outside Carlisle. William of Malmesbury reported the finding of a grave for Gawain along the coast. It was a giant's grave, but no giant's bones have been found in Britain. Saint Kentigern of Scotland (called "Mungo") is the only near contemporary described as gigantic, or the tallest man in those parts.

Failing objects from the past, the historian must make do with testimony from as many diverse persons as possible, particularly when they tell, independently of each other, the same story.

Working by crosssection we can descend past thought and deeds through the consciousnesses of several witnesses. This method involves reading the same texts over and over until two things happen: (1) the author becomes familiar to the reader, and (2) the discrepancies in his account demand deeper scrutiny.

A good example of one such study lies in the many Grail manuscripts. Why does no one text include complete directions to the Grail castle? The various cold-shoulderings of this segment of each account caused me to decide that King Arthur himself must have refused to authorize such a road map, with its telltale sea crossing. One land route runs into another, but the sea intervenes, either from the Solway Firth or from the Wirral Peninsula (adjacent to the modern port of Liverpool). Each text provides the questing hero, his departure on the quest, various recognizable stops along the way, familiar landmarks, and arrival at the Grail Castle, usually at nightfall. Now, if this castle is built upon an island in the sea, and furthermore hidden from sight until the hero stumbles down a steep grade inside a narrow cleft, how did he get there from the mainland? Where in the real world are such a grade and cleft? Why wasn't his entire route laid out?

It is time to recapitulate. The hero came to a "stony passage," then to a fountain where he saw a comb lying on the earth. He passed castles, spent a first night, saw a sandy shore or beach before a very prominent place in front of which a broad body of water stretched to the horizon. At this point each author lapses. Then follow the improbables: Lancelot crossing some "sword bridge," Gawain tossed off some "water bridge." All along the authors know, of course, that most bridges go *over* water and are not causeways through it, much less under it! It would seem obvious that we are here confronted with several cases of lost knowledge.

We fail to understand the hero's reactions, such as the irrational behavior triggered by the comb. We can no longer get away with calling the medieval authors naive (which only means "native" anyway). It is more likely that Lancelot and Gawain were leading two invasion forces, one by land, one by sea. Why does Lancelot start at the sight of the comb? Why does it mean that the queen has passed by recently? Why should Lancelot be so

BRITAIN

HEBRIDES

DALRI..

Inverness

PICTLAND
(CALEDONIANS)

ANGUS

NORTH
SEA

Loch
Lomond
Dumbarton
Stirling
Firth of Forth
ANTONINE WALL
Firth
Clyde
STRATHCLYDE
Edinburgh
NORTH
Melrose   Bamborough
Galloway
HADRIAN'S WALL
Carlisle
Solway
Firth
BRITONS
Penrith
UMBRIA
ISLE
OF
MAN

IRELAND

IRISH SEA

York

Chester

Lincoln

WALES

ENGLAND

Isca (Caerleon)

ATLANTIC
OCEAN

London
Winchester
THE SAXON SHORE
Canterbury
Dover

CORNWALL

ENGLISH CHANNEL

FRANCE

stricken? Has she dropped him a clue? Art historians puzzle about carvings of combs on ancient Pictish monuments in Scotland. Symbol? Hieroglyph?

Why does the author (and he is not alone) specify that *a sandy beach* fronted the castle where Lancelot saw the queen pass away from him? He is identifying the castle, it would seem, to the initiated. Authors are frequently sensitive to such graphic detail and repeat information even though it may be meaningless to them; intuitively they feel it may have great, albeit hidden, significance. Will there still be a sandy shore before a castle mound? Why so precise? One suspects that the castle's name has to do with this sandy strand. The first author was revealing a secret when he told his readers how to recognize this castle from the land or from the sea. Why? Was this King Arthur's birthplace? Was it a much sought-after site?

Detection depends upon the ability to reconstruct from clues consisting of odd behavior or misplaced objects. A good detective understands that a crime in the present can be solved from the past, which survives in the present, and which also informs the future. Scholars have been very interested in the crimes that were reported in the vicinity of King Arthur.

In the cases of abduction, treason, and murder implicating Arthur, King Urien of Gorre, Lancelot, Gawain, and Modred, the preliminary investigation was done by authors of the Middle Ages. While their sincerity was, as André Gide observed, a "matter of talent," their work comes to our aid today. It is a matter of faith that authors write in order to discover the truth. Their voices, distinguishable and separate, become familiar as the truth of their findings becomes apparent, or not. Many such medieval authors were, in absentia, hauled into the witness box to testify to their findings.

The writers of the twelfth century—Geoffrey among them—demonstrate their individual attitudes toward the world in which they lived as toward the world of King Arthur in the distant past. Today we see the reasons for their admiration for true nobility, their scorn for women, and their contempt for adultery, and for lust. We see the enmity for Arthur creep into the poems written by Marie de France. Eventually we will be able to theorize about her unknown source that it came not from England originally, nor from France. Through author after author we can track these same mysteries, and see the authors recognize in various actions the mainsprings of human behavior. Their inferential logic leads them to hypothetical reconstructions of events in King Arthur's world. Our meditations concerning epistemology and our training stand us in good stead.

My admiration for the textual scholars of the twentieth century knows no limits and is equaled only by praise for those critics who showed no scorn for the past and those who refused to ride to prominence on the shoulders of medieval scholars. And local historians should not be overlooked. It was from them that I learned, for example, that King Lot took his name from

Lothian in the Edinburgh area of Scotland and that his name was probably Loth. They pointed out the hill fort once commanded by him. All the more reason to believe that Loth was not king of the Orkney Islands, as was often claimed. At his fort called Traprain Law, an obvious place of refuge for local people, a silver hoard, one piece of which is engraved "CON" (for Constantine) was recently unearthed.

For years I have disagreed with those who saw in King Arthur a cult figure, harvest god, or Irish fairy, and I have found many reasons for having undertaken this long process of substantiating King Arthur from a word-by-word rereading of the Arthurian manuscripts of quality. First, there is the peculiar, annalistic nature of these accounts. As in *Gawain and the Green Knight*, calendar dates recur in Chrétien de Troyes and Marie de France. Second, the geography proves accurate and familiar, making it virtually impossible *not* to recognize topography, landmarks, and sites. Such unexpected realism of place combats any idea that Arthur was some sort of god.

A third clue comes from the growing proof that many French and German manuscripts contain deformations of proper names. In the French manuscripts it stems from two faults: the failure to read Celtic languages very well and the general lack of regard for accuracy. The German texts like to mystify with puns and anagrams, saying, for instance, that the river is called "Der Kal," when their source had said that it was the "Calder River" (pronounced "Cauder" in Scotland). Obviously the German Ulrich von Zatzikhoven read his source and did not depend upon itinerant bards or singers for it.

The first theory about the typical Arthurian plots, in which adventures seem strung together like beads on a string, was that their linear structure represented Christian or linear time progressing at the same pace toward a promised end. Upon closer examination this structure reveals itself to be circular. The same places occur upon each line of march, as if Gawain, Lancelot, and Perceval in turn were dispatched by Arthur upon a military expedition. The three plots are the same or cover the same territory: the recapture of the Grail Castle, the investiture of Perceval at the Grail Castle on the Isle of Avalon, and the surrender and consequent capture of Queen Guinevere.

And then there is the reality of the characters. Lancelot, for example, is identified too closely to have been fictional. We know too much about his childhood, his education, and his exploits concerning the recovery of his father's lost dominions. He was neither Leo the Lion, as the *Prose Lancelot* claimed, nor an elderly ruler killed in the red sunset of the *Mabinogion*. Lancelot died young, in the full power of his maturity. Despite the marvelous legend about him—which means that he was revered because of his saintly lineage—he acts and rules like a real king.

What rings most false is the psychological treatment of women, especially when they are viewed as sex objects. Here the medieval authors become crazed, accusing King Arthur of incest, Gawain's mother of infanticide, Queen Guinevere of adultery, Lancelot of treason, and Modred of patricide. Regarding Modred, the voices of the Scots, raised in protest over the centuries, were drowned in contumely. "Modred was no traitor, nor a murderer," they argued during the Renaissance. "He was our beloved king." A foray into anthropology reveals that in fact there were unknown, supposedly barbaric people in the north of Britain who lived under customs other than those of the better-known Celtic peoples to the south.

Let us suppose, then, that in some of the Arthurian manuscripts there are traces of another society and of another, different culture—not Roman, not Welsh, not Anglo-Saxon, and not French. Was there another language in the far north of Britain, which has not yet been found in a written form? Does that explain why so many names of the Arthurian material—*Arthur, Guinevere, Carlisle, Britain, Picts,* and *Pictish,* for example—are of unknown etymology? Might it be that real arcana have at last emerged from the vast Arthurian literature?

Some of the behavior, relationships, and ceremonies of the Arthurian world seem unduly strange, to wit weddings, marriages, severed heads, phlebotomies of women (continued until they bled to death), peculiar laws of inheritance on the distaff side, and warrior queens. It would appear that in Arthur's world the sons of kings did not automatically inherit their fathers' crowns, which perhaps throws a new light upon the Arthur-Modred tangle.

If we were only dealing with a new and imaginary culture, we might agree with recent scholarship that the Arthurian was truly a never-never land; but referents draw us unmistakably back into the fifth and sixth centuries. Outside the world of the king, the rest of the continent seems familiar. We welcome reassurances from these strange people that Constantinople is still in place, that the Roman Empire heaves in the throes of dissolution, and that Jerusalem and Nazareth (which one wants to recognize in the medieval "Sarras") are still the Golden Cities and center of the known world. We also recognize without too much disorientation that Celtic Christianity is a law unto itself, far distant from Rome. Among the "sea-green Britons," as a scornful Church Father termed them, doubtless there were outstanding heresies, some of them stunningly beautiful, which are no longer considered so very heretical.

At the point where the clues seemed to merge into some Gordian knot impossible to untangle, a British scholar discovered that one of King Arthur's castles was real—a ruin that can be clambered over today. R. L. Graeme Ritchie actually found and identified Caerlaverock Castle and its Dark Age castle mound, both of which can be seen on the north shore of the Solway Firth, near the modern city of Carlisle.

This magnificent discovery, which Ritchie reported to Oxford University in 1952, alerted scholars that a new search should be made at once into the entire Arthurian corpus. It is likely that there in Caerlaverock, one deduces from many testimonies of authors, King Arthur was born. The original name of that castle and sandy shore may have been something like "Tintagel," but in a British and not a Cornish form, like "Dun Dagel."

The geography of Britain yielded the first clue that led to this breakthrough. Surely that geography could not change completely from the fifth and sixth centuries to now! Both O. G. S. Crawford and I. A. Richmond had been on the right track after all. Further clues followed rapidly and substantiated them too. Now should follow a reexamination of the literary texts, which will surely furnish new evidence in this rigorously comparative approach.

Given the vast body of written texts, the progress has been slow. At first a system of notation allowed the reader to move haltingly from one text to another, a process that gained speed only when one was able to retain the material without the use of notes. Certain texts were discarded along the way as being too corrupt, poorly written, and generally unreliable. In those cases the authors were found wanting in intelligence and talent. The comparative approach showed which texts were admissible into prime positions, whose authors were to become the major witnesses in the box. Thus, for first evidence I selected those texts which recount multiple versions of the same stories: the life of King Arthur, the abduction of Queen Guinevere, the inauguration of Perceval at the Grail Castle, the death of King Arthur after the Battle of Camlan, and the transporting of the wounded Arthur to his place of final refuge.

The modern literary critic is familiar with the phenomenon of distancing, which shows either irony on the author's part or sometimes even hostility, as is the case in certain Arthurian texts. Marie de France stands out as a hostile witness, which makes one think she was in the pay of King Henry II of England. Her hostility is evident in both *Lanval* (which became James Russell Lowell's "The Vision of Sir Launfal") and in her much better story *Yonec*, whose hero had to avenge the slaying of his father by Lancelot. The latter tale is told from the point of view of Arthur's enemy, King Urien of Gorre, who once and maybe even twice kidnapped Queen Guinevere. The unreliable testimony in some accounts actually deepens our knowledge. The sources of Marie de France, which have always been thought to be Breton French, from her espousal of "la matière bretonne," turn out to be more probably Manx and Q-Celtic.

A second breakthrough came from the historians R. G. Collingwood and J. N. L. Myres, who decided in 1963 that the historicity of King Arthur could "hardly be called into question." The fact that an immense legend had grown up over the centuries, with Arthur as its chief hero, no more proved him fictitious than the legends concerning other figures such as Moses and Aristotle, they argued, proved them not to have been historical personages. The reason that this statement from such widely respected scholars created a breakthrough is that no fact exists until someone has affirmed it. Therefore the new research restates the problem, reexamines the primary sources and then the later or secondary sources that seem pertinent, and argues the evidence all over again in the light of the new disciplines and these recent discoveries in Britain. This program will enable us to discover new elucidations for past actions, new arguments, and new explanations for Arthur and his queen, for Lancelot, and for Perceval.

The defense of King Arthur as a historical figure involves, in a way, the defense of that literary man who first wrote a biography of Arthur, Geoffrey of Monmouth. As Melville said of Ishmael, he is the only begetter, without whom there is no story at all. Geoffrey's *History of the Kings of Britain* placed King Arthur in the north of Britain, where the scholars Crawford, Ritchie, Piggott, and Rachel Bromwich of Cardiff University have also recently placed him.

This new defense of Arthur also involves the defense of Britain in the Dark Ages. From the view of geography—terrain, coastlines, settlements, rivers, and mountains—only one certain military strategy imposes itself upon commanders. Since Arthur was said by the ancient historians of the Dark Ages to have executed the defense of Britain against invasion from Ireland, from Scandinavia, or from the continent of Europe, and then to have taken the war across to the shores of Europe, we must consider what British military historians have had to say about defense and attack.

Arthur will also be examined in the only places where he is actually recorded—in the ancient works of Gildas and Nennius, in the archives of Wales, and in the pages of Geoffrey. From there the investigation will move to a crosssection—to Arthur, Lancelot, and Guinevere and their relationships with each other, in frozen stasis. For the first time they can be viewed realistically, and not through the insane optic of "courtly love," that scholars invented for want of better entertainment.

The fourth part of this book will focus on what has always been found troubling—the early form of Christianity practiced in Britain during the lifetime of Pelagius, for Uther Pendragon is said to have followed in his observances this doctrine called the Pelagian heresy. Here again the practices at the Grail Castle, possibly an educational institution for British princelings and chieftainesses, will be examined and we will watch Perceval as he leaves the world and accepts the crown of the Grail Castle. Finally, we will pick up Arthur again in his last, continental warfare, follow him through it to his final, tragic battle in the west, and watch the three or four queens, who are supposed to be his sisters or half sisters (unless one of them was his mother), receive him upon their funeral barge and ferry him away to safety on Avalon. That isle, it seems, is the key to the whole affair. If it can be located, the entire warp of the material will finally come clear at last.

Finally, there is a last question that demands address: Why the great affection for King Arthur?

Years ago one might have said it was because he was a charismatic leader—until Hitler demonstrated the dangers of such an answer. Perhaps the reply should be amended: because King Arthur fulfills the ideal of man-hood. Although no great writer has ever chosen him as a supreme epic hero, he does adhere in some respects to the epic type and stature of man. Like the epic hero he is beloved of the gods, pious and honorable, an active and military hero, and like the true epic hero he is a man whose death becomes him as much as his deeds in life raised him daily in the reverence of his followers.

In fact he is that manly man; son, brother, husband, father, uncle, sponsor of youths, and righter of wrongs.

To Geoffrey of Monmouth Arthur was the savior of his country and of the oppressed Celtic peoples. Like Moses and Christ, he departed—la-mented, celebrated, praised, and unburied. His legend has it that he will return.

Gerda Lerner said recently that history means a kind of collective im-mortality. An unknown and disordered past is more than distressing; it is abhorrent. We labor to fill the vacuum of knowledge lost through the mali-ciousness and ignorance of barbarians. We wish to push ourselves to the limits of this lost knowledge. Ultimately we have some goal in mind, per-haps of being, as Shakespeare said, "in Arthur's bosom."

PART I

KING ARTHUR

1

The Historian:
Geoffrey of Monmouth

Geoffrey of Monmouth brought King Arthur from the depths of the Dark Ages and introduced him to the world. Alone among medieval historians and writers, it was Geoffrey who attempted to chart Arthur's life; almost everything we know about it comes from the last half of Geoffrey's *History of the Kings of Britain*.*

Without Geoffrey, it is safe to say, there would be no schematic format, no light to follow through one of the greatest bodies of literature in the world. His impressive lead was followed by many, who continued to present new material until the end of the Middle Ages, a point marked by Sir Thomas Malory's *Le Morte d'Arthur*.

In book 7 of Geoffrey's *History* Merlin begins speaking in the future prophetic tense about an evil King Vortigern and about invasions of Britain by the Saxons, by the Scots from Ireland, and by the Picts from north of Hadrian's Wall. Arthur's ancestors, Aurelius and Uther Pendragon, will undertake in turn the defense of the realm, but both will soon succumb, laments Merlin. Everything will go very badly until the fifteenth year of Uther's son, Arthur.

From Geoffrey's account it would seem that Merlin was the original narrator whom Geoffrey was translating into Latin, so that, when we read the English, we are reading at least a translation of a translation (and probably of a translation). Geoffrey speaks through and on behalf of Merlin, and for Arthur also, and thus appoints himself a premier spokesman for the Dark Ages.

*See Appendix 7.

There are two major blots upon the otherwise glorious reputation of Geoffrey of Monmouth: (1) the original text, which he claimed all his life to be translating, remains unsubstantiated and has never been found; (2) he seems to have made many huge errors in geography. For example, a notable error was placing King Arthur in Cornwall. However, his other errors may not be errors at all.

Since 1929 what appears to be a vindication of Geoffrey has been building steadily. It is my purpose here to offer new evidence in his defense.

It will be instructive to consider some of his geography to get an idea of the problems. When an author is translating, the misreading of a single letter in a word can throw his whole geography off. Obviously, Geoffrey was having a terrible time just reading the handwriting of his Merlin text. He may even have needed reading glasses. (The sort of magnification needed for the microscope was discovered in Holland during the Renaissance.) It is therefore imperative that we follow Geoffrey into his mistakes and suggest corrections, for the problem is acute: whoever does not believe Geoffrey of Monmouth cannot believe in the historical King Arthur.

The action Geoffrey mentions seems to skip from "Armorica" (Brittany) to "Totnes" on the Saxon shore (southern England), to the Boar of Cornwall, who is supposedly Arthur.

The general movement of place-names in book 7 of the *History* continues overall from south to north, by way of York, to a place that can definitely be situated: the ancient fortress of the Britons, Kaer (Fort) Alclyd (on the Clyde River). This is a known mountain fortress atop a volcanic plug, and it was a known garrisoned fort even in the Dark Ages. This aerie, which is now close to the north shore of the Clyde River at Dumbarton, near Glasgow, was once in the middle of the river. Geoffrey's Welsh translator, whom he authorized, agreed here that this place was Dumbarton, but he had let "Armorica" (or Brittany) stand in Geoffrey's text, not suspecting that the name was a mistake for North Wales (Armonica). He was aware that Scotland was the locale. But suddenly the place changes to the improbable London-Winchester-Salisbury area of southern England, and it is clear that Geoffrey has strayed again, or that he has thought he recognized these places because he knew of no such names elsewhere. Geoffrey's notion that "the City of [the] Legion" is Caerleon in southern Wales only compounds his errors. The Welsh translator cannot decide whether he is in Scotland or in Wales and England. He is soon at home again, however, back inside Scotland at Trimontium, where Uther Pendragon suffered his great defeat. This, says the Welsh translator, is the Roman station and fortress at Trimontium (those triple Eildon peaks which were Sir Walter Scott's favorite vista).

No sooner has it been established that the locus is the north-north-eastern provinces ("aquilonaribus provintiis") than unaccountably a description of Tintagel Castle in Cornwall is given. Hence the zigzagging up and down Britain from the southwestern tip to Scotland when Arthur is born. The Welsh author translates "Arturus" as "Arthyr," tells us his mother was daughter to the commander, Amlawdd Wledic, and recognized (King) Lot (*recte* Loth) of Lodonesia as prince of the hosts of Britons. It is likely that Geoffrey's "London" was an error for Lodonesia, the Lothian area of Edinburgh and King Loth's hill fort at Traprain Law.

It is not probable that Aurelius, Uther, and Arthur dashed back and forth during their tenures as commanders from one remote corner of Britain to the area of the Roman walls in the north. But this erroneous and even ridiculous geography is responsible for Geoffrey of Monmouth's low reputation over the centuries. If for the moment his errors can be held in abeyance, or even forgiven, it can be proved what a genius he was in fact.

When Geoffrey writes about the life of King Arthur, he plays upon our heartstrings. Here he works methodically, dividing his life of Arthur into five parts:

Arthur's ancestry and birth
His battles
His coronation
The continental campaign
The defeat of Camlan, Arthur's wounding, and .
his departure overseas to the Isle of Avalon

His account is gripping and brilliant in every way.

In Arthur Geoffrey saw the greatest leader the world had ever known. This king took as his goal the defense of his country. He lived in such bad times as we cannot imagine, "when the very sky was falling down and when the wrath of the stars dried up the crops in the very fields." At such an awful hour this man with a vision founded a company of youthful warriors such as Gawain, his father King Loth, and King Anguselus, and defended Britain. King Arthur restored order and peace to the realm of which, when he became king, he shouldered the first and final responsibility.

What is marvelous is that Geoffrey realized what he had in hand. With few reference books and with only a very scanty knowledge of geography—and then only that of southern England, for his acquaintance with continental France proves very limited—Geoffrey still grasped the significance to the world of what he had found: the life story of one of the world's greatest kings. King Arthur was a man after his own heart: loyal, brave, honorable, Christian, truthful, undaunted, and supremely resourceful.

Geoffrey's philosophy of history is apocalyptic and visionary, ergo Christian, prophesying a day of wrath (*dies irae*) when the world, locked into sin, will be changed by the hand of God. Geoffrey saw the coming of King

Arthur as the coming of a holy person to the rescue of a world in the throes of fire and flood. Geoffrey chose Merlin as his mouthpiece, or auxiliary narrator, which is a procedure customary to Christian writers of Apocalypse (Revelation).

Thus, in *The History of the Kings of Britain* Merlin stands in the past predicting future events that in fact have long since come to pass. In this same way, John of Patmos in the Book of Revelation spoke of the destruction of Rome. History is perceived as age after cataclysmic age, with only God, or his minions, in control. For Geoffrey, then, the lord over evil is King Arthur.

Everywhere Arthur will rise, Geoffrey assures us, to conquer the Isles of the Ocean and the Forests of Gaul. Six kings of his line shall follow him. After many other cataclysms, and long before the New Heaven shall appear on earth, there shall come a disturbance of the fixed stars among which angry winds shall battle until in their wrath the stars shall leave their wonted tracks across the sky, and the inverted dome of Heaven shall withhold rain, and crops shall wither.

What ardor and enthusiasm Geoffrey brought to his struggle with the lack of reference books and his ignorance of British and French geography. He writes consistently like a Christian historian of his time, informed throughout by one particular literary model: the Book of Revelation in the New Testament.

Arthur was the Red Dragon of the Celtic peoples, and he fought the White Dragon of the Saxons. "I will write the history of the Britons," Geoffrey proclaimed. "Let the Saxons write their own history." In concluding his history, Geoffrey recommended to William of Malmesbury and to Henry of Huntington that they mind their own business since they were not capable of studying the Celts. They had no source, as Geoffrey had.

His source, claimed Geoffrey, was a small book lent him by Walter, archdeacon of Oxford, who was himself an antiquarian and book collector. Walter had found the little book, which was written in a "British tongue," inside "Brittany." The hue and cry against Geoffrey for making this statement without proof has never ceased.

But parts of Geoffrey's statements are probably true, for he was from 1129 an Augustinian canon of Saint George at Oxford. He was a master, or *magister*, so one assumes that he had studied in France, where he had earned the master's degree. To translate Merlin, however, he would have needed to study Brythonic, like his friend Caradoc of Llancarvan, and to have been educated in Gwynedd. His friend Walter probably was provost of the College of Saint George, in Oxford. It is also certain that Geoffrey worked on the revision of his *History* for twelve years after its first appearance in 1136. He finished his *Vita Merlini*, a poem on the life of Merlin (which has recently been edited at the University of Cardiff), in 1148. He also mentioned that he knew the Welsh writer Caradoc of Llancarvan, who, he said, was writing the continuation of his history. As will be shown, Caradoc did write the history of Wales in Brythonic, and is said to have written (but probably did not) the earliest account of the abduction of Queen Guinevere, whom he had taken to Glastonbury. For his part Geoffrey did not mention Glastonbury, or any other Benedictine foundation, even though some people think that he may have been educated in the one at Monmouth. Geoffrey also said that he worked on the history with texts of Bede and Nennius at hand, but, of course, Bede did not mention Arthur (so far as is known).

Geoffrey's *History* was not criticized during his lifetime, but it came under virulent attack for the first time in 1198 from William of Newburgh, who called the life of Arthur "fables" and "fiction," without a grain of truth, made up by the early Britons. Even today many scholars doubt that Geoffrey's friend passed him a rare book so that he could write from it the life of Arthur. Nobody doubts the popularity of the *History*, however, of which 191 handwritten manuscripts survive in forty-nine libraries in eleven countries. For elegance, interest, and charm it was hardly surpassed in the entire Middle Ages.

In 1929 Acton Griscom and Robert Ellis Jones supplied a much needed, diplomatic text of the *History* and openly stated their belief that Geoffrey eventually would be vindicated, once his proper names had been unscrambled. They further noted that archaeology had already come to his aid. No one had ever believed Geoffrey's story about Vortigern's son having fled to Ireland; now a pillar stone and an inscription found in Ireland support Geoffrey's assertion. In 1935 the famous historian and geographer O. G. S. Crawford, who founded *Antiquity* magazine in Scotland, took up the cudgels in an article called "Arthur and His Battles," proving brilliantly that Geoffrey's "Camblan" was really on Hadrian's Wall.

In his recent edition of Geoffrey's verse *Life of Merlin*, Basil Clarke of the University of Cardiff also supports Geoffrey. Clarke nowhere ignores the tendentious theories of Faral, Fletcher, and Tatlock as to whether or how much Geoffrey disliked the English, the Welsh, or the Scots or whether he favored the Bretons, the Normans, or this or that Plantagenet. Clarke states that King Arthur's enemies, when in this world of shifting affiliation they were not his allies, were identified correctly by Geoffrey as Saxons (which means Anglo-Saxons), Scots, and Picts. Second, on the whole Geoffrey located these foes correctly—to the north of King Arthur. Even the battles of Arthur's youth seem to have been on the time-worn battlefields of the north, where Briton met Scot, Scot met Pict, and all met the "Saxons."

The twentieth century has provided yet another champion for Geoffrey: Stuart Piggott, who founded a new area of historical inquiry in *Ancient Europe*. In 1941 this historian moved to the defense of Geoffrey in "The Sources of Geoffrey of Monmouth." The attackers of Geoffrey, said Piggott magisterially, have been stirred "more [by] professional jealousy than [by] critical faculty," particularly whenever they judged Geoffrey to have been a "fraudulent romancer." His history made, on the contrary, "a considerable contribution to historical literature." Thus, Piggott too saw the gap between history and literature so narrowed in Geoffrey's case as to become fused.

Geoffrey's sources existed, Piggott continued. He then proceeded to expand Sir Edmund Chambers's learned evaluation of the *History*: the "little book" in British, plus verbal information or oral tradition, old ballads, Gildas, Bede, Orosius, Livy, Virgil, Saint Jerome, and Eusebius, hagiography, name sequences, regnal lists, Welsh archives of a lower order, Saxon genealogies, and the famous "Nennius" compilation completed by the year 550. These studies, available only at such a center of learning as Oxford, perhaps obviously created their own "indigestibility," observed Piggott. Still charitably inclined toward Geoffrey, however, he was struck by the brilliance of the passage Geoffrey wrote about King Arthur's coronation. Piggott believed that these pages hit the reader with convincing impact. Such vivid re-creation of an ancient ceremony of kingship could not have been invented from whole cloth, he said, and certainly not at Oxford in the twelfth century.

Stuart Piggott then moved to one specific example in Geoffrey's text. The case is among the most troublesome: What did Geoffrey mean by the geographical precision of "Breton"? How could Bretons have so quickly come across the English Channel, which is no mean feat in any day, to launch themselves in warfare with Arthur? And if they came, why are there no written Breton sources for this superhuman feat? Why are there no King Arthur manuscripts at all in Breton or in Breton French? Very well, hypothesized Piggott, let us for once suppose that "Breton" is an error; Geoffrey probably meant "Britons."

If we are no longer obliged to read "Breton" in the Arthurian material, then many problems are immediately solved. If "British" can be substituted for "Breton," and "Britain" for "Brittany," King Arthur and his rapidly arriving allies stay inside the British Isles and, what is more, actually are in communication with each other within a few minutes by beacons. This would also solve the problem of the dearth of Channel crossings in the Arthurian material, with Marie de France remaining the isolated case. It would further obviate the centuries-long, unsuccessful search for Arthurian sites in Brittany.

When Geoffrey spoke of Arthur's major ally, a prince whose name was perhaps Hoel, or perhaps Alain (*Alan* means prince), this warrior, unless he had to cross the Channel and then travel the length of Britain, came to Arthur's aid from somewhere nearby. When Geoffrey had this prince convalesce in Dumbarton, outside Glasgow, then he did not lay him too impossibly far from his womenfolk at home; for they surely came to care for their lord. We know how fast his relatives, the four queens, rallied to the wounded Arthur, even having a royal barge at their disposal. We also know how eagerly the young women watched Lancelot receive from Queen Guinevere the sign to kill his foe. And with what glee they claimed the head. Again, these substitutions render such points believable.

"The Breton episodes attributed to Arthur by Geoffrey," Piggott suggested, "may in part be due to misreadings of *Armorica* (which is Latin for Brittany) for *Armonica* (which is Latin for *Arfon*, now called Gwynedd, or North Wales)." Such an idea makes marvelous sense for several reasons:

1. King Arthur had close relatives in North Wales, at least on his mother's side.
2. North Wales is in sight of the Isle of Man, which is in sight of the coast of Cumbria and in sight also of the Rhinns of Galloway, the coast of southwestern Scotland.
3. North Wales is also in easy access by sea to Dumbarton, by way of the Irish Sea, in sight of land all the way into the Firth of Clyde.
4. North Wales is also close by sea to the hidden loch on the coast of Scotland that the Welsh archives now tell us was the king's harbor, Loch Ryan; here King Arthur was well hidden but poised to cut the sea route of the Scandinavians.

With this suggestion Stuart Piggott joins the eminent Anglo-Saxon historian, R. H. Hodgkin, who said in his book of 1935, *A History of the Anglo-Saxons*, that Arthur was not in the south of England or in Cornwall.*

Historians are not the only ones who have attempted to vindicate Geoffrey of Monmouth; assistance has come from a famous English archaeologist, the late T. C. Lethbridge, who was director of excavations for the Cambridge Antiquarian Society. He read Geoffrey's descriptions of ancient giants in Britains, believed him, and following his directions uncovered giant chalk figures buried centuries ago by the turf on the Cambridgeshire hills.†

---

*According to Hodgkin, "the Cornish traditions of him must be erroneous, since Cornwall was quite outside the fighting area" (vol. 1, p. 122).

†He told of his search in *Gogmagog: The Buried Gods*.

❧ 2 ❧
Geoffrey's
Life of King Arthur

Geoffrey of Monmouth agrees with the church historian Bede that in Arthur's time Britain saw bloody conflict between four peoples: the Britons,, Picts, Scots, and Angles. The Picts lived in the Highlands of Scotland, with their capital at Inverness, and raided the lands south of the Firth of Forth. The Scots were the new immigrants into western Scotland from Ireland; their center of power was at Oban. The Angles were pushing northward from York toward Northumberland, past Berwick and what we suppose was Lancelot's home near what is now Bamborough, and threatening Edinburgh and East Lothian. After the Romans evacuated their walls (the Antonine and the Hadrianic), the northern of these was manned by the chieftains of the Britons at two ends of the line, near Edinburgh on the east, or at the Firth of Forth, and at Dumbarton Rock on the west, on the Firth of Clyde. Those tribesmen specifically calling themselves the Men of the North, Gwyr y Gogledd, lived near the ancient hill fort of Traprain Law (Dunpelder) in East Lothian. We hear of them early in the Arthurian chronicle of Geoffrey, particularly of their leader King Loth of Lothian, whose wife is King Arthur's sister, sometimes called Anna, and whose oldest son is the famous Gawain.

King Arthur himself came of mixed blood, being royal or noble Roman on his father's side and royal or noble British on his mother's side. Both his father and his paternal uncle were illustrious commanders in chief; his maternal grandfather and uncle were commanders in chief of the native Britons. King Arthur married Queen Guinevere, who bore him one son named Lohot and/or a son named Amhar (Amr) and, some say, even a third son; Geoffrey does not give us this information. Anna married the chieftain King Loth of Lothian and bore several children. Geoffrey admires the oldest, the military

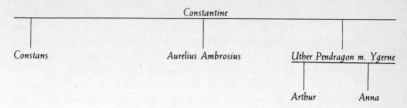

man Gawain. King Arthur also had a second (half?) sister, the Widow Lady of Camelot, who was a personage of great prominence and status in their world; she is the royal mother of Perceval. It is sometimes said that another sister of King Arthur married Arthur's most determined foe, King Urien of Gorre; it was in any case her husband or widower who abducted Queen Guinevere.

Geoffrey does not expand upon the maternal connections of King Arthur, but his Welsh translators know them, at least partially. They were recently reconstructed by Rachel Bromwich as follows:

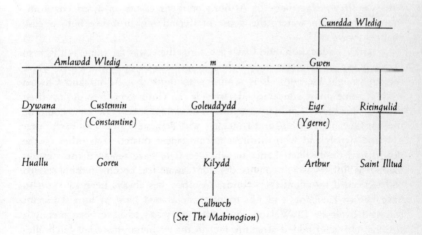

(See *The Mabinogion*)

And his paternal antecedents? According to Edmond Faral, Nennius listed seven Roman "emperors" (or generals = *imperatores*) to have been inside Britain over the five hundred years of Roman occupation: Julius Caesar, Claudius, Severus, Carausius, Constantinus, Maximus, and Maximianus. Both Severus and Constantinus (Constantine) reportedly died inside Britain. During the coronation of King Arthur in Geoffrey's text, Arthur refers to his blood relationship to both Constantine and Maximian. The "emperor" or general Constantinus is said to have been the son of Constantine the Great and to have been interred in North Wales, near the Menai Straits. There was also the Roman named Constantius Chlorus, however, who was the father of Constantine the Great; he died in the city of York. Geoffrey pursued the matter no further than to cite the name *Constantine*, however.

With such an ancestry, which is probably historical, and by process of elimination, we can conclude that King Arthur likely was born in the British *caer* (castle) of his mother, a queen and the daughter and granddaughter of British commanders in chief. It was undoubtedly a very safe fortress. Since King Arthur is customarily called "noble Roman" (Queen Guinevere is also so called), Arthur must have been born inside the ancient Roman province, probably near some Roman military installation, such as a training camp for British recruits. Chances are that he was educated nearby and that the proximity of the training camp was the key; King Arthur, like King Loth, Gawain, and Lancelot, was highly trained as a field officer in his youth.

We know from the Nennius gloss that Arthur had a reputation for cruelty, even in boyhood, and that he was difficult to control and warlike. Lady Gregory reports that he made a raid into Ireland when he was still a boy and stole some dogs from a local king. This would appear to square with Geoffrey's placement of Arthur's mother's castle on a seacoast, surrounded by ocean water; the coast of Ireland was probably but an easy channel away.

Arthur's education (and Gawain's, too), then, was the same as a Roman field officer's, as Geoffrey makes clear in his account of Arthur's first twelve (or so) straight victories. It is tempting to think that Arthur and Gawain were at some point educated side by side, so close were they during their decades of successful military operations of various sorts. The same could be true for Queen Guinevere and Lancelot, who communicated with each other by hand signals and who in direst circumstances trusted each other to the death. It is the brilliant Lancelot who seems to have replaced the steadier Gawain as Arthur's assault commander, for Gawain had become terribly scarred and weakened by countless wounds. Geoffrey has always been said not to have known Lancelot, and not to have mentioned him. In turn, Lancelot was said by Jessie L. Weston some fifty years ago to have been merely a fictional character added after the fact to the Arthurian material. Such allegations are as wrong as they are unthinkable. Thus, Queen Guinevere and Lancelot are scrutinized separately and in later chapters.

Believing that King Arthur was a noble Roman and at the same time a grandson of the illustrious Cunedda Wledig,* who founded the royal House of North Wales, the Welsh historian of Wales John Edward Lloyd con-

---

*(Note: The term *wledig* means commander in chief in Brythonic or Welsh. It is the equivalent of the Roman rank of *dux*.)

cluded that King Arthur was also a commander in chief, like four of his ancestors. When he is called *dux bellorum* in the Nennius or Welsh archives, it means that his title was "duke of Britain."

As duke of Britain, so elected in plenary session by the British chieftains, Arthur would have commanded both the Antonine and the Hadrianic walls, comprising thirty-six fortresses of the line, and after the year 446, the remnants of the Sixth Roman Legion. His headquarters would have been their old station, or the city and vast fort of Carlisle, anchoring with lines of fortifications extending along the south shore of the Solway Firth, the western end of Hadrian's Wall.

Off and on in the Arthurian material one meets King Arthur's mother, an old white-haired grande dame whom he has not seen for extended periods of time, in her own castle. Most frequently this royal mother is attended by her daughter and several granddaughters. It is easy to recognize her castle, which today is a nature preserve on the north shore of the Solway Firth, where the River Nith spreads out into the quicksands and marshes of the Solway. Today the medieval castle, which stands uphill, is called by a very ancient Pictish word: Caerlaverock. Walking down toward the river edge one can still see the castle mound of the Dark Age wooden fortress and even the channels along which ships could have circled the ancient fortress.

North of Caerlaverock, at an intersection of road and river, is the city of Dumfries, whose name occurs frequently in the oldest texts, such as the Béroul *Tristan*. Nearby were Roman training camps, and a Roman harbor. Across the Nith River (the only bridge was at Dumfries) is the old abbey called Sweetheart in the Middle Ages and New Abbey today, where, if a similar institution existed in the Dark Ages, both Arthur and Gawain could have been educated. To the west of the River Nith, through the hamlet called Beeswing, stretches the solitary loch where local historians still say King Arthur spent time: Loch Arthur. The place is silent today, still, isolated—a wooded bowl heavy with blackberry bushes, a lake in its center. A perfect place for a princeling to practice hunting, water sports, arms, and forestry.

Dumfries stands at an intersection of road and river, with Caerlaverock down the east bank of the Nith a few miles below it, and Sweetheart Abbey down the right bank, each isolated from the other by the River Nith. The only bridge or crossing is at Dumfries, still a Royal Burgh.

The geography argues in favor of this area as King Arthur's early boyhood residence. From the river crossing at Dumfries the old track runs due west to Castle Douglas, then west again to Loch Ryan, said by Welsh archives to have been the King's Harbor. Today it is still the shortest route into Ireland.

From the junction at Dumfries the route also runs north and east to

Moffat and Peebles, diagonally still to the source of the River Tweed. Then the stream takes the traveler down past the two ancient abbey sites and ruins of Melrose in the Eildon Hills, past the Roman Trimontium, farther east to the sea at Berwick.

The *Sone de Nansai* manuscript also traces the circumnavigation of northern Scotland in the Dark Ages, the route of the Vikings. By land, the road from the southwest (Dumfries) to the northeastern seaboard (Berwick) crosses the Great North Road of the Romans at Trimontium. There at the triple peaks of the Eildons King Uther Pendragon suffered a crushing defeat while his son Arthur was still a lad.

Geoffrey commences before Arthur's birth, at the reign of the old traitor Vortigern, whom the Welsh called Gwrtheyrn. Geoffrey sets no date for Vortigern's actions, but modern scholars place them between 425 and 459. As the story begins, Vortigern has slain not only the Constantine who is Arthur's grandfather but also Constantine's oldest son Constans. The seer Merlin warns Vortigern that he will be annihilated in the crossfire between the Saxons on the one side and the sons of Constantine on the other. This prophecy proves true. The evil old king is burned to death in his tower, proof that fortresses built during the Dark Ages were for the most part of wood.

This conquerer of the Saxons and destroyer of Vortigern was the second son of Constantine, the new commander in chief, Aurelius Ambrosius. His name and feats are honored by historians and remembered to this day. Geoffrey paints a vivid and touching picture of this great commander/chieftain and records his laughter and his words to Merlin.

Once the area between the walls was pacified, Aurelius Ambrosius set about restoring the churches that had been torn down by the pagan "Saxons." Then he turned his attention to the three hundred Britons massacred during a banquet and truce. Aurelius desired to construct a memorial to them, which will last for all eternity, he proclaims. He goes to an unidentified city named "Guintonia" by Geoffrey of Monmouth, but apparently translated incorrectly into English as Winchester, in the south of England. A historian of that city, W. Lloyd Woodland, denied it: "The tradition that King Arthur rallied the British forces at Winchester . . . is utterly wrong" and wrong also that Aurelius built a lasting memorial in stone there or thereabouts.

A closer look at this section of Geoffrey's *Historia* is warranted. "Guintonia" is very near a fortress alternately called "Salesburia" incorrectly rendered into English as Salisbury in southern England. Second, at "Salesburia" is a mountain called "Ambrii": "in monte ambrii." Now comes the most troublesome of Geoffrey's translations from his little book.

Aurelius Ambrosius made it perfectly clear that he wished to construct a monument in stone that would last forever. It was to stand near a city, another place called Salisbury, and beside a mountain. Not a hill, but a mountain: "Send for stones to make a circle about the route" (most likely a processional path). After consultation, Merlin volunteers to go to Ireland for especially healing stones, and this journey requires the military services of Uther Pendragon, youngest of the three sons of Constantine. War breaks out in Ireland, but Uther wins and with Merlin's supernatural powers manages to transport the stones to "Salisbury" and to the mountain.

Geoffrey understandably also selected Winchester, Salisbury on the Salisbury Plain, and perhaps then Stonehenge in southern England as this astonishing and vast site. Certainly Stonehenge would appear worthy of the pious intent of Aurelius. As one hundred thousand tourists discover each year, it stands at quite a distance from Salisbury, on the downs north of the city. But *there is no mountain, properly speaking, in that vicinity*, only the rolling downs and dry Salisbury Plain. And in any case both Stonehenge and Avebury are prehistoric sites so much more ancient than the reign of Aurelius Ambrosius as to make ridiculous Geoffrey's choice! Geoffrey's nonexistent source, then, must be reinterpreted.

The initial connection that Geoffrey made with the Winchester-Salisbury area probably seemed doubly justified to him, however, if he knew the various Roman roads in that vicinity. Their system of highways, such as numbers 7, 13, 14, and 15 (London to Chichester, thence to Caerleon [or Isca in Wales], thence to Exeter on the south coast) would make these sites appear logical. The Roman city of Calleva Atrebatum, now called Silchester, was a hub of seven roads; the Arthurian manuscripts are always setting rendezvous points at such an intersection. From Calleva Atrebatum roads led to London, Old Sarum, Alchester, Chichester, Saint Albans, and Winchester. Since Silchester represented in Geoffrey's day the most extensive Roman remains in Hampshire, it probably struck him as a likely area for Aurelius. George C. Boon's book *Roman Silchester* talks about his discovery that no such stone memorial there, such as Aurelius had built by Merlin, was there. But Geoffrey must have been reinforced in his wrong opinion by the mention of Saint Albans, for he knows King Arthur will be crowned in a city of the martyrs Julius and Aaron (both still unlocated).

It's time to weigh the facts: a city called Guintonia, a nearby place called Salisbury, a mountain standing close by, a monastery at Salisbury, a principal church there also, stones set in a circle around a route or processional path, a large or very rich cemetery where Aurelius and his brother Uther Pendragon are preparing their burials in royal style. Aurelius tells Merlin to send for the giants' healing stones in Ireland: "mitte pro chorea gigantum." Then the text recounts the well-known Irish legendary history that giants from Africa settled Ireland. Later Geoffrey repeats his Latin, so that unfortunately there is no mistake about his meaning: *Aurelius was interred at Guintonia* "prope cenobium ambrii infra choream gigantum quam vivens fieri preceperat." He repeats the name of the city: "urbe guintonie." Aurelius was interred in a cemetery: "in cimiterio." Uther Pendragon, dead from poison as was Aurelius, was also so interred: "ad cenobium ambrii & infra choream gigantum iuxta aurelium ambrosium."

Thus, Aurelius is being interred beneath the circle of the giants that when alive he had ordered made for him in a cemetery near a monastery of Ambrii. Uther Pendragon was taken after death to the monastery of Ambrii and buried below the circle of the giants, next to Aurelius Ambrosius.

In good faith one cannot excuse here any translation into English referring to Stonehenge. Thus, Geoffrey should be exonerated from such nonsense; *he never wrote it.*

Second, Geoffrey of Monmouth was perhaps one of the most accomplished Latin prose writers and poets of all time. His Latin is unassailable. In only one instance does he waver, unsure whether to spell *giant* "gigantum" or "gygantum"; either way it is a perfectly correct Latin genitive plural. And yet something is altogether wrong in this passage.

What is wrong is the circle of stones. If King Arthur and his family are recognized as Christian and Arthur himself as the first Worthy of the Middle Ages, first even before France's Saint Charlemagne, *it is not likely that Aurelius would have been building stone circles to the pagan gods.*

Whatever is pagan in the Arthurian material was knowingly put there by medieval authors. They may even have done it in jest. Many of them learned mythology at schools of the Dark Ages and of the Middle Ages that specialized in it. Thus, the story of the giants is Irish legend or mythology, no giants having actually been found in Britain. (Constantine the Great *looks* from his bust like a giant, and probably King Arthur appeared gigantic in frame and strength.)

One is left nursing a massive dissatisfaction with Geoffrey's text, which itself is accurate. He must have misunderstood his source. What other alternative is there? He must have had to choose between two Greek words: *choreia* (dance) and *choros* (choir). He chose the former and wrote that Aurelius had constructed a circle, a round, *a dance of the giants*, as the passage is translated. (And, as the height of the ridiculous, even Stonehenge is often so termed!)

Had Geoffrey opted for the latter word, he would have written that Aurelius Ambrosius was interred beneath the choir, or quire, of the abbey, or abbey church, and that the royal graves were near the processional way as the clergy entered their eastern end or choir of the church. And, in fact, the choir of a church is semicircular.

When Geoffrey goes on to say that the clergy from all over were invited to the Pentecost celebration in which for three days Aurelius Ambrosius sat in state wearing his crown and being congratulated upon the succes-ful completion of his memorial to the three hundred British dead, it's difficult to imagine him sitting inside a circle of stones ("circa plateam") in the middle of the road!

On the other hand, it was customary in olden times to steal or pur-chase cut stones with which to build churches. It is likely that Ambrosius got some stones from Ireland and that he considered them beautiful. Merlin must have thought so too, if here he was the master builder, a kind of Abbot Suger *avant la lettre*. All this is argument, before the dawn, of course.

A hitherto misunderstood passage from the *Mirabilia* or Marvels of Brit-ain in the Nennius compilation came to join Geoffrey's troublesome text:

Est aliud miraculum in regione quae vocatur Ercing. Habetur ibi sepul-chrum juxta fontem qui cognominatur Licat Amir, et viri nomen, qui sepultus est in tumulo, sic vocabatur.

This passage from the *Historia Brittonum* of Nennius translates as follows:

There is another miracle in the region called Ercing. They have there a tomb next to the fountain [or font] that is known as "Licat Amir," and the name of the man who is buried there in the burial mound is so called [i.e., "Amir"].

Then Nennius adds one other puzzling sentence:

Amir [vel Amir mur] filius Arthuri militis erat, et ipse occidit eum ibi-dem, et sepelivit.

Amir [or Amir the Great] was [the name of] the son of Arthur the Soldier, and he killed him in this very spot and buried him [there].

According to the Welsh *Mabinogion*, King Arthur had a son named Amhar. The *Perlesvaus* manuscript tell us that the courtier Kay killed Arthur's son, that King Arthur buried him temporarily in the tomb of his ancestors and later that Queen Guinevere removed the head of her son to the Grail Castle, where she was having built the tomb for herself and for King Arthur.

Until now, the words "Licat Amir" have made no sense to anyone; when studied in connection with the Geoffrey passages on the memorial to the British dead, Salisbury, and the Mount of Ambrii, they have astonishing significance.

The Mountain of Ambrii must mean the Mountain of Ambr(os)ii: the Mountain of Ambrosius. Ambrosius is also called Amir the Great by Nennius. His name, also spelled "Amhyr," comes from his name in Welsh: Emrys. The second name of Ambrosius is his agnomen, or surname, usually indicating in a noble Roman the title accorded for outstanding merit and service to the country, like Scipio *Africanus*, or C. Julius *Caesar*. Actually his name means Aurelius the Immortal. The mountain, therefore, is the Mountain of the Immortal Aurelius.

This brings us back to the Nennius "Licat Amir," where the name of Ambrosius appears again. Unless the remark, by itself cryptic, is taken alongside the story by Geoffrey of Monmouth, the reference to the mountain is neither clear nor apparent. However, by the rules of linguistics that govern the Romance languages, which coming from Latin were fronted in the mouth by the native Celtic speakers, the Latin noun *lectus* (*bed* in English), becomes the French word for bed, *licat* (now *lit*).

In the context of monarchs like Aurelius Ambrosius, the word *bed* assumes a special meaning, as a Bed of Justice. In olden times kings sat upon a *lectus* (or bed) as they dispensed justice, or wore their crowns. Thus, the otherwise incomprehensible Nennius gloss becomes the Bed of Ambrosius, and the Mountain of Ambrosius becomes the Seat of the King: Ambrosius's Seat.

Is there a mountain called the Seat of Ambrosius, situated near Salisbury, an abbey, a sacred burial place for royalty? No, that mountain is today called Arthur's Seat. It towers above Salisbury, the northeastern suburb of Edinburgh. King Arthur reputedly was jealous of Ambrosius's fame. He once removed the body, or the head, of an ancestor from the White Tower, which seems to mean Guintonia. Presumably he also changed the name of the mountain from "Ambrosius's Seat" to "Arthur's Seat." It was said of Arthur that he particularly wished to be indebted to no ancestor for his own skill, might, and exalted reputation.

Authors writing about Edinburgh hold that the mountain in question was called Arthur's Seat because the king sat there to direct a battle. This seems unlikely. In the first place, King Arthur did not direct his battles from the top of extinct volcanoes but engaged the enemy from the assault line. His battles were all fought in the north in his extreme youth, except the last one which was fought on Hadrian's Wall. It is probably true that one of his early battles was fought near Edinburgh, another at nearby Linlithgow.

By "Arthur's Seat" is probably meant his palace, where he sat to dispense justice, a palace so lavish and so splendid that an encyclopedist in distant France marveled at its opulent treasures. Today the British royal seat, Holyrood Palace, is directly downhill or *below Arthur's Seat*.

The immortal dead are still honored in huge stone monuments across from Arthur's Seat, on Calton Hill summit. Sir. Walter Scott customarily escorted visitors to Calton Hill, or Hill of the Royal Caledonians, whence they could look across, especially in the good morning light, to see King Arthur's profile on the Salisbury Crags above Holyrood Palace.

On September 14, 1128, on that site King David I encountered the stag with the holy cross between its antlers; as a result he reconstituted the Abbey of the Holy Rood, near the palace. The first church may have been built on the foundations of the church dating back to the times of Aurelius and Arthur and may have utilized many of the same stones. In King David's church, there was a Rood Screen and a royal burial vault. We read that the Rood Screen, containing a piece of the cross upon which Christ was crucified, may also have been inherited. It was donated by the empress Helena, mother of Constantine the Great, who had found the Holy Rood (Cross) in Jerusalem where she had built the Church of the Holy Sepulcher. Or it was donated by King Arthur himself, who was said to have gone to the Holy Land for that purpose.

In the Treasury of the Abbey of the Holy Rood there once reposed a piece of the Lord's Cross, a silver cross with a piece of the True Cross, a new cross of pure gold with thirty precious stones (this as of 1493), silver crosses and chains, plus a chalice of the pure gold. Such treasures correspond well to the description of the immense riches contained in King Arthur's palace, noted as being in the "land of the Picts," that is, in Scotland.*

A glance at the floor plan of Holyrood shows that the burial vault for royalty was just inside the East Processional Doorway, adjacent to the Rood Screen and opposite the choir and choir screen. The chapter house and font were located south of the processional way. Since churches were customarily built on the holy or consecrated sites of earlier churches, Geoffrey of Monmouth's text concerning the burials of Aurelius Ambrosius and Uther Pendragon appears to be accurate.

Geoffrey gives no term for the heroic struggle against enemies and approaching death of Uther Pendragon (by poisoning); but he seems to have enjoyed an old wives' tale about Arthur's birth being presaged by fiery events in the heavens and his conception which was worthy of the early Greek hero Heracles (Hercules). He repeats the famous and amusing legend of Hercules, son of Alcmene and Zeus, but son also of the earthly Amphitryon, which had long ago so inspired Sophocles, Euripides, and Seneca. While over the centuries scholars have taken credit for having made a hero-god of King Arthur, Geoffrey's use of the ancient source doubtless started it all.

---

*Some of these same treasures were saved during the revolution of November 5, 1688, when the bones of the kings and queens were cast out and most of the abbey torn down. A few walls and stones have survived. They are presumably in the Treasury of the Glasgow Cathedral.

Uther Pendragon passed away long before his son reached manhood. During Arthur's minority King Loth of Lothian acted as regent of the realm, which included much of what is today the region of Scotland called Borders. Loth was also earl of Carlisle.

Arthur probably spent much of his youth around the Caerlaverock Merse. (Visiting his mother years later, he remarked how changed it all looked to him.) A fatherly and strong hand was provided by King Loth, Gawain's father, from his stronghold at Dunpelder or Traprain Law in East Lothian. A silver hoard from that site buried during Arthur's lifetime, contains one piece marked "CON," one supposes for Constantine.* The mount called Traprain Law (*law* = peak) can be clearly seen from Calton Hill in Edinburgh. Presumably there, a hundred years or so after Arthur's death, the poem *Gododdin* mentions him. The name *Gododdin* comes from the Latin name of King Loth's clan or tribe: *Votadini*.

When Arthur was fifteen years old, he attended a convocation of the chiefs of the Britons, who elected him as their commander in chief. The meeting was held at what Geoffrey called "Silchester" in southern England, but which was most probably at *Silchester on the Wall of Hadrian*, or the Chesters fort on that wall. Furthermore, this north British site is about halfway across the wall, or close to the midpoint of the east-west axis, also adjacent to five Roman roads, one running east-west below the wall and two (which branch into four) running south-north. The fact that this site is so close to Carlisle suggests that Arthur, the summoned guest of honor, came from the area adjacent to Carlisle, as from Dumfries and the Caerlaverock Merse. Without realizing it, Geoffrey mentions the chiefs of the Britons, Arthur's Welsh kinsmen from the line of Cunedda Kings, who had migrated south from the Firth of Forth some time after 400.

Assuming command, Arthur waged what seem to be six campaigns, according to Geoffrey. After his first victory he rewarded the three northern chieftains who had ruled freely before the Saxon invasions of their territories. Here Geoffrey, first of all authors in the Middle Ages to do so, announces the three famous brothers, principal figures in the Arthurian sagas:

1. Loth of Lothian, the father of Gawain and Modred
2. Urien (of the many spellings), the father of two sons both named Owein (Yvain in French); his kingdom is Murray (murefensium) in western Scotland, and/or the western Isles
3. Anguselus, king of the Scots (?)

*Part of the silver hoard is in the Edinburgh Museum today.

In Geoffrey's text, this third brother remains the most vocal, the most supportive, and the most important of the three (until the wounding of Arthur). Yet Geoffrey knows the least about him by way of actual facts.

That following winter Arthur ordered the construction of a fleet of ships for the purpose of conquering Ireland the following summer. It seems most unlikely that such boats were built on the river in York when the Clyde River or Clydebank would have offered Arthur a closer harbor, a wider and deeper river, and a proximity to materials and labor. Still at "York," according to Geoffrey, Arthur wedded "guenhuueram," the spelling of whose name Geoffrey can never decide upon, "of a noble Roman family." We know her as Guinevere, the older version of the modern name *Jennifer.*

The next summer Arthur launched his naval operation in the Irish Sea, conquering what are routinely mistranslated as "Iceland" and "Gothland," instead of the more obvious Islay and Scotland. He passed the succeeding winter at his island base in the Irish Sea—clearly not Iceland this time, but more probably Islay, or the Isle of Man.

Arthur maintained the peace for twelve years, a kind of Golden Age for himself and his kingdom. Then he renewed a naval campaign, this time against "Norway" and "Denmark." Instead of being struck here by such unlikely conquests, we should remember that the names probably designated British territories occupied by Scandinavians, or Vikings. The Isle of Man was called "Norway" well into Geoffrey of Monmouth's day, for instance.

Then Arthur launched naval operations against Gaul, the name of that region only becoming "France" later during Arthur's lifetime and that of King Clovis. This campaign lasted nine years.

Returning to Britain King Arthur enjoyed a magnificent crowning ceremony, probably something akin to the triumphs accorded victorious Roman commanders. Geoffrey assumed that this ceremony took place at "Caerleon" in modern Wales, which was the old Roman rest-and-recreation center. But surely Geoffrey erred again: Caerleon for Carlisle. The splendid coronation ceremony ends this part of the *Historia,* of which it stands as the culmination.

The last part of Arthur's life deals with his European campaign in which some, but not all, of his chieftains participate. Here the king loses both Bedevere and Kay. Just at the point where victory seems assured, Arthur hears that Modred and Guinevere, whom he had left as joint regents of Britain, have married and usurped the throne. But Queen Guinevere is supposed to have died long before Arthur left for the continent! Obviously the original archives represent two opposing points of view.

In the matter of Queen Guinevere and Modred even Geoffrey of Monmouth seems to be mouthing antifeminist material. He has Arthur land in the south of England, which would have been correct if he had been talking about Julius Caesar, but where Arthur certainly did not land. Then he picks up the terrible story of war, Modred attempting to stop the king from landing. As Arthur's men tried to come ashore, casualties ran high. Three days later Arthur pursued Modred and his forces to the battlefields, Hadrian's Wall. There, it is now believed, the Battle of Camlan was fought, and Arthur was fatally wounded. It was the year 542, adds Geoffrey. Many renowned rulers died there that day.

Of all the authors to have treated the Arthurian material, only Geoffrey has provided a rough chronology of the events of King Arthur's life:

1. Antecedents
   King Aurelius Ambrosius
   King Uther Pendragon
2. Career
   Election at Chesters . . . .   *Aged* 15
   Northern campaign
        Battle of Badon Hill . . . .   c. 500
   Island campaign . . . .   1 *year*
   Peace . . . .   12 *years*
   Gallic campaign . . . .   9 *years*
   Crowning at "Caerleon" . . . .   (?)
   Roman/European campaign . . . .   20 *years* (?)
   Return and final campaign
        Battle of "Camlan"   542

The twenty years for the Roman campaign and the date of 500 for the Battle of Badon Hill, which completed the northern campaign, derive from the supposition that Geoffrey took into account the famous reference by Saint Gildas to this very battle at Mount Badon, or at Badon Hill. Gildas for some strange reason did not give the date; everybody else, said Hodgkin, within a century and a half forgot what had happened inside Britain at the end of the Roman occupation. Faral came to the rescue here and figured out the date of the Battle of Badon Hill:

1. Two facts alone about Gildas are certain:
   a. he was born in Strathclyde, and
   b. he was called into Ireland by King Ainmericus (reigned 565–68).
2. The *Annals of Ulster* (Annales Tigernachi) inform us that Gildas died in 569, *recte* 570.

3. Gildas wrote his epistle about the fall of Britain (*De Excidio*) before Maglocunus died (King Maelgwn of North Wales) in 547, or 549. Gildas was 44 years old when he wrote the book, and he was born in the same year as the Battle of Mount Badon.
4. Therefore Gildas was born around 500, which is probably the date of the Battle of Badon Hill.

It is interesting to look at the dates of King Arthur and his antecedents as derived by two modern scholars, the historian John Morris (1973) and the archaeologist Lloyd Robert Laing (1975):

I. Antecedents
    Aurelius Ambrosius, c. 460–c. 475
    Uther Pendragon, c. 475–c. 490
    Birth of Arthur, c. 475
II. Career of King Arthur. . . . total = 25 years
    Election, c. 490
    Northern campaign
    Island campaign
    Peace = 12 (?) years
    Gallic campaign = 9 (?) years
    Roman campaign = 2 (?) years
    Wounding at Camlan, 515

Many historians, including R. G. Collingwood and J. N. L. Myres in *Roman Britain and the English Settlements*, revised at Oxford in 1963, have accepted the statement of Gildas to the effect that forty-four years of peace followed Arthur's twelfth victory at Badon Hill. On the other hand the *Annals of Wales* allow Arthur only twenty-one years of peace. And Geoffrey grants Arthur a peace of only twelve years. In summary now, we have the following estimates:

Badon Hill		Camlan	
Bede	493	Morris	515
Morris	c. 495	Bede	537
Gildas	c. 500	*Annales Cambriae*	539
Annales Cambriae	516	(Annals of Wales)	
Matthew of		Geoffrey	542
Westminster	520		

This preview would not be complete without a rapid glance at the *Anglo-Saxon Chronicles*, despite the fact that they do not honor Arthur with so much as a mention. *Ethelwerd's Chronicle* lists the arrivals into southern England, on the Saxon shore, of Hengist and Horsa, of Ella and Cissa, and of Cerdic and Cynric as between 449 and 556. John Morris in *The Age of Arthur* placed the landing of Hengist and Horsa earlier, perhaps around 428. The Anglo-Saxon records claim that everywhere the Britons fled before them like fire, as in 473, that the ancient Roman coastal fortress of Anderida (Pevensey) fell to them in 491, and that the Isle of Wight fell in 530. King Cynric of the West Saxons was able by 534 to become a king and reign for twenty-six years inside England. King Ida of Bernicia (Northumberland) was able to surround the fortress of Bamborough with a thorn hedge and commence rebuilding it by 547. Thus, by that date the new arrivals, Angles and Saxons, had established their kingdoms. It is true that the early Bernician kings enjoyed rather short tenures, their regions averaging not more than six years apiece.

Bamborough Castle Rock seems once to have been a British fortress called Dinguardi, according to Herbert A. Evans's *Castles of England and Wales*. Theoretically, Dinguardi became Joyous Garde in the French romances about Lancelot and Guinevere.

By the year 542 or thereabouts, the Angles, Saxons, and Jutes had settled the coastal areas east of a line drawn, roughly speaking, from Southampton to Edinburgh. King Arthur's victories, then, either happened very early in the century, as John Morris seems to have concluded, or were victories far north of the Humber River, as our evidence would seem to indicate.

As Kenneth Jackson has pointed out, Somerset fell to English-speaking peoples between 658 and 682, Cornwall not until 838. Therefore, as Hodgkin argues, they were outside the area of conflict in Arthur's time. The Battle of Badon Hill, as Lloyd seems to have argued correctly, around the year 500, cut Phase I of the Saxon migrations into Britain from Phase II. Phase II, after the career of King Arthur and probably largely because of it, will conclude the separation from England of the Celtic realms of the north and of the northwest. Lloyd reasons convincingly in this way in his *History of Wales.**

After Arthur's death the Angles were again driven out of the far north. The Pictish king Bridei mac Bili reconquered Edinburgh from them in 685. By 844 "Kenneth mac Alpin" had united the Picts and the Scots. King Kenneth Macalpin begins the line of early kings of Scotland, then, which leads to King David I who reconstituted Holyrood Abbey (843 to 1153). Scotland's line of kings is tabled in John Prebble's *The Lion of the North*. Prebble

*(Vol. 1, chapter 5)

speaks of the North Britons, "of whom one may have been Arthur." Yet there were three kings of Scotland between Alpin and David I who were named Constantine. The name Arthur *was* perpetuated, but in the line of the early kings of the Dalriadic Scots, on the west coast of Scotland.

Those who tend to discount Geoffrey's dates of Arthur's last stand at Camlan slight the heroic traditions of North Wales. Someone emerged victorious there, his eye on the main chance—the vacuum created by the passing of Arthur. That someone appears to have been King Maelgwn of Gwynedd, whose biography was written by Saint Gildas, who anathematized him in *De Excidio*, his lament upon the fall of Britain. Sharon Turner in *The History of the Anglo-Saxons* argued that King Maelgwn fought against Arthur at the Battle of Camlan—that he fought alongside Modred, in other words—and that he survived the carnage. As Turner presented the case, Maelgwn stood to win; his son became King Brude (Bridei) of the Picts soon after the death or departure overseas of King Arthur. In those days inheritance of the throne was not always dictated by primogeniture but also obliquely, by the law of tanistry. Turner's argument supports Welsh heroic tradition: Arthur was still alive in 530 when he fought alongside Gereint (Erec) at the Battle of Llongborth, and he saw Erec, whose coronation he had attended in Edinburgh, fall there to his death.

It is now possible to state that Geoffrey's reporting of Arthur's life tallies with the general history of his century. Geoffrey appears to have understood well the annalistic nature of his sources, seizing upon the major points of the king's life and career: his antecedents; his election by the chiefs at Chesters on Hadrian's Wall; his early battles; his island campaign off the west coast of Britain; his coronation at "Caerleon"; his Roman campaign against what may have been Vandals and/or Visigoths; and his final attempt to resume command inside Britain.

For some strange reason Geoffrey did not find the story of how Merlin raised Arthur, how he taught Arthur to draw the sword from the flintstone, and how Arthur by lighting the fire was recognized by the chieftains as their future king. All this is embroidered in the pages of Sir Thomas Malory, but it comes almost directly from *Merlin* by the French poet Robert de Boron. Most likely Merlin was in Arthur's time the name of the Lord Abbot of some monastery like Sweetheart near Dumfries and was therefore called "Father" by the boy Arthur. (The clergymen who attended the boy candidate were called "Brothers.") Or, the whole story came from some Dark Age author who had read it in Plutarch's life of Theseus.

Second, Geoffrey's geography tallies with the geography of Britain. He refers to islands off the west coasts of what are now northwestern England and western Scotland; he mentions Dumbarton, fortress of the Britons,

several times; and also Lothian, the Caledonian Forest (the Romans designated noble persons of the far north as "Caledonian"), Loch Lomond, and
the River Clyde; and with Geoffrey's lead we are able to recognize Hadrian's
Wall, with its fort of Chesters and later its fort of Camboglanna or Camlan.
From these points directions into the Caerlaverock Merse, Dumfries, Galloway, Loch Ryan, and then across the shallow fords of the Solway into the
string of Roman fortresses along the swampy south shore, all the way from
Carlisle to Bowness-on-Solway, appear to be within our grasp. Proximity to
the Irish Sea remains a sine qua non of Arthurian place directions. If Geoffrey falls down at all, it is with regard to time and distance; here we will
require some of the French calculations if we are to finally locate the various
"castles" of King Arthur.

Geoffrey has also displayed a knowledge of ancient documents, such
as those of Gildas and Nennius, though not of the arcane Welsh *Triads*.
Geoffrey's Arthur is very much a Roman, a highly civilized military man—
hardly the Red Ravager of the *Triads*.

From Geoffrey we hear of "real" people, historical figures—King Loth,
King Urien, King Anguselus, King Vortigern, King Uther Pendragon, the
Lady Ygerne, Queen Anna, the Widow Lady of Camelot, the Lady of the
Lake, the Loathly Damsel of the ancient ballad, Prince Modred (beloved in
the history of Scotland), and Gawain, who fought a king called the "Green
Knight" not far from Ireland.

And through Geoffrey's efforts we have been led to royal sites dating
from Arthur's day; along Roman roads to Roman ruins; and into Christian
sites inside northern Britain. All greatly assist in pinning down Arthur. And
where Geoffrey doesn't lead he points, as for example in the case of Vortigern. A disciple of the Irish theologian Pelagius, Vortigern was declared by
Rome to have been crazy, a "sea-green Briton" whose theology was nothing
but heresy.

Thus, from Geoffrey we have many leads—and a new feeling of con-
fidence in this witness from the long-lost past.

❧ 3 ❧
The Twelve Battles

Arthur's twelve battles immortalized him. It is here, at this particular point, that Geoffrey collates at least two different sources. his "Merlin" manuscript lent him by Walter, archdeacon of Oxford, and the much older "Nennius" compilation of Welsh arcana.

The report that in his youth King Arthur fought twelve battles first derives from this Latin manuscript ascribed to someone called Nennius. This volume chronicles the history of the British, *Historia Brittonum*. Its oldest and most trustworthy copies, the Chartres Manuscript (no. 98) and the British Museum Harley (no. 3859), date from no later than the mid-tenth century.

The best Arthurian scholars from France and from England, Faral and Chambers, have already proven that Geoffrey worked from the Harley copy. It contains some *Annals of Wales*, some genealogies, and a section on the marvels to be seen in Britain. These last pages read like a modern travel brochure of the *Mirabilia Britanniae* ("When you get to England, be sure not to miss seeing Loch Lomond up in Scotland. Loch Lomond measures . . . "). The subject of the so-called twelve battles of King Arthur is no less serious a topic. (See the table on page 66 for the listing of the battles in the British Museum's Harley Manuscript 3859.)

It is probable that no words in any Latin archives have furnished so much challenge and labor to scholars as have those cryptic ones in Harley Manuscript 3859 designating once well-known place names. The results of this study are very interesting in themselves, but we must look through them in order to find King Arthur's kingdom.

The Glein River of battle 1 has not been located officially, and the same is true for the Dubglas River, where battles 2–5 took place. In the case

Battles Numbered	Sites	Translation
1	"ostium fluminis . Glein"	= mouth of the River Glein
2, 3, 4, 5	"aliud flumen . Dubglas . . . in regione Linnuis"	= another River, the Dubglas . . . in the Linnuis area
6	"flumen . Bassas"	= River Bassas
7	"in silva Celidonis, Cat Coit Celidon"	= in the Celidon Wood, Battle of Celidon Wood
8	"in castello Guinnion"	= in Fort Guinnion
9	"in urbe Legionis"	= in the City of the Legion
10	"in litore fluminis . . . Tribruit"	= on the banks of the River Tribruit
11	"in monte Agned"	= on Mount Agned
12	"in monte Badonis"	= on Mount Badon

of the sixth engagement, while there is no Bass River today, there is a Bass Rock. Bass Rock and the ruins of Tantallon Castle are located, the first in the Firth of Forth, the second on the south shore or entrance to that firth. The two are so striking that they are often painted by watercolorists.* If we accept Bass Rock as a possible Arthurian battle site, we should speculate about Arthur's having to defend the entrance to the Firth of Forth; Arthur's Seat; the Edinburgh area; and the fortress or fortresses at Stirling across the Firth of Forth to the north.

It is true that the Firth of Forth over the centuries has been the site of major naval operations, such as the preparations by the British fleet for the Battle of Jutland.

In the cases of battles 7 and 8 we can be more assured, for they yielded their secrets in 1945 to the linguist and historian Kenneth Hurlstone Jackson. Fort Guinnion, he discovered, indicated the Roman Binchester, only twenty miles south of Hadrian's Wall.

The Celidon Wood, he also discovered, pointed directly to the modern metropolis of Glasgow. It was probably not, as some had theorized earlier, the city of Penrith, which is the first large town south of Carlisle, on the present M6 Freeway, but farther to the north. Both Faral and O. G. S. Crawford were in agreement with Jackson's findings.

*See Arthur G. Bradley's beautiful book *The Gateway to Scotland* and the watercolor by A. L. Collins.

The Nennius papers had said that Arthur bore (or wore) the image of the Virgin Mary and slew great numbers "through the power of Our Lord Jesus Christ and the Holy Virgin" then, there at Binchester.

The Nennius documents state elsewhere that King Arthur had undertaken the pilgrimage to Jerusalem and had brought back a holy statue for the treasury of the "Wedale" monastery, near "Melros." Where to look? The very distinguished medieval Melrose Abbey stands at the foot of the Eildon Hills. It was at this spot that Uther Pendragon had lost his terrible battle, so we are in battle country and near the mark after all.

The medieval Melrose Abbey, the ruins of which can be visited today, stood very close to the huge Roman fort of Trimontium, there on the Great North Road, or Roman road from London to York to Stirling in Scotland. The fort was called Trimontium from the triple peaks of the Eildons, an exceptionally dramatic panorama. Almost no traces of Trimontium (now called Newstead) exist today. Faral was quite certain, however, that the lost *Northern Annals* of Scotland, and the Annals of King Arthur, were composed, kept, and first stored there at an earlier or Dark Age Melrose Abbey.

King Arthur appears to have been fighting where Geoffrey of Monmouth put him, that is, north of York, close to Hadrian's Wall, and no farther north than the Antonine Wall, which connected what is now Glasgow on the west to what is now Edinburgh on the eastern side of Scotland. It also connected the Firth of Clyde on the west side of Scotland to the Firth of Forth on the eastern side. This narrow line is also Britain's narrowest point and, as such, the best place to make a stand.

The "City of the Legion," which Nennius names as the site of the ninth battle, no longer seems to scholars to be the small Roman walled city of Deva, now Chester, where the Twentieth Roman Legion was quartered. The question becomes one about the Roman legions stationed in Britain before Arthur's day. The Twentieth was at Chester. The Second Augustan Legion was stationed at the rest-and-recreation center for Roman troops, Caerleon-on-Usk in southern Wales. The Sixth Roman Legion was quartered in the city of York. Thus, York, Chester, and Caerleon were all cities of the legion. But all three are too far from the places now believed to be sites of Arthur's battles and are not positively identified as sites of Arthurian wars.

The term "City of the Legion" is too vague in the Nennius papers. It now appears more probably to refer to the newly or latest constituted capital city of the Romans: Carlisle. The Carlisle area came under fire, as it were, as early as 368. Maps show it as a ring of heavy Roman fortresses stretching far to the west beyond the modern city of Carlisle.

The great Roman system of fortresses at Carlisle included much of the lowlands lying at the end of the Solway Firth, and the forts on its southern shores. They were for centuries the headquarters of the most fierce and daring, the most warlike and the most successful of the ancient tribes of the

Britons, the Brigantes. By Arthur's time these tribes had spread victorious to the northern or Pictish shores of the Solway. In fact, they had spread into the very area where, presumably, King Arthur was born and nurtured.

So important to the Roman occupation of Britain was this center of Carlisle that the Roman itineraries 2 (Dover-London-Chester-York-Carlisle) and 5 (London-Lincoln-York-Carlisle) ended there. We also know that the place mentioned most frequently as the headquarters of King Arthur, in the French manuscripts, is this same Carlisle.

Thus, Carlisle and its fortresses maintained not only the western ramparts of Hadrian's Wall, at the center of the fiercest fighting during the last hundred years of the Roman occupation of Britain, but also the major junctions of the main roads going (1) east and north into the Edinburgh area, and (2) west into Glasgow and the fortresses of the Britons, especially at Dumbarton Rock on the River Clyde. Furthermore, after the Roman withdrawal, two centers witnessed the regrouping of the native British forces: (1) Carlisle–Glasgow–Traprain Law, and (2) Stirling–Edinburgh–Traprain Law. Carlisle remained a powerful and independent center of British power, for long periods of time a capital of Strathclyde, well into the seventh century. It even has been more than once the capital of Scotland.

Battle 11 has been thought, but by no means unanimously, to have taken place in the Edinburgh area, which was then a hill fort on the Edinburgh Castle Rock, overlooking a plain. There are reasons, besides Arthur's Seat, for placing the king in that city.

For Battle 10 Nennius gives us in Tribruit two place names, O. G. S. Crawford decided, referring to the sandy shore of a river as well as to a system of three rivers flowing into an estuary. He reached this conclusion after having compared the variants in several Nennius manuscripts, testing them against the principles of linguistics. Some manuscripts specified the Latin *tractus* and its Welsh original *traeth* meaning a tract of sand lying on one shore of the river. The second root *bruit*, he felt, came from the Latin rendering of the Old Welsh name for the River Frew in Scotland.

This remarkable river flows through the Vale of Menteith as it broadens toward Stirling Rock, and in this upper valley the River Frew joins the River Forth. After their confluence the Forth and Frew rivers swell down toward the rock and then wind in loops beyond it into the Firth of Forth. Their roughly eastern course butts up against the rock, having by their course cut the Lowlands of Scotland from the Highlands to the north. As Crawford saw it, Battle 10 stopped the invading Picts from the north.

The once spectacular Fords of Frew were long considered one of the Wonders of Scotland. North of them extended the wild lands of the Northern Picts, all the way to Inverness and the Macbeth country. This land of black sheep, say the Perceval texts, was cut, by a Middle River, from the southern land of the white (Christian) sheep. The Fords of Frew were the only, single crossing of these waters.* In Arthur's day the Fords were so steep that horses had to go down them Indian file.†

The word *Tribruit* refers, concluded Crawford, to these three dangerous waters, which traverse the Vale of Menteith just west of Stirling Rock. In fact, three streams swell the deep waters, creating on the other side of Stirling Castle Rock the wide Firth of Forth: the Forth itself, the Goodie Water, and the Teith. "No more suitable place for a fort or a battle could be imagined," summarized Crawford in "Arthur and His Battles."

Fourteen years later Kenneth Jackson, in another article, placed this battle along the marshes between Carlisle and the Solway Firth, at or near the sites so insisted upon by the continental writers of the Middle Ages. Carlisle is known variously as Karidol (German); Karleolum (Norman French), Caerluil, or Caerleol; Luguvallum (Latin), capital of the Roman *civitas Carvetiorum* (province of the people of the Deer?) after 368, as Rome became more and more worried about losing the north.

In summary, then, the battles of Arthur have been identified as follows:

7. Celidon Wood = the Glasgow area
8. Fort Guinnion = Binchester, south of Hadrian's Wall
9. City of Legion = Carlisle
10. River Tribruit = (a) Stirling or (b) Carlisle
11 Mount Agned = Edinburgh (or perhaps High Rochester, north of Hadrian's Wall)

The last battle, Mount Badon, remains the most challenging since this combat inaugurated the long period of peaceful reign by King Arthur and established his military reputation. The site of this mountain fortress has been sought above all others. Such was its fame and reputation that three of the ancient sources mention it. Saint Gildas records it as the siege of the Badonic Mountain, "Badonici montis," where the Saxons failed to "beat down the northern powers." Nennius calls it a war or the battle of Mount Bado, "bellum in monte Badonis," characterized by the bloody slaughter of 840 men in one day—a battle so terrible that people, including Saint Gildas, remembered it in relationship to their natal day. The *Annals of Wales* employ the same sort of terminology, adding that there were three engagements in this battle over a period of three days and nights. During the encounters King Arthur wore the Cross of Christ.

---

*Today the fords lie where the Goodie Water flows into the Forth, in farmlands and country roads crossed at the point of river junction by a small bridge.

†The French authors of the *Prose Lancelot* were agog when Lancelot performed this marvelous feat on his way to safety in the north.

The composite references give us the following clues:

1. There was a mountain that had a fortress on the summit.
2. Against this fortress a siege operation was mounted. Thus, the Saxons were entrenched.
3. King Arthur led and organized the repeated waves of assault.
4. Under King Arthur were allied forces of the north.
5. King Arthur is represented as Christian, but his foes are pagan.
6. The number three is characteristic of all accounts.
7. The carnage was massive, so much so that the secret Welsh lore marked Arthur with it. The battle was savagely fought, as if it was a turning point.
8. The victory of Arthur was so decisive as to have crushed the enemy for one or even two generations.

What sort of victory is that?

Customarily the Battle of Mount Badon has been placed at Bath in southwestern England. Geoffrey of Monmouth probably started this ascription, which has been followed somewhat routinely by military historians, such as Charles Hardwick in his *Ancient Battlefields in Lancashire*. One sympathizes with Geoffrey, of course, since place names commencing with the syllable *Ba* are virtually nonexistent. Bath is nonetheless a very poor guess. This Welsh Caerfadon (note that it is *fa* and not *ba*) is a Roman spa, a watering place; it was never a fortress and is not on a mountain. Furthermore, it is immensely distant from King Arthur's wars.

It is entirely possible that Geoffrey of Monmouth had seen one of the original Gildas manuscripts. In one of these the pair of scribes who copied it inserted their own hook: "qui prope Sabrinum ostium habetur" (which is believed to be near the mouth of the Severn River). This cuts no ice now, for "Severn" is routinely mistaken for "Solway" in early Arthurian texts.

Two recent scholars follow Geoffrey for no apparent reason. *The New Historical Geography of England* puts the Battle of Mount Badon, correctly ascribed to 500, on the English Channel near Poole Harbor. Thus, Arthur would have rushed down from Edinburgh-Glasgow, transporting with him all the northern tribes and clansmen, to fight Saxons at Saint Aldhelm's Head, where the chalk downs reach the sea at the Isle of Purbeck and he would have lost; the Saxons quite sure that they won all the battles in southern England.

In her book on King Arthur, Helen Hill Miller still placed King Arthur at Bath. She thought that the Saxons were invading Somerset, but they had not arrived that far west yet, of course. She further tried to make a case for King Arthur's coming down through the Swindon Gap in the Chiltern Hills. While the Romans were occupying England, they brought their galleys into the south coast, not too far from Portland Bill. One does not see how any-one but Saxons got to Bath by water, although King Arthur was a ship-builder. Transporting men overland to Bath could never have been done at short notice, not in those days. Pitched battles on land, as fought in the Dark Ages, had to be hosted years ahead of the designated date of combat.

In any case, we can now say with fair certainty that eleven of the twelve battles were probably fought in the north, and numbers 7, 8, 9, 10, and 11 positively so.

The only way to make further progress in either Nennius or Geoffrey is to take them together, collating each episode of their separate accounts. In Nennius several battles are unaccounted for; left over in Geoffrey is the rest of the war. What becomes apparent first is that Nennius lists only Ar-thur's twelve youthful battles inside the two walls. Geoffrey does not at-tempt to number these engagements, but stands aside to take a longer look at them.

Very briefly, Geoffrey gives in the twelve pages of his very dense and compact report the following revised scenario:

1. Arthur is near his capital city (which Geoffrey thinks is York).
2. He hears that the Saxons have invaded Albania, which is Scotland. Since they have come by sea, it is obviously eastern Scotland.
3. Arthur defeats them and rushes to the largest city in the area for rein-forcements from North Wales. (Geoffrey thinks he must have gone to London, which is very unlikely.)
4. Arthur fights, alongside his reinforcements, three battles in Scotland.
5. Then Arthur goes down to Binchester, below Hadrian's Wall, and works his way north to Carlisle, where he fights two more terrible battles. Geoffrey calls this region the land of "Somerset," which is in southern England. What he *must* have meant was the land of the Welsh, which sounds like "Somer" but which is *Cymry* (Old Wales, or Strathclyde). All this time Arthur is aiming for Dumbarton, which the Saxons have be-sieged and taken.
6. Having swept through the southern province, Binchester to Carlisle, Ar-thur returned to Edinburgh and won a battle there. He then swept the Saxons out of the Border area and westward into the one fortress on the north or right bank of the River Clyde.
7. He fought the Battle of Mount Badon, afterward destroying the fleets of the Saxons in the Clyde estuary there.

In order to show how this reasoning came about, we must return to Nennius and recapitulate his twelve battles in reference to Geoffrey's five or so cam-paigns of King Arthur.

The Twelve Battles

Nennius	Geoffrey
I.	
1. Mouth, River Glein	
2–5. River Dubglas, Linnuis region (Retranslating the "Mouth of the River Glein" into ancient writing we would have "Aber-Glein," which might be "Aber-Gullane" on the south tip of the Firth of Forth.)	1–2. River Dulgas near the city of York (?). Arthur learns that the Saxons have invaded Albania (Scotland). After battle 2 Arthur goes to London (?) to meet his reinforcements from North Wales.

6. River Bassas
   [Bassas = Bo'ness?]
        = Bass Rock?]
	3. Battle at Kaer-Luid-Coit, or "Castle-Lothian-Forest." Here 6,000 Saxons drowned in the river. The rest wasted the land to the Severn Sea (*recte* Solway). Saxon survivors fled to the woods. The Saxons disembark new forces at Totnes in southern Britain (?). Geoffrey may have meant to say at Bo'ness on the Firth of Forth. It is the only port there with a *litus*, or sandy shore backed by a rather high sea cliff. Arthur had been preparing an expedition against the Scots and Picts. He was obliged to fight new Saxons.

II.	
7. Cat Coit Calidon (Battle of Celidon Wood)	4. Forest of Celidon Arthur realizes he must aim for Dumbarton, already seized by the Saxons.
III.	

8. Fort Guinnion
   (Binchester)
9. City of the Legion
10. River Tribruit
   (Carlisle, or Stirling)
	5–6. City of Legion, a battle fought for two days, on a hill. The second day Arthur killed 470 men. Carlisle.

IV.	
11. Mount Agned (Edinburgh)	
V.	
12. Mount Badon	7. Dumbarton

Geoffrey refined the Nennius list thusly:

I.   Campaign of East Lothian
II. Caledonian Forest
III. March north into Scotland, from Binchester, and Carlisle
IV. Edinburgh
V.   Dumbarton/Glasgow

Geoffrey's overall account rings true from two points of view—history and geography. He actually makes three major errors that can be disposed of: York, London, and Somerset. Somerset is the easiest of all, because for reasons of phonetics "Cymry" and "Somer" are close, and "Somerset" actually means Land of the Cymry, or Welsh, in any case. Thus, by Somerset we now decide that Geoffrey meant Strathclyde, the Carlisle area.

The matter of York is more difficult. Geoffrey speaks of its noted churches, which sounds like York. He puts it close to a river where Arthur had his fleet built, which does not sound like York and the small Ouse River. He has Arthur wed the queen there, but York was not Arthur's home church or the home of his ancestors, nor was it the place of his palace. Arthur would have no reason to winter in York if he was to fight Saxons in Scotland. Time and distance are both wrong.

We need instead of York an eastern coastal city with famous churches, where shipbuilding took place, near the seacoast and landing place of the Saxons, close to the action inside Scotland. The answer seems obvious now, that by "York" Geoffrey meant "Guintonia," the Salisbury and Holyrood area of Ambrosius and Uther. Their church was then far more famous than York-minster, which was the later Saxon center of the Roman Catholic church.

However, we now are privy to more information—hidden from Geoffrey of Monmouth, who was not a member of the bardic order in Wales. The *Welsh Triads* pick up a reference in Geoffrey that confirms his use of a private source. In speaking of the church that Ambrosius had rebuilt (at the site of the present Holyrood Abbey ruin), Geoffrey said that "Guintonia" was also called Caer Caradoc or Castle of Caradoc. The Welsh *Triads*, which (again, let us be fair to him) *Geoffrey absolutely could not have seen or heard*, also tell us this: *

> Three Perpetual Harmonies of the Island of Britain:
>   One was at the Island of Afallach,
>   and the second at Caer Garadawg,
>   and the third at Bangor.
> In each of these three places there were 2,400 religious men; and of

---

*Ms. Penarth 185, called R. Vaughan's Ms., *Triad* 90, trans. by Rachel Bromwich.

these 100 in turn continued each hour of the twenty-four hours of the day and night in prayer and service to God, ceaselessly and without rest for ever.

Older translators said "Three Perpetual Choirs," which brings us back one more time to Geoffrey's probable mistake of *choros* (choir) for *chorei* (dance). What Ambrosius founded, then, was a Perpetual Choir. It must have been Arthur who founded the same at the Isle of Avalon (spelled "Afallach" above), where Queen Guinevere planned that he would rest after his life had ended. It was also the Welsh *Triads* alone that recorded what Arthur had done at the White Tower, Guintonia perhaps, and his reasons for moving the head of his ancestor Bran (the word means king).

Once the scene begins to make sense, the other pieces fall into reasonable places. The "London" where King Arthur met his reinforcements from North Wales was most probably Glasgow, or if not that city, then some other harbor inside the safe, very long estuary of the Clyde. Dumbarton itself is only a few miles downstream from Glasgow, on the north bank of the Clyde just where the River Leven, draining Loch Lomond, flows into the Clyde. It is only four miles from Dumbarton up the Leven to Loch Lomond. Arthur may have had his ships built on both coasts, a North Sea fleet at the Firth of Forth, where shipbuilding continued until very recent times, and an Irish Sea fleet in Glasgow. If the Saxons came ashore at Gullane and at Bo'ness on the Firth of Forth, then one understands very easily why so many of them drowned. The waters are deep, dangerous, cold, and very stormy. Reading Geoffrey, one sees how clearly he grasped King Arthur's problems, menaced as he was on two fronts at once. The few pages of Geoffrey, which are so difficult to decipher, almost explain that the first war should be called the defense of Britain.

Geoffrey rises to true epic stature as he tells about this war, giving us Arthur's harangue to his men, and the encouraging words of Bishop Dubricius at the City of Legion, or Carlisle. That this ecclesiastic should sanction King Arthur confirms the early conversions to Christianity in this area.

Stephen Johnson's *Later Roman Britain* shows what a very considerable accumulation of Christian evidence and objects distinguished Carlisle itself. This evidence attests to a bishopric, many churches, lead baptismal tanks, and Roman town buildings. Only Cirencester, says Johnson, has yielded a greater concentration of Christian objects in all Britain. And nearer to Dumfries, where King Arthur may have grown up, was the earliest center of Christianity inside Scotland, a center founded by Saint Ninian in honor of the beloved Saint Martin of Tours. Traces of Saint Ninian and of his churches will probably emerge from the continental manuscripts concerning King Arthur.

So, the Romans seem to have had five capitals: London, York, Lincoln, Cirencester, and Carlisle.

A consideration of Arthur's return to the more northerly line at the Antonine Wall should recall the precision about the Battle of Mount Badon set down earlier. The Fortress of the Britons at the Rock of Clyde, or Dumbarton Rock, answers the first criterion; it is the most famous fortress upon a mountain in the Dark Ages of Britain. The Saxons could very well have been entrenched about the sides of this double volcanic plug, which then stood surrounded by the waters of the Clyde River. Throughout the course of history the rock was besieged and was stormed over and again. It was a site which the allied forces of the north at any time would have considered imperative to regain and hold.

Geoffrey's Latin makes it clear that he understood the significance of Dumbarton. He calls it what it was, the *civitas alclud*,* the state called Rock of Clyde. By *civitas* Geoffrey indicated its importance as a large administrative unit of people, a nation, a commonwealth. It included the Loch Lomond area, which he will soon have King Arthur take his cousin Hoel around to see. Then Arthur will speak about the *mirabilia* of Scotland, like any host to his guest. Geoffrey later calls Dumbarton the *pagum badonis*, the country of Badon, the canton, or the district. The Loch Lomond, called *stagnum* to distinguish it from the waters of the Clyde, will soon see Arthur's ships cruising there.

Arthur himself presumably stormed up the steep rocky banks at Dumbarton to the tops of the double peaks, or as Geoffrey says, "ascendit arturus." His "nephew Hoel," as Geoffrey has it, lies ill within the fortress, another reason for urgency and fierceness. Thanks to his own efforts and the customary violence of his methods, King Arthur delivered the rock from "barbarica oppressione."

The Welsh *Triads* seem to have Mount Badon in mind when they characterize Arthur's battle frenzy as red:

> Three Red Ravagers of the Island of Britain:
> Rhun son of Beli,
> and Lle(u) Skilful Hand,
> and Morgan(t) the Wealthy.
> But there was one who was a Red Ravager greater than all three: Arthur was his name. For a year neither grass nor plants used to spring up where one of the three would walk; but where Arthur went, not for seven years.†

*Or "Alcluith," originally three miles from the Rock of Clyde at Dumbarton, at the Old Kirkpatrick Ferrydike.
†*Triad* 20 W, trans. Rachel Bromwich.

At Mount Badon Arthur fought and won a decisive battle that stopped the Saxon incursions for forty-four years, said Saint Gildas, who was born at Dumbarton. What sort of victory could have guaranteed a peace of such long duration, in such an area as Dark Age Britain? Enlisting the assistance here of a noted British military historian, one reads in the pages of Sir Halford J. Mackinder's *Britain and The British Seas* that "the defence of Britain rests fundamentally upon the theory implied in the command of the sea." If Mackinder had given him directions Arthur couldn't have followed them better.

What Arthur patrolled first, according to Geoffrey of Monmouth, was the shallow Narrow Seas along the east coast of England and Scotland. This is what every commander in chief should do first, according to Mackinder. Arthur cleaned out the flat, low shoreline from Berwick-on-Tweed, it would appear, northward at least past the Firth of Forth. Then on the oceanic and older side of Great Britain Arthur engaged to defend the jagged coasts and vast red promontories that sweep out into the stormy seas, and more than five thousand islands. There in the Irish Sea he established a naval base upon an island; especially after he had conquered the Isle of Man, Arthur would have stationed himself almost at the exact center of Great Britain. From the Isle of Man Arthur could see with the naked eye Ulster, Cumberland, Wales, Dalriadic Scotland, and Strathclyde. The Isle of Man, never ruled or conquered by the Romans, is called the Navel of Britain. Its symbol is the sacred tripod, three legs in a wheel, as at the Delphic Oracle.

Or one may turn to the geographer Ian A. Richmond for instruction and background to Geoffrey's history. According to this scholar, the defense of the coasts of Britain, after the withdrawal of the Roman legions, was of first consideration. It was urgent to launch sea sweeps up the east coast to the Orkneys and Scapa Flow. From the year 388 it was also urgent to stop such Irish searaiders as those who captured the future Saint Patrick from his native England, or Strathclyde. Naval operations out of Dumbarton, which Geoffrey tells us Arthur had organized, would have had to maintain control of the inland sea as far south as Great Orme and Anglesey. The Romans had always patrolled such waters, for they had to protect their copper shipments, which sailed along those coasts.

The problem of Arthur's decisive victory is becoming clearer. At what places could Arthur have caught the Saxon invaders and stopped them for years? If Geoffrey had said Scapa Flow, we would believe him; for a study of British geography would certainly indicate that a sweeping victory in the rough waters of the Pentland Firth could have stopped them.

The route of the Scandinavians, historians tell us, brought them through the tidal race at Dunnet Head, down into the north and then the Little Minch into the Gulf of the Hebrides, directly to the Islay, which Geoffrey gave as an island base for Arthur. At Islay and Jura Arthur was ready to swing around and launch his next punitive expedition against the Dalriadic Scots pouring in from Ireland.

If Arthur did not stop the Vikings at Scapa Flow, and if he did not get them at Cape Wrath, then he would have had to engage them outside Dumbarton in the Firth of Clyde. Geoffrey has placed him there after his youthful, other campaigns.

Arthur could never, it seems pretty clear, have held the Scandinavians anywhere inside the long sea channels between Cape Wrath on the north side and Dumbarton to the south. These channels are as much as one hundred fifty miles long, and often as much as thirty miles wide. Whole flotillas of the low-riding Viking ships could have darted about in those channels forever.

But it was more likely a naval victory that stopped the long harassment by the Vikings in the northern seas. A naval victory would have meant the loss of highly trained Viking seamen. Pilots and navigators cannot be trained overnight. Further, it took the Vikings decades to build an entire fleet, what with the necessity of skilled labor and the great expense of imported timber.*

If the peace Arthur won at Mount Badon lasted even seventeen years, which is the lowest estimate, he must have killed a whole generation of Scandinavian mariners. If this was the case, then why has Geoffrey said only that Arthur's general pursued the Saxon ships and destroyed them? Why did Geoffrey let it go with the liberation of Dumbarton from "barbaric . . . oppressions"? Something remains unclear.

Geoffrey's reticence might lead us to suspect that all was not entirely well at Badon Hill. Geoffrey tips his hand there, whetting our curiosity until we start searching elsewhere, as in the *Prose Lancelot*.

A description of a real landmark—especially one as memorable as Dumbarton Rock—is not apt to be mistaken even in literature. It is huge, red, vertiginous, awesome. There is nothing on its sheer face to hang on to.

Therefore, when the *Prose Lancelot* refers to the culmination of King Arthur's "War in Scotland," Dumbarton Rock and the Clyde banks emerge recognizable. The author is working either from a superior source or from personal knowledge.

The French author was presumably writing in France, although he may have written this section in Holyrood, Melrose, or Jedburgh, or in Stirling at Cambuskenneth Abbey, and he was not much interested in the military genius of King Arthur. Perhaps he saw little evidence of it. What he says is that the king besieged "Arestuel."

---

*An idea of how slowly and at what great expense in skilled labor also comes from Sharon Turner's *History*. He speaks very thoughtfully and at great length about Anglo-Saxon shipbuilding on the continent.

In the foreground flowed a very wide, long river. On the opposite shore rose a long mountain peak, or a British hill fort, a Celtic *dunn (dum)*. The place was called "the Rock of the Saxons," because they had seized it. Thus, it may very well be the Rock of Clyde, Fort of the Britons (Dumbarton).

King Arthur's camp, with a viewing tower for the queen, had been set up on the opposite shore of the river, here called the "nearer" shore. Circumvallation of the rock had failed to wrest it from its occupants.

Between the opposing forces, in the middle of the river at a ford upstream from Arthur's camp, the warriors met daily in deadly hand-to-hand combat. The river water washed away the blood. The queen's general, Lancelot, one day lured the defenders out into the ford in force and there hacked them to pieces.

King Arthur himself, explained the *Prose Lancelot*, had been taken prisoner and was being held inside the fortress on the rock. *Certain Irish allies of the Saxons planned to take him into Ireland.* The Welsh *Triads* confirm that Arthur was even more exalted than the "Three Exalted Prisoners of the Island of Britain" (*Triad 52*).

> And one [Prisoner] who was more exalted than the three of them, was three nights in prison in Caer Oeth and Anoeth, and three nights imprisoned in Gwen Pendragon, and three nights in an enchanted prison under the Stone of Echymeint. This Exalted Prisoner was Arthur. And it was the same lad who released him from each of these three prisons— Goreu, son of Custennin, his cousin.

This account differs from Geoffrey's version because here it is not Arthur who releases his cousin lying ill in Dumbarton, but the other way around. It seems to be the same cousin from North Wales, however, named not Hoel, as Geoffrey had it, but Goreu.

Several traces of this imprisonment subsist in Welsh and Irish lore, but the one closest to the *Prose Lancelot* comes from the latter. According to Irish sources there was a real prison made of the bones of slaughtered Romans, where political prisoners were incarcerated, Arthur among them. This many-chambered structure was in the land of Gorre. This places does not figure in Geoffrey's account, but the stories about it are so numerous in the Lancelot adventures that it must be heeded. Here Queen Guinevere was taken as a prisoner, and here she, like Arthur, was held until Lancelot rescued her.

There was another reason for Arthur's having been taken prisoner: the Saxon princess who commanded the forces inside the rock wished to wed him. In the *Prose Lancelot* version, the first part of the Battle of Badon Hill was fought by the Saxon Camilla against the British battle queen Guinevere. The *Prose Lancelot* yields that King Arthur was not kept inside the rock but was conveyed by ship into Ireland. It behooves us then to look for the land of Gorre to the west of Dumbarton, across the sea. Both Saxon commanders, a king and the woman Camilla, commit suicide by leaping from the ramparts at the rock, said to be at the Ford of the Gaels' Shore. Once victorious here, King Arthur received into "The Round Table" those of his commanders—Lancelot, Hector, and Galehaut—who had won the day.

It would seem that this account does not contradict Geoffrey's source but rather supplements it, although it transfers the focus to Lancelot. It supports the view that Badon was fought in part on the Clyde River Valley (*strath* Clyde), between Dumbarton and Glasgow. The Rock of Clyde was and is *Dum* (*dunn, mons,* mount) + *Barton* (*Britannorum, Breatan, Bretan, Britton, mBretan* = of the Britons), also called *Alclut* (Rock of Clyde) in Geoffrey of Monmouth. Geoffrey had started his story of King Arthur there, with the evil King Vortigern for whom Merlin built the fortress on the rock. The *Prose Lancelot* agrees: this was the fortress of Vortigern, when he espoused the Saxon Hengist's sister, which explains the Saxon commander Camilla. Once King Arthur had installed himself within the huge red lava mountain, he could consolidate the Celtic realm and hold it.

At Dumbarton Arthur held the largest natural refuge south of the Scotch-Irish kingdom of Dalriada and controlled the seas in and beyond the Clyde estuary, plus the border area between the Clyde and the Solway. His strongholds extended from Dumbarton and Glasgow in the northwest to Carlisle with its Roman ruins in the south. From Dumbarton, according to Geoffrey, the king moved up the Leven River to Loch Lomond and then due east into the Rock of Stirling. From there he had a direct line of sight to Arthur's Seat and the Holyrood Palace area of northeastern Edinburgh. The military road from Stirling to Loch Lomond to Dumbarton is much used today, its track sunk deep into the soil. Between Edinburgh and the North Sea Arthur counted upon the hill fort of Traprain Law and the Gododdin as the first line of defense.

Few landmarks in the world impress the eye and the mind like Dumbarton and Stirling and Arthur's Seat. Traprain Law, near Haddington, is almost as ghastly and haunted. Seen from the high ground at the southern shore of Loch Lomond, the Rock of Clyde down in the river valley swims in front of the blue water like a massive red dragon. Far below in the Vale of Monteith is the gray, brooding western cliff of Stirling.

These ancient landmarks are not hidden, but obvious. And unquestionably Arthur's battles in that vicinity were dictated by geography. Dumbarton continued to be seized by the Vikings long after Arthur's death and again "liberated," as Geoffrey had it, and returned to what Nora Chadwick called the Celtic realm. Stirling is garrisoned today.

The *Lancelot* text supports Geoffrey's impression that King Arthur's early battles constituted a northern campaign, called a War in Scotland. The French

Grail romances, which will be considered in detail in Part III, also support Geoffrey—that Arthur was in Scotland at "Winchester" and at "Salisbury" and that King Arthur's War in Scotland commenced in the eastern marches, when Lancelot's father lost his fortress of "Joyeuse Garde" (believed to have been Bamborough). Then it was that Arthur commenced his victorious career, at the dire news, as Geoffrey says, that Scotland had been invaded.

It's time for the historians to set it all in perspective. In his history of Wales, John Edward Lloyd explains that the defense of Britain in the Dark Ages would have involved a triple threat from enemies who were, upon short notice, also allies: Irish, Saxons, and Picts from the north. This state of affairs developed from as early as the year 360. After 446 it worsened, when the Britons' appeal to the Roman governor Aetius in Gaul failed substantially to put the military problem in Britain upon his shoulders again.

Under the Romans, three high-ranking military officers had divided the command inside Britain:

1. the count of Britain (*Comes Militum Britanniarum*) commanding 2,200 infantrymen, 200 cavalry, and 37 forts (*castella*)
2. the count of the Saxon shore (*Comes Tractus Maritimi,* and later *Comes Litoris Saxonici*), commanding 3,000 infantrymen, 900 horsemen, and 9 fortresses
3. the duke of Britain (*Dux Limitum Britannicarum*) commanding 14,000 infantrymen, 900 horsemen, and 36 forts of the Antonine and Hadrianic walls

Since no reports were dispatched to Rome from these officers after the year 400, says Nora Chadwick, then their offices must have fallen vacant, their forts perhaps partially abandoned and deserted. Sir John Rhys, one of the most respected Arthurian scholars, believed that when Arthur was designated *dux,* it meant that he had been appointed to the office of count of Britain. In *A History under the Anglo-Saxon Kings* J. M. Lappenberg studies the question of the Roman military administration inside Britain. Professor Lloyd of the University College of North Wales at Bangor more or less agreed with Lappenberg.

The defense of Britain seems to have been Geoffrey's assessment of the twelve battles of King Arthur, a series that in his mind constituted a northern campaign. Geoffrey functioned like a modern military historian, emphasizing location, terrain, type of action, and strategy. He has shown his readers pitched battles, sieges, an ambush, a tactical retreat, forced marches, encirclement, blockade, and the use of cavalry and a fleet of ships. The ships are maneuvered inside Loch Lomond as well as in the Clyde estuary and probably also in the Irish Sea. Arthur's naval base inside the islands of the western coast of Britain seems the logical headquarters for such a campaign. According to Geoffrey, the Britons preferred to fight upon the heights, in the mouths of rivers, or at the fords. His Arthur has excelled in drawing out his foes for hand-to-hand combat, followed by rapid pursuit and slaughter. The king's emphasis was always on the enemy's total surrender. Speed, resourcefulness, and energetic action have characterized the young king's style.

Geoffrey's Arthur has also shown skill as an administrator; as field commander he had to oversee reinforcements, victualing, supplies, rewards, officers of the line, and salaries. Arthur and his warriors became rich from the booty taken from the Saxons when they surrendered. Turning over treasure was, in fact, a condition of the surrender. In negotiations and in psychological warfare, a third requisite for a great general, Geoffrey's Arthur also merits admiration. He seems to have been able to keep his foes off balance, manipulating them at every turn.

Geoffrey knew of no disaffection in Arthur's ranks, at least not before the battle of Badon Hill. Thus, even this early in the century, the *principes iuventutis*, or young worshipers of Arthur, thronged to his side, ready to die for him. They helped launch the king's second campaign which, according to Geoffrey, took place entirely in the islands off the west coast of Britain and began with the summer conquest of Ireland. As "gallant knights," a twelfth-century modernization, they wait in the wings for the French romancers to immortalize them, however.

As the modern historian Halford J. Mackinder explains, there are always the same three problems in the sort of situation in which Arthur found himself: (1) the command of the sea, (2) the defense of Britain if that power is lost, and (3) the separate defense of Ireland. Once the seas were secured and the rear protected, Arthur could move to an offensive action on the continent of Europe. His final opponent is there. Accordingly, Geoffrey gives Arthur nine years in Gaul, which he spent also destroying coastal fortresses and fleets based along the Friesian, Danish, and Saxon shores. Arthur's home ports, then, must have been along the Narrow Seas, well within safe harbors. The inner waters of the Firth of Forth would seem perfect for Arthur, as modern admirals would surely attest. Nearby Edinburgh is still one of the three marshaling centers for the transport of British troops abroad.

4

The Coronation
of King Arthur

We still wish to know, as we unwind the thread, whether we are dealing with the records of a real king. Where did he live and fight his wars and reign in peace? Who were his allies? Who were his enemies? Can we give a name to their leader? What reality, in short, underlies Arthur? Can we still find confirmation in the brief final sentences of Geoffrey, before he gives the bloody ending at Camlan?

There appears to be reason to believe. Arthur's chronology is coming clearer. His ancestry seems verified, at least on his mother's side, and in the case of Aurelius Ambrosius. His battle sites have been located in part. Best of all, the ancient hill forts from which he looked down are places from which we too can look. Furthermore, the general history fits the circumstances of Arthur's alleged life, military career, and associates.

The places where Arthur was said to have lived—by more than fifty authors from different centuries and in different languages—turn out to be places we can visit. Here he lay wounded, here he lies buried, here he lay beneath the stones of his prison, here he stood and looked out over the waters, here he ran through the Holy Woods as a boy, here he outfitted some small craft and sailed these waters, here he wielded his hammer, smashing the gates to the lochs, and here he ravaged the foe until the earth swam in blood long after. We also know, from archaeologists who have worked in England, that he was not in *England*—all the more reason to believe he was in the north.

At the height of his power, says Geoffrey, Arthur enjoyed a wonderful coronation, to which, in a manner of speaking, he dragged his vanquished

enemies. He made them process and participate so they would be obliged
to bear witness. Even supposing that Geoffrey brought his imagination to
bear on his sources, there is reason to believe his account. To paraphrase
Albert Einstein, the eternal mystery of Geoffrey's source is its comprehensi-
bility.

An in-depth examination of Geoffrey of Monmouth's text is in order.
Such a procedure remains consonant with medieval methodology, for in the
Middle Ages two theories of time were commonly held: that time is a linear
continuum stretching longitudinally to its promised end; and that time is
relative and therefore cuts at points into a vertical descent, or stasis. Before,
we looked at Arthur from birth to maturity, and then from his first to his
twelfth battle. In the pages where Geoffrey speaks of his coronation, we
shall see Arthur as he would have been caught by a modern novelist, held
fast in time, perhaps even larger than life.

Geoffrey regrets the lost days when he writes, "Britain was then exalted." Then there was a king of wondrous might. He stood after Caratacus
of Caer Caradoc, who was the son of Bran. In those times, however, kings'
names were not used or spoken. Lancelot was already a famous warrior and
a great man before he guessed that his name was "Lancelot," and that he was
descended from many kings of Britain whose names were Lancelot I and
Lancelot II. Whatever his tenure, octennial or other, Arthur came to some
great Roman city for a second crowning in the pages of Geoffrey.

We know from Saint Gildas that kingship existed among the British
princes of the fifth century. In his diatribe Gildas lashes out at those very
kings who succeeded Arthur in the 540s, after the Battle of Camlan, for
failing to rule properly (as Arthur had done). We know that Arthur distrib-
uted riches and venison to his allies. His supporters stretched back, generation by generation, to the Roman occupation of Britain. His presence at a
High Ceremony, which was his second coronation, graced his land. The
harmony of his gestures blended human existence, divine order, and the
immutable transits of the fixed stars. Therefore his power would be felt beyond the grave. Because of Arthur, society and nature moved in quivering
consonance. His name was probably Father, as in Old Irish *athair* and *athir*,
and the Latin *pater*. Lancelot's name in youth was Galahad.

We do not know that naval battles were fought against the Saxons by
the ancient Britons. Previous Arthurian scholars have thought that Arthur
won by the use of cavalry; but really, of what use are horses on Dumbarton
Rock? Or on Traprain Law? Or on the triple peaks of the Eildons, where
Uther Pendragon was whipped? We do not know that Christian churches
mantled the land; we know only of the poor, wattled structure of Glastonbury. We can only see some bits of stone at Whithorn on the coast of
Galloway, where Saint Ninian supposedly built Candida Casa. Yet, says
Geoffrey, Arthur built ships, or craft of some sort. He was also crowned in

a Christian church. We do not know that bishops and archbishops, whatever those terms meant in the Dark Ages, presided at Arthur's second coronation. Yet Geoffrey says that they did officiate. We do not know much about the Catholic church, then called Culdaic or Celtic, because it existed in Arthur's day, before the arrival in Canterbury of Saint Augustine, sent by the pope at Rome to convert the Saxons. Most distressing of all, we still do not have any idea of the extent of Arthur's dominion.

But we have a chance to find out, in the dense passage wherein Geoffrey details the coronation. How? Because he furnishes the guest list. A coronation was not to be missed, both conquered foes and trusted allies attended. Everybody who was anybody in Arthur's world had to be there. And Queen Guinevere was crowned, too, so the ladies attended, although British custom decreed that the sexes be separated from each other.

The roster of the honored guests will furnish us with the hardest riddle of all: Who was who? What was his home? From how far away did the guests arrive? Ergo, what was the extent of Arthur's realm at the end of his decades of peaceful reign?

Until now, the critics reviewing the second coronation of Arthur in the pages of Geoffrey of Monmouth have been dubious. Their skepticism has by now almost effaced Geoffrey's testimony; for they have not even accepted the possibility of a Pentecostal feast and crown-wearing rite, or even that such pomp and circumstance could possibly have attended British royalty prior to the establishment of the Plantagenet dynasty. Why not?

Why should not King Arthur, Geoffrey asks, who had years previously struck stark terror into their hearts, summon his utterly vanquished foes to whatever place he designated? Why must "splendor and elegance" be restricted to a twelfth-century age of chivalry? Were diadems and laurel wreaths, such as those worn at the coronation by Arthur and Guinevere, placed only upon the brows of Norman dukes before 1136? Surely not, for even in Roman republican times great public benefactors were honored in Rome, as were victorious military men. Thus, the occasion of Arthur's second dignification, coming after battles, island conquests, and nine years of victories on the continent, offered him the opportunity to return home for reinforcements and well-earned rewards: a triumphal procession, and what seems in retrospect to have been a promotion to the military, Roman rank of *imperator*.

Even the Welsh keepers of secrets were certain that Arthur, finally, was declared emperor, *Yr Amherawdyr Arthur*. Sir John Rhys speaks of this title in his *Studies in the Arthurian Legend*. Many Roman generals received this advancement to the supreme command after a first signal victory.

In Geoffrey's account King Arthur has just set foot again upon British soil. Like any conquering hero after sustained and arduous combat, he rides high. Therefore he receives a triumph, something akin to what Fabius Maximus, Caesar, or Pompey received in the streets of ancient Rome. As *dux* riding through his city, King Arthur was entitled to carry a swagger stick in his hand before striding in full panoply into the church. Arthur will wage a continental campaign, enlisting those who have the stomach for it, and offering them gain.

Geoffrey decided that Arthur chose the city of Caerleon-on-Usk (*Kaer Illion ar wysc*) in southern Wales as the site of this most important rite. The critics pounced upon him for this, claiming that Geoffrey chose Caerleon because it adjoined the domains of his patron, Robert of Gloucester. There is, of course, no proof that Geoffrey was Gloucester's toady or even his debtor. We can only suppose that Geoffrey's source again stipulated "City of Legion."

The simple fact of its size may have argued for Caerleon in Geoffrey's mind. Ten thousand Roman soldiers, nine or ten generations of them, had been quartered in this Roman site called Isca (from the Welsh word *usige* or water), which was far enough away from the Severn estuary to be relatively safe from sea raiders. The guests of King Arthur, however, could arrive by ship—an important consideration.

The Roman Isca had been for three hundred years a major fort, known now to have consisted of a rectangular area of fifty acres (1600' × 1400'), entered through four gates, of which the southeastern led to the Usk River, the bridge, and the main roads. Beyond the southwestern gate there was an amphitheater which once held some six thousand spectators, and which now is called Arthur's Round Table. To the northwest was a semicircular British camp, which is now called King Arthur's Chair. Nearby was the native fortress of Caerwent, or Venta Silurum, now Chepstow. By the southeastern gate of Caerleon the large mound came to be called King Arthur's Palace. Here he was said to have held court seven times at Easter and five times at Christmas, and here he was crowned on a Whitsunday. The palaces of Caerleon had golden roofs, added Geoffrey, at which point archaeologists refuse to follow him further.

The most troublesome point concerns the churches, said to be those of Christian martyrs Julius and Aaron, where King Arthur and Queen Guinevere were crowned. Church scholars place those martyrdoms, along with that of Saint Alban, during the reign of Decius (249–51) in Rome. But where were the churches dedicated to them? Here Geoffrey followed the Christian theologian and historian, the Venerable Bede, who wrote that these first two martyrdoms occurred in Caerleon, Wales. In his *Itinerary* the Welsh churchman and friend of King Henry II, Giraldus Cambrensis (Gerald of Wales), stood by his contemporary, Geoffrey of Monmouth. He personally verified the vestiges of ancient Roman splendor of Caerleon, their magnificence, he said, surrounded by three miles of brick walls, provided with aqueducts, hypocausts, and lofty towers. He also said that he saw there the churches of Julius and Aaron, just as Bede and Geoffrey had said. Nobody else saw the churches, unfortunately for the reputation of Gerald of Wales, and no trace of them has ever been found. Thus, it is not certain that Gerald of Wales authenticates Geoffrey of Monmouth.

In all fairness it should be added that in Roman imperial times there were three archdruids in Britain and that they are supposed to have been replaced by three archbishops of the Celtic church prior to the arrival of Saint Augustine in Kent. The Celtic archbishops presided at London, at York, and at Caerleon. In light of this, then, Geoffrey's choice of Caerleon as answering to the ubiquitous term "City of the Legion" makes good sense.

The first or second hint that Geoffrey may have erred comes from King Arthur's contemporary Saint Gildas. For no particular reason, Gildas claimed that Julius and Aaron were martyred in Carlisle, which was called "City of Legion." It should be pointed out here that Gildas was a British historian and Bede an Anglo-Saxon writing at Jarrow in Northumberland some two hundred years after the death of Arthur. Geoffrey's contemporary historian Henry of Huntington followed Gildas's "Aaron and Julius, citizens of Carlisle," with his "Kair Lion, which we call Carlisle."

But there comes another bit of evidence bearing out Bede, Geoffrey, and Gerald of Wales. A similar connection between Caerleon and Saint Aaron was made by another contemporary of Geoffrey's, the mysterious writer of fiction and theology Marie de France. In her British (called "Breton") poem *Yonec* (Johnnie), which was composed some forty years after Geoffrey's *Historia*, Marie mentions a ruler called Muldumarec. His kingdom lay either at Caerwent or between it and Caerleon. According to Marie, on the feast day of Saint Aaron there was a great celebration at Caerleon (Karlion) and also at other cities.

Now why should the hero's great adventure happen at Caerleon upon this special day? What had Yonec to do with Saint Aaron? Nothing, in fact. Therefore the thought occurs that this poem, translated by Marie de France, as she admits, could once have been a part of the adventures written to entertain King Arthur and Queen Guinevere at their coronation. Perhaps the story in the Welsh *Mabinogion* that tells the adventures of Gereint (Erec) also formed a part of a longer set of works. Therefore Marie may have mistaken "City of the Legion" for Caerleon. If not, she must have read it in Geoffrey or heard it from Gerald of Wales. Marie is said to have worked under the patronage of King Henry II. While it was not in *his* interest to emphasize the importance of Wales, it was certainly to the benefit of his friend Gerald to have done so. Finally, of course, Caerleon was bypassed in favor of Canterbury, and Gerald was bypassed in the church, as he was for the princedom of Wales.

Although this is conjecture, further analysis will demonstrate that Marie de France made one capital error—in placing the kingdom of Muldumarec at Caerwent in what is now southern Wales. It will be essential to identify this British king, who in fact attended King Arthur's coronation, though probably not out of any fondness for Arthur. Muldumarec is widely known in Arthurian literature as King Urien of Gorre, whose son becomes the hero named Yvain in the French romances, and whose kingdom is the land of the giant Gorre. People used his name in the oaths "By Gorrey," and "By Golly," neither one of which appears now in Webster's. Marie's allusion fails also to confirm Geoffrey's choice of Caerleon, then.

Caerleon was a city, claimed Geoffrey, that much resembled Rome. The church of Saint Julius, with its convent for women, was located there. So was the cathedral church of Saint Aaron, with its affiliated school for two hundred astronomers and philosophers. Geoffrey pursues this identification of astronomy and prophecy in his last work, the *Vita Merlini* or *Life of Merlin*, where that seer retires to an observatory the better to learn from the heavens the secrets of the future. In claiming further that Caerleon constituted the Welsh See of Great Britain, Geoffrey seems to be striking, as Gerald of Wales did, a blow for Celtic Christendom. It was futile, for soon after Geoffrey's time the medieval archbishoprics were established by Rome: Canterbury, York, Saint Andrew's, Glasgow, Armagh, Tuam, and Dublin.

In his book *The Legacy of Arthur's Chester* Robert B. Stoker argued for Chester as the city of the king's coronation, but this reasonable argument is still unsupported by the many continental manuscripts. Apparently it would have been too distant a location for the honored guests anyway. Still a small, Roman city surrounded by stone walls, Chester is on the River Dee, which is navigable to that point. The city certainly quartered the two Roman legions, the *Adjutrix* for a time, and the *Valeria Vitrix* for some three hundred years.

But the case for Carlisle grows stronger. First, there is the testimony of Arthur's contemporary Saint Gildas. Second, there is the very ambiguity of the name *Caerleon*, particularly since the etymology of *Carlisle* is still unsettled. In the third instance, Carlisle was a city of refuge for queens during the wars in Scotland, as when Saint Cuthbert escorted the queen of Northumberland there in the seventh century. They saw the huge ruins of the Roman Carlisle: fountain, aqueduct, mural defenses twenty feet high, and they perambulated its walls. One can imagine how much more splendid Carlisle was two hundred years earlier. Furthermore, one can probably argue that Carlisle would have been an ideal city of refuge for the ill-fated Queen Guinevere during the Battle of Camlan.

Carlisle was moreover the second most important Christian center in Britain in Arthur's day, judging from archaeological finds. It was also the fifth Roman *civitas*, or Roman capital constituted after 368, and thus the most recent Roman capital. Like London, Caerleon, and Chester, it had previously been a *vicus*, or Roman military center. William of Malmesbury, another contemporary of Geoffrey's and a much more famous historian, testified to the existence of a noteworthy Roman temple to Mars or Victory there.

Speaking from a logistical point of view, Carlisle was the kind of center capable of supplying foodstuffs and fodder for many coronation guests, their attendants, and their horses. Situated on the Cumberland Plain and Eden Firth, it is still an agricultural center. And Carlisle is eminently a safe place. From the point of view of military security for the king and his guests, Carlisle would have been Arthur's choice. The city is so protected by the natural geography of the land that access by any large number of soldiers would have been extremely difficult. It is separated from the Irish Sea on the south and on the northeast by the wilderness area today called the Kershope Forest. On the east and south, Carlisle is separated from Yorkshire, from Lancaster, and from Northumbria. One has only to recall *Gawain and the Green Knight* and the unforgettable wintry journey of Gawain south out of Carlisle to Penrith and then down into the Liverpool and Chester area to see what a difficult terrain lies in that direction. An old English ballad attributed to King Arthur verifies the direction. Even today the sense of wild scenery all but overwhelms one on the M6 Freeway or the Glasgow-London Express.

The size of Carlisle is also in its favor; in Roman times its seventy-four acres were enclosed by walls against the fifty acres apiece of both Chester and Caerleon.

The many road junctions of ancient Carlisle, which may answer to the Arthurian texts' cryptic designation of "the seven roads" would have been protected by Hadrian's Wall stretching to the north. Furthermore the more secluded northwestern coast of Britain would have afforded a greater measure of security than Chester or even Caerleon could have offered.

And, Carlisle was not one of the ancient druidical centers of Britain— an advantage from the point of view of the Christian King Arthur.

Lastly, Carlisle was the ancient home of the Welsh people, the Walenses. Thus, it would have been called "Wales" in Arthur's day, or "Galles" in the French texts. The latter always refer mysteriously to "Galles," and then to North Wales as "Norgalles," and then to outer Wales, "Outregalles," or "Estre-Galles." They do not, of course, mean modern Wales. Even today the southwestern coast of Scotland is called "Wales," or Galloway. The Carlisle Plain formed the center of the Welsh peoples in Arthur's day and was ruled by British kings well into the eleventh century. Therefore, King Arthur was probably crowned at Carlisle, a city he chose personally as the scene of his greatest moment.

So flamboyant was Arthur's glory there, so lavish his feasting over three whole days, that Archbishop Dubric(ius) placed the crown on Arthur's head, then, exhausted, begged to leave the world for a small hermitage. Geoffrey's information about Saint Dubric, whose remains were found and brought to Llandaff in Wales from Bardsey Island in the twelfth century, agrees with the *Book of Llandaff* that Dubric became bishop of Llandaff around 470 and archbishop of Caerleon around 490. (The *Annals of Wales* do not confirm Geoffrey, however.)

The next prelate whom Geoffrey extolls is none other than the patron saint of Wales. The beloved "Devi Sant" (c. 520–88) was an uncle of King Arthur and, like him, descended from the Cunedda Kings. Other monastic tradition joins Geoffrey here to assure us that three or four great personages of the Dark Ages journeyed to Jerusalem: the empress Helena Augusta, who was the mother of Constantine the Great, King Arthur, and Saint David of Wales.

Through Saint David, who certainly became a primate of the Cambrian church, King Arthur is forever connected with the present South Wales. Saint David's teacher was Saint Illtud, a cousin of Arthur. Saint Illtud later became a soldier in Arthur's army. Thus, in the pages of Geoffrey, King Arthur becomes more and more a pivot and pillar of ancient British Christianity as nephew, cousin, and associate of the most celebrated of the desert ascetics. Their deeds and works, such as the fifty-three churches in South Wales dedicated to (and founded by) Saint David, now far surpass in number the deeds of the king.

Old verses tell how (presumably at this coronation) King Arthur sanctioned his uncle's retirement from the world. Saint David moved to the Brecon area where the Cistercian Abbey of Llantony stood in Geoffrey's day:

> *Here it was that the patron saint*
> *Of Cambria passed his age of penitance,*
> *A solitary man, and here he made*
> *His hermitage, his food of roots, his drink*
> *Of Honddi's mountain stream.*

Every word of Geoffrey's account is laden with significance. Even in distant France, in Geoffrey's time, Chrétien de Troyes grasped the details of Arthur's reality, always placing first among the list of conquered kings the very one Geoffrey places first and foremost. One king at this coronation is the pivot of Arthur's realm. Because of him, and because Arthur is crowned before him, King Arthur's new office is proclaimed before the most select witness. These other kings are witnesses, if not electors, and the most important Britons of their age.

King Arthur's office was known and heralded as "the Crown of Britain." The day of his coronation King Arthur was said to have been exceedingly joyous and, added Geoffrey, exhilarated by the celebration of his victories.

A careful reading of Geoffrey's text shows that the most important guests attending the coronation processed according to a strict protocol.

First came King Angus of Scotland. First in rank, invited first by Arthur, and his presence announced first, he was the cherished High King of Scotland, the "Rí Alban." He is called "King Angus of Scotland," or in Latin, Auguselus [sic] of Albania. (In some later accounts his name is even syncopated into "Angel.") This great man ruled Scotland, then Alban, "nunc scocia," or now called Scotland, Old Scotia. The authority on ancient Scotland is still W. F. Skene, who explains that the area designated here is eastern Scotland north of the Firth of Forth. This geography must be borne in mind, for it explains how Angus came to the coronation from Stirling, north of the Firth.

In the case of Angus, the critics, most notably J. S. P. Tatlock, have gone astray. Tatlock identified the High King of Scotland as "very likely" to have been Angus of Moray, "a notorious rebel" killed in 1130 as Geoffrey was writing his *History* in Oxford. Thus, he missed the point, called Geoffrey a liar, and stopped the search by other scholars for half a century. Tatlock did not even see that the second king comes from Moray.

Following King Angus came King Urien of Moray, King Cadwallon Lawhir (Long Arm) of North Wales, King Stater of South Wales, and King Cador of Cornwall. Geoffrey's Welsh translator repeats the names in Welsh: Aaron, Yrien, Kasswallawn Lawhir, Meyric, and Kattwr.

The princes of the Celtic church—the three Celtic archbishops of the ancient, sacred centers: London, York, and Caerleon—followed the five chiefs of state. Although all three bear witness, only one of them places the crown upon the head of King Arthur while the other two support him at either arm. The dignitaries present and the solemnity of the occasion have no doubt contributed to King Arthur's renown.

Geoffrey lists rank and title for these most honored participants: "Rex Albanie," "Rex murefensium," "Rex Demetorum," "Rex Venedotorum," and "Rex Cornubie." He specifies that the first and fifth are kings of territories, the other three kings of peoples. Cornwall and Albania are considered territories. The people of Moray, now called Dalriada by historians, and the Welsh peoples are considered tribes or clans not yet integrated into kingdoms.

When Griscom and Jones edited Geoffrey at Columbia University in 1929, they believed that each of these personages would eventually be proven historical. In fact, King Angus appears in the *History of Great Britain* written by John Major around 1526. King Urien of Moray and King Cadwallon Lawhir are attested in the Welsh genealogies of the British Museum Harley Manuscript 3859. King Cadwallon Lawhir is one of the Cunedda Kings, perhaps the father of the King Maelgwyn Hir, or Maelgwyn Gwynedd, who survived Camlan. He died, in 547 or 549, of the plague, during an epidemic in Anglesey. He was excoriated as an evil, immoral king, by Saint Gildas. The King Cador of whom Geoffrey speaks later distinguished himself in King Arthur's European campaign. He is also the same king who raised Queen Guinevere. He will therefore never be found in southern Britain, in what we know as Cornwall.

Next process eleven noble consuls, "nobiles consules," says Geoffrey. The phrase has troubled Geoffrey's critics, who try to equate it with Anglo-Saxon earls and earldoms, with a noticeable lack of success. The "cities" which they represent as delegates have been even more problematic for the critics. Their names do not occur in the List of Thirty-three Cities of Britain given in the Nennius archives. Furthermore, the names do not exactly correspond to the names of the Roman cities of southern England. Critics flounder as they attempt to translate them into Gloucester, Winchester, Salisbury, Warwick, Leicester, Canterbury, Vaddon, Silchester, Oxford, Chichester, and Dorchester or Dorset. By "Vaddon," of course, they think Geoffrey means Bath again. And there is another, greater difficulty. each of the above-mentioned cities, except Canterbury, lies west of the line of the Anglo-Saxon advance into Britain. It is therefore doubly hard to see them as victorious allies of Arthur, and even less as conquered allies of Arthur.

Such confusion must send us back to the original list of Geoffrey, where we have also, thanks to Griscom and Jones, his alternate spellings from the other manuscript copies of the *History*. We find the problem of the cities set out thus:

1. Claudiocestrie
2. Wigornensis, or Guigornensis
3. Salesberiensis
4. Guerensis, or Warewic
5. Legecestria
6. Kaicestria
7. Dorobernie, or Galluc Guintoniensis
8. ex badone, or Badone
9. dorocestrensis, or dorchecestrensis
10. ridochemsis, or Ridocesis
11. Oxenfordie, or Oxinfordie

We should be able to solve the problem of these cities without even having to point out the discrepancies between the names given by Geoffrey and the names of the cities in southern England with which scholars have traditionally associated them.

First of all, on Geoffrey's list there are four Roman forts, or *castra*, (#s 1, 5, 6, and 9). Now, there are three forts on Hadrian's Wall designated as *castra*: Chesters, Chesterholm, and Great Chesters. The fourth is located to the north of these, on the Antonine Wall. That is the easiest of all to recognize, the names being very close:

6. Kaicestria, Kaercestria = Castle Cary

The evidence presented thus far, particularly in the sites of the youthful Arthur's twelve battles, supports these sites as those conquered by Arthur, ruled by him, and maintained as military outposts by him. Now we are closing in on the real King Arthur.

Among the seven remaining names, we have also one *vicus*, or large city garrisoned and fortified by Rome: Guerensis, which Geoffrey says was then called Warewic. We have already presumed that Arthur was crowned at Carlisle, which was for centuries a Roman *vicus*. A glance at the Ordnance Survey Map of Ancient Britain, North Sheet, shows that, in fact, Warwick is east of the city of Carlisle, or else the name of its eastern suburb.

By "ex badone" we have already supposed, for the reason that Dumbarton Rock was probably the site of the Battle of Badon Hill, that Geoffrey designates the Glasgow area. Now, if *anyone* came to the coronation of King Arthur, it would be a representative from this large and important city. More important then was the nearby fortress of the Britons at Dumbarton.

The names *Dorobernie* and *Salesberiensis* indicate the Edinburgh area and that of the Seat of Ambrosius and Arthur's Seat, and Holyrood Castle. We have already given the reasons for *Salisbury*, the name still in use in Edinburgh. As far as *Dorobernie* is concerned, Geoffrey explained it by adding "Galluc Guintoniensis," or Guintonia, or Caer Caradoc, or "Winchester" at Holyrood.

Two remaining names manage to sustain our attention for a little longer, but 2, *Wigornensis/Guigornensis*, seems to refer to some place called "White," such as Whitley Castle, well known as a Roman road station on the main road north into Carlisle and Hadrian's Wall. The linguists A. F. L. Rivet and Colin Smith have shown how persistent were the Celtic place names, and how rarely, if ever, they were replaced by the Latin. Thus, Whitley Castle satisfies more than Geoffrey's labored translations.

The name, *ridochemsis*, apparently troubled Geoffrey more than all the others. He specifies that it is also, or could also be spelled either *Ridocesis* or

Oxenefordie. In so doing, he displays a knowledge of linguistics that is truly as astonishing as it is impressive.

Our only clues are the word roots, and the most important one is the Welsh *rhyd*, which means a ford of a river. This alerts us to the fact that in those days after the departure of the Roman bridge builders and maintenance crews the bridges inside Britain were no longer maintained. Arthur's forces would have crossed the many rivers at the fords from more ancient times. Thus, the ford mentioned in this word must have been well known to Arthur as well as to his commanders, and heavily used.

Therefore, in order to identify *ridochemsis*, we must refer to the European manuscripts, which tell about the great fords inside Britain, what they were called, and who passed them under what circumstances. We have already seen how Lancelot caught the Saxons at Blood Ford on the Clyde River just upstream from Dumbarton Rock and how he slaughtered them. Now, since the Welsh word for *blood* is *gwaed*, Blood Ford on the Clyde River cannot refer to *ridochemsis*. Nor should it; there is already a representative from Dumbarton Rock!

Besides telling us about the *Gué du Sang*, or Blood Ford, the French-language manuscripts and the German *Parzival* contain lengthy descriptions of other fords in Britain. These texts also describe a very dangerous river crossing, sometimes called the Perilous Ford, or *Gué Perilleux*. It is often Gawain who braves this crossing, which lies near a military post or castle at the junction of two rivers, where a fast river flows into a tidal river. By accumulating testimony to Gawain's perilous adventure, we learn also that this ford bars the route into "Galvoie," which is probably Galloway. *Galvoie* translates easily as *Galles*-Wales + *voie* = way. It is the castle of King Arthur's mother, rebuilt at the death of Uther Pendragon, which guards the western reaches of the Rhinns of Galloway, and which also guards the confluence of the Nith River and the Solway Firth, which is a tidal estuary. Furthermore, that shoreline is eminently dangerous, consisting of quicksands. This, then, would seem to be *ridochemsis*.

Geoffrey's "Oxenefordie" does not designate the city of Oxford. His critics to the contrary, Geoffrey would have known that Oxford is *Rhydychen* in Welsh, *Rhedecina* in Old British.

Geoffrey's *ridochemsis* consists of two root words, both very common in Indo-European languages: *rhyd* = ford + *ac* = sharp, difficult, or dangerous. The Celtic derivatives of the root *ac* were studied by Joseph Loth in the *Revue Celtique*. The root occurs most commonly in the Latin adjective *acer*, which gives the English family of words such as *acrid*. The *ac* root transforms regularly into *ox*, just as Geoffrey suggested—a linguist well before linguistics, as a discipline, was founded. What Geoffrey did not seem to know is that the older British name was never replaced by the educated, Latin or Roman place name. Thus, Geoffrey wasted his time translating these old British names into Latin. He also deprived us in some cases of the Old British name.

Scholars have always maintained that Old British was never written, but this case in Geoffrey proves the contrary, as Rivet and Smith hypothesized at Princeton University in 1979.

By *ridochemsis* Geoffrey meant that a representative from the castle of King Arthur's mother, where it is thought King Arthur was born, attended the coronation as an official delegate.

The names of these "noble consuls" have yielded the extent of King Arthur's kingdom at the time of his coronation. What we have to do now is to coordinate the other dignitaries. If they fall into a logical geographical area, then we shall have offered a new proof of the veracity of Geoffrey of Monmouth. He could not have invented these names that thus far fit so well. It is only recently that the forty names now known for forts on the Hadrianic and Antonine walls were taken from inscriptions on the Rudge Cup and on the Amiens Patera (skillet), but new finds are being examined for further evidence. Thus, Geoffrey could not have known about the four Chesters he names except from the pages of an ancient little book, as he claimed.

The next personages to process in a line after King Arthur are the six kings whom he conquered in the islands during his second campaign, which lasted a year. To date scholars have failed to credit Geoffrey here, too. So, to make some progress in another thorny matter, we shall confront Geoffrey with two of his most accomplished translators, on the theory that four heads are better than one. First, a look at Geoffrey's Latin names for these conquered rulers, followed by the version prepared, doubtless with much labor and thought, by the Welsh translator edited by Griscom and Jones along with the best of the Geoffrey manuscripts, and the Anglo-Norman cleric Wace's explanation. Wace worked under the auspices of King Henry II and theoretically had access to privileged information.

The use of this comparative method has clarified Geoffrey's text, reducing the conquered islands to places adjacent to the western coasts of Scotland and Cumbria. In the names of his personages here, Geoffrey seems to have struggled unsuccessfully with Gaelic; as a result he often confuses the title of the king, as in the first instance, with his actual name. Recalling Sir John Rhys, we see that Geoffrey calls the king either Gilla or Gillamaurus, which means that the king was designated "servant of the Virgin Mary," or that he was Christian: *Gilla + muire*>*Gilmore*. When the Welsh translator gives the same name to the second king, we suspect that again the title has misled him. He was probably a functionary in the coronation ceremony,

The Island Kings

In Geoffrey of Monmouth	In the Welsh Translator	In Wace (the French Translator)	Location and Conclusion	
1. Gillamaurus (Gilla)	Gillamwri	Villamus	Hibernia	= Ireland
2. Maluasius	"	Malinus	Hislandie Isslont Alawnt	= Islay
3. Doldavius	Doldaf	Doldamer	Godlandie Goudlandie Gudlandie Yssgottlont	= Scotland
4. Gunuasius	Gwynnwas	Gonfal	Orcadum Orchadum Ork	= Orkneys
5. Loth	Llew mab Kynvarch	Lot	Norguegie Nor Wegie Llychlyn	= Argyle and the Isle of Man
6. Aschillus (Ascillus)	Achel	Acil	Dacorum Denmark	= Denmark in Caithness

something like an official sword bearer, or an armor bearer perhaps. In the ceremonies of the Scottish clans such a person is called "An Gille Môr," in fact. It is this sort of possible misapprehensions on the part of Geoffrey and his translators that prompts us in passing to look at the ceremonies traditional to the Carlisle area, or to ancient Scotland.

Another problem for the translators was the geography. Wace simply left the place of conquest in the second island blank in his pages, rather than put Geoffrey's "Iceland." Coming to Geoffrey's rescue here in 1929, however, Griscom and Jones pointed out that Geoffrey never meant Iceland. If he had meant Iceland, he would have spelled it correctly and written "Ynys yr ia," instead of correctly indicating Islay. By the same token Geoffrey never meant Gothland as the third island. The "s impure" clearly indicates that it is Scotland, which the French could not pronounce without prefixing a vowel. "Yssgottlont." Danish settlements in Britain were routinely called "denmark," just as Argyle was routinely called "Llychlyn" the area north

The Eleven Kings

Geoffrey's History	Le Roy Artus	Le Morte d'Arthur
1. Auguselus, albanie	Aigusel of Scotland	King Anguish of Scotland
2. Vrianus, murefensium	Urien of Galles, or Gore	King Uriens of Gore (Gorre)
3. Caduallo laurh, venedotorum	Tradelinan de Norgalles	King Cradelment or Cradelmas or North Wales
4. Stater or Eddelin, demetorum	Belinan de Sorgalles	King of West Wales (?)
5. Cador, cornubie	Ydier de Cornuailles	King Idres of Cornwall

Island Kings

6. Gillamaurus, Hibernia	_____	_____
7. Maluasius, Isslont	_____	_____
8. Doldavius, Ysgottlont	_____	_____
9. Gunuuasius, Orcadum	_____	_____
10. Loth, Llychlyn	Loth	King Loth of Lothian and Orkney (?)
11. Aschilllus, Dacorum	_____	_____

of Loch Lomond, which is in "Prydyn." Now that area is called Dalriada, from the name of the Irish peoples who settled it in Arthur's lifetime. When Geoffrey says "Norway," he refers to a land of sheep and shepherds. In Geoffrey's time the Isle of Man was called "Norway" from its line of Norwegian kings who came in after the death of King Arthur. The Isle of Man still has a special breed of sheep native to that island.

To search for details concerning Geoffrey's eleven kings, let us turn again to the comparative method and examine a French manuscript, which is early and yet different from Geoffrey. Then we can look at the late version of the same subject in Sir Thomas Malory's Le Morte d'Arthur.* The early French manuscript, which is called Le Roy Artus (King Arthur), uses a different terminology, labeling these kings "defiant." Up until the king numbered 6, Geoffrey's source seems fairly close to that used by the French-language

*(I, xii, but also I, iii; I, viii; V, i, et passim).

author. It is interesting to see that the French author understands that "Galles" and "Gorre" are not Wales and Gower but older terms for some other places.

The twenty-two noblemen attending King Arthur's coronation can be followed in the pages of Geoffrey, sometimes to tragic ends. Others have to be sought in the pages of the continental writers. In Arthur's continental campaign one of these kings is most prominent—King Angus of Scotland. He is the last and the only personage besides Hoel and Arthur to speak at length during the coronation ceremonies. In Europe he will later command an infantry division, as will also Kings Loth and Aschil, Duke Hoel (Howell), and "Sir" Gawain.

When King Angus falls, he causes the kingdom of Arthur to fall shortly afterward. He is the most important single personage in the realm.

Sir Gawain falls alongside King Angus of Scotland. Geoffrey says that Angus died when Arthur returned to Britain and was stopped from disembarking by the regent Modred. Geoffrey does not know any Lancelot, but Malory says that Lancelot killed Gawain. A king of Norway named Olbricht fell at Camlan along with Kings Aschil of Denmark and Cador of Cornwall. It was Yvain (Owein), son of King Urien of Gorre, who succeeded King Angus on the throne of Scotland. Eight other kings died with Modred, whom Geoffrey calls "the Perjurer." After the passing of Arthur, King Maelgwn I lir of North Wales at Anglesey reconquered Arthur's six islands and united them under his rule. As we can see, there are discrepancies here that must be cleared up. But thanks to Geoffrey the main personages, with the exception of Lancelot, are already identified and in place.

It is clear that Geoffrey thought long and hard about all of this. He alone saw that Arthur's realm depended to a great extent upon three brother kings. He emphasizes their solidarity and then their disunion. First among them is King Loth of Lothian, who seems at times to have been stationed elsewhere inside Britain.

With the roster of names complete, and with their places of origin in mind, we have the extent of King Arthur's kingdom at its highest point. The coronation hails the beginning of Arthur's last summer on British soil. He is challenged by Rome at the ceremony. That challenge is answered by Arthur first, then by Hoel, and finally at greater length by King Angus of Scotland. Thus, the events of the end are set in motion. Arthur, Hoel, Cador, Loth, and Anguselus will set forth for the continent in August. Modred and Guinevere have been named co-regents. Notably, one king is missing: King Urien of Gorre—King Arthur's foe and the source of the Arthurian material of Marie de France, which is anti-Arthur, probably sufficiently anti-Arthur to have pleased King Henry II of England.

In Arthur's speech, Geoffrey of Monmouth either found or composed a masterpiece of political writing and a set piece of oratory that would have

KING ARTHUR'S KINGDOM

pleased Cicero or whoever wrote the rules of Roman oratory in *Ad Herennium*. In Geoffrey's oration, King Arthur comes off as extremely deft in the art of persuasion.

Arthur's first appeal was a reminder of the riches they had gained through serving him. "Confederates in prosperity and adversity," Arthur begins. "Confederates in arms and in counsel . . ." Then he appeals to the listeners' common or gnomic wisdom: "Wise men foresee calamity in order the better to bear it." Arthur continues: "We are now being attacked by Romans who demand tribute." Then the *interrogatio:* "Why? Because Julius Caesar once invaded and conquered the ancient Britons?"

"In so doing," continues Arthur, "he took tribute unjustly." Stropping his sword he again disarms the listeners with a *sententio* full of popular wisdom:

> What is seized by violence is unjustly seized . . . Therefore since he is unjust, we have the right to be unjust . . . So let the better man win! . . . Since he demands tribute of us, I demand tribute of him. . . . Why? . . . It is my ancestral right:
>
> My ancestors:
>   1. Belinus and Brennus of the Allobroges took Rome,
>   and they also hanged Roman nobles in the forum,
>   2. Helena's son Constantine, and Maximian were both
>   Emperors at Rome.
>
> Furthermore, did this Roman defend Gaul and the islands we have just taken?

From the first words, wherein he emphasized money, King Arthur moves on into one flattering falsity after another. For "we are asked for money" he substitutes "we are being attacked." For "since he was unjust" he substitutes "since he is unjust, then I can be unjust." After such a fallacious exposition, he moves on to another appeal: "Let the better man win." His ancestry is the coup de grâce, for now he is indisputably the son or descendant of Constantine the Great. The Parthian shot follows: "Furthermore, . . ." Thus, the conquered kings are enlisted against the Romans who had allowed them to be conquered by Arthur of the whetted axe and ducal hammer.

By this philippic worthy of the ancient Greeks and Romans, of whom he was one, of course, King Arthur calls his present enemies and his allies, and especially his young princes, to arms under his command.

In his speech Arthur's cousin Hoel reminded all present that a sibylline prophecy once foretold the conquest of Rome by three men, Belinus, Constantine, and Arthur. Falling into line, the six island kings, who have no cavalry, promise foot soldiers. Again, in this minor point Geoffrey seems to be right, for Lancelot, who was raised on an island, did not know how to ride a horse when he first arrived at Arthur's court. A thousand youths flocked to Arthur's standard, which was a golden dragon.

Geoffrey gives several details about the coronation, which need to be examined separately to see whether they correspond to similar details in the ancient ceremonies of Scotland. We learn that at the feast Kay and the butler Bedevere passed the meats and drinks to the royal guests. Geoffrey considers them superior in rank to the Cador who, according to the Welsh *Mabinogion*, dressed Arthur for battle. While both Kay and Bedevere died on the continent in the last campaign, their offices continue today in the Earl Marshal and Chief Butler of England. Geoffrey gives Kay's function as *dapifer* or distributor, something like a herald or even like the High Sennachie of Scotland.

One feature of this coronation may seem puzzling—that the guests should rise from table and adjourn to the playing field. This on the Sunday of Whitsuntide? However, it must be recalled that the Lord's Day was not sanctified until after Arthur's death, and then by another prince of royal blood, Saint Columba; so here, too, Geoffrey was accurate.

While it is said that Saint Columba in the generation after Arthur inaugurated a king of Dalriada according to an ancient druidical rite, the same cannot be said of Arthur's coronation. King Arthur's rites were sanctioned by the church. First, the king was clothed with the ensigns of royalty, and he stood to show that he would follow in the footsteps of his predecessors. Then, to proclaim his innocence and integrity, he was robed in white. We do not know if he carried a red and white rod, or if Excalibur was borne before him. Recognized as a candidate, Arthur was preceded into the church by his honors—four golden swords—which were carried by a king of Scotland, of Cornwall, and of the two Wales. King Urien was excluded from performance here. Nor does King Loth join this select group. We do not know if seventeen elders had convened in council at a stone table to elect Arthur solemnly. Nor do we know if the king sat on either the Bear Stone of Castle Forbes, or on the Stone of Scone. Geoffrey mentions no stone on which he would have sworn, such as the black stone of Iona in Saint Columba's time.

Geoffrey also omits the "Ascertainment-of-Right" formula, but the Keeper of Genealogies must have been Kay the Sennachie. Arthur wore a royal diadem, although medieval illustrators always showed him wearing a mural crown, perhaps with five towers (one for each conquered city).

Queen Guinevere was preceded by archbishops and other princes of the church. She was crowned with laurel, doubtless signifying that she was in her own right a victorious battle queen. This was already a British tradition. The fact that she is so immediately appointed vice-regent makes one think she may also have been a chieftainess.

If she was, in fact, a chieftainess of the north of Britain, then the clansmen in attendance would have walked backward before her. Geoffrey is clear that she wore the personal ensigns of her royalty. He does not identify them or elaborate, which is a pity, but the French writers certainly do, albeit failing to recognize them for what they are. In any case, Lancelot recognized them and knew the queen by that cognizance.

Four queens preceded Queen Guinevere into her church, that of Saint Julius, each bearing a white dove. These birds were her honors, then, just as the golden swords were Arthur's.

The French romancers pick up the idea that Guinevere is a sex symbol, a sort of queen of courtly love, which fashion was all the rage in the twelfth century—or that she doubled for the constellation Virgo. Fortunately, Geoffrey never bows to such a silly notion. And it never occurs to Geoffrey here that Queen Guinevere should be construed as indebted in some way to the doves of Venus.

The pages of Geoffrey of Monmouth are filled with regnant queens of Britain, some known, most of them unknown but for Geoffrey's mention of them. It was Geoffrey, in fact, who introduced us to Cordelia, to Gwendoloena, and to Marcia and who lauded Helena, seeing her as Matilda, the daughter of King Henry I. In no place does Geoffrey presume to censure or to slander Queen Guinevere. He limits himself to saying that her second marriage to Modred was not sanctified by the church.

The four white doves appear wonderfully significant, and it is fortunate that Geoffrey left them in his account. He did not invent them. They refer to Guinevere's first greeting to Lancelot as he leaves the Grail Castle at the age of fifteen to join King Arthur and to renew his vow to defend the queen to the death. He and she had been reared together in the Grail Castle. The turtledove is the heraldic bearing, long before systematized heraldry, of the Grail Castle. Gawain's red and white horse was branded with the turtledove. Only the most select damsels were raised at the Grail Castle, said Wolfram von Eschenbach, and they were to be wedded only to kings and noblemen with royal or with sacred pedigrees.

From Geoffrey's pages, scant though they are, we have gleaned an idea of the life of King Arthur. We also know the names of his closest associates and of his bitterest enemy. The extent of his kingdom looms clearer for us, as does the importance of his coronation. The personages who attended the king and who pledged their support lived in places that exist even now. Their stories are consonant with the general history of the Dark Ages, its customs, and its protocol.

Geoffrey apparently knew nothing about something his own translator, Wace, called "the Round Table." He did not solve the mystery of Lancelot, for Chrétien de Troyes had not yet sprung "Lancelot" upon the unsuspicious Middle Ages. Geoffrey closed his lips upon the abduction or abductions of Queen Guinevere. He also skirted the problem of what seemed to him to have been her second marriage to Modred. Alone among the writers of the Middle Ages Geoffrey did not do much to slander Modred, although he could not resist the epithet "Perjurer." It was probably something he failed to understand. He felt the deepest sorrow at Arthur's wounding, for Geoffrey believed the prophecy of Merlin that even in the wrath of the stars God would again send an Arthur into Britain.

It is with regret that we leave Geoffrey of Monmouth, who sought lost knowledge, whose eyes were generally unclouded by passion, whose attitude toward the world was thoughtful and reflective, who refrained from abuse of others, and who in the interests of truth tried to avoid myth and fiction. Geoffrey of Monmouth was the only writer of the Middle Ages to cling to King Arthur, first to point the finger and claim that it was Arthur who drew the sword in defense of his country, Arthur who saved Britain for all the ancient peoples, and Arthur who slew Modred.

PART II

❧ ❦ ❧

THE
ABDUCTION
OF
QUEEN
GUINEVERE

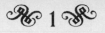

The Romances

The fascination with King Arthur and his Queen Guinevere swept across the literary circles of northwestern Europe in the mid-twelfth century, attracting the most able writers of the day. In this instance, the poets followed the historian; Geoffrey of Monmouth had made great literature out of history, and it was the sort of literature that cried out to be continued. The race for old material was on, and it intensified as more venomous tongues joined the throng.

The long section on King Arthur in Geoffrey's *Historia* had tremendous appeal. Writers amended, adapted, verified, and expanded Geoffrey's text. The first was Wace, who came from the Channel Islands to the court of King Henry II around 1100. His courtly *Brut*, a history of the Britons, who were said to be descended from the Roman Brutus, dates from 1155. The best of the Anglo-Norman adaptations or versions of Geoffrey's text, it was written in Old French (the language of the Plantagenet rulers of Great Britain at that time) and achieved the status of literature.

Wace was followed by the austere Layamon. An Anglo-Saxon monk from Worcestershire, Layamon had by 1190 added his own material and doubled Wace's number of verses. Layamon depicted King Arthur as stern and fatherly. Whereas Wace had joined the court of King Henry II from the Channel Island of Jersey, Layamon came from the area around the "Severn" estuary in western England. It was probably Layamon who induced his successors in Wales to adopt that area as King Arthur's kingdom, leading them into such geographical errors as "Gloucester" and "Worcester."

Neither Wace nor Layamon, both talented adapter/translators, wrote a word about Queen Guinevere having been abducted. Nor did Geoffrey write anything about the Queen having been kidnapped, taken far away, and held

hostage or prisoner of war. At first this omission, on Geoffrey's part particularly, appears very odd. Roger Sherman Loomis, the noted mythologer
from Columbia University, was sure that an account of the abduction had
appeared prior to 1136. If that was the case, it seems unlikely that Geoffrey,
whose *Historia* was already finished in 1136, would not have read it or heard
of it.

I think it is safe to assume that Geoffrey knew of the abduction. His
omission, however, may be traceable to a peculiarity of his as a man and as
a writer. Unlike Layamon, who was a misogynist, the magister at Oxford
admired the brave queens who had reigned in Britain.

It has long been common knowledge that Geoffrey furnished Shakespeare with a courageous queen or *regina* named "Cordeilla," daughter of
King Lear (Leir). Having first restored her father to the throne, Cordelia
succeeded him and reigned in peace for another five years. Geoffrey also
held up to his readers another unknown, Queen Marcia of Britain, who
succeeded her husband upon the throne and drafted a code of laws, the *Lex
Marciana*, which was so good that King Alfred himself translated it.

Of course, Geoffrey bowed before the most honored and venerated of
ancient queens, Queen Helena, also called Augusta and Venerabilissima.
She was later immortalized for having found in Jerusalem the *Vera Crux*, or
True Cross of Christ, and for having built over the tomb of Christ the first
magnificent Church of the Holy Sepulcher. This church was rebuilt during
the twelfth century at the expense of the royal family of France and was
inaugurated in their presence. This could be construed as testimony to the
growing popularity of King Arthur, since he was reputedly her descendant.

Queen Helena was also immortalized in the thirteenth century by the
sacred Welsh stories, the *Mabinogion*. The young princess who was to become queen and the mother of Constantine the Great (and thus the ancestor
of King Arthur) was educated in Britain by her father King Coel, or Old
King Cole. He intended her to succeed him upon the throne, but she married and moved to the Near East. If Constantinople was built before her
death, perhaps Helena was the "empress of Constantinople" of the Perceval
texts. And the name *Helena* occurs frequently in the Lancelot texts; his mother
and his wife were both called Helena (Elen, or Elaine, depending upon the
native language of the authors).

Geoffrey of Monmouth also wrote about another unknown queen of
Britain whom he seems to have resurrected—Guendoloena, granddaughter
of Brutus, who ruled alone for fifteen years and then was succeeded by her
son.

When such a unique historian as Geoffrey displays such interest in
female sovereigns and such knowledge about their obscure reigns, is it really
so astonishing that he might have suppressed a sad story about Queen Guinevere's abduction? He admits tersely that Queen Guinevere was declared

co-regent during the absence of King Arthur. He admits that she ruled
alongside Modred. He does not say why Modred was chosen to rule with
her. The older brother Gawain was, of course, going overseas with Arthur,
as was their father, King Loth. Geoffrey mentions that Queen Guinevere
also married Modred but not according to a Christian ritual. If so, she brought
about the final and terrible Battle of Camlan between Arthur and Modred.
After Arthur's fatal wounding, the Queen retired to a convent and there she
died. During the battle she waited at "Caerleon," at the "City of Legion,"
now identified as Carlisle. She went there from what Geoffrey calls "York,"
which we have identified as Edinburgh, or Holyrood Castle.

Did Geoffrey decide to remain silent? Did he find this material incon-
sistent with his knowledge of British queens? Did he sense a mystery behind
such suppositions? That would seem to be the case.

Wace felt no such sense of honor where British queens of old were
concerned. Working for King Henry II of England, who feared King Arthur,
Wace intervened boldly and supplemented Geoffrey here. "Guinevere was
barren, and that's a fact," he added waspishly. For his part, Layamon hinted
darkly that King Arthur had personally murdered his Queen Guinevere. He
then added a curse upon her name and memory. Guinevere appears to have
inspired the same sort of hatred in the writers of the Middle Ages as she did
in the Victorian poets.

Perhaps authors must be judged by their hearts, by what they include
and what they omit. Geoffrey of Monmouth allowed Queen Guinevere the
benefit of the doubt, or maybe he never doubted her at all. But Geoffrey's
hour is past, and the clouds of suspicion gather about his lack of a source.
After Geoffrey come the multitudes of French-language authors, for whom
Queen Guinevere was the target of choice, but their attacks lack verisimili-
tude. The more they attacked her, the more mysterious, fascinating, and
tantalizing she became. And consequently, the real Queen Guinevere vanished almost totally from their pages.

The French-language romances began to appear around 1150, only
fourteen or so years after Geoffrey's *Historia,* which says something about the
popularity of Geoffrey's history book.

By definition the romances are verse narratives that deal with romantic
love in a "Roman" or Romance tongue. The French poets felt no compunc-
tion to deal tenderly with a long-dead British queen, but looked upon her
with "modern" eyes, and applied to her more relaxed or "courtly" standards
of morality. They judged her by her ability to stoop low enough to play the
"love game" in a "courtly" way, so that the besotted "knight" was neither
driven crazy by sexual frenzy nor mortally offended. Their accounts coincide with troubadour poetry, which fashion lasted for centuries and which

is supposed to have a lot to do with the money spent by noble women on enthroning the Virgin Mary in Gothic cathedrals, with courtly love, and adultery—*if* courtly—and with chivalric settings. All this is in the first, brilliant flush of the High Middle Ages.

For his part Geoffrey had peered intently over the centuries, all the way to the lost Dark Ages, occasionally finding unreliable fragments of knowledge in Gildas, in the Nennius compilation from the Vatican library, in the Harleian genealogies, the Welsh archives, and whatever Roman books he had. Generally he abstained from explaining what he failed to understand. He also said nothing about what he failed to discover, and recorded, therefore, what for reasons of his own he judged worth repeating.

The writers of the romances, on the other hand, modernized, pirated, and updated Geoffrey's ancient material and created an unbelievably difficult tension between that society and personages of ancient Britain and an idealized and nonexistent society of knighthood, of chivalry, of stupid, clanking knights, and sex-mad men and women. But it is in this anachronistic world they created that the abduction or abductions of Queen Guinevere occur.

The French-language authors had a more modern vocabulary. War is called "assembly." Hand-to-hand combat to the death is called "jousting," or even a "Round Table." Campaigning is termed "choosing the leaf instead of the flower," doubtless from the old northern habit of carrying branches to the battle so that in the confusion of combat the chieftain could be recognized. In the French pages Queen Guinevere is dismissed as "gentle" and "courtly." The laws, the politics, the bloody customs, and the hard realities of the Dark Ages are all ignored; worse yet, they are unknown.

Worst of all, in the pages of the French-language romances, proper names and common nouns are translated willy-nilly, wholesale into Old French. *Arturus* becomes Artus or *Artur*. *Gawain* becomes *Gauvain*. And suddenly, as if emerging full-blown out of the brain of Jove, there comes somebody called Lancelot.

Finally, reading the Anglo-Norman romances and those others in Old French from the continent generally requires a peculiar mind set: familiarity with each author's mentality, vocabulary, and vernacular; constant adjustment of time and epoch, research into geography, retranslation back into Latin and the Celtic languages in order to discover about whom and what he is talking, and constant interrogation of the text—the training and the province of the literary scholar. Then, perhaps, the real or at least the probable facts underlying the particular cases are open to sifting, accepting, or rejecting.

Fortunately, two criteria provide frames of reference according to which Queen Guinevere as she is presented in the Old French romances can be measured. First of all, we must dispel the traditional image of some ordinary wife who functioned at King Arthur's court primarily as a cupbearer or as a mistress of the wardrobe. Those images derive from two of Queen Guinevere's contemporaries: King Hrothgar's Queen Wealtheow in *Beowulf* and the young Kriemhilde in the *Nibelungenlied*. Since King Arthur is a contemporary of both Beowulf and Theodoric of the Ostrogoths (called Dietrich in the Austrian poem), such comparisons could have been valid.

At her coronation Queen Guinevere bore branches, more like a Plantagenet king. Geoffrey therefore suggested that she was another traditional warrior queen, more like Brunhilde, someone able and willing to lead fighting forces. Geoffrey also had her as a duly crowned queen of Britain.

The French romance writers agree in one detail with Geoffrey—that Guinevere was immensely prestigious and that she was sacred to her contemporaries because she had been duly anointed, face and head, and crowned. This first criterion places her, then, in an acknowledged tradition of such fierce British battle queens as Cartismandua (c. A.D. 50) and Boudicca of the Iceni (c. A.D. 61).* Queen Guinevere also resembled other similarly renowned princesses, like Shakespeare's Imogen, daughter of the high king Caratacus (Arviragus), for whom Aurelius Ambrosius's *caer* or castle in Edinburgh may have been named. Caratacus was a royal personage of exemplary personal courage and was much admired in imperial Rome.

Queen Boudicca's exploits are the most famous, however. She was an original Queen Victoria, her name "boudi," or victorious, referring to her victory over Rome. She was recognized and saluted by the Roman historian Tacitus for her victory in the Boudiccan War: how she drove her battle chariot through the ranks, how she hauled her ravished daughters along and angrily paraded them among the British warriors so that all could witness their condition, how she showed the soldiers her own bare flesh that had been cut by Roman lashes. That day, she told the warriors proudly, the women of Britain would die or conquer. The men might do as they pleased.†

Queen Boudicca eventually resorted to suicide, a final solution and an expedient considered most honorable in the Dark Ages, according to Saxo Grammaticus's history of Denmark. Whenever a chieftain was faced with unthinkable dishonor, which might be the usual hideous death meted out to the vanquished, he or she was allowed instant suicide. Thus, Queen Boudicca avoided being dragged naked, captive, and in chains through the streets of Rome.

Thinking of Queen Boudicca perhaps, or of the lovely flowing blonde locks of Imogen, called Gladys Claudia, the Roman poet Martial compli-

---

*Queen Boudicca's statue stands on the embankment opposite the Houses of Parliament in London, and at Oxford University.

†(*Annales* of Tacitus, XIV, 32–35).

mented the province of Britain. He said that for its mountains, rivers, churches, and its fair women, those islands were truly past compare. Everyone agreed that Queen Guinevere was the noblest and the fairest of the fair. What was her fate?

Scholars have made much recently of a sculpted archivolt of the Modena Cathedral in Italy, showing some scene from the Arthurian material. Over the north doorway, cringing and helpless in the corner there is a woman whose name is given as "Winlogee." They have speculated that this person carved about 1120 is the abducted Guinevere. Not so. It is another woman from the Cornish stories, someone called Guinloie, who shrank and trembled before her fate. None of the texts say that Guinevere cringed or trembled. She went down, it is true, but proudly and in silence.

The real British queens were honored, so much so that the poet Martial might have added to his list the highways of Wales, called "Fford Elen" or "Sarn Helen" in honor of Constantine's mother, whom the emperor Maximus met in Wales at Segontium (now Carnarvon). King Arthur's ancestor ordered these roads constructed in honor of his British bride. She was only one of the ancestral queens so honored; Others have given their names to places: Brigantia of the Brigantes of York; Cambria Formosa of Wales, daughter of Belinus (c. 373 B.C.); Queen Mebd of Connaught; Queen Skatha of Skye; Queen Macha of Ireland; Queen Taillte of Teltown, Ireland; and Etin, Fola, and Banba, the three eponymous queens of Eire.

Not to be outdistanced in this respect, the later Anglian queen of Bamborough is well remembered as having toured the ruined city of Carlisle not- long after the death of King Arthur. King Alfred's warring daughter, Queen Ethelfleda, restored that other city of the Legion, Chester, and stormed nearby Derby. But she refused to be addressed as "Queen" or even as "Lady." Instead she demanded that she be called either "King" or "Imperial Lord." And it was to this group of proud monarchs that Queen Guinevere belonged.

A second criterion applicable to the mystery of Queen Guinevere comes from a consideration of her other peers in those "calamitous times." Saint Cesarius of Arles, a contemporary, speaks of the age of Arthur as so calamitous that he had to write a book, one of the first on the subject, of descents into Hell. In fact, he enunciated for the Catholic church the now well-known doctrine of Hell. The criterion is this: that both the coronation and the wedding of King Arthur and of Queen Guinevere are remembered all these centuries afterward.

King Ataulf and his bride Galla Placidia have remained historical and were much more known in that same age; and they were wed in the great ancient Roman city of Narbonne in southern France. That city was a center for the writing of medieval epics. But what of their wedding? We know that Ataulf assembled for his bride a basket heaped full of precious gems taken during the sack of Rome. She is almost forgotten except for her mausoleum and other structures in Ravenna and in Rome.

But the bards of the Cymry have not let us forget Queen Guinevere. In fact, they say that there must have been at least three queens of King Arthur (so confused is the case of Guinevere), and all three named Guinevere! The bards furthermore regularly preserved the pedigrees of their own twenty old Welsh tribes, five of which they declared royal. It was their confederated princes of the north who had elected Arthur *dux bellorum*. The wedding of Theodoric the Great allied him to the Franks, to the Visigoths, to the Vandals, and to the Burgundians. Queen Guinevere brought King Arthur the Round Table in her dowry. Whatever it was, it stood *inside her own real property*. Neither Arthur nor Lancelot had real property of his own, it seems. Only she owned two vast sections of Great Britain.

On the continent during the age of Arthur and Guinevere, abducted queens could safely steal inside the powerful Catholic church and remain there. Roman Christianity was even then in the firm grasp of prestigious churchmen like Saint Rémi of Reims and Saint Germanus of Auxerre. The latter had salvaged the man who would become Saint Patrick, and sent him to Rome for an education. Thus, both Radegunde from Thuringia and Clovis's Queen Clotilde in Gaul (soon to be France) were, after abduction and forced marriages, able to live on quietly in the church. Henri Pourrat in *Saints of France* spoke movingly of their sad lives.

A few other outstanding women, near-contemporaries like Saint Geneviève of Paris and Saint Brigit of Ireland, feared marriage so much that by their own frantic efforts they finally reached sanctuary in the church.

The early Celtic saints in Britain tried their hardest to protect young brides, whose husbands routinely killed them as soon as they became pregnant.* Even in the fifteenth century husbands often forced their pregnant wives to gallop to their deaths on horseback. Another sad tale involves the daughter of King Loth, a girl named Thameta (in one version). She was abducted and, unless her story is apocryphal, gave birth to Saint Kentigern (or Mungo), the patron saint of Scotland. The accounts vary as to what death was meted out to this girl after the delivery.

Thus, in Guinevere's day—abductions were common but *not in the case of a crowned queen of Britain*.

The more we reason it out, and the more the evidence accumulates, the more interesting this reported abduction of a British queen from the

---

*This remains a puzzle.

Dark Ages becomes. The repercussions of this mad and inhuman act must have rung through the ages.

The cruelty is well attested. Not only do the saints' lives speak of terrible cruelties inflicted upon married women, of tortures and of the deaths of noble young women at the hands of their husbands, but certain romances notable for their bloody excesses corroborate them. One such is the anonymous Glastonbury or Perceval manuscript *(Perlesvaus)* translated by Sebastian Evans as *The High History of the Holy Grail.*

In this romance the author dwells overlong upon the case of a jealous husband who stripped off his young wife's clothes, drove her into a forest pond, and whipped her with branches broken from the trees. The water ran red with her blood. When Gawain attempted to rescue her, he was unable to stop the husband, who, pretending to take aim at Gawain, murdered the girl instead. When Gawain tried to give her a Christian burial, the husband threw the girl's body to the forest animals. The same author, who was a monk at Glastonbury Abbey, tells how maidens, despite their nobility, were regularly scourged by their (male) tutor. He also tells how Queen Guinevere was sitting enthroned in court when the head of her beloved son Lohot was thrown in her lap.*

Returning to his own sick taste for bloody scenes the *Perlesvaus* monk, who is otherwise a most talented author, adds that this hero's sister was doomed to be beheaded by her husband as soon as the marriage had been consummated.

The same author knows in this world of violence four outstandingly heroic women, who absolutely cannot be dishonored or daunted: (1) Queen Guinevere, (2) Princess Jandree of the Grail Castle (who is the same person in P-Celtic, but there called Cundrie), (3) the nameless Chatellaine of the Castle of Beards, who holds prisoner the mutilated warriors, and (4) King Arthur's (half?) sister, the Widow Lady of Camelot and its fifteen castles and the mother of Perceval (Perlesvaus).

Queen Guinevere becomes more and more familiar as she threads her way ahead of the four queens who attended her and as she prepares the

*The romances speak so often of the sons of Queen Guinevere that the evidence needs to be established now, in the face of Layamon's charge that Queen Guinevere was barren. A rumor of Arthur's son called Llacheu comes from the story "The Dream of Rhonaby" in the *Mabinogion,* and also from the Welsh *Triads.* In the French romance called "Erec and Enide" by Chrétien de Troyes, a son is named as Lohous (v. 1732). In *Perlesvaus* and *The Alliterative Morte Arthure* he is murdered by Sir Kay, and this identical version is given us in the German Lancelot manuscript called *Lanzelet.* Again in the *Mabinogion's* story called "Gereint Son of Erbin" the son is called Amhor, which one supposes is in honor of his great uncle Aurelius Ambrosius. Sharon Turner speaks of a third son in his *History of the Anglo-Saxons* but does not give the source. Lady Charlotte Guest in her pioneer translation of the *Mabinogion* devotes time to this question in the notes to her edition.

Arthurian adventures for storing in their archives. All the way through Malory at the end of the Middle Ages, the other queens are also more or less
known. There is, says Malory, a Queen Morgan of the land of Gorre. There
is a queen of North Wales, Gwynedd. There is the queen who is King
Arthur's mother, who is attended by her daughters, also queens. Then there
are four or three queens who attend King Arthur to the Grail Castle at his
fatal wounding. By Celtic custom these must be not strangers but close blood
relatives of the king himself as he sets out on the westward journey into
death.

The mystery of Queen Guinevere always presupposes royalty, a recognized rule in ancient Britain holding that none of the blood royal could
raise to royal honors those subjects by birth unroyal.

The Welsh *Triad*, which claims that there were three queens of King
Arthur, all three named Guinevere, has inspired much speculation and some
jeers. The first Gwenhwyvar, said the *Triad*, was a daughter of Gwythyr ap
Greidol, the second's father was Gwyrd Gwent, and the third's father was
Gogyvran Gawr. These three fathers provide three possible areas for Guin-
evere's estates.

It seems possible that this cryptic *Triad* refers to the three separate
areas of Britain where authors claimed three separate queens during the three
ages of Guinevere: birth, marriage, and death. There may once have been
three poems about her at these ages. The *Prose Lancelot* gleaned, or recalled,
one or two details of her childhood, just as Caradoc and his neighbor Layamon had things to say about her wedded state, and as the German-language
Lanzelet more than hinted, about the manner of her death. Thus, the *Triad* in
question situates her in three areas of Britain: "Cornwall," "Gwent" in Wales,
and the unknown "Gorre."

Looking at "Cornwall," we begin to suspect another mistranslation.
The Latin place names of Damnonia, Domnonia, and Dumnonia indicated
on Roman maps three distinct areas of their conquered territory: a "Cornwall" somewhere in Scotland, a "Cornwall" in southern England, and a
"Cornwall" in Brittany (France).

Here are the reasons for preferring Scotland as Queen Guinevere's hypothetical birthplace:

1. Guinevere was married in "York," which both Geoffrey of Monmouth
   and the Welsh *Mabinogion* ("Peredur") wrongly but routinely accepted for
   the more likely Holyrood Palace in Edinburgh.
2. "Cornwall" was reputed to be one of the "three thrones" in ancient Britain; thus a truly royal palace such as Holyrood, nearby Stirling, or Linlithgow.

3. According to Layamon, Guinevere brought to King Arthur as part of her dowry "the Round Table," which eventually probably lay inside his conquered kingdom, and the Lowlands of Scotland would have been inside his kingdom of Strathclyde.
4. Queen Guinevere seems to have been foreign, or Pictish, not only because of her unpronounceable name but also because of her strange manners, tastes, and customs.
5. Queen Guinevere was obnoxiously warlike, even a leader of war bands, traits that had been instilled in a northern chieftainess.

The *Triad* speaks next of Gwent, which seems to be the area—at least it is so on ninth-century maps of Wales—around the Usk and Severn rivers, off the Bristol Channel. Many writers placed the coronation of King Arthur and the abduction of Guinevere there, and there Layamon wrote that Queen Guinevere was barren. The material of Layamon, of Caradoc, and of the *Mabinogion* comes to some degree from this general area.

As far as the mystical land of Gorre is concerned, and it remains mystical, we are told to think of a far distant land, perhaps once belonging to an ancestor of Queen Guinevere but recently conquered by the evil enemy of King Arthur. The king took Gorre from enemy hands, later hid his treasure there, and there built or removed to Gorre his older Grail Castle. The queen also had King Arthur's tomb and her own constructed there. In this way she resembled her contemporary, the Roman princess in Ravenna, Galla Pacidia. Today popular tradition says that Queen Guinevere lies buried in Angus, north of the Lowlands. It may be that her body was removed farther north for safety. Lancelot was always moving the bodies of his ancestors. It is a measure of how dangerous the times were that the bodies of ancient sovereigns had to be removed periodically. It follows that King Arthur was fighting at times a delaying action, forced off and on to retreat farther and farther into the north of Britain.

We know the vivid picture of King Arthur visiting Queen Guinevere as she lay in her coffin at the Grail Castle, interred in "Gorre" along with the head of her son Lohot. King Arthur prayed over her body and gave the priests there her vestments, robes, personal treasures, and worldly goods. No father of Guinevere or other relative is mentioned as attending the king in his mourning.

However, we must conclude that since Queen Guinevere does not appear in the Cornish genealogies of the present Cornwall in England or in those of the present Gwent in Wales, the third father is the one to be taken most seriously. This is the great black giant, or the third evil raven or Ogre Raven from the foreign land of Gorre. (Here in Gorre Malory had also put Queen Morgan as the evil wife of King Arthur's foreign enemy King Urien of Gorre.

Hateful old verses taunted this Queen Guinevere:

> *Gwenhwyvar, the daughter of Gogyvran the Giant,*
> *Bad when little, worse when great.*

Both Robert Graves and Sir John Rhys have believed that the name *Guinevere*, from the Welsh spelling given above, indicated that she was never human but a pagan White Goddess. Her stranger name in Geoffrey, Roger Sherman Loomis to the contrary notwithstanding, seems oldest. Geoffrey had no idea of the spelling, but something like "Guanhumara" seems to be the oldest and most authoritative version. Geoffrey tried it every way, never able to approximate it in Latin. Thus, he made it pretty clear that her original name was not Latin, and even that its native form predated Latin.

If Queen Guinevere was born, as now seems the case, inside some Pictish territory called in Latin "Cornwall," then her name must have been repeated only by word of mouth. Pictish seems not to have bothered with a written language; hence the confusion in Geoffrey about her real name.

Her own excessive cruelty argues the very ancient, very primitive origin of this virtually barbaric queen, albeit educated for a certain time in ancient Christianity. There seems little softening of Queen Guinevere's manners. Her decisive manner, her quick command of situations, and her dauntlessness point to the theory that she was a dangerous, haughty chieftainess and the sole possessor of large territories of her own.

Queen Guinevere's hobby was the collecting of human heads, which had in life belonged to her bitter enemies. She had them embalmed so that she could carry them around and gaze upon them often. The *Prose Lancelot*, a superior text, thought this bit of information well worth recording for a posterity that has not heeded it.

When the queen's name is transliterated into Welsh, it does come to mean something like "White Goddess." This is not news, however. The French romancers of the Middle Ages were perfectly able to grasp the significance of such an etymology: *Gvan* (White) + *Weüre* (*vipera>guivre* = dragon, serpent). But when they thought of Queen Guinevere as the Dragon Queen with the golden head and golden crown, it was not an innocent association. When they visualized for their select reading audience some queen of Britain lurking about the forests of Gaul dressed as the French *Wouivre Blanche*, they knew that she was the same dragon beheaded by Saint Michael, who was slaying an enemy of the Catholic church. (We remember that Joan of Arc was also called the *puella Gallica*, girl from the eastern forests of Gaul, and that she died for it.) Thus, yielding to the mythological parallelism built up around this Queen Guinevere, the last authors in the composite romances called the *Prose Lancelot* spin the most revolting stories of the "second," evil Guinevere.

Before turning to the actual accounts in the romances of the abduction of the British Queen Guinevere, we must deal with the equations between her and these mythological personages, or ghostly white goddesses. Too many scholars have believed this nonsense, repudiating any real Queen Guinevere of the Dark Ages. As an example, in her pioneer *Lancelot* Arthurian scholar Jessie L. Weston nonetheless understood the abduction of Queen Guinevere to have no basis in fact. It was all a myth, she thought. Weston saw the story of the abduction of Queen Guinevere as duplicating that of the Greek Proserpine, which she termed the original "Pluto-Proserpine abduction tale".* In 1927 Roger Sherman Loomis of Columbia University concurred.

Later scholars of the Irish fairy tale have not failed to see in the abduction of Queen Guinevere a pale copy of the delightful Irish fairy tale known as "The Wooing of Etain." *Ancient Irish Tales* tells the story of how Etain's first husband, who is the god Mider, or the Roman Pluto, god of the nether regions, claims his bride in the underworld and takes her there away from her second and real, earthly husband. It is a familiar theme of the Demon Lover echoing all through world fiction as in the later Don Juan stories.

If we look at the morphological pattern of these ancient abduction tales, we must see that the abduction of Queen Guinevere does not, in fact, follow them. Both Weston and Loomis were too eager to pass Arthur into limbo. The abduction of Queen Guinevere has to be studied as a real event; it is not mythological at all.

There are at least five reasons why the abduction of Queen Guinevere fails to fit the classical and also the Irish pattern common to all such mythological tales:

1. Queen Guinevere is not abducted from her childhood home.
2. She is not wrested from her mother (there is no reference anywhere to Queen Guinevere's mother).
3. She is not a young maiden.
4. She is not, in most versions, rescued by her husband.
5. She is not taken to the dark underworld but to a fortress where her rescuer sees her plainly several times, in broad daylight.

The chart on page 117 makes even clearer the differences between the abduction of Queen Guinevere and those which are traditionally mythological.

*P. 118 and Note 2.

Classical Myths of Abduction

Home	Mother	Heroine	Abductor	Rescuer and Kinship
Greece	Leda	Helen of Troy	Paris	Menelaus/husband
Phoenicia	Telephassa	Europa	Zeus	Cadmus/brother
Thrace	————	Eurydice	Hades	Zeus
Sicily	Demeter	Persephone	Hades	Helios
————	————	Kore	————	Jupiter
Rome	Ceres	Proserpina	Pluto	Dionysos/husband
Crete	Pasiphae	Ariadne	Theseus	————————
Crete	Pasiphae	Phaedra	Theseus	

One has to look only briefly at M. Terentius Varro's *Res rusticae*, where Roman religious customs and observances are explained, to see why Guinevere's mother is absent from her story. Guinevere had no connection to a mother, to the earth, or to the mother and earth goddess Ceres. Even less could she have figured in any sacred rite connected with the establishment of Greek or Roman civilization.

The queen of ancient Britain was to all intents and purposes a motherless child, raised by an appointed guardian or *nutritor*, perhaps the Lady of the Lake. One precision about her childhood is reported in the *Prose Lancelot*, which adds this curious detail to the otherwise undocumented early life of this great princess: like Lancelot himself, she knew the safe way to the castle of the Lady of the Lake. Specifically, Queen Guinevere knew how, by wading into treacherous sea water from one certain point on the shore, to reach this haven quickly and safely. Such an interesting detail tends to support the notion that this concealed fortress was, indeed, on a stormy, rough sea. Because its approach was so well guarded by natural geography, it was a safe place in which to raise the princelings Lancelot and Guinevere.

Only one account tells us that Queen Guinevere was rescued by her husband, and that one is the one false and/or mythological account of Caradoc which we have.

Finally, only four accounts speak of the abduction or abductions of Queen Guinevere: *Vita Gildae, Lancelot ou le chevalier de la charette, Lanzelet,* and the *Vulgate* or *Prose Lancelot*. The first is a life of Saint Gildas, the second is the famous Old French Lancelot manuscript called *The Knight of the Cart*, and the other two are authoritative Lancelot manuscripts.

The *Vita Gildae*, written possibly as early as 1130, is a Latin account of the life of Saint Gildas, perhaps by someone called Caradoc of Llancarfan. Geoffrey of Monmouth knew him and believed that he would continue the *History of the Kings of Britain*. What Caradoc actually wrote, contrary to Geoffrey's expectation, was the life of Saint Gildas. This unannounced text seems to have originated at Glastonbury Abbey and to have been written to publicize that foundation and tourist attraction. Thus, we already have two reasons to doubt its accuracy. Caradoc treats the abduction of Queen Guinevere graphically but in passing only, his main interests being elsewhere. What he manages to say about the queen is both false and derogatory. What he implies about King Arthur is much worse than that.

Lancelot, or the Knight of the Cart was written around 1177 by that man who is probably the most widely admired writer of romances in Old French. He is called Chrétien de Troyes, perhaps because he was converted to Christianity from Judaism, but he referred to himself as "li Gois," which seems to mean "Gentile." Speculation has it that he worked in Champagne for Eleanor of Aquitaine. If so, he was paid to poke fun at King Arthur.

His material reads as half serious and half unearthly, as if he were at times utterly bored to be writing a fairy tale, or taking leave of his world, as it were. Since he is the most admired French writer of the Middle Ages, however, he should be accepted as a worthy competitor to Geoffrey of Monmouth. The spookiest aspect of his otherwise erratic account is its apparent familiarity with terrain, landmarks, and places. How that could have happened is very much the issue. Unfortunately, Chrétien is the sort of author instructed by his noble patroness to be mostly interested in plot and in the wealth and social standing of his noble characters. He never tells us how he knew what he knew.

Fortunately there is now a much longer and more labored narration of the same abduction episodes, with an even greater expanse of time studied and an even greater interest in plot, outcome, and circumstance. This is the German Lancelot account, called *Lanzelet*, written around 1194, or rather translated from a lost original in Old French, by Ulrich von Zatzikhoven. Since this text relates material of the first order, and in the greatest detail, it will not only expand the Chrétien manuscript but elaborate upon it. Although this author has no apparent familiarity with the actual terrain involved, he does manage to avoid concealing the ancient names for places.

The fourth account comes from the encyclopedic compendium of Old French romances called in English the *Prose Lancelot*. Composed between 1220 and 1230, and marking the change from poetry to prose in an Old French language, this book ought to stand as the greatest achievement of the French Middle Ages. Many authors seem to have been involved in its composition, for the work is often diverse and uneven in quality.

The opening section or "Childhood Lancelot" is a beautiful book on the education of a prince. One wonders if it could have been written by Queen Guinevere herself, or by the Lady of the Lake, in its original Old British form. The educational theories and practices expressed in this section would put the modern progressive-education movement to shame.

Supporting data concerning Lancelot and Guinevere come from the poet Marie de France and also from the anonymous authors of such other texts as the *Didot-Perceval* and *Perlesvaus*. These two last works treat specifically the life and adventures of King Arthur's nephew Perceval (see Appendix 2).

The abduction of Queen Guinevere has been studied previously, and by a noted Arthurian scholar. Shortly before his death, Kenneth G. T. Webster was preparing a book, *Guinevere: A Study of Her Abductions*. He did not live to complete the book; it was finished by Roger Sherman Loomis, who added the foreword. (Omitted here are many of the manuscripts studied by Loomis and Webster, as not having to do with Queen Guinevere, but with other heroines such as Guendoloena, Guinloie, and Guimer.)

Geoffrey of Monmouth seems to have known that Queen Guinevere was not "courtly" but was one of the stalwart, ancient warrior queens of Britain. The mystery surrounding her, her limitless real estate, and her "marriage" to Modred remains as tantalizing as ever after all these centuries. When the equally mysterious, unexplained personage of Lancelot is added, the unfathomable demands to be cleared of its mists.

What if Queen Guinevere resembled Brunhilde, whose devoted attendant Gunther parallels Lancelot? Surely Brunhilde did not come from Iceland but perhaps from Britain in the Dark Ages. What if the plumed warrior Queen Guinevere, waving her laurels and her palm branches, resembled Boudicca, who was forced into suicide? Was she reddish blonde like Boudicca, tall and large-boned, of a similar flushed and reddish complexion?

This powerful queen, her son's head on her lap, or lying in her sarcophagus with his head beside her, or in her arms touches the heart. This was the queen who inspired the devotion of the nonpareil Lancelot.

All the good was interred with this gallant queen. When Arthur left for war, he left her to his enemies *and* to hers. Queen Guinevere herself may have died like Arthur and most heroes.

As we open the two Old French texts (and others) now, we encounter one discovery, perhaps the single most important one of all the years of application to Arthurian texts: the proper names have been translated from the old British tongues. Thus, there is no point looking in Geoffrey of Monmouth for the new Arthurian hero introduced, it seems, by Chrétien de Troyes, for the word and name *Lancelot* must be a translation. He was not Queen Guinevere's lover but her supporter and her avenging angel.

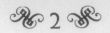

2

The
Glastonbury
Abduction

Readers in the twelfth century must have been shocked to learn of the abduction and rape of Queen Guinevere in Glastonbury. This story is as follows:

One time, when pirates from the Orkneys robbed him on his desert isle, Saint Gildas took refuge in Glastonbury. Sorrowfully he took his servants and his effects and travelled there, with great grief in his heart. There in the summer region ["in aestiva regione"] the reigning King was named Maluas. Now, Glastonbury is known as Glastonia, id est, "Urbs vitrea," which is City of Glass.

It was besieged by the Tyrant Arthur with a countless multitude of fighting men because of "Guinevere his wife," who had been raped and stolen away by this aforesaid evil King. She had been led to this refuge because the place is virtually unreachable because of its defences, its river and swamp, there to be kept safely.

Now the King [Arthur], who had sought his Queen for around a year, heard that she was being held in that place. Thence he moved his whole army consisting of all the fighting men of Devon and Cornwall. Battle is about to be joined between these foes.

Having seen this, the Abbot of Glastonbury, along with Gildas the Wise, made their way between the battle lines. They counselled King Meluas to return the captive peaceably. Therefore she was returned, as well she should have been, peacefully and with kindness.

Afterwards the two Kings came to the temple of the Holy Mary and there swore to obey the Abbot of Glastonbury.

Saint Gildas was often sought out for advice near Glastonbury after that, on the river bank where he built the Church of Saint Mary of Glastonbury.

> Glastonbury is also called "Inisgutrim," from "Inis," which means island and "gutrim," which means glass. After the expulsion of the Britons and the coming of the Angles, it got called "Glastingberi," whence "Glastiberia, which is Glassy State."

There are two copies of this twelfth-century account, rife with errors and falsehoods. Saint Gildas did *not* reside at Glastonbury, Somerset, but in Dumbarton on the Clyde River, in Ireland, and in Brittany, France, where he founded the monastery of Rhuis and where he died. *Somerset* does not mean the "summer region," but seat of the Somers, or Welsh. "Urbs vitrea" does not even mean City of Glass but, more likely, a town where indigo dyes were manufactured.

The account of the rape and abduction of Arthur's wife is almost too ridiculous for consideration. Arthur never brought an army into southern England, and the West Saxons were not even there that early in the sixth century. Arthur is nowhere else called "Tyrant." Nor was Arthur the kind of man who would have waited a year to avenge such a crime against his queen, or to say to the monks of Glastonbury, "Well, boys will be boys." Further, Glastonbury Abbey was not founded until two hundred years *after* the death of King Arthur. Gildas never said that Arthur led the fighting men of Devon and Cornwall; what he said in his *Epistle* was that a King Constantine in the decade following the disintegration of Arthur's realm ruled in "Domnonia," which was Devon and Cornwall.

The assertion that the abbot (unnamed) and Saint Gildas walked between the battle lines probably comes from an earlier exploit in Britain of Saint Germanus of Auxerre, France. The fanciful or "folk" etymologies add the final straw. What is to be made of such a text?

In final review it is clear why only two copies of this text—Burney 310 and Regis 13—were made and preserved. The latter (or Royal Manuscript) bears the Latin marginal note: "Auctore ut fertur Caradoco Lancarvanensi." In other words, "By the author, it is said, named Caradoc of Llancarvan." Thus, the text is virtually laid at the doorstep of Geoffrey of Monmouth and could almost be blamed upon him, derive some authority from his mysterious source, and ride upon his illustrious shoulders. This text was meant to be authoritative. For this reason, the fewer copies the better, and the more closely guarded, the better. Best of all would be to refuse access to it and claim authority. Nobody has ever believed a word of it. The text is an out-and-out forgery and a ridiculous one at that.

It was certainly not written by Caradoc of Llancarvan, not while in his right mind, at any rate. In the closing sentence of his *History* Geoffrey said that Caradoc of Llancarvan would be continuing his history of the Britons. For all we know, Caradoc did not do so. If he was already dead by the time of the Glastonbury abduction text, then his name was used simply as another authentication of the spurious text.

Geoffrey did not mention any abduction of Queen Guinevere, for various reasons, as I have already argued: because of his admiration for queens regnant, because he sensed a mystery here, because there were awful rumors floating about, and most of all, because Geoffrey could smell a forgery just as we can all these centuries later. Furthermore Geoffrey was a trained scholar with the title of magister, the equivalent of an M.A. degree. His degree must have been from the University of Paris, for the only other university in the West was Oxford, though it was not founded until after Geoffrey had completed his *History*. However, both Geoffrey and Caradoc seem to have been Augustinian canons, members of the same monastic order.

This hoax, apparently perpetrated at the Benedictine Abbey of Glastonbury in the twelfth century, has fooled none of the Arthurian scholars to date. All have seen the purpose of the maneuver—to place King Arthur at Glastonbury Abbey. Henceforth, who would know the truth of the matter, or who would care? Pilgrims thronged then as they throng now to worship King Arthur in Glastonbury.

An even greater hoax was created out of whole cloth at the Benedictine Abbey of Glastonbury. The grave of King Arthur and of Queen Guinevere was found far underground during the twelfth century. Three incompetent eyewitnesses were brought to see it. And the greatest historian of the twelfth century was invited over from Malmesbury, another Benedictine foundation only a walking distance away. He was asked to change his *History* to accommodate the "new finds" about King Arthur. The historian was William of Malmesbury.

In order to proceed among these false testimonies and faked eyewitness accounts, we should refer to Saint Gildas. After all, the abduction story comes from the first, earlier *Life of Saint Gildas*, which the monks at Glastonbury probably decided to store and keep it private. Fortunately, there is a second, more complete version. The second *Life* comes from the very abbey in Brittany, France, that had been founded by Saint Gildas. It can hardly be contested.

The authoritative *Life of Saint Gildas*, called the *Other Life* or *Alia Vita Gildae*, makes no mention of King Arthur, and none of Glastonbury, or of Queen Guinevere. It tells the life of Gildas, how he was born in or near Glasgow on the Clyde River, how he was educated by Saint Illtud (who we know was the nephew of King Arthur and a soldier in his armies at one time). We know that Gildas was born around the year 500, giving by his birth date the date of the Battle of Mount Badon, about which he said he ought to know. He wrote his famous *Epistle* castigating the five kings of the Britons around 540. King Arthur died in 542. Gildas went to Ireland in 565, and he died at the foundation that he built at Rhuis near the Breton city of

Vannes, in 570. As was the custom, his body was floated out to sea. Apparently the bodies of great men were not buried at all in those days. His dried bones were then later recovered and shared out among those Houses venerating him. His bones became precious relics.

The Welsh historian Lloyd scoffed at the earlier *Life of Saint Gildas*, which he said first was from Glastonbury Abbey and a figment of the imagination of the monks therein. King Arthur was never near Glastonbury with an army, at any rate. It is, of course, barely possible that he visited that shrine, if it *was* a shrine then, and if in his days it was called, as now, "Jerusalem."

Saint Gildas was truly a very great man in his day and long afterward. Since he is the only extant British historian of Arthur's day, of the writers the only possible eyewitness to Arthur, and since he was also a great writer, he should be studied carefully. He was called the Scot (Albanicus, Albanius), the Dumbartonite (Badonicus), the Welshman (Cambrius), the Irishman (Hibernicus, Hibernius), the tearful Historian (Historicus), and the Wise (Sapiens). His proverbs are still admired: "The worst is yet to come. . . ." "When the ship is about to founder, let whoever can swim swim." "A wise man knows the glint of truth no matter who utters it." "The Picts and Scots," he gibed, "come out into the spring sun like worms from their holes." That for King Arthur's enemies! Although he never mentioned Arthur, he did admire Arthur's uncle, the historical Ambrosius Aurelianus, whom Geoffrey of Monmouth called Aurelius Ambrosius.

A Christian miracle is still attributed to Saint Gildas. Because Saint Helena, the mother of Constantine the Great, had found the rock cave in which the body of Christ had been laid, Saint Gildas sought a rock cave in which to pass his last years in penitence and adoration. He made his home inside such a rock, which he painfully and slowly hollowed out. Suddenly the Lord gave him glass windows and a spring of water for his use!

Far from condoning early Christian practices in Britain, such as those reported as being from Glastonbury, Gildas condemned them: "The Britons, opposed to all the world, hostile to Roman usages, not only in the Mass, but even in the tonsure, sheltering themselves under the shadow of the Jews." For the Britons tonsure meant shaving the front of the head and leaving the back hair long. Gildas's remark about the three religions—pagan, Christian, and Judaic—brings to mind the symbolism in the Perceval manuscripts and the caskets in *The Merchant of Venice*: gold, lead, and silver.

Although the history of Glastonbury is very well known, there is no mention of any abduction of Queen Guinevere to that place. Instead, the history of Glastonbury recounts a fast-growing tradition of holiness, intended to attract pilgrims to what would otherwise be a small market town hidden in the marshes, at a considerable distance from any main highway. The road leading to it from the coast makes innumerable right-angle turns every quarter of a mile or so, so that it takes an endless amount of time to travel what as the crow flies can hardly be more than fifty miles. Drainage ditches line the road about each farmstead. In the distance is a queer spur of land, the Glastonbury Tor. On its top is the ruin of a medieval chapel. Cows graze along its side, and the upper reach of the small town is called Bove or Cow Town, and also Mount Avalon. In the hollow land below this tor lie the ruins of the old Glastonbury Abbey, once said to be the largest religious foundation in the world. This abbey was suppressed in 1539 by King Henry VIII, who changed from the Roman Catholic church to the Church of England. Since that time the pilgrimages have only increased.

In Glastonbury, people will tell you that the little River Brue there still holds in its narrow, grassy waters the sword Excalibur thrown there by King Arthur himself. They will assert that he died in Cornwall some hundreds of miles to the south. Their piety stops all questions of how he walked to Cornwall from the mere village of Glastonbury, wounded to death as he was. They will also maintain that the barge with the four queens conveyed him all the way to Glastonbury and that water stretched the whole route. The reason: Glastonbury was called the Isle of Avalon. Who called Glastonbury the Isle of Avalon? Why, Glastonbury, of course.

There was and is a great miracle at Glastonbury also, one that is renewed at least once a year. It has to do with a thorn tree that blooms once or twice a year in memory of Saint Joseph of Arimathea, who took Christ from the Cross and who later converted the Britons to eastern Christianity, direct from Jerusalem. Today the thorn (*Cratageus oxycanthia praecox*) still stands inside the ruins of the Glastonbury Abbey.

The story of the Glastonbury thorn was told by the monks who, after the death of William of Malmesbury, reedited his *History* of Glastonbury. That history says that Joseph of Arimathea was sent to Glastonbury by Saint Philip, the Apostle of Gaul, to preach the gospel there. On reaching "Ynis witcin" (another spelling for "Island of Glass"), he stuck his staff into the earth. It took root. Every year on "Old Christmas" and May (which may be the same date), it blooms. This "Levantine hawthorn" had two trunks.

Among the dozens of Glastonbury historians, the Reverend R. Warner, F.A.S., wrote in 1826 that pilgrimages never have ceased throughout the centuries. It is a most holy site. Today it is perhaps rivaled only by nearby Stonehenge, and also perhaps by the holy island of Iona off the coast of Scotland.

Today many cults own property there and hold meetings for their worldwide membership. They will explain how the Glastonbury Holy Thorn symbolizes the Nativity. They will also show the Holy Well or Chalice Well, where Saint Joseph of Arimathea buried the Holy Grail, which has not yet been recovered. (During World War II Adolf Hitler sent a whole team of archaeologists into occupied France to find the Holy Grail.)

At Glastonbury one is also told that Cadbury Castle, an ancient hill fort twelve miles away, is Camelot. And one is informed that the ruins of Glastonbury Abbey are the remains of the Head Church of Britain and that buried there, in and under the ruins, are Saint Joseph of Arimathea, Saint Brigit of Ireland, Saint Patrick of Ireland, Saint Gildas of Brittany, King Arthur, and Queen Guinevere. William of Malmesbury may be cited as the authority.

Authorities in Glastonbury will tell you that the people of Britain are descended from ancient Phoenicians who mined tin in Cornwall and also from the most elect of the ancient Jews. Their primitive and oriental Christianity predates the Roman form of Christianity. Like the religions of the ancient Near East, it is heavily astrological. The late Katherine E. Maltwood is the most recent authority on the Glastonbury Zodiac, through which she saw earth effigies ride: King Arthur is Sagittarius, Queen Guinevere is Virgo, Perceval is Pisces, Gawain is Aries, and Lancelot is Leo. In Glastonbury it is said that stars shine into lakes or pools at the summer and winter solstices and at the spring and fall equinoxes. Mrs. Maltwood's theory or vision of the Zodiac came to her from examining aerial photographs made by the American Army Air Force in World War II and deposited in the Taunton Museum near Glastonbury.*

History knows the phenomenon of Glastonbury with its accretion of tradition still flourishing, its holiness still building. Real history pinpoints its origins as a lake village raised above swampy ground. The first monastery there was founded by King Ini of the West Saxons, long after King Arthur, around the year 708. Here is an account from an old book, *A Short History of the English People:*

> Ini, whose reign covered the long period from 688 to 726, carried on during the whole of it the war . . . [with the Britons] . . . The West-Saxons thus became masters of the whole district which now bears the name of Somerset, the shire of the Sumer-soetas, where the Tor rose like an island out of a waste of flood-drowned fen that stretched westward to the Channel [Bristol Channel]. At the base of this hill Ini established on the site of an older British foundation his famous monastery of Glastonbury. The monastery probably took this English name from an English family, the Glaestings, . . . ; but it had long been a place of pilgrimage, and the tradition of its having been the resting-place of a second Saint Patrick drew thither the wandering scholars of Ireland. The first inhabitants of Ini's abbey found, as they alleged, "an ancient church built by no art of man"; and to this relic of a Roman time they added their own oratory of stone. The spiritual charge of his conquests

*Mrs. Maltwood's artwork, books, and papers are now the property of the University of British Columbia, in Vancouver.

Ini committed to Ealdhelm, the most famous scholar of his day, who
became the first bishop of the see of Sherborne, which the King formed
out of the older diocese of Winchester so as to include the new parts
of his kingdom.

Here the difficulties faced by the historian in dealing with Glastonbury and
the opposition between the seen and the unseen, between fact and faith, are
clear. Everything that King Ini had founded was destroyed by the Danes
around 940, when they put Glastonbury to fire and sword.

Glastonbury was taken into the church around 940, when Saint Dun-
stan became the Abbot under Benedictine rule. He was buried at Glastonbury, and for centuries his tomb drew pilgrims. It is said that many kings of
the Saxons were also interred there, including King Edmund I in 946, King
Edgar, and Edmund Ironside. Thus, in the tenth century a fusion occurred
there, melding the Black Monks of Saint Benedict with the Cluniacs and
Cistercians from the continent, and the Oriental asceticism of the Benedictines, Irish ascetics from such monasteries as Tintagel on the Cornish coast,
Saint Patrick of Ireland, and later, the Venerable Bede. Historians from the
Benedictine order, the most important being William from nearby Malmesbury, wrote lives of saints for Glastonbury and its many histories. Few vestiges of this period remain, however, since Glastonbury Abbey was again
burned to the ground in 1184. At that time it had long been a problem for
the royal historian William of Malmesbury and for the king, Henry II.

When William of Malmesbury wrote his first history of Glastonbury,
completed around 1125, he dated the foundation to 708 and not before. He
made no mention of King Arthur, Saint Patrick, Saint Brigit, Saint Gildas,
or Queen Guinevere. In 1135 William was persuaded, after a visit to Glastonbury, to move his material back to a founding date of 472. That year he
put Saint Gildas at Glastonbury and also King Arthur, but not his grave.
Between 1240 and 1250 the monks of Glastonbury rewrote the *History* of
William of Malmesbury, adding the information about the Apostle Philip of
Gaul who sent Joseph of Arimathea in A.D. 63. Eventually they moved the
date back to A.D. 30, when they said that Jesus Christ himself founded the
original old church or "vestusta eglesia." The pope sent missionaries, they
claimed, from the years 166 to 430. Saint Patrick died there in 430. Now
King Arthur was buried there and also Queen Guinevere. Glastonbury, they
concluded, is the mother church of all Britain.

Over the centuries the pilgrimages to Glastonbury have steadily increased. In France, the Bretons continue to echo this same old tradition,
claiming that both Saint Peter and Jesus visited Brittany. Glastonbury insists,
in addition, that it is founded upon a rock (Peter) and therefore not subject
to earthquakes.

The dealings of Kings Henry II, Edward I, and Edward III with Glastonbury would fill many volumes, but it is instructive here to recall that King Henry II ordered the monks at Glastonbury to disinter King Arthur and that they obeyed him. The king sent down three supposedly impeccable witnesses, who each recorded that event. King Edward I paid a much publicized visit to Glastonbury in 1275, after King Henry II had raised the money to rebuild it. King Edward III sent a seer down there in 1331 in order to launch a search for the tomb of Saint Joseph of Arimathea. One can only wonder what new evidence prompted that search, which proved fruitless.

As R. F. Treharne, the historian of Wales, said recently in *The Glastonbury Legends*, one hesitates to "lay sacrilegious hands on devoutly held beliefs. . . . Grievous loss, we must . . . dismiss Arthur . . . from any proven historical connection with Glastonbury."

The three eyewitness accounts of the excavation drawn up for King Henry II and the finding of the tomb containing the bodies said to be those of King Arthur and of Queen Quinevere exist. The witnesses were gulled by the Abbot of Glastonbury, Henri de Sully. What seems to have happened is that a curtain was placed about the deep excavation, so that the witnesses could *not* see what was going on. It must have been dark when they were shown the leaden cross found in the tomb; these three prominent persons from the court of King Henry II all saw something different.

They saw a leaden cross brought out from the tomb. They could not tell exactly where it came from, but they understood that it had come from under the slab of the tomb, except that the tomb was an oak log that had been hollowed out to contain the bodies. All in all, it was a strange place for a cross to have been placed.

The first account is by Gerald of Wales, Giraldus Cambrensis, the famous writer whose account is easily available today in Appendix 3 to his *Journey through Wales*. His account, *Concerning the Instruction of the Prince*, was written shortly after 1191, when King Arthur's supposed grave was opened. He begins by saying that Arthur was a famous patron of Glastonbury Abbey, which remark is in itself enough to dismiss the account as anachronistic. Anyway, Gerald saw the lead cross and reported that it said: "Here in the Isle of Avalon lies buried the renowned King Arthur with [Queen] Guinevere his second wife." He then gives all the folk etymologies, much expanded, and states that *Avalon* means Isle of Apples.

The second witness, Ralph of Coggeshall, in his *Anglican Chronicle* quoted the inscription as saying: "Here lies the tomb of the renowned King Arthur, buried in the Isle of Avalon."

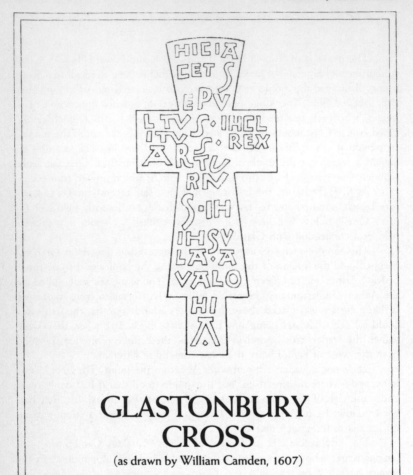

GLASTONBURY
CROSS
(as drawn by William Camden, 1607)

The third witness, another Glastonbury historian, named Adam of Domerham, put into Latin verses something to the effect that there in the tomb lay Arthur, flower of kings, glory of the realm, alongside his second wife, who also merited Heaven.

It is most interesting to recall the exact Latin seen by Gerald of Wales. The point is that he saw something different from what was seen by the last two witnesses to go to Glastonbury and see this lead cross before it disappeared forever in or around the year 1700. Gerald quoted the Latin inscription as follows:

"HIC JACET SEPULTUS INCLITUS REX ARTURUS CUM WEN-
NEVARIA UXORE SUA SECUNDA IN INSULA AVALLONIS."

The English scholar John Leland, chaplain to King Henry VIII and King's
Antiquarian from 1533, saw the cross in Glastonbury around the year 1542.
He said that it was about one foot high.

The last person to report on the cross was Queen Elizabeth I's historian, William Camden (1551–1623), who made the drawing opposite. It
says, in his *Britannia* of 1607:

"HIC IACET SEPULTUS INCLITUS REX ARTURUS IN INSULA
AVALONIA."

The lettering of this inscription is called "debased uncials," which means that
it is bastardized from the majuscule script usually about an inch in height,
used prior to the tenth century, and then mostly for copying Bibles. It is
not, in other words, the type of carving found on tombstones of the sixth
century. And the Latin is very curious: "Here lies buried the famous King
Arthur in the island Avalonia." Gerald of Wales had quoted Geoffrey of
Monmouth correctly; Geoffrey had said "the island of Avallo." Geoffrey did
not say, as Gerald did, that a cousin called Morgan bore Arthur away to the
Isle of Avallo.

One can only speculate about Glastonbury's real role in all of this; for
pilgrims, however, it was *the* place to worship King Arthur. Even when the
second Patrick of the ninth century, recorded in Irish archives as the abbot
of Ireland, fled to Glastonbury to be interred, it is still said in Glastonbury
that the person interred there is the adored, first Saint Patrick of the fifth
century.

Interesting too is the fact that Marie de France translated the famous
Purgatory story of the second Saint Patrick. One wonders again whether she
was the abbess of Shaftesbury, next to Glastonbury.

Realizing what may have been a deliberate confusion (and this charge
has been leveled at Glastonbury by historians), one would do well to look
at a map of southern England in the twelfth century. The Benedictine houses—
Glastonbury, Malmesbury, Shaftesbury, and Amesbury—are located only a
few miles apart. Each one has been connected falsely, but over and over
again, with the Arthurian legends placing Arthur and company in those areas.
He is also placed time and again, and falsely, in the bishoprics that admin-
istered those abbeys: Salisbury, Winchester, and Bath. And he is placed,
again falsely, in the Benedictine abbeys of Westminster (London) and
Gloucester on the Severn estuary. And J. Armitage Robinson, because he

was a bishop of Wells, is considered the most eminent of Glastonbury historians.

Alone against this massing of evidence from the Benedictines—the greatest of them is the *Perlesvaus* author, despite his excessive cruelty—stands Geoffrey of Monmouth, Augustinian canon of Saint George at Oxford, later named bishop of Saint Asaph's in North Wales, and his patron, Walter, archdeacon and provost of the College of Saint George.

The Augustinians believed that knowledge stemmed from reason applied to belief. They also thought that one could arrive at truth by the exercise of intuition. They held that knowledge could be acquired by the power of the will, by wishing to know. They felt that illumination came from understanding.

Nothing Geoffrey had found led him to believe that Queen Guinevere had been taken to Glastonbury to be raped and held prisoner for a year.

Edmond Faral argued in France in 1929 that the spurious Glastonbury tradition stemmed entirely from a desire to cut short the popularity of Geoffrey of Monmouth. It is possible that the monks of Glastonbury waged a campaign to discredit Geoffrey of Monmouth. Or that the death of King Henry II in 1189, before the Benedictines labored sixteen feet underground to disinter the gigantic skull and giant's bones, spawned the sort of confusion that produced the reports alleging that the disinterred *was* King Arthur. King Henry had wanted to rebuild Glastonbury. The finding of King Arthur's body would have attracted more tourist money and would have stilled rumors that Arthur would return to seize the throne. King Henry II was justly worried and near his own tragic end. He said that he had heard the Arthur story from Welsh bards at his court, and the tale had interested him. It is also possible that he heard the Arthur story from his mother, Queen Maud, who was said to have been much fascinated with it.

At first glance, the first life of Saint Gildas, especially the abduction story that it contains, would seem to be a forgery. And much of it *is* doubtless untrue. It would also appear to be mythological, particularly since the husband of the victim is the rescuer. However, this first account of what later will be called a real abduction contains certain elements that intrigue, and it raises some questions.

First of all, it was in this early decade of the twelfth century that people were saying that Queen Guinevere had been abducted and taken to a sanctuary of great renown. This holy place was certainly not Christian, for *no Christian sanctuary would have countenanced any abduction, most especially not that of a crowned queen.* The writer of the *Vita Gildae*, or Glastonbury abduction account, knew that she was a queen, and called her "reginam." The man who abducted her was a "king." No one has reported a king of the Britons at Glastonbury, which is everywhere considered a "Teutonic sanctuary," because it was founded by King Ini.

Thus, we have a clue: the sanctuary to which Queen Guinevere was led prisoner likely was not Christian and was not Glastonbury. Then it must have been a pagan sanctuary ruled by a king hostile to King Arthur. This is confirmed by the language of the text; the word *rebellis* refers to King Arthur's foe.

The word *rebel* applied to *king* recalls the Rebel King whom Arthur defeated in his first twelve battles, according to the *Prose Lancelot*. The king who abducted Queen Guinevere in the *Lanzelet* text is called Valerin, which easily corresponds linguistically to King Urien (Latin capitals = Vrien < VRIANUS) of Gorre, off the west coast of North Britain, a place as yet unidentified.

In the *Vita Gildae* there is one aspect of the pattern that separates it from the mythological treatment, a new character who can be called the Intercessor—Saint Gildas himself. We know, however, from the second life of this holy man that he resided in Ireland during the middle part of his life, when he was physically active, and not in Glastonbury. Hence the question: are there other allusions in the first *Vita Gildae* to Ireland?

The name of the king who abducted Queen Guinevere sounds like an Irish name, which presented the same difficulty to this "Caradoc" author that the names beginning with *Gilla* (as in Servant to Mary) gave Geoffrey of Monmouth. The name commences with a very familiar syllable from the Irish, *mál*, meaning prince. The word is often seen on tombstones in the genitive, *magli* (of the prince). The form *Meluas*, as given in the *Vita Gildae*, represents the Cornish spelling or version of the same name. (In Welsh it is Melwas; in Malory, Sir Melias de Lile or Sir Meluas of the Island.) The *Vita Gildae* seems part and parcel of the Cornish material that claimed for King Arthur's birthplace the Irish monastery for desert ascetics on the cliff at Tintagel. There was no such early place, no Tintagel even when William the Conqueror after 1066 surveyed Cornwall.

The island to which King Arthur was taken after his wounding was called "the Island of Apples." Gerald of Wales speaks, in his report to the king, of Glastonbury being called "Island of Apples" because long ago there had been apples there. In his last work, the *Life of Merlin*, Geoffrey of Monmouth says that the dying king was taken by ship to the Fortunate Isle, a land of summer, called the "Isle of Apples." It was not Glastonbury, however, because it was an island in the sea. The trip to this island was hazardous since it required the services of an oceangoing pilot named Barinthus. Morgen received Arthur there, and Gerald of Wales agreed but called her Morgan. Geoffrey says: "Insula pomorum que Fortunata vocatur" (v. 908) [The Island of Apples which is called Fortunate]. Again, Glastonbury does not fit the picture. From an agricultural and climatic point of view, Glastonbury is not a remarkably fortunate place. It is even subject to drought.

Finally, the Glastonbury abduction story lacks an essential part: an ending. As presented, it sounds like an example of oral tradition, where the author has heard only part of the story or took so long to sell it or find an abbot willing to support him while he wrote it that he forgot the end. Or perhaps he wasn't even interested in the problems of Queen Guinevere. If this story has any chance of being treated as real, it needs an ending, which means that somebody would have had to die. Of the two candidates, Meluas is the likely one. If, on the other hand, Meluas did not die, certainly Guinevere would have. For his part, King Arthur could not be characterized as pusillanimous.

In a matriarchal society, the queen sets the standard of beauty and womanliness. In Guinevere's world all feminine beauty would have been measured against her and found lacking. And anyone who abducted such a queen would have lost his life for it.

The story of the exhumation of King Arthur releases Queen Guinevere from at least one slanderous accusation. It was not she, if the monks were right, who wedded Modred. She was already dead and buried before Arthur's continental campaign.

William of Malmesbury noted that he saw at Glastonbury an old manuscript about King Arthur. It was called *Gesta incliti regis Arturi* (Epic of the Renowned King Arthur) and yielded much information about Joseph of Arimathea. The story of the burial may have come from this lost work; the language on the cross could be construed as a clue. The cross supposedly found inside the grave of King Arthur *should* have read "Hic iacet sepulcrum incliti regis Arturi . . ." ["Here lies the tomb of the renowned King Arthur"]. The cross must have been a rush job, with nobody supervising the carver.

If the Glastonbury story did not come from a lost Arthurian work, and if it did not come from oral tradition or stories told by Welsh bards or Irish scholars attending Abbot Patrick of Ireland, then it may have come from King Arthur himself *if* he visited Glastonbury. If Glastonbury was, in fact, an early Christian center, and if it was then called Jerusalem, it might account for the tradition that King Arthur visited "Jerusalem."

Glastonbury alone has claimed King Arthur, as long ago as the Middle Ages. The exhumation of his body was offered as proof, and the story has been relentlessly maintained in the face of a hostile world. An English King Arthur exerted a powerful pull on pilgrims, not to mention poets. The "Glastonbury Hymn" was written by William Blake (1757–1827) and is called "Jerusalem": *

> And did those feet in ancient time
>   Walk upon England's mountains green?
> And was the holy Lamb of God
>   On England's pleasant pastures seen?

* # 499 (*Oxford Book of English Verse*) Jerusalem (from 'Milton').

And did the Countenance Divine
 Shine forth upon our clouded hills?
And was Jerusalem builded here
 Among these dark Satanic Mills?

Bring me my bow of burning gold!
 Bring me my arrows of desire!
Bring me my spear! O clouds, unfold!
 Bring me my chariot of fire!

I will not cease from mental fight,
 Nor shall my sword sleep in my hand,
Till we have built Jerusalem
 In England's green and pleasant land.

The Abduction
of the Queen

In order to track the story of abduction back to its possible origins in history, we need to examine again and more closely the first Old French—and the most peculiar—account of it in the *Lancelot* written by Chrétien de Troyes. The title of the work is perverse: *Lancelot, or the Knight of the Cart*. It would appear that someone was being funny.

This odd title suits the custom of novelists and their precursors—the poets like Chrétien de Troyes—who feel free to title a work of the imagination as they please. This *Lancelot* should at least have been called *The Quest for Queen Guinevere*. This queen, Chrétien tells us, wished to humiliate her "knight" Lancelot and so required him to mount upon a common cart and be drawn by an evil dwarf into the center of a town. This must be considered a silly interpretation. Would the queen have wished to humble the very man who was trying to save her?

The story begins at Camelot, the most romantic of Arthur's castles. That such a crime should take place there seems unlikely, but the date is accurate. It is forty days after Easter, and a party is still going on.

Enter the spoilsport, an unknown challenger. We guess without straining that it must be King Arthur's archenemy, King Urien of Gorre. He claims Queen Guinevere—a formal declaration of war. The pretext? Perhaps Guinevere and her territories had been promised to King Urien.

Queen Guinevere is to lead a war party out of the castle with Kay as her champion and defender. King Arthur lets her go, which means it must have been *her* fight. The Easter party breaks up, and the inhabitants of the castle weep for Guinevere as if she were already dead.

The queen sets out smartly enough with Kay, whose bleeding horse returns shortly without its rider. It is learned that the queen has also fallen hostage. Hastening after her, Gawain meets an unknown knight, dusty and distraught. The knight's first horse foundered during the hot pursuit of the captive queen, as does a second horse borrowed from Gawain. For want of better transportation, the hero mounts a cart drawn by an evil dwarf.

Chrétien did not consider this at all ridiculous; rather, that act or some previous crime caused the mysterious hero to be condemned to death—by hanging, drowning, burning, or flaying.

The sensible reader cannot venture further into the slippery meshes of such a fairy-tale narration without asking the question which the author has artfully concealed: What was the crime of the unnamed rescuer? He seems to have been absent from court when the queen was challenged to battle, judging from his speedy gallop to her rescue. His crime must have been that he was meant to be the guarantor of her safety, and probably responsible because he was the host of King Arthur, then, at Camelot. The seizure of the queen has in some way dishonored him irrevocably. He will never achieve the Grail Quest or some such heartbreaking eventuality.

Chrétien's second knight, then, must be the brand-new hero: Lancelot.

But Chrétien presents such an unfortunate Lancelot, a sorry youth who has committed adultery with the queen, and this crime while she is helpless in prison! We cannot believe that all this came down to sex, that the affairs of a people turned on that. Chrétien has Lancelot and the queen succumb to a salacious diversion, a one-night love affair, with blood displayed afterward on her bedsheets. It might have been vulgar, but the French writers of romance loved it and cried, "Adulteress!" As long as they slandered a British queen, all was fair.

This version of the situation in far-off Britain seems confined to the French authors, for it does not occur in Caradoc of Llancarfan or in Ulrich von Zatzikhoven.

Thus did Chrétien lead the French and unquestioning readers all over the world into mere inconsequence, slandering both Lancelot and the queen, accusing them of moral turpitude in the face of their imminent deaths and a national emergency, not as it were, but as it was. The allegation is frivolous and absurd.

Chrétien carries on with this nonsense, however, relating how the unknown knight met Gawain at the castle on the water where the dwarf-drawn cart had taken him. The fortress was remarkable, and actually described, which is a rarity. There Lancelot and Gawain drew up their strategy. The former would take the more dangerous course overland to the

Island Fortress where the queen would be held. Gawain would set off by water for the same place.

After Gawain's departure the unknown knight fought a terrible battle at a ford, emerging victorious (as Lancelot always did). Of course, we do not know for sure that this is Lancelot. Nor do we know the fortress by the water for sure, but it is beginning to seem as if we have been here before.

So we are in no way surprised to learn that the queen has been taken to the same place King Arthur was supposed to have been taken (had he been captured instead of her and not released at Mount Badon): Ireland.

Caradoc supplied Irish clues about the abduction, and they multiply in Chrétien.

At this point someone cried halt. During lectures at Oxford University in 1952, the renowned Arthurian scholar L. G. Ritchie announced his entirely original discovery: Scottish elements in the romances of Chrétien: in *Erec et Enide* (c. 1170), in *Yvain* (c. 1175), in the Grail romance (*Conte del Graal*, c. 1185), to which we can now add *Lancelot* (c. 1170).*

Ritchie established the following equations, which are so valid that one cannot imagine not having seen them before:

Isle de Voirre = Island of Gorre, where there are no serpents, or *some part of Ireland*. This abduction tale should tell us why there were henceforth no more serpents ever inside Irish territory

Escalados = Carse of Falkirk (between Edinburgh and Stirling)

Cotouatre = Scot's Water, or the Firth of Forth

Cardeol or *Carduel* = Carlisle, a series of fortresses on the water, or the Solway Firth

Estregales = Outside Galles, or old Wales = Dumbarton area

Uriien = Evrain (=Valerin) = King Urien of Gorre

Galvoie = Galloway, Rhinns of Galloway

The source of Chrétien de Troyes is nothing less than the lost history of ancient Scotland, said Ritchie. The names within his tales are all Old British and Celtic. The names of persons have been translated into Old French by Chrétien but come originally from Celtic languages:

1. Artu, Artus = Arthur
2. Guenièvre = Guanhumara = Guinevere
3. Bademagu = Bademagus = the magician or Druid named Bade
4. Maelwas = Meluas = Meleagant = Prince Something-or-Other
5. Lancelot (?)
6. Kay

*His lectures were published as *Chrétien de Troyes and Scotland*.

7. Yders
8. Yvain = Owein

The geography also is Celtic: Britain, Cornwall, Ireland, Gorre, Logres, and London. Chrétien, said Ritchie, had access to privileged information about the history of Scotland in the twelfth century and in the Dark Ages. He talks about the political realities surrounding the reign of King Arthur in Strathclyde, at Carlisle, and at Dumbarton. He also knows accurate details about the reign in Scotland of King David I. He probably got this information from the Augustinian or Austin canons at Jedburgh Abbey, Melrose Abbey, Holyrood Abbey, or Cambuskenneth Abbey in Stirling. Geoffrey of Monmouth also had access to the same or similar lost knowledge, and he too was a member of the Augustinian order.

Chrétien admitted having taken one manuscript from Beauvais Abbey in northern France. The monks from Beauvais were the very administrators who helped King David I of Scotland reconstitute his abbeys inside Scotland. Chrétien talks about Saint Kentigern of Scotland, about King Arthur and his queen, and about the same set of circumstances that Geoffrey of Monmouth, an Augustinian canon in Oxford, studied in his *History of the Kings of Britain*. Furthermore, Chrétien wrote only fifty or so years after the reorganization by King David I of these same abbeys, where, reasonably, the archives of Scotland in the Dark Ages were most recently stored.

Why did Chrétien make such a sad mystification in his *Lancelot*, which reads more like a series of unmotivated, incomprehensible blunders? King Arthur is portrayed as a craven, as he was in Caradoc. The queen is besmirched forever with the charge of adultery. And Lancelot comes off as a mawkish fool. Why?

The circumstances behind the *Lancelot* and its composition are known and can be reconstructed with some accuracy. The work was commissioned by the countess Marie de Champagne, who supplied the author with two resources: (1) the material of the account and (2) her wishes regarding the form of narration and the interpretation. She apparently asked for a story in which the lover enhances the sexual appetite of the lady if he obeys her commands to the point of personal humiliation, pain being the essence of courtly love. But who was this perverse lady, Marie de Champagne?

The countess Marie was the daughter of the queen of France, who later became the queen of England in the twelfth century, the helpless Eleanor of Aquitania (1122–1204). She married King Louis VII in 1137, accompanied him on the Second Crusade to the Near East from 1146 to 1149, bore

him two daughters (Marie and a sister named Alix), and was "repudiated" by King Louis, the French say, in 1152. Her first marriage was annulled because she bore no son.

Eleanor then married Henry Plantagenet, duke of Normandy, count of Anjou, and soon thereafter Angevin king of England. By this marriage King Henry II acquired one-third of France, inheriting two provinces from his mother, two from his father, and seven from his wife Eleanor.

After the murder of the archbishop Thomas Becket in 1170, Queen Eleanor retired to France, where she established courts at the several provincial capitals of her extensive domains. Her French daughters married and established courts at Troyes, at Bar-sur-Aube, and at Blois on the Loire River. Each vied with the other for the most famous authors of the day. The countess of Champagne won with her Chrétien de Troyes.

With Queen Eleanor at Poitiers, ignored and unwanted by her husband, he ordered King Arthur's grave excavated at Glastonbury and conquered Ireland (1171–72). Both of these actions caused Arthurian texts to be commissioned and read during the years ahead.

Queen Eleanor favored her two English sons who survived the death of the eldest, Prince Henry, and particularly because they rebelled against their father; her profligate sons were Richard Coeur-de-Lion and John Lackland.

King Richard shared his mother's passion for romances of courtly love and was something of a troubadour poet himself. While on the Third Crusade he once lost one of the best Arthurian romances in a card game in the Holy Land. The Forester of Cumbria, in the Carlisle area, lost another romance of King Arthur, the now famous *Lanzelet* known only from its translation into German.

The dean of Arthurian and medieval scholars in France, Gaston Paris, once said that Chrétien de Troyes was probably the King Herald at the court of Champagne. Or he was a monk. But either way he was told to oblige his patroness. At the court of Marie de Champagne, plain, ordinary married love was condemned. Adultery was all the rage.

The countess of Champagne chose wisely in Chrétien, who was already a specialist in stories of rape, murder, kidnapping, torture, and cannibalism. An experienced author, he saw right enough what Marie required: a fairy tale. For him it was a happy choice initially.

Working within the tenets of the fairy tale absolved Chrétien from any sort of coherent explanation, psychological or otherwise, of his material. Chrétien's account never explains why King Arthur let his queen leave the castle of Camelot. We never know why Queen Guinevere treats her knight Gawain with respect and her unknown knight with disrespect and then falls into bed with him. We do not understand the series of tests and trials of this unknown knight, whom she introduces finally as Lancelot. How did she know that he was coming after her? Why did she let him be captured after he had rescued her? How did she recognize him through his disguise at the tournament? Why did she make no effort to release him from his prison? How did he know that she had been captured in the first place? Why was the queen mourned by her courtiers? Why did she leave with the incompetent Kay? Why do all assume that she will never return alive? What was the mystery of the dwarf and cart? Why did the townspeople assume that Lancelot, for it was Lancelot, would be executed?

How did Lancelot know in which direction to pursue her? In fact, he followed a real route. The question has been asked: did Chrétien de Troyes have directions supplied by the countess? Or was Lancelot a Scot? We can follow Lancelot on a map of Scotland.

The fairy tale of Chrétien reveals something that is distinctly not a fairy tale: the map of Scotland. Yet the fairy-tale aspect absolved Chrétien of all logical links, the fairy tale being a series of episodes hinging upon a young girl's desire to grow up and marry a prince. It includes admonitions to the girl and lists taboos for her to observe as she matures. Thus, Chrétien has ready-made his sex angle, his perverse undercurrents, and his love angle. He only had to add two new characters, for the fairy tale always follows the stereotype and always works on the principle of seven characters.

When he added Lancelot and the princess Jandree to his list of five characters, Chrétien painted himself into a corner. Obviously, he could not finish the tale. The hero is Prince Charming, and Chrétien was not willing to give him the center of the stage. Prince Charming cannot marry the heroine because she is already King Arthur's wife. Second setback. Worse yet, Lancelot will have to marry the princess Jandree if it is a fairy tale. Therefore, Chrétien de Troyes left the *Lancelot* unfinished, as a bad job or as an impossible assignment made by the countess of Champagne, who had probably already paid him.

Therefore we are back where we left off with Caradoc of Llancarvan's prior account: Who died?

A continuator finished the story of Chrétien, which is a botched job. A fairy tale must end with the young girl marrying the prince. Even frogs and monsters can become princes. A fairy tale tolerates no unhappy ending, but how can there be a happy ending in a story of rape and kidnapping? We insist: Who died?

There are the usual seven characters in any prototypical fairy tale, said Vladimir J. A. Propp in his book on the morphology of the fairy tale. In this case of the *Lancelot* the seven occur, in fact: (1) the hero, Lancelot, (2) the donor, the Lady of the Lake, (3) the antagonist, Prince Meleagant, (4) the auxiliary hero, Gawain, (5) the king, Arthur, (6) the queen, Guinevere, and (7) the princess, Jandree. The rather wide variations indicate how difficult it was for Chrétien to force his material into the characteristic format.

The Lady of the Lake, who gives Lancelot a magic ring so that he can perform the dangerous deed or feat always required of the second hero, remains offstage. The figure of the king is doubled by another king named Bademagus, governor of the Island Fortress, where the queen is held prisoner. He is not only a magician (or a pagan priest), he also doubles as the Intercessor. In the account by Caradoc of Llancarvan, the Intercessor was Saint Gildas. Since the second king functions as a peacemaker, most uncharacteristically for King Arthur, one suspects that Arthur has been, or was, altogether absent. However, in Chrétien's version, as in the usual format, the first king serves as the dispatcher of the hero. In Chrétien, the princess of the Island Fortress, which was later to be the prison of Lancelot, remains unnamed; we know from the Perceval tellings, however, that her name is Jandree. Lancelot weds the daughter of the Grail King, and her name is Helen, since all the Lancelot figures marry women named Helen, and this from father to son. That being the case, they must constitute a dynasty. Finally, the figure of the king, which is both Arthur and Bademagus, is tripled because in the shadowy background it is understood that Bademagus is the deputy for King Urien of Gorre and that the Island Fortress is in Gorre.

However kind and honorable the pagan priest Bademagus may be, he is still a pagan priest, and his kingdom is pagan. Thus, we have underlying the tale a rationale for war and conquest on the parts of King Arthur and his commanders, Gawain and Lancelot. The Perceval manuscripts confirm: there was a sacred island fortress and a holy sanctuary surrounded by the sea. At one time it had been Christian; in Arthur's time the inhabitants relapsed, requiring its reconquest. Queen Guinevere claimed descent from some ancestor, father, or black giant thereabouts.

A pagan priest similar to Bademagus appears to be practicing after the death of King Arthur, in the far north of Scotland, at the old Pictish capital of Inverness on Loch Ness. There, sometime before 584, Saint Columba took steps to stop him. The saint, famous for the strength and beauty of his Irish tenor, scared the whole pagan company by standing one night in the pitch dark outside King Brude's Hall and singing at the top of his voice one of the Psalms from the Old Testament. He made this priest Broichan, also called the Magician, sick to death until he released his hold over the Pictish kingdom.

Chrétien's *Lancelot* appears at first sight to be valueless as history. It closely follows the outline or morphological pattern of the fairy tale, which format was established recently from the collation of a hundred such tales by the Russian scholar Propp. The account of Chrétien commences with an evil deed (called X in the formula), which brings about a void or lack of presence in the community: the abduction of Queen Guinevere.

This causes the departure of the hero (Y). The hero decides to remedy the situation (W). In his extreme need some donor gives him a magic talisman—Lancelot's ring (Z). His route (R) is followed in chapter 5. A battle ensues (L). The hero is victorious. In the case of the *Lancelot*, Chrétien makes Lancelot victorious several times; but we see that we are really dealing with the several battles of a military campaign. One such victory (V) on the hero's part eliminates the evil deed.

The author then proceeds to turn himself about with a "Return of the Hero": ↓. If he has the wits, he writes a "Pursuit of the Hero" (P) and his subsequent imprisonment, which is the case in Chrétien. Since Lancelot did not kill the queen's jailer Meleagant the first time they met in single combat, he is imprisoned by Meleagant on the Island Fortress and is only liberated a few stages before his own death. His liberator is Meleagant's sister, the princess (Jandree), who is enamored of him.

Lancelot's reintegration into his own circles is accomplished by the arrival of someone incognito (o). Still one terrible task awaits the hero (T). Lancelot must meet the criminal adversary again, at which time he must kill this prime antagonist, Meleagant. The end of it all should be the nuptials (N), and accession to the throne of the princess's country by the hero Lancelot. Thus, the easily recognizable formula of the universal fairy tale is:

$$X—Y—W—Z—R—L—V—↓—P—o—T—N$$

After Propp had completed his examination of the fairy tale and established formulae, he remarked that the fairy tale and the medieval romance both stemmed from a unique source. They developed everywhere and over the centuries, he decided, along virtually parallel lines. He did not venture a guess as to the ultimate source of these literary forms.

It can be suggested now that both the romance and the fairy tale originated in the Dark Ages. Sometimes that history is mingled with classical mythology and with biblical literature, as in the *Lancelot*. Whenever the heroine is rescued by her husband and, especially, whenever she is drawn as an earth goddess rescued by the husband from the arms of the god Pluto of the underworld, the picture or prototypical pattern followed is mythological.

An example of the biblical influence upon Chrétien can be seen in the English translation of the *Arthurian Romances* by W. W. Comfort. The editor of that edition, the biblical scholar D. D. R. Owen, whose specialty is descents into Hell, saw the journey of Lancelot to the Island Fortress as based upon the Gospel of Nicodemus. There is no doubt that Chrétien was so influenced. The doctrine of Hell had been established by the twelfth century, and it was very much upon the minds of writers, scholars, and monks like Chrétien.

If Chrétien was thinking of Christ harrowing Hell as he portrayed Lancelot, perhaps he also had another clue. The *Prose Lancelot* will describe Lancelot in such detail that he is immediately recognizable. Other authors will have him speak so clearly that his style is instantly recognizable. It was essential that a hero be trained in oratory, a point well documented in ancient Ireland, for instance.

Furthermore Lancelot occupies a permanent position of the highest honor in King Arthur's court; he often sat on King Arthur's right, or even on the same level—equal to Arthur. Several times Chrétien mentions how exalted this royal Lancelot is. Nobody in the realm equaled him, either in birth or in courage. Therefore one should not be surprised to find Lancelot equated, as in Chrétien, with Christ. Like Charlemagne and Roland in the ninth century, Lancelot is at the least a soldier of Christ, a *miles Christi*. We grasp some idea of his stature in Arthur's world by the repeated attempts of the most beautiful heiresses to bear him a child. And one of his sons will be the most holy Galahad, of course.

The story of Lancelot at the Island Fortress should have ended with a nuptials scene, but Chrétien hides the ending of his tale, which we must suppose cannot be made to fit the pattern he was supposed to follow. To discover the elusive ending, we shall have to look into the German *Lanzelet*, which came originally from Carlisle, and which was a translation from some Old British text.

At this point in the analysis it can only be said that Chrétien will have to redeem himself, or we shall never accept him as the most talented French writer of the twelfth century. When he followed the dictates of the countess Marie de Champagne, he acted dishonorably toward himself and his source. Queen Guinevere was no lovesick married woman in search of titillation, like the usual adherents of courtly love. It is particularly instructive at this juncture to turn to the essays of Michel Butor, one of France's leading avant garde writers, for a modern interpretation of the fairy tale.

The fairy tale is written, and this applies directly to Chrétien, says Butor, at that point where the oral tradition calls the writer to rescue it before extinction. It is a narrative intended for childish women, like the French countess Marie, who have managed to acquire only the most narrow apprehension of reality. Or it is intended for children, more or less. Its account of life is in direct and "flagrant opposition" to the real world of men and women.

Between reader and real world the fairy tale waves its curtain of mystery, wonder, and unreality. Its readers demand happy endings. Not for them the world of adulthood. They wish to remain permanently sheltered and liberated from real life. The fairy-tale characters, all superlative and all of them artificial, appeal to such readers; the characters are always the most beautiful girls, the most royal kings.

Most of all, the fairy tale fails to correspond. In Chrétien it fails to correspond to the reality of Queen Guinevere's predicament: abduction and prison. Being a warrior queen, she herself fails to adhere to the "vertical inequality" that Michel Butor finds in the fairy tale. Its architecture, he says, is one of inversions: "The status of women is [experienced] as an inferiority, and this inferiority, contrary to the others, is definitive." The fairy tale of Chrétien, then, was meant to compensate the countess of Champagne for her imperfect life, and probably for her imperfect husband.

Chrétien compensated for his serfdom by inserting all the truths and all the symbols that we find so contradictory today because they oppose the patent and latent meanings in the text. There is a passing funeral cortege and a bier. There is the mirror, which always represents death; if one wishes to see one's own approaching death, one has only to look at oneself twice in the mirror. The voyage over water of Gawain, Lancelot, and the queen symbolizes the trip to the western world from whose bourne no traveler returns, says Chrétien forcefully several times. In his text all the clarity comes from beyond the grave, from the back side of the mirror. When he first sees Lancelot, even though the hero is disguised, the King Herald crosses himself. "Here he comes," he whispers. The comb at the fountain almost breaks Lancelot's heart. Why? We do not need a dictionary of symbols, for these are universal, spanning time and space. But why the cart? This part of the tale remains troubling.

In Chrétien's *Lancelot*, then, the reader's stance is rather more than less uncomfortable. There exists, first of all, the tension acutely experienced between material from the Dark Ages and a text that has been casually but only partially modernized. The twelfth century stands between the reader and the world portrayed. The Dark Ages have been modernized in the sense that they have now been set in a twelfth-century dream of dazzling knighthood, romantic love, a hint of pornography, and a sweet but horrible version of chivalry. It is a chivalry that barely masks an ugly, uncompromising ferocity. Lancelot hands Jandree the severed head of her enemy, for which service she daintily promises to help him in his need.

The reader is stranded between overt paganism and a pale Christianity, between the kindly pagan priest who tries unsuccessfully to save his son from death and the supposed Christian descent of the challenger Lancelot into the realm of Hell. The worst is the confrontation between the real heroic figure of a British battle queen, doomed yet unafraid, and her alter ego, here an overripe older woman seducing a lusty boy lover. The fairy tale is notorious for its lack of morality; the same flat tone informs all occurrences: "So they cut off her head. So they sat down to dinner." It is a "Once-upon-a-time" world, a never-never land of immorality, divorced from right and wrong. We see why Chrétien could not finish the text. That was honest of him.

Chrétien's introductory explanation (vv. 1–250) of the circumstances behind the queen's abduction remains cursory but adequate. The strange knight claims the person of the queen and challenges King Arthur to send his queen out with an armed escort. His intent is to ambush her and offer her combat at an arranged battleground. If she loses the surprise battle in that forest glade, she will become his prisoner. Grieving, King Arthur entrusts the queen to Kay, who has volunteered or demanded the assignment. The courtiers mourn the queen as if she were already dead.

At first both King Arthur and Gawain escort the queen's party; after a few miles Gawain continues alone until he meets the Knight of the Cart. They pass Kay's horse returning riderless to the stable. The queen's men lose the combat, and the queen falls hostage, probably on her own recognizance, to the foreign challenger. If her party had won the battle, the challenger would have been obliged to release from perpetual imprisonment those persons captured from King Arthur's realm. Their captivity in his land is awful, and their suffering endless.

With a little effort we should be able now to place this battle into one of the twelve or so campaigns described and listed by Nennius and Geoffrey of Monmouth.

It would seem that this episode forms a part of King Arthur's island campaign, where the queen and her forces constitute a subordinate command. King Arthur remains at headquarters, after the short ride in the direction of the queen's command, less than a day's ride from Camelot. The castle identified as Camelot is situated near Carlisle, not inland like that fortress, but right on the water's edge.

Centuries later, Sir Thomas Malory, who may have been a military man and who in any event knew a few things that would have caused Chrétien's eyes to widen, emended the earlier reports by attributing the initiative to Queen Guinevere.* In the month of May, according to Malory, the queen led a squad of ten queen's men into the forest: Sir Kay the Seneschal, Agravain, Brandiles, Sagramore, Dodinas, Ozanna, Ladinas, Persant, Ironside, and Pelleas. These men were all wounded and taken captive along with the queen.

The queen's men wore green, *as had Lancelot and Gawain in Chrétien's account.* War parties inside Scotland characteristically wore green leaves on

---

Le Morte d'Arthur, vol. 2, book 19.

their lances and on their helmets when they set out for war on Whitsunday, says John Prebble in his history of Scotland.* We recall that Queen Guinevere had worn laurel leaves during her coronation at Carlisle.

Malory understood the circumstances of the engagement in a more military fashion, claiming that the queen volunteered to go as hostage in order to save the lives of her ten men. Her captor was the same as in Chrétien, now spelled "Meliagraunce," which reproduces Malory's spoken language or his accent in the fifteenth century, rather than "Meleagant," which represents Chrétien's accent. (Spoken language always takes priority over written language.) Malory knows more immediately, namely, that Meliagraunce is the son of Bademagus, to whom King Urien has entrusted his subkingdom, the Island Fortress.

In Caradoc of Llancarfan the purpose of Meluas (Meleagant) was rape. In Malory, the purpose is similarly sexual relations, but we begin to see that more may be involved here than mere sexual appetite. The unclear story of Brunhilde comes back to mind. She was overpowered by Siegfried, who acted as agent for his king, Gunther. After having been deflowered, Brunhilde lost all her strength and her independent status, or property. She changed from a proud sovereign and warrior queen to a shrew and a jealous woman, haggling with Kriemhilde about who would precede whom into the church. In other words, Gunther, whose deputy was Siegfried, overpowered Brunhilde, thus depriving her of her kingdom. That seems to be the case with Queen Guinevere.

King Arthur allowed his queen to lead a war party because she was an independent chieftainess, royal in her own right, mistress of her person and real property. By some law unknown and unused nowadays Queen Guinevere lost her inheritance to Meliagraunce (or Meluas, or Meleagant).

Sir Thomas Malory worked closely with the *Prose Lancelot*, whose authors probably were the first to grasp the significance of these events in the legal status and life of Queen Guinevere. They agreed that Carlisle and Camelot were adjacent, in the north of Britain, and that King Arthur was in residence at the latter when the matter of Queen Guinevere's inheritance arose. King Arthur was at that time deep in war against three powerful northern kings: King Galehaut of Sorelois (Sutherland?), King Bademagus of Gorre, and King Loth of Lothian. Although as combatant and ally Lancelot remained loyal to King Arthur, he had already been accepted as heir presumptive to two of these same northern kingdoms: Gorre and Sorelois. When he went on the quest for the queen, Lancelot also went to win the land of Gorre for himself. Gawain went on the quest for the queen but also to rescue his brother Agravaine, King Loth's second son. The political situation becomes tangled, indeed.

*(p. 93).

Queen Guinevere's situation in the *Prose Lancelot,* while never explicit, allies her also to King Arthur's northern enemies, so closely, in fact, that she must have been by birth a northern chieftainess. More than once, Queen Guinevere along with Lancelot passed north of the Forth-Dumbarton line or into the kingdoms of the Northern Picts. Once there, she seems to have become their overlord, even of the Out Isles and of Sutherland. Only after the death of Prince Galehaut did King Bademagus dare send to King Arthur's court for the queen. In some ways now the story is rounded out albeit complicated.

Throughout, the characterization of Meleagant remains fairly consistent; that he was the rapist and abductor appears to be so well known to all that it needs to be explained by none. Chrétien interprets Meleagant's behavior as dominated by an overpowering or psychopathic sexuality. Strangely unfamiliar with human passions other than sexuality, medieval clerics and intellectuals easily attributed concupiscence to the people they wrote about and appear to have calmly accepted human depravity as the norm.

In the German text of *Parzival* Wolfram von Eschenbach stands up to Meleagant, whom he calls Meljacanz, son of King Poydiconjunz of Gore (books 3, 7). The boy Parzival, who had never before met a knight, one day encountered Meljacanz in the forest, in the act of abducting an heiress named Imane. He wore, scolded Wolfram, the crown of discourtesy, since the only love he ever won he took by force. So at least someone in the Middle Ages besides the saints Gildas and Columba disapproved of kidnapping women. Aside from that sort of crime, said Wolfram, Meljacanz acted the part of a courageous and manly warrior. Wolfram saw no contradiction there. For the sake of comparison, it should be pointed out that the death sentence for kidnappers was not established in the United States until after 1932!

Is it possible for a man to be manly and a rapist at the same time? What can lie behind the sordid acts of Meleagant? Could Chrétien and the others have stumbled across some unfamiliar culture, another code of morality, and failed to realize it?

In his book *The Welsh People* the Arthurian scholar Sir John Rhys explained that personal relationships were once quite different from those we know today. In ancient Ireland, for instance, courtship was frequently initiated by the lady. This custom is illustrated in such Irish tales as "The Pursuit of Dermat and Grania."*

It seems that among the Pictish peoples of ancient Scotland the crown passed to the royal daughter, who was called the heretrix chief. She was free to bestow it upon the consort of her choice. Thus, the kings of the Picts were most frequently noble sons of non-Pictish origin. It would also

*Other such instances occur in the *Old Celtic Romances* translated by P. W. Joyce.

appear that consummation of a marriage with a chieftainess conferred the rank of prince consort upon the male. This goes far to clarify Queen Guinevere's situation with regard to suitors—King Urien, Meleagant, and then Modred—and also that of the unfortunate Brunhilde and her two husbands, Siegfried and King Gunther. It might also explain the hearsay evidence concerning "Morgan le Fay," or Queen Morgan, reputedly the mother of two sons by different fathers. The word *Prince* in the name *Meluas* or *Meleagant* means that he was the consort of the heretrix Imane, and perhaps of the tortured Queen Guinevere.

Chrétien's confusion and his accusation of adultery may have resulted from his failure to realize that northern Britain, especially the Rhinns of Galloway but also the whole northern part of Scotland above the Forth-Clyde line, was once Pictish. Meleagant's desperate attempts to establish himself upon a throne have perhaps been misconstrued as excessive or psychopathic sexuality on his part.

Sir John Rhys claims that other peoples, long before the time of Chrétien de Troyes, also failed to comprehend the ancient civilization of this remote and far northern part of Britain:

> . . . the Greeks and Romans . . . could not understand the relations of the sexes among the peoples of that race, except as mere license and wanton promiscuity . . . Dio Cassius (lxxxvi. 16) . . . introduces . . . a Pictish lady . . . on Pictish morality . . . she thought the Pictish custom the better, since . . . Pictish ladies openly consorted with the best warriors of the race. . . . Further the Pictish succession cannot have always been confined to the Pictland of the North, for the ancient literature described abounds in heroes who are usually described with the aid of the mother's name.*

Thus, as Lancelot said, he was a king's son and therefore without inheritance except as he conquered it for himself. Idem, Meleagant.

To summarize, Queen Guinevere is being taken to an island surrounded by ocean water. It was written on the stone, we are told. This is an old, famous, well-preserved story, once known to everybody.

Every account of the abduction concurs that the island is of glass, looks like glass, gleams like glass, and/or has on it a crystal mountain. It is the Fortunate Isle of dreams, where the month of May is exquisite and lasts all year. Its gateway is a solid diamond, wrote genial Geoffrey of Monmouth, spouting symbolism in his old age. There is there a cluster of golden

*The Welsh People, p. 14.

stars, and a land abloom with flowers and tropical trees. It is the summer land of Voirre, or Gorre, *where no serpents are*. Before it lies a swamp, and before that a river, and around that the sea. It must be seen before one leaves this world. Its castle is called the Castle of Death.

Gorre is ruled by a king, enemy to King Arthur. His name is Urien, and his deputy governor is the magus or magician named Bademagus. That unfortunate seer has a willful son bent on his own destruction despite everything his father can do to stop him. This is Meleagant, a prince. Bademagus is the Intervener, called Mabuz the Enchanter by Ulrich von Zatzikhoven, or "Der wise Malduz," or "Der wise man." It is only a small jump backward to Gildas the Wise, of the Glastonbury manuscript. The Irish connection remains solidly the same.

Queen Morgan is somehow connected here—whether or not she is the Lady of the Lake or the sibyl of Ulrich—and therefore connected to Lancelot and to Guinevere.

We still do not know who dies, but we are closing in on it.

4

Lancelot's Quest

Several attempts have already been made to reduce Chrétien's narrative to a scheme that would make it more comprehensible. Mario Roques, who edited this text in 1967, saw it as divided into thirty-nine episodes, but earlier Gaston Paris had realized that the more one worked at this sort of schematization the more meaningless the whole became. The welter of events, encounters, and adventures constitute a real tangle out of which nothing in the way of logical format has yet emerged. It is therefore imperative to take a new approach; instead of persons encountered and tasks performed, plotting Lancelot's journey upon a map will perhaps reveal his progress and his purpose.

There are only ten stops along the way:

1. Abduction of the queen: royal castle, Carlisle
2. Dwarf and cart: Castle Marvelous
3. Perilous Ford: near Castle Marvelous
4. Damsel's home, a castle upriver: royal castle
5. Fountain and *Perron*: sacred site
6. Old abbey and cemetery: royal necropolis
7. Stony passage: Hadrian's Wall
8. Pitched battle: Carlisle
9. Challenger at the ferry: near Castle Marvelous
10. The sword bridge: Land of the Gael

Even at first glance it is obvious that Lancelot is making some sort of royal progress, from castle to castle, as if he were circling his realm, or some realm belonging either to him or to another prince. The former theory is probably closer to the truth. Aside from Gawain, who makes an early departure at or near the Perilous Ford, Lancelot is accompanied by nameless persons. Even the kings who receive him remain nameless. Ancient kings used to make a circuit of their realm, after their accession to the throne, and they often made this circuit in strict ritual fashion, taking right-hand turns only. At last, our first real clue to the identity of Lancelot: he seems to have just become a king. In fact, Chrétien, who is a shameless name-dropper, is staggered by the magnificence of Lancelot. And Chrétien dealt preferably with royalty.

Another traveler to the north, Dr. Samuel Johnson, had some qualms about the "instability of the vernacular languages." Chrétien's French is only so-so, and we don't know the language of his source. To make matters worse, Chrétien is not really interested in Lancelot or the cart, chariot, or vehicle upon which he rode, which was supposed to cause him humiliation.

Chrétien has no use for the initial situation and no intention of clarifying the resultant military situation. The facts are that a challenge to war was delivered in person at Arthur's court during a session at Carlisle, more properly at Camelot, which is adjacent to the former and is on the water. As a result Queen Guinevere is taken prisoner. Gawain and King Arthur rush off in pursuit. They are joined by Lancelot, who rides so hotly to the rendezvous point that he causes two horses to founder, in one afternoon. Geographers of the Carlisle area reveal that there was in ancient times a rendezvous point on the shoreline between Carlisle and Gretna Green, at the huge granite boulder called the Clachmabenstone (properly, Clachmabenstane). The stone is still there, and that seems about right, as far as distance and direction are concerned. Once Lancelot has arrived, which means once he has taken command, King Arthur is free to return to other business at Carlisle.

King Arthur had begun his military career as a Roman *dux* and was promoted to *imperator*, or supreme commander. As such, he would have worn the distinctive scarlet mantle of that rank, and, in fact, King Arthur's mantle was always one of the Thirteen Treasures of Britain. When wearing it, he often moved so fast as to become invisible. The supreme commander appointed, as in this case, two lieutenant generals from the upper class of that society, Gawain and Lancelot. As here, they were assigned in battle wherever the commander saw fit.

Chrétien was not in the least interested in Lancelot's overtired horses or in his rate of speed. He does note later on in the text that Lancelot met a local king disporting himself with his son and courtiers in a meadow. The king and his companions were mounted on splendid Spanish and Irish horses of great price. But Lancelot must have been riding a common utility horse descended from the wild forest horses native to that region. They were small animals, measuring only thirteen hands (52 inches as compared to 60"—or fifteen hands—mounts we ride today), judging from a skeleton found beside a chariot's wheels in Yorkshire, over a hundred years ago. Lancelot's horse would not have been a draft horse of later times, like the famous feathered Clydesdale, but perhaps the ancestor of the sturdy Galloway, suited for long rides along forest paths, an animal with an easy, loping gait, really just a fast walk. It is no wonder they foundered when pushed to a sustained gallop. Their usual gait covered something like five miles an hour, giving a maximum perhaps of thirty to thirty-five miles per day under optimum conditions.

The month was May, with good weather and good grass for the horses. The distances in the country where Lancelot was heading are not excessive, given the speed and stamina of his mounts:

Carlisle to Glasgow: 95 miles
Carlisle to Edinburgh: 94 miles
Carlisle to Stranraer (ferry point): 80 (?) miles
Edinburgh to Hawick: 51 miles
Edinburgh to Stirling: 36 miles
Edinburgh to Dumfries: 73 miles
Edinburgh to Jedburgh: 48 miles

Specifically, the time is late May. In ancient Irish territory at least, the first of May was the famous celebration of Beltane with bonfires and horse races for all. May Day was the ancient New Year's Day in Gaul, and perhaps in other Celtic lands. The tenth is doubly sacred, with the much observed heliacal rising of the Pleiades; today that only announces the coming of summer in those latitudes and the rapid lengthening of the daylight hours. It is true that Lancelot may have followed an ancient route of pilgrimage as he went toward "tu thall," the other shore. While the mounted rider is an ancient heroic symbol in European legends, Lancelot is making a practical and a military journey. His circuit of the realm serves the purpose of recruitment also, for it culminates in a pitched battle near Carlisle. And we know that King Arthur fought several days there, as one of his famous twelve battles. Lancelot's quest is therefore not mythological. His commission from King Arthur was multiple, consisting of recruitment of youths, tracking the queen and the prisoners, reconnaissance, and rescue.

Lancelot's situation on that first afternoon must have been of the utmost desperation. Having exhausted his transportation, Lancelot came upon the dwarf and the cart. And it is here that Chrétien himself foundered. He does not tell what sort of cart, how many wheels it had, what was in it, or why Lancelot was or was to have been so humiliated.

The dwarf was not driving a war chariot, or two-wheeled *essedum* of the Celtic warriors. Nor was it that of the "car-bourne British King Arviragus . . . dropped from his battle throne." It was not some four-wheeled cart

SCOTLAND
and Lancelot

such as that described by Stuart Piggott as a burial vehicle of an ancient warrior or one like the cart that took away the queen in a world where women could expect at any minute to become routine prizes of war. And the dwarf was certainly not driving any four-wheeled bronze chariot, the ritual vehicle pictured for the ride of the sun god.

Chrétien does say that the cart Lancelot rode in was *unique in its city of those times,* whereas by the twelfth century there would be thousands such in France. It served as a farm tipcart, one supposes, and also as the local pillory or tumbrel. The word *tumbrel* makes one wonder if that was the original word in Chrétien's source, for if it was, the picture would change drastically. The word *tumbrel* or *tombereau* also indicates a military machine for use in a siege operation. If Chrétien saw *tombereau*, he might have thought it meant a two-wheeled farm cart while in fact it might have signified a trebuchet, which is a machine for demolishing walls and other stone structures.

The trebuchet is a military engine similar to a wrecking crane, with an iron ball suspended on the tip of its vertical axis so that it swings back and forth on the projecting arm. It was worked by one man, the dwarf, seated at the front so that he could pull back a lever, which when released propelled the rope and hanging ball forward to demolish the wall. This was a primitive jet propulsion machine. The rearward rocking motion of the vertical axis opposed the hoisting and releasing of the front axis. A windlass (the word is Icelandic) and horsehair ropes wound up the rock on the front axis and then let it fall forward and into the structure to be knocked down. In King Arthur's time the ball could have been of stone, but one is inclined to think it was of iron. There were iron foundries (and still are) in the Falkirk area, halfway between Edinburgh and Stirling, the Carron Iron Works. We are told that Perceval's famous sword was forged there—and so perhaps was Excalibur.

The question of King Arthur's siege methods arises here. Nennius had heard of them. In the Nennius documents there is an odd sentence: "Artur Latine translatum sonat 'ursum horribilem,' vel 'malleum ferreum,' quo confringuntur molae leonum: . . ." Now it makes sense, in view of what could have been Lancelot's trebuchet: "The name *Artur* sounds like the Celtic word for shaggy bear, which is *arth,* or 'iron mallet,' with which the walls of the seas were demolished." That is to say, not "molae leonum," but *moles llion.* The Welsh word *llion* (of the waves) was mistaken for *leonum* (of the lions), which has up to now made no sense at all. By "moles llion" the translator may have been trying out an etymology for *Carlisle* (the word is not decipherable otherwise). *Carlisle* to him meant Castle of the Waves, or Camelot, Castle of the Hammerer: *Caer + llion,* and *Caer + Mallet.* Our word *demolish* derives from this Latin word *moles* or structure. We know that King Arthur took Carlisle, which was surrounded by Roman walls twenty feet high.

Therefore taking it must have meant breaching the walls. Now, if the queen was being taken to a neighboring castle adjacent to a ferry point, Lancelot could very well be bringing up the siege machinery. We know that King Arthur was not the type of commander to let his queen go into slavery. Nor would he have sent Gawain and Lancelot barehanded to bring her back.

A modern lieutenant general might have done the same thing as Lancelot: jumped upon the piece of siege equipment and let himself be hauled into the nearby castle precinct. Or he would have leaped gracefully into the dwarf's tumbrel, disdainful of the menace presented by "the plebeian" wielding the birch rod. W. W. Comfort, the English translator of the *Lancelot*, thought that the dwarf was driving an oxcart and used the word *goad* for the whip in his hand. But the text does not say "goad"; rather, and more threateningly, it says that the dwarf held a birch rod. The word is *verge* (Latin *virga*), a badge of office of the *lictor* or minor dignitary attached to a Roman officer, the official "bircher," like a beadle. Thus, what Chrétien never caught was that the dwarf was a royal officer, and Gawain's brother.

But Lancelot was in no peril. Whatever the vehicle, Lancelot ignored the driver. The reader cannot do likewise, for Tristan suffered greatly from the dwarf of Tintagel Castle. His name was Frocin, and there is another dwarf at the Island Fortress where the queen will be held. The dwarf, as hostile or Pictish princes are often described, seems to have held some minor office at such places.

In fact, Lancelot is nearing the castle sometimes identified as Tintagel in Cornwall. Since the queen was to be held there, and since King Arthur could not know it would be for one night only, it is likely that siege machinery was rushed to the site. And if it was rushed there, then all the more reason why the queen was moved in the morning. As a noble Roman himself, King Arthur would have been familiar with Roman siege machinery: the catapult or scorpion (small catapult) and the *ballista*, which hurled stones of enormous size at an angle of 45°.

We can certainly suppose that King Arthur sent an armed force after the queen and that this force was commanded by Gawain, who outranked the much younger Lancelot. Gawain seems to have taken the point, commanding the vanguard in this emergency or the main column of light-armed foot soldiers preceded by cavalry. Thus, he was able to lend Lancelot an extra horse. Later on, he would have been too far ahead of him. Presumably Lancelot was the artillery officer, who brought up the rear guard and baggage van. The Romans marched this way, the baggage train in the rear so as to turn and face the pursuers, protecting the main force. Since they started in the middle of the day, they cannot have gone more than between eight and fifteen miles, in Roman marching terms, by nightfall. Each soldier carried his own gear on a forked stick over his left shoulder: blanket, rations, utensils, and a pot for cooking.

Lancelot and Gawain arrived at a castle by the seashore and spent the first night there, assisted, accompanied, and instructed by the first among a series of damsels—royal maidens of marriageable age. This is the royal castle, often described by Chrétien in later works such as the *Perceval* or *Grail* romance, and identified in most Arthurian texts. Sometimes it is called Tintagel, as in the Béroul *Tristan* manuscript. In Parzival's time King Arthur's mother resided there with her royal granddaughters.

It is also called Castle Marvelous. Ritchie identified it as Caerlaverock. King Arthur, then, was born there. Four queens resided there at one time: Arthur's mother (whom Wolfram von Eschenbach called Arnive); Gawain's mother, called Sangive; and Gawain's sisters, named Cundrie and Itonje.

Various writers stumbled over its name, sometimes using *Roche* (Rock) *Sabins* (mistaking Severn for Solway), or *Roche de Champguin,* as Chrétien finally had it: Rock of the White Field, the Irish *Mag Find.*

The castle is located in such a way that it can hardly be mistaken. It faces a great water and looks toward Ireland. It is insulated by another water, the river with the dangerous crossing, or the River Nith with its quicksands. The Perilous Ford designates the crossing, where crowds accumulate to ford the river. Here Isolde underwent her test for veracity, and here Lancelot will perform a hand-to-hand combat witnessed by a large crowd. It is becoming clear that people are thronging from all over to see the heralded young Lancelot.

We know that the ferry crossing is near, for Gawain will opt for the water route and leave Lancelot here. Gawain once had to leap his horse over the river nearby in order to pluck a wreath for his demanding sweetheart Orgeluse, the Proud Lady. Lancelot will choose the harder—or land—passage to the Island Fortress, and the terrible sword bridge. The first castle is on a white plain, which lies between it and the water of the Solway Firth. The other water, the River Nith, flows on the second side of the castle, which is one square mile in area. On these two sides the water broadens into a lake. The castle is fortified on the third side and was customarily entered, one supposes, from the Carlisle side, or the east. The ferry runs outbound from the Solway. The opposite shore and perhaps even Port Carlisle of the Romans is visible from the front of the castle grounds.

This castle is also called the Castle of Wonders, for the Wonder Bed lies there, as Gawain and Lancelot know very well, both having survived the test of its burning lance that descends from the rafters at night. Lancelot survived without a glance at it. He rose from bed, only slightly wounded, and threw the lance away from him. With similar disdain he endured the damsel's taunts. In the morning Gawain left for the attack on the Island Fortress by water, and Lancelot remained there where Castle Marvelous guarded the coast to the west, or the "Ports of Galloway."

Lancelot's next adventure is the combat at the Perilous Ford. There he falls into the hands of another royal damsel, with marriage on her mind, however, and is obliged to accompany her upstream to another castle. We know that this supposition is probably correct for two reasons. First, Béroul speaks of a king of Dumfries, an enemy of the Scots; Lancelot could have recruited him. Second, his castle is described as a *dunn*, ergo Dumfries, the main royal site near Caerlaverock and a river. Instead of proceeding west across the ford, Lancelot now turns north again. During a night of lurid threats of sex, with Lancelot resisting the damsels, he is attacked by men wielding swords, axes, crosses, and hammers. Again it is a royal site, for these are four symbols of royalty.

Lancelot's subsequent journey with the royal damsel and her father takes him toward what appears to be a sacred precinct. First Lancelot undergoes an emotional upheaval, as he recognizes the comb of the queen lying at the edge of a fountain. The word taken to mean stone edge, or parapet, is *perron* in the Old French. A mysterious word of uncertain meaning, it occurs at a pagan temple in *Gawain and the Green Knight*, where the English translator is also stumped and renders it as "hard rock." Lancelot takes to his heart tresses of the queen's golden hair.

The comb symbolizes the Pictish chieftainess. It also conveys a symbolic meaning of boat and embarkation. Thus, the queen seems to have left him a clue to her whereabouts. For some reason not given to the reader, Lancelot veers north again. He turns up next miles away outside the castle area and Rock of Stirling.

When Lancelot arrives at an old abbey, he performs rites that are recognizable today: the laying of wreaths on graves. Lancelot goes to a sacred burial place to honor his ancestors and the other war dead. Fortunately the writers of the *Prose Lancelot* omitted no details. Writers of the Middle Ages thought that Lancelot would have gone to the Old Abbey, their further precision placing it near the Castle of Stirling today and, even more precisely, on the very battlefield of Bannockburn.

The old abbeys of Scotland were founded in the Middle Ages: Jedburgh (1118), Kelso (1128), Holyroodhouse (1128), Melrose (1126), and Cambuskenneth (1147). And yet in the accounts of Lancelot's visit prior to the year 542 details pinpoint the old abbey as Saint Ninians, just south of the Castle Fortress of Stirling, approximately in the middle of the battlefield and national monument to the dead of Bannockburn, a battle of 1314. Today no one at Saint Ninians associates it with King Arthur. Yet it is true that earthworks called "King Arthur's Knot" lie just below the cliffs of Stirling Castle. Stirling was Lancelot's chief seat and the chief prize of any war. Then as now, it loomed high on its gray cliff, overlooking the most ancient battlefield, the "Cockpit of Scotland."

Lancelot came here to the "Old Abbey" of Saint Ninian, who was a saint of the ancient Celtic peoples, around the year 397, said W. F. Skene.

A missionary trained at Rome, connected to the Christian church inside Gaul, Saint Ninian built a stone church "vulgarly called Candida Casa" (White House), after the death of his beloved Saint Martin of France/Gaul. His goal was the conversion of the Southern or Galloway Picts to Christianity, with the hope that he could at the same time persuade them to cease their bloody attacks upon the Strathclyde Britons.

The ruins of Candida Casa have been found at Whithorn on the southern tip of Galloway, on the promontory from which the tip of the Isle of Man can be seen across the Irish Sea. In 447 Saint Patrick founded the bishopric of Man in this area, called the oldest inside Britain. In 838 Pope Gregory IV reestablished it and called it the bishopric of the Western Isles.

The earliest date given for Sweetheart Abbey, near which King Arthur may have been born and raised (since it is across the River Nith from Caerlaverock Castle, perhaps also near the Perilous Ford) is 1373. Candida Casa cannot be the old abbey visited by Lancelot, for it was called the "Great Monastery." Saint Ninians is mentioned more than once in the Arthurian manuscripts, however, and it stood and stands today beside the Roman road from the south into Stirling and the Stirling Castle precinct. Today it is a small cemetery surrounded by a round wall, "round," just as the Lancelot accounts describe it.

Lancelot paid a ceremonial visit to an old abbey beside a cemetery containing thirty-four tombs. The place, adds the *Prose Lancelot* of the thirteenth century, stood near the Perilous Forest and a boiling fountain guarded by two lions. The lion is, of course, the symbol of Scotland today, and the Scottish flag shows a red lion on a yellow field. Here, now that he is a man and a commander, Lancelot is formally instructed in his royal family and royal history; this ceremony resembled an ascertainment of right to the throne. Galles (Wales) is named from Lancelot's grandfather, he is told, whose name was Galaad (Galahad), and he was the son of Saint Joseph of Arimathea. His name is Galahad, Lancelot is also told. Up until now he has not known his real name.

Before the time of Lancelot's grandfather, the country was called either Hofelise or Hostelisse. (This is very strange, and one wonders if it could have been *hof* + *selig* = Holy Hill.)

The names of kings were tabooed until the third generation, Sir James Fraser tells us in *The Golden Bough*. Thus we understand why Lancelot did not previously know his own name.

We learn with some shock that Lancelot is descended from Saint Joseph of Arimathea, contrary to the Glastonbury legend, which places that personage in Glastonbury. The sixteen-volume *Lives of the British Saints* by the Reverend Sabine Baring-Gould, yields the following: the legends concerning Saint Joseph of Arimathea "are wholly worthless, [and] they must be passed over." This saint is reputed to have lived in Britain in the first century, to have taken the body of Christ from the Cross, and to have brought the Holy Grail to Britain. His feast day is March 17.

A Joseph of Arimathea, supposed to have been a member of the Sanhedrin, was known to Matthew, Mark, Luke, and John. Lancelot's appearance at the holy cemetery either coincides with the Christian celebration of the Ascension of Christ or followed soon after that date. Lancelot was asked to see if he could lift the slab from the tomb of his grandfather Galahad, who had reigned under the name of King Lancelot I. The young hero easily lifted the slab. He was thereafter enabled to transport the body of his ancestor.

We are not told to what place he was permitted to transport this body, but we can infer from his subsequent stops that it was either to the vicinity of Carlisle or to the Island Fortress where Queen Guinevere lay hostage. The fact that he transported the body of his revered ancestor to any place indicates that things must have been going badly. If King Arthur was losing the north, along the Firth of Forth (then known as the Frisican Sea), then the sacred tombs would have to be removed to safer places. Now, since the Celtic peoples are always reported as moving west before the thrust of warriors arriving on the eastern coasts, one supposes that Lancelot was conveying this body to the western island. If that is so, then one can understand why no directions to that place appear anywhere in the Arthurian texts. Particularly troublesome have been the omissions of sea crossings in the texts. The idea of the mythologists that Lancelot, like a mythical horseman, could ride horseback over land *and* sea is not very helpful.

The visit of Lancelot to this old abbey does not cease to astonish, for there in the text are some very interesting dates. They are given after the young hero has descended to the crypt or Perilous Hall. There lies the tomb of Saint Joseph of Arimathea, surrounded by flames as high as a lance. Lancelot draws back. At his involuntary movement a voice from the underground proclaims that he is not destined to end Perilous Times.

Lancelot replies: "Quel deuil et quel dommage." What grief and what a shame! He has not been pure? No.

Only the destined one will by his presence alone extinguish the flames.

There are thirty years yet to go, says the voice of the apocalyptic prophecy. Lancelot may not sit in the Siege Perilous. The voice says no more about this Round Table Seat at this time, unfortunately. But it is near.

From the death of Christ, we are told, there will be 454 years until the coming of the destined one. There are now 30 more years to go in the life of Lancelot (15 years from the birth of Galahad). The sum is not added for us, but we can work it out: A.D. 33 (if that is the death date of Christ) + 454 + 30 = 517 (the lifetime of King Arthur). Young Lancelot is bowed with grief at the thought that he will not achieve the Grail Quest.

We do not know that he recruited clansmen at this ceremony or even whether there were clansmen in those days; but he left for a pitched battle soon afterward. The king of Dumfries and his royal daughter, who had accompanied Lancelot to this ceremony, leave him. The ceremony had commenced at about 3:00 P.M.

Before arriving at the southern or Stony Passage, which one takes to have been Hadrian's Wall, Lancelot meets a knight who counsels him, and he recruits his two young sons. The Stony Passage consists of a wooden milecastle with men on guard duty who attempt to prevent Lancelot's crossing. One assumes that Lancelot took the shortest route from Falkirk to Carlisle, through the Kershope Forest, which even on the modern road maps of this area is plainly marked in at least three places: King Arthur's Camp. This was the king's staging area and food supply, consisting largely of cattle driven into the deep glens, such as the one marked on the map between Moffat and Peebles as the Devil's Beef Tub.

After having crossed the *Passage de Pierres*, which is just what Hadrian's Wall is, Lancelot has one last adventure with a hostile knight. Then he fights the pitched battle, probably that of Carlisle, or a part of it. He fights, says Chrétien, alongside Logres. King Arthur's name is not mentioned here, but the king will eventually join Lancelot at the Island Fortress.

Lancelot's last adventure reveals what we have been looking for all along—that the passage to the Island Fortress lies over water. Lancelot meets the Bull challenger. He seems to be taunting the hero when he says that he can "ferry him west" over water. That seems to mean that he can kill him, or send him to the land of no return, which is what Gorre is called.

His is the severed head claimed in ancient times as legal recompense by the Loathly Damsel, who is the king's daughter from Gorre. Hideous and unladylike, she comes jauntily into the castle outside which this final duel takes place. She is riding a tawny mule, as is her custom. She is loud and uncouth, with beetling eyebrows and broad buttocks, dark-complexioned, and yet perversely appealing in her boisterous ugliness. She must have just got off the ferry, and she is the last and not the least of the king's loathsome daughters to claim Lancelot as her husband. On top of that she is ready to earn him by promising to save his life at some future date.

In this combat Lancelot is compared to the hawk killing the lark. Curiously enough, the name of the castle is probably *Caerlaverock*, which means Castle of the Lark. Lancelot gives the knight a second chance to save his life, defeats him again, and then gives Jandree her due, the severed head. She throws it into a snake pit. (If it was the use of snake pits that Saint Patrick forbade, that injunction obviously did not apply to Caerlaverock.)

Thus, Lancelot has come down to the ferry point himself. Chrétien remains mum. There is no sea crossing at all. Suddenly Lancelot is in the land of Gorre and approaching the dreadful sword bridge, whose blade he must cross. And beyond that lies the challenger. The definitive solution will be witnessed by King Arthur.

Lancelot arrives at the sword bridge late the next afternoon. Chrétien would have us believe that this entire quest took place in the period of a week, six days on land and one day left over (for the sea crossing).

What are the achievements of Lancelot to date, before he commences his greatest feat? At the beginning of the emergency he came on fast, without waiting the usual twelve hours after the burst of the first alarm flare. We think he took command of the rear guard. We know that he rode upon the cart with the evil, surly dwarf. He even rose unruffled from the Perilous Bed, taking no notice whatsoever of the slight wound in his side.

At the Perilous Ford he performed marvelously again, and this time in the presence of a crowd of people, who had come from all around to watch him. After this meet, he accompanied the second king's daughter to her home and castle. He may there have taken possession of her real estate and first demonstrated his virility.

Moving rapidly up to the adventure and test of the fountain and mysterious *perron*, stone marker, basin around the spring (Chrétien's idea), or mounting stage (Marie de France's solution), or keystone to a vault (*Gawain and the Green Knight*), Lancelot demonstrated his tracking ability. It was he who recognized the meaning of the queen's clue.

It was only at the old abbey and cemetery that Lancelot suffered his unique setback—that he would never sit at the Siege Perilous of the Round Table and that he would never achieve the Quest of the Holy Grail. Neither Round Table nor Grail is as yet mentioned by Chrétien, but a text of the Dark Ages mentioned the latter and gave formulaic directions to the Grail Castle. After having ascertained his right (to the throne?), Lancelot set about one of man's oldest occupations, the hauling of stones. Like the respectful Aeneas of classical literature, here Lancelot showed his reverence for the dead. In so doing, he sacrificed the present to the past and to the future, which is considered noble.

He easily pierced the Stony Passage, defeated its sentries, and supposedly led his forces into battle at or near Carlisle. In the last adventure, he slew the knight who had offered to "ferry him west" and gave the head to one of the Loathly Damsels. She is the sister of Meleagant, and she will leave the ship as it is about to founder. Even this early, she wishes to ally herself with Lancelot, in marriage, if possible. Once married, according to her defenders, she will turn into the lovely maiden of a man's dreams. The ballads tell us she had already tried her wiles on King Arthur.

Then Lancelot went west over water and survived this passage whence none previously had returned, it was believed. Throngs gather, and maidens diet in order to purify themselves at his approach. Badly wounded at the sword bridge, he admits no pain and no inconvenience. He is so seriously torn and bleeding that King Bademagus willingly accords a month for him to recover. Lancelot haughtily refuses. He would fight Meleagant the next day. How could he disappoint all these people who had come from such distances to see him perform, or all the lovely maidens who had so painfully got themselves in shape for him?

There is reason to be suspicious of Lancelot and of his real purpose at the mention of these throngs who have gathered more than once for his coming. He is not a healer. So, why so many people? How do they all know about his coming? Of what lives do we never tire? Of whom do we wish to know the slightest bit of news? Whom would we all wish to see in real life?

There is the clincher, it would seem. Lancelot must have been a great royal personage.

King Bademagus bowed low before Lancelot, deferring to him in utter humility, offering him all his resources, and extending to him all courtesy. And he was the father of Lancelot's challenger—in need of a position in life, and preferably of a kingdom. Lancelot's first castle was that of King Arthur's mother, where he was almost slain on the Perilous Bed. That test proved him to be who he said he was—not Lancelot, of course, but a minion of King Arthur. Behind this abduction of the queen stand King Urien of Gorre and his Queen Morgan, called le Fay. Now it was the "Fairy Queen" who had raised Lancelot on an island in the sea. Why would she who is Queen Morgan hate Gawain, Yvain, and Lancelot? Or does she hate someone else, and not Lancelot?

Something complicated must have happened for this Queen Morgan to be filled with so much hate. Two, perhaps three, things were always much feared by the Celtic peoples: that the sky would fall down, that thunder would strike, and that twins would be born. This last was feared only by women, since it was thought that the firstborn twin was the son of the earthly father and the second twin the son of the Devil and thus, the mother of twins was put to death. Now, we know that there were two sons both named Yvain, both called sons of King Urien. We also know that Lancelot's mother died soon after his birth, while running alongside a lake and holding her baby in her arms. We have also heard that the baby, or a baby, was thrown in the lake. As soon as that happened, the baby was pulled from the water by a queen, called Lady of the Lake. She was a fairy, or, as the Irish say about their ancient kings, she was a priestess, but anyway a king's daughter. The Lady or Queen of the Lake who raised Lancelot protects him along his way, but so does Queen Guinevere. The hair from her head must have healed Lancelot, (Guinevere being the healer). The ring from the Lady of the Lake must be considered as able to clear his head. He needs that badly, for he is subject to delusions.

The other people with whom Lancelot associates along his way are kings and the children of kings. The king he met in the forest was royally robed in red mantle and furs, and his saddle and bridle were of solid gold. He had to truss up his son to keep the lad from following Lancelot and risking death in his service. The abbot of the old abbey took upon himself the instruction of Lancelot, and he was a royal abbot at such a necropolis. Even the dwarfs were royal officials and functionaries. These persons were all witnesses to the progress of this great personage named finally, by the abbot, and then by Queen Guinevere, as Galahad/Lancelot. Even the lands of Wales/Galloway and Gaul are named for him and his ancestors.

Chrétien's account of Lancelot sounds very much like a first-person narrative, as if recounted by Lancelot himself according to his custom whenever he had a minute at court. A specialist could probably distinguish between the real experiences of Lancelot and his nightmares, for Lancelot appears to have an artist's eye!

Thus, the special touches: the nobleman riding on the big gray hunter; the smell and sight of new-mown hay at the old abbey; the healing medicines (treacle and crushed pearls); the golden ring before the eyes; the sarcophagus surrounded by high flames; the nightmare cart or trebuchet. We also learn what only Lancelot could have said—that he could not swim, that he resented being addressed as "thee/thou," that he hated decapitating the defeated warrior.

If Lancelot was the second twin of a queen, she would have been put to death for bearing a son of the Devil. If he was the son of Morgan le Fay, she would never have recognized him for fear of being put to death. When the multiple birth occurred to the mother of Lohengrin, she put golden chains about her babies' necks as she surrendered them to be thrown into the lake. As the story goes, they survived as swans and were later recognized because of the golden chains. They grew up to found the royal House of the Netherlands, it is said. Did Morgan Le Fay give Lancelot the golden ring for the same reason? Or was Lancelot the firstborn and Modred the second? According to some sources, Modred was cast out to sea in a floating cradle and washed ashore like Scyld, the ancestor of the royal family of Beowulf. Fortunately, the *Sone de Nansai* manuscript written for the Lady Baruch in Cyprus during the Crusades will provide some much needed assistance here.

When we tell stories, we transform reality, never so much as when we tell our own story. When things are too hideous to bear, we turn them into fairy tales; when they are too complicated to grasp, we leave them mysterious. And so it went with Chrétien.

Further, Chrétien was without dictionary and grammar book, rendering his narrative doubly hard to read. He hated anything to do with mathematics, engineering, or military affairs. But what impressed Chrétien and what he really enjoyed was anything to do with money and wealth: jewels, clothing, palfreys, furs, precious fabrics from the Orient, food, dinners, menus, banquets, tablecloths, cushions, fireplaces, servants, carpets, and especially fine saddle horses. He adored mentioning sex and love, in that order. He also raved about sports and contests in the field where there were lots of banners and comings and goings. He got a particular thrill out of ceremonious manners of all kinds, at all kinds of public gatherings. He knew all about feats of arms in fun, but with blood and death running freely at the end. He knew all about the seduction of the white chemises worn by the damsels promenading their wares. Maybe Chrétien owned a scarlet cloak of his very own. He knew where the richest ones were made, and that the best helmets came from Poitiers, and that the Angevin Empire extended from Dombes to Pampelune on the Spanish border.

Chrétien de Troyes was perhaps not the writer that Lancelot would have chosen.

5

King Lancelot

We have now come to a moment long anticipated, the confrontation between Chrétien's account of Lancelot, supreme in his strength and glory, and Ulrich von Zatzikhoven's independent version written a hundred years later—after one hundred years of Arthurian fever and Arthurian research. We cannot congratulate ourselves that we are the first to have tracked the great Lancelot backward from apogee to the commencement of his quest or the first to have pondered his journey or sought his real line of march.

When Ulrich names the places Lancelot conquered, we can check him against today's excellent maps. If he says that here Lancelot learned his name, we will make the corresponding adjustment, realizing that he has reached what resembles the old abbey at Saint Ninians in Stirling, near the ancient battlefield, and very near Stirling Castle—within sight of the shire center and major prize of any war. As he takes possession of kings' daughters along his quest route, we shall see whether he first killed their fathers and how he acquired real estate. Did the hero conquer the kingdom assigned him by the Lady of the Lake? Did he reconquer his own father's lost realm? Or did King Arthur lose the borders of Northumberland? Isn't that the *Logres* where Lancelot claimed he was born?

Accompanied by enthusiastic native warriors, *all the countrymen* who had watched him fight on the plain, Lancelot proceeded to the fortress where Queen Guinevere was being held. His followers formally wished him reputation, position, and wealth, as if he were seeking these primarily and as if they coveted them along with him. A day's ride and a night separated them from the fortress in Gorre, which presumably lay no more than twenty-four hours from the South Galloway shore. Lancelot's long-dreaded ordeal would be what Chrétien calls the sword bridge.

This bridge was a very peculiar contraption. Linguists indicate that the craft of bridge building was temporarily lost when the Romans and their chief religious leader, called "Bridge Builder" or Pontifex, withdrew from Britain. For centuries one bridge remained unrepaired, it is thought, at Pontefract—*ad pontem fractum* (at the broken bridge)—another at Gatesheads, another at Ends-of-the-Road. The dangerous fords of the Medway, the Darent, the Tyne, the Aire, the Lea, and the Severn, it is believed, were not bridged again until after the Norman Conquest. The names of few towns in Britain present the suffix -*bridge*, while many end in -*ford*. Isaac Taylor said:

> It should be noted that *pont*, the Welsh word for bridge, is derived from the Latin, probably through the (Christian) monks, who were the great bridge-builders. Nevertheless it has been thought that the art of bridge-building was known at a very early period of the Celtic nations, and was subsequently lost.

Readers of Chrétien de Troyes and his many manuscript illustrators adopted without protest his account of Lancelot crossing the famous "sword bridge," resulting in the *Lancelot* text's being assigned a place among the world's treasured tales of fairies and beasts—or pure fantasy.

Two shining sword blades the length of two lances and rigid, claims Chrétien, bridged a devil's stream that flowed swift, cold, and fearsome, and was bottomless. Anyone who fell into it would be lost, drowned, and swept out to sea. The brilliant, polished blades of this bridge were at both banks thrust into tree trunks. So sturdily were they anchored that they could without bending at all support a huge weight, and they were sharper than scythe blades.

The two warriors who accompanied Lancelot up to the bridge, added Chrétien, sagely advised him not to attempt the crossing. Theirs may be the only sensible words in the whole account.

Actually, continues Chrétien, there were all told (for he is not yet satisfied that he has confounded his reader) three perils: the bridge itself, the stream, and two chained lions panting to attack whoever arrived on the opposite shore.

Even if Chrétien was modernizing and adapting an ancient account to please his patroness Marie de Champagne, what reality, if any, could have lain beneath this account? Surely Queen Guinevere and her captors had not crossed sword blades, any more than had their horses, supplies, and luggage. Surely the inhabitants and their livestock, including the two lions—if they were lions—did not subsist on fish, bark, grass, and water. In medieval times provisions were hauled in baskets or sleds up ramps cut into rock faces below abbeys and castles, as in Mont-Saint-Michel. It would hardly have been feasible to transport goods across a metal blade by means of a simple system of pulleys fixed to tree trunks! Even Chrétien conceded more than once that the "bridge" was bad, that it had been poorly constructed, and that it was so difficult as to be impossible for such a prosaic purpose as crossing.

A simpler possibility suggests itself—that Chrétien had leaped upon a droll idea because it delighted him the way it delighted his contemporaries, the medieval illustrators. The French are disposed, it would seem, to find things that the British do comical. That Lancelot should cross sword blades wakes up the children in the audience and amuses all to some degree. For cross them he did, says Chrétien, wounding his hands, his knees, and his feet. When he got to the other side, he found that there were no lions there at all!

Chrétien rendered the bridge as "pont-espee" (sword bridge). What if his original had said "pont," meaning "pontoon," or "punt"? Had Chrétien's source been French, it would probably have said ferry, or "bac," from the Latin *baccarium*, which means a flat, bucket-shaped boat or raft used to transport passengers and vehicles short distances, across a river mouth or other narrow waterway. Even an inlander like Chrétien would have understood.

But what if Chrétien had never seen a *punt*, a chiefly British system and word? Sir Thomas Malory, for the same crossing says, "pounte."

Passengers and freight may have crossed this channel regularly in a narrow, flat-bottomed boat of considerable weight and size, such as would be required to service a major defensive fortification. If, however, Lancelot were left to maneuver it alone, presumably his hands and knees *could* have been skinned. Most certainly, Lancelot was not often required to haul himself and his steed across ocean channels.

Perhaps Lancelot propelled the usual square-ended British punt by means of a pole, or perhaps he pulled it overhand along a chain. In the latter case, he would have needed, against such unbelievably powerful currents as surge into the bays and channels of western Britain, all the superhuman strength of torso with which he was, if the *Prose Lancelot* can be believed, uniquely possessed.

Chrétien's literary fortune was doubtless much advanced with his sword bridge. But now the voice of reason ventures to raise a protest.

One medieval illustrator also made his fortune here, as subsequent art historians have observed. One particular *Prose Lancelot* copy, made around 1310, contains colored pictures of Lancelot's main adventures: riding in the cart, rescuing Queen Guinevere from the fire, lifting the slab on his grandfather Galahad's tomb, and crossing Chrétien's sword bridge. This copy is the manuscript formerly belonging to Yates Thompson, now in the Pierpont Morgan Library in New York City.*

The sword bridge picture as illustrated in the *Prose Lancelot* during the Middle Ages is brilliantly colored. The artist proceeded polyscenically, dividing his picture into two parts by a sapphire tower, crenellated in brilliant red, where King Bademagus of Gorre and the captive Queen Guinevere stand exclaiming, seemingly quite at ease, admiring Lancelot. The king of Gorre wears a red gown and red crown with three raised leaf clusters, and the dainty queen is dressed similarly but in pale rose. Her blonde hair is long and loose and very lovely, like her open countenance. Behind the tower, and against a darker blue background, the blonde Queen Jandree of Gorre, wearing a red robe, an emerald green cloak, and a similar leafy crown, stands before three maidens, all hailing Prince Meleagant.

Armed with a shield, wearing knee stockings and a kilt, this ravisher darts around the corner of the castle to encounter his challenger Lancelot. Against a mottled brown sky, in the left half of the painting, Lancelot (in the middle ground) crosses a broadsword on his hands and feet. The hilt rests on the castle bank, the blade extends toward the land side. Lancelot has forgotten to take off his chain mail, as Chrétien thought he would have done.

The rolling waves beneath Lancelot are a telltale emerald green, like a certain Turner seascape, but heavily stressed with black ripples, as Van Gogh would probably have painted them. The two oriental-looking trees are pure ornament here, their blonde trunks barely the height of the attendant who holds the leash of the two lions. Meleagant and the lions occupy the foreground.

One beast is tawny, the other a dark brown. As Loomis observed, they resemble puppies rather than lions, despite their short manes and tufted tails. A person who did not know that these were lions might think that he was seeing two affable English dogs—no canine gladiators, but rather lovable bulldogs cross-bred with ruffled griffons. Their handler has about him neither weapon nor protection, only a leash. In any case, these "lions" had, by the time Lancelot arrived at the gate, been returned to their cages or kennels.

By the same token, it is easier to believe that Yvain's best friend and defender in Chrétien's earlier romance was a dog than that lions had been

---

*The major work on medieval illustration in Arthurian texts, written by Roger Sherman Loomis and his wife Laura Hibbard Loomis, is *Arthurian Legends in Medieval Art*. See illustrations numbered 250 ff. and the textual commentary, p. 98 ff. See also Margaret R. Scherer's *About the Round Table*, Metropolitan Museum of Art, pp. 54–55, et passim. Scherer calls Chrétien's lions "imaginary," and "enchantments." Three of these pictures, including Lancelot crossing the sword bridge, are reproduced by Elizabeth Jenkins in *The Mystery of King Arthur*, opposite p. 81.

domesticated in ancient Britain. The fifteenth-century Queen of France, Isa-beau, had lions in her menagerie. They traveled with her but were not trained; they did not heel nor walk on leashes.

The medieval artist's honesty impresses us, however, for he has no idea of the landward side of the castle in Gorre or of its shore, neither of its elevation, nor of its character, whether deserted or inhabited. A point must be made of this, for one subsequent manuscript, the *Sone de Nansai* of the thirteenth century, states as fact that there is something monumentally important on the land side of this fortress. The medieval artist assumes or knows that the season is summer and has therefore painted the sward along the castle shore not as cultivated and green but as sere and tufted, as if grown over outcroppings of stone. His medieval castle, which he repre-sented as red and blue, anachronistically depicted English and French roy-alty in the later, medieval days of armorial bearings.

Although he foreshadowed it, Chrétien neglected the second passage, but he later remembered Gawain's invasion choice of the alternate bridge, the "pont evage," the almost equally celebrated "water bridge." Originally the reader had been alerted to expect it at the castle where the queen waited. In that case the reader also accepted it as a possible second approach to the castle, by boat instead of bridge, as Chrétien understood it, except that if it is actually under water, it makes a poor crossing.

In their notes to the Webster translation of *Lanzelet*, Loomis and Webs-ter theorized that the water bridge was in actual fact subaqueous, a *crannog* or causeway to an artificial island situated in a lake. They based this theory on their assumption that the Lady of the Lake lived in a lake and not on an island in the sea, which the Latin language would have designated a "lake." Or they thought that it was a wooden bridge sometimes visible and some-times, by magic, invisible. The *Prose Lancelot* calls it the "pont perdu," the lost bridge. The *Lanzelet* author, so bent upon the marvelous, situated this "water bridge" at the magician's castle. Chrétien opted for only one super-natural intervention here: Lancelot, athwart the sword bridge, consulted his magic ring to see if the lions still awaited him.

A reader today might be disposed to believe finally that the midsea castle of King Bademagus and his son Meleagant, which Malory said had been entrusted to them by King Urien of Gorre, and which Malory also said had a "pounte," might have had a second or postern gate on the sea side. Such gates frequently stand above a long, deep channel cut down a cliff face, deep enough to afford access and protection in calm weather to a boat of shallow draft, as passengers disembarked, or while goods were unloaded. Above the buffeting of the waves, and flights of narrow stone steps, there often stood not a "water bridge" or "pont evage" but a trapdoor, a drawbridge of sorts, or a "pont levage."

As it turned out, Gawain fell off the "water bridge." Had he fallen armed into the sea, he might have drowned. In this case he only got stuck in the narrow shaft, from which he was extricated, Chrétien explained, by men using branches of trees and long poles with hooks at their ends. Gawain's was by far the less successful penetration.

Was Chrétien again and again in error? The possibility exists that he encountered more than once in his source the recurrent problem of when to use a definite article in Old French, particularly in cases where the Old French *li* elides to *l'* before a masculine noun beginning with a vowel, as whether to write *evage, l'evage,* or *levage.* Was not the more sensible word *levage,* lever bridge, or drawbridge?

Now that Chrétien seems caught in one error, we recall that it was he who introduced to the world a new hero with a French name: Lancelot. After years of research Jessie L. Weston called Lancelot a nobody—an unknown, fictional, and invented person. She found no trace of Lancelot before he was "created" by Chrétien in 1177.

The character of Lancelot, said Weston, was a late addition to the Arthurian material, where he served merely as one anchor for a conventional, triangular love story. Weston also refused to accept the findings of Loomis and Webster that Lancelot was a memory of the prehistoric Irish solar deity. She cannily refused to see Lancelot as a Lleu Llaw Gyffes, or sun god, from the Welsh *Mabinogion.* No less was this personage the unnamed knight carved on the Modena archivolt in Italy, and not of the ilk of those heroes authenticated in the Welsh *Brut:* Gawain, Kay, Yvain (Owein), and Bedevere. The only constant part of his biography, she observed, was his having been taken from his queen mother's arms by a water fairy. The *Prose Lancelot* (and here Weston has exaggerated) says nothing about a fairy.

On the whole Weston found Chrétien's account of "guilty love" between Lancelot and the queen unpalatable at best, as a love story frankly poor, and as an account incoherent. With characteristic vigor based upon her very extensive knowledge, Weston also rejected, perhaps too hastily, an old worry of French scholars about the correct use of the definite article. It was a nineteenth-century Breton French scholar, Count J.-C.-H de La Villemarqué, one of the first persons to study Arthurian romances and a first translator of the *Mabinogion,* who noted Chrétien's probable error in 1841–42. Then Villemarqué advanced the theory that Chrétien erred in the spelling of Lancelot's name, which explained to him why nobody had ever found this hero or his name in history. He should have spelled the hero's name without the definite article *l',* or as *Ancelot,* said Villemarqué.

Villermarqué thought that *Ancelot* meant, coming from the Vulgate *an-*

cilla dei, handservant of the Lord, which is an epithet otherwise of the Virgin. He was only partly right. An ancillary would not have sat equal to King Arthur, nor would he have been crowned at some site not more than five days' distance from Carlisle. Therefore we cannot perceive Lancelot as an *ancillus dei,* nor as the Virgin Mary. And yet, we *can* agree with Villemarqué's statement that the hero's name does not commence with a capital *L,* but with a capital *A.*

Since Gawain and the others existed in Geoffrey of Monmouth and in William of Malmesbury, while King Loth and King Urien existed along with their families, and while Perceval and/or Peredur/Parzival also existed in many accounts, which spoke of him as having lived, it seems unlikely that Lancelot should alone of all these be a fictional character. This is borne out by Chrétien, who must have received privileged information, and whose text will stand up, as we are now seeing, under the harsh light of today's scholarship. The theory of Webster and Loomis that Lancelot was the memory of the ancient Celtic sun god makes him too unique. It also denies the historicity of all these other personages of the Dark Ages, which was, indeed, the thrust of earlier modern scholarship.

Meanwhile it has not been possible today to repudiate the picture drawn by Geoffrey of Monmouth or the words attributed by him to those three brothers who attended King Arthur's coronation, especially not the personage who preceded the other dignitaries present: KING Anguselus of Albania. He stood foremost and equal to KING Arthur. Why? Because he alone was a great sovereign. We remember his bold words and his prompt offer to accompany King Arthur to the continent.

So must we look again at his name. The name *Anguselus* occurs in Latin in Geoffrey of Monmouth. But Chrétien is writing in Old French. However, when the name *Anguselus* comes from Latin into Old French, as we suspect is the case here, it loses in perfectly regular, normal fashion its middle syllable. Thus, its second consonantal group, *gu,* which is in weak and unaccented position within the word, drops out. We are left with this: *An + sel + o* (*o* = the normal masculine ending in French, and it is often written *ot*). We pronounce the French word resulting from this syncopation: *An-sel-ó.*

The name *Ancelot* derives normally, then, from *Anguselus* and according to the laws of linguistics. We have only to see details in M. K. Pope's text, *From Latin to Modern French.* Pope's chapters on the palatalization of velar consonants and the reduction of consonantal groups yield such examples as *vigilare, regina, regula, margula, nigrum, fragare,* and *legere* (where the middle syllable drops from the Latin word as it comes into French).

The *Prose Lancelot* furthermore makes it clear that we are dealing here with a line of kings named *Anguselus,* or some derivative of that name as first established by Geoffrey of Monmouth. Our young Lancelot is a son or a grandson of the earlier king of the same name.

A reexamination of the *Lanzelet* will confirm that Geoffrey of Monmouth did not invent but reported accurately concerning three of King Arthur's coronation guests, including the Anguselus who appears to have been the *Rí Alban*, an exalted personage known to later Scottish historians as the High King of Albion, or Scotland. This *Ard-righ Albaínn*, or High King, seems to have been not only Lancelot but also his grandfather Galahad before him, who was called in the Arthurian romances king of *Galles* and was also named Lancelot. The Arthurian hero Lancelot was a son of a King Ban or of a King Briadan. The *Lanzelet* text also mentions two other contemporaries of King Arthur, and they too appear among Geoffrey's coronation guests—Sir Mauron and King Gilimar, the latter a mute lord who resides on a mountaintop, or dunn, three days' ride from Arthur's court at Carlisle.

Knowing Chrétien's awe of the nobility, we can accept the possibility that he erred to amuse them, substituting "water bridge" for drawbridge as he plunged Gawain into a cleft of the rocky shore. We can see that similarly he took little care with his translation into "sword bridge," which was, as he wanted it, the very arduous access into Hell. Perhaps he even chuckled to himself as he dangled between his neologism *evage* and *levage*, between *punt* and *pont*, and between *espee* and *espiet* (pole).

That he should have made an error in the proper name of a prince, however, is unacceptable. Chrétien writes that Lancelot's name was *"the* Ancelot." We can take the name from the Latin *Anguselus*, into the Old French *Ancelot*, and into the modern Scottish place name *Angus*. What would it mean if a personage were called "The Angus"?

Even today "The Angus" would mean that the personage was a clan chieftain in modern Scotland. Thus, we conclude that Lancelot was royal and in his own country.*

The German *Lanzelet* text commences with another touching account of Lancelot's birth, the death of his father, and his education by what this author translates poorly also as "mermen" and "mermaids" on an isle in the sea. The Lady of the Lake or sea raised the infant and trained him to conquer the realm of "Beforet," at which point he would learn his name. Again, he seems to have been called Galahad as a child and Lancelot as a man. In a sense Lancelot is to be considered as having been programmed in boyhood for a specific royal mission and dispatched early to accomplish it. In this

---

*Hector Boece wrote that Queen Guinevere lay buried in Angus, in the town of Meigle ("Megile"); that is, he added, 20 miles from Dundee. This information is given today in guidebooks to Scotland.

telling he lacks the humanity with which the *Prose Lancelot* had enveloped him, where the Lady called him Fitzroy (King's Son), also as in Scotland, and crowned him daily with red roses.

Lancelot's father has been understood from the *Prose Lancelot* to have been a Ban de "Benoïc," or otherwise unidentified place name which the *Lanzelet* spells "Genewis." Lancelot's new or conquered kingdom is called the White Land, which was in Latin called Albion, and then Scotland, Scotia, and now "Norgalles." "Norgalles" seems to translate North Galles, Galles itself being King Arthur's kingdom of Strathclyde to the south.

This geography contradicts the old theory advanced by F. Lot in his 1918 study of the *Prose Lancelot*, whose erroneous conclusion was adopted recently by another French scholar, L.-F. Flutre in his index of Arthurian proper names. They believed that "Benoïc," or Lancelot's birthplace, designated the present North Wales, basing their opinion on the prefix *gwyn-* or *Gwynedd* (North Wales), which also means white. But *Albion* also means white from the Latin prefix *alba-*. It comes down to the fact that Lancelot is never called "Welsh" and was not accepted among the Welsh bards as a native son. His older name, Anguselus/Lancelot, comes from Scotland and to us from Geoffrey of Monmouth and also from writers like Chrétien who composed in Old French. The "Benoïc" is more likely a Berwick on the east coast of Britain.

The *Lanzelet* gives us one more chance to follow this same Lancelot throughout his career and his series of adventures, including the abduction of Queen Guinevere. Although Ulrich's theories are sometimes even more fantastic than Chrétien's version, still he does not manage to turn Lancelot entirely into smoke. He has Lancelot's series of conquests begin in what seems to be western Scotland, a domain beside the sea in Morois, Moreiz, or Murray. He indicates that the mature Lancelot came back into Britain proper from the western sea.

Rapidly moving up in the world, the young hero swiftly conquers a "Patrick of the Hill Fort." Because the stakes are very high, he has first to overcome a giant, two "lions," and the uncle of the resident heiress, or chieftainess. This second place is called "Limors" and is usually identified fancifully, though one wonders why, since the name "Limors" is so close to Lammermuirs or Lammermoors. Thus, here Lancelot has almost returned home, to his birthplace, presumably between Bass Rock at the edge of the Firth of Forth and Berwick. In this case he returns to the place where local tradition has always wanted him, near the rock of what would later be the medieval Bamborough Castle.

Chrétien also knew this place, and he also spelled it recognizably as "Limors" and "Lymors," (Sir Walter Scott's territory, if you will). We can now see, after having collated the texts, that Lancelot has carved himself a kingdom bordered on its four corners by Edinburgh, Tantallon, Berwick, and Melrose. His lightning rush is not over yet, however, and it will take him all the way from his birthplace in Berwick, Logres, as he says, into the northern Bannockburn Corridor.

His third conquest went poorly for a time; he so overextended himself that he landed in prison. From his prison he could see in the distance the mysterious final conquest of Beforet. We sense excitement in the text of Ulrich. Lancelot's goal is actually in physical sight. He has almost reached the revelation of his name and the wonderful scene at the old abbey, which we recall from Chrétien.

Now Ulrich fails us. Although he gives eight geographical precisions, so that the reader knows for sure how important this part of the conquest is, Ulrich himself fails to comprehend and falls into a literary convention. He too slips into the same comfortable slot: the descent into Hell. All of a sudden he begins calling the next-to-last castle the "Dead Man's." The river is "Der Kal," or River of Torment, tantamount to saying that Lancelot must now cross the Triple Rivers of Hell (minus the sword bridge).

Here Lancelot's confinement in an underground prison reads right into the hands of the mythologists, like an eclipse of the red, leonine sun god, or like any other Dantean journey into the Otherworld Realm of Hades, Pluto, and Persephone. And yet one must be grateful to Ulrich for having filled out Chrétien's account somewhat and for having placed Lancelot geographically where we can put him today—between Dumfries and Stirling.

If Ulrich really wanted to keep Lancelot in the realm of Hell, he should have taken out of his text all the ensuing geographical precisions: the broad highway, the beautiful panorama, the plain flat as a wall, or flat as the top of a wall, and the brightly "painted" castle. He should not have written that Lancelot's host now is Morgan le Fay's cowardly son whom Lancelot defeats in single combat. This, in concert with another text, indicates that Lancelot is in Lothian, having come from East Lothian west into Midlothian, and west again into the Edinburgh area. (Again, this is familiar Scott country.)

As mentioned above, from his prison Lancelot can gaze out over the countryside. He sees twenty reivers burning villages thereabouts. They have come from the magical fortress of "Dodone"! It is the place of Lancelot's youthful dreams, and the end of his toilsome journey.

From his jail cell he can look out upon the borders of that promised land of Beforet, and the fortress of Dodone, both of which the Lady of the Lake has raised him to repossess. His lifetime goal and mission are in plain sight. With renewed vigor Lancelot negotiates his release, falls upon the raiders, kills one of the band, and watches him collapse *upon the sand of the shore*. For us, it is an unparalleled moment. Ulrich has told us where Lancelot is—not Hell, but Edinburgh.

This chief seat lies, in fact, not far from a sandy shore: the Firth of Forth. The place is traversed by a winding river, the Almond, so named today, although Ulrich calls it something else. That the castle seat is major there is no doubt. Nor is there any doubt that the castle proper is ornate, lavishly ornamented, rich, and marvelous. Below it a plain extends panoramically, a plain well known to the whole world. Lancelot is to be crowned there, neither lost nor insecure any longer. He has come home.

Ulrich managed to throw us off the scent and even to stump us for a time with his winding river, for we know that the winding river snaking up into the Edinburgh area is the Almond. Ulrich calls it the Kal, or "Der Kal," and thinks of it as one of the rivers of Hell. There is no such river in Scotland as Derkal. We must begin all over again.

It is necessary to go back, in fact, to the place name specialists, from whom we learn that rivers throughout western Europe commonly contain one of the original Welsh words for "river," such as *dwr*. Now we see that this is the case here, the Welsh *dwr* giving Ulrich the German *der*. The Welsh *cal* then gives him *Kal*, or winding. Thus, we have in Ulrich: *Cal* (winding) + *der* (river) = *Calder* (and not *Der Kal*). Today we find two places named "Calder" to the southwest of Edinburgh city itself, both of them on the sandy shore of the Almond River. This water flows north-northeast into the city of Edinburgh and thence into the Firth of Forth. It was a battlefield in Lancelot's time, and it would remain a battlefield for centuries to come.

Lancelot has moved westward along the south shore of the Firth of Forth, probably from Nennius's Mouth of the River Glein (Aber-Gullane), consolidating his conquest of East Lothian by adding Midlothian, which he has encircled and entered from the west, passing through Calder and even following the course of the Almond River. Chrétien's names for Edinburgh (Tenebroc and Teneboc) are not mentioned, but the site overlooking the plain recalls Erec's tournament in Chrétien "desoz Teneboc an la plainge" (v. 2083 of *Erec*), or below Edinburgh on the plain. Years later, Lancelot (Geoffrey of Monmouth's Anguselus or King Angus of Scotland) attended Erec's wedding to Enide here. He was then accompanied by his two sons, named Cadret and Coi. From the heights of the ancient, "painted" ("painted" translates "Pictish") castle, Lancelot could look down upon the plain where tournaments or battles were engaged.

South of the Forth River in ancient times were 90 percent of the fifteen hundred ancient forts of Scotland. They were called "Keirs," reports William J. Watson, whose *History of Celtic Place-Names of Scotland* has deserved the reputation of Bible for Arthurian scholars ever since its publication in 1926. These smallish forts crowned the summits of the hundreds of small eminences along an oval plain, the whole surrounded by a palisaded rampart. Thus, Lancelot had penetrated, it seems reasonable to believe, across the plain to the south shore of the great Forth River. He had conquered the forts all the way to the Firth of Forth, the "magnum flumen Forthi," which the Angles were soon to name the "Scottewattre." And they renamed it so during the Arthurian period, for the latter name also occurs in the Arthurian romances.

The modern geographer O. G. S. Crawford in his *Topography of Roman Scotland North of the Antonine Wall* shows by his Index Map the probable ancient route from the coast at North Berwick all the way north into the Edinburgh area. Thence Lancelot departed for the great, final conquest of his life.

From the Roman fort of Cramond Lancelot would have crossed the Antonine Wall at Camelon near Falkirk, at this fort between Wall Stations 13 and 14, and proceeded northwest to West Plean in order to arrive before the Royal Castle of Stirling, which Ulrich has called "Dodone." Ulrich's choice of word has thus far pointed scholars toward Greek mythology and the site of the Oracle of Zeus at Dodona. That is not where Lancelot went, of course. Traveling this only road into northern Scotland, the Great North Road of ancient times, Lancelot would have had to pass right by a stone building of Roman-style construction called "Arthur's O'on."

Lancelot fell next, Ulrich says, into a great, wide valley. As Crawford explains the geography of this area, Lancelot would have entered the terrible north-south battle corridor of Stirlingshire.

To the west rises the hilly region of Bannockburn (from *bannauc* = hill), falling at sea level into fertile clay lowlands and peat bogs. On its tidal estuary Stirling stands atop majestic gray cliffs, two hundred fifty feet high, accessible to ships but well inland and therefore relatively safe from sea attack. In Lancelot's day this almost impregnable fortress, walled precipitously by nature, site of prehistoric and Roman forts, commanded the narrowest crossing of the Forth Valley, which was one mile wide at that point. Two roads led out from Stirling, the first westward into Loch Lomond and then south into nearby Dumbarton on the Clyde, now a suburb of modern Glasgow.

The second road crossed the Forth at the Fords of Frew, which are (so far as I know) no longer visible but which in Lancelot's day were one of the Wonders of Scotland. This road forked northeast into Angus, Scone, and Aberdeen and northwest again toward Loch Ness and into Inverness, capital of the northern Picts. The latter route flanked the Stirling crossing of the Forth. The first is still a military road, and Stirling, on its gray, westward-facing cliffs, is still garrisoned today.

The ancient Ford of Kildean, called in Gaelic the "pass of the cleft," answers to a graphic description in the *Prose Lancelot*, the path descending a narrow defile, fording the Forth, and heading into the virtually uninhabited far north.

This passage was described long before the *Lanzelet* manuscript mentioned that Lancelot conquered his final fortress of "Dodone." When Lancelot and Prince Galehaut set out once under King Arthur's displeasure and

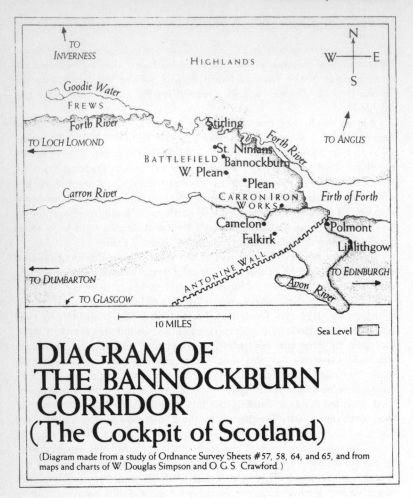

DIAGRAM OF THE BANNOCKBURN CORRIDOR (The Cockpit of Scotland)

(Diagram made from a study of Ordnance Survey Sheets #57, 58, 64, and 65, and from maps and charts of W. Douglas Simpson and O. G. S. Crawford.)

started for the Out Isles and/or Sutherland, they descended this same precipitous path from a fortress and followed the riverbank until they came to a wonderful ford, whence they gained access to safety (the Outer Hebrides?). Thus, whoever held Stirling Castle, then as now, possessed, say the geographers of Scotland, the key to Scotland.

The "west castell" at Stirling is still preserved carefully and called the "King's Knot." "Knot" comes from the Gaelic *cnoc*, a hillock or castle mound. From the modern castle and cliff one looks down upon it and across the

Vale of Menteith, the emplacement of the ancient Fords of Frew in the distance.

As late as the fifteenth century William of Worcester still recorded about King Arthur: "custodiebat le round-table in Castro de Styrling, aliter, Snowdon west castell" ["King Arthur presided at the Round Table in the Fort of Stirling, otherwise known as Snowdon West Castle"].

Snowdon (Sinaudone, Senaudon, Isneldone, Dodone, Sinadone) occurs only a few times in medieval manuscripts as one of King Arthur's residences, and it was disputed by Loomis and Webster, both of whom identified Snowdon Castle improbably as Segontium at the foot of the desolate range of Snowdon Mountains in North Wales. As the name of a fortress, "Snowdon" occurs in four Arthurian texts, including the Béroul *Tristan* and Ulrich's *Lanzelet*.

Ulrich explains that King Arthur and his court visited "Dodone," then, which is "Snowdon," when Lancelot invited them to his coronation. It was solemnized in that castle. Whereas Chrétien in *Yvain* gave it as a trip by horseback of three days to the Firth of Forth from Carlisle, Ulrich specifies four days from Carlisle to the borders of what appears to be Stirlingshire, and an extra day (to cross the Bannockburn sands) to the Castle Rock itself. Both estimates to this refuge and royal seat of the Kings of the North are close.

The *Prose Lancelot* confirms even a third time, naming Lancelot's queen there as Sebile, whom one takes to have been the heretrix chief. Her name in Ulrich is an anagram: Yblis. In Stirling Castle Lancelot painted his famous murals recounting his adventurous life, but whether he "painted" or was "Pictish" remains in doubt. His realm is called Norgalles, Terre Blanche, or Albania, and not modern North Wales. King Arthur's realm to the south is Galles, centered at Carlisle and at his Camelot on the coast. The *Prose Lancelot* further, and once more, confirms the visit of King Arthur to Lancelot's Snowdon Castle after the king's return from Gaul. It also supplies a chronology.

We know now, then, that Lancelot was inaugurated at Snowdon after King Arthur's first campaign abroad, during which time Queen Guinevere was abducted.

We read again that King Arthur much admired Lancelot's "paintings." The illuminator of the particular *Prose Lancelot* copy (around the year 1470) shows King Arthur looking at King Lancelot's paintings.*

Wearing a velvet robe with a wide ermine border and a scalloped ermine bertha, crowned in gold, right hand raised in an admiring gesture, King Arthur stands in a hall inside Lancelot's castle. He gazes intently at

---

*(Ms. fr. 112, vol. 3, fol. 193) of the National Archives of France, in Paris.

one of Lancelot's murals painted upon the inside of an exterior wall that is pierced by a Romanesque grilled window. The scenes are in two rows, the painter having again worked polyscenically to show in the upper row three scenes: Lancelot bidding farewell to his tutor (with whom as a boy he once quarreled over the beating of his dog), Lancelot first paying homage to Queen Guinevere, and the queen standing beside two attendant ladies, whom she clearly outranks. On the bottom row he shows only one scene: Lancelot leading a war band in fierce combat, the warriors mounted and wielding broadswords, against a giant warrior and his party. There are dead men strewn upon the ground. The scene is in clever perspective. King Arthur stands sideways to the mural, which is painted upon a wall diagonal to the foreground of the picture, the palace floor made of square tiles receding into the corner of the apartment. The second wall of this unfurnished chamber or hall is made of wooden laths, as is the ceiling of intricate design. Through the barred window one sees very distant hills.*

This unknown artist represented Queen Guinevere as visibly older than Lancelot, which must have been the case. We know she was twelve when Gawain enlisted in King Arthur's army, for she was the same age as Gawain. Lancelot came to court after Gawain had served for some years and had long since reached his full maturity. According to the *Prose Lancelot*, at the time of King Arthur's formal visit to Lancelot's castle, which we have decided was Stirling in Scotland, the queen was still a beautiful woman, although fifty years of age. If Lancelot was then at the height of his conquests and powers, he was at least ten to twenty years younger than Guinevere.

By all accounts Lancelot survived Queen Guinevere, whose tomb he visited in Avalon. That is about the only point upon which the various accounts of his last years agree.

---

*(Margaret Scherer reproduces this picture as heading to her chapter on "Castles Painted with Arthurian Scenes," in her *About the Round Table*, p. 10).

6

Meleagant's
Death

The abduction of Queen Guinevere
has brought into prominence the personage of Lancelot, whose prime characteristic has been his service to King Arthur, to the queen, and to the
realm. His entry there after a childhood in the "Lake" was dazzling and swift
like all his actions. His functions combined to make him a champion but
also a leader of men, a liberator of prisoners, a winner of wives with large
landed estates, and a defender of the right. His flamelike quality as a person
set him apart from the other members of King Arthur's circle, for Lancelot
was volatile, energetic in the extreme, swift, daring, and verbally brilliant.
As such, he was beloved. Authors pictured him variously, as a warrior in
white armor on a white horse, as a crimson-stained hawk, as the red lion of
sunset, or as the deadly leopard.

Like the red sun Lancelot suffered eclipses during his long imprisonment, when he starved, lost his health and vigor, became thin and weak,
and suffered madness. Like others of royal blood, he underwent phlebotomies or venesections from time to time, and for an unknown purpose having
to do with healing practices. Lancelot formed liaison after liaison with women,
marrying several, apparently all at the same time, being the ward of several,
being courted assiduously and simultaneously by several, and finally fathering a great son by the Grail King's daughter.

Lancelot's fury in combat was only slightly less than that called "battle
frenzy" among primitive Irish warriors. He struck such awful blows that men
crossed themselves when they saw him arriving on the battleground. He
actually lifted his antagonists off the ground, and he often leaped from
horseback onto them, crushing their helmets and their skulls. He took unerring aim. In combat he often raged so hard that he could not be stopped.

Through the tremendous force of his pride and will power, he felt no pain himself. His own person was sacred, which speaks volumes about his origin and position in the world.

The various functions of Lancelot, when they are summarized and listed and studied for what they are, have all to do with his service to King Arthur, to Queen Guinevere, and to the Round Table. He was very early in his career elected to that organization. During meetings of that chapter, he sat on King Arthur's right hand and was equal in elevation to him. Thus, he surpassed everyone else in honor, dignity, and pedigree.

Lancelot performed kingly functions. For example, he fought judiciary combats, where right was plainly seen from wrong. He settled open issues of land and rule. He buried the dead and honored their graves. He led armies and fought wars, one after another. He was crowned at Stirling.

In his *Studies in Medieval Literature* Roger Sherman Loomis decided that there must have been a genetic connection between Lancelot and Irish nobility, and specifically between him and King Lugh Loinnbheimionach of Ireland. Both, he pointed out, had been raised by queens and trained by persons called "mermen," whom we would call plainly "sailors." Both personages remained nameless during infancy; Lancelot was referred to merely as "King's Son," or "Fitzroy." As soon as each prince arrived at court, he occupied a certain seat of honor, sat upon a special stone of destiny, was deferred to as royal, and was much admired for physical beauty, bearing, strength, and prowess. Neither showed fear or felt pain.

Each personage performed a certain specific feat involving the lifting of a huge stone or stone slab, meaning that he could and would deliver prisoners from bondage. Through clandestine affairs of the heart, each personage sired a son of high renown. Each was intimately associated with the color red, a red lion, or red armor, or a red device. One was a king of Ireland, and the other, Lancelot, was a great-grandson of a king of Ireland.

This evidence only goes to show that Lancelot also became a king and that he was probably raised, or fostered, on the same island in the sea and by the descendants of the same sailors. Thus, the royal princes of ancient Britain were raised in safe isolation somewhere between the two islands of Ireland and Cornwall/England/Wales/Scotland.

The second half of Chrétien's *Lancelot* deals with the three duels that Lancelot fights against the queen's captor, Meleagant. Here Chrétien develops the psychological treatment for which he has always been so admired. The governor of the fortress that Lancelot has penetrated is, as we know, the subking called Bademagus. He administers this Island Fortress for his relative and sovereign, King Urien. Prince Galehaut of the Out Isles so respected Bademagus that he also named him regent and heir of his own kingdom during the interregnum that would follow his, Galehaut's death.

The dignity and honor of Bademagus recur in Chrétien as beyond question. This exceptionally noble ruler receives the wounded Lancelot from the "sword bridge," welcomes him with all due respect, treats his wounds, supplies him with a horse, and at length and in every way loudly laments the coming combats.

Great interest is generated by the juxtaposition between such a fine king and his headstrong, rash, and ungovernable son Meleagant. The father, firm and noble ruler that he is, has lost control of his beloved son. This violent, choleric Meleagant is bent upon his own ruin, recognizing in his intransigence only two possible outcomes for his situation: victory and death. In vain King Bademagus warns his son, remonstrates with him, attempts to appeal to his better nature, even resorts to shaming him. Nothing avails. Since no person before Lancelot has ever crossed the "sword bridge," he is obviously the greatest champion in Britain and Meleagant's superior. King Bademagus has realized from the first that his dear son is doomed.

Convinced by Bademagus that the queen's privacy has been and continues to be guaranteed by him, Lancelot even so regretfully consents to postpone his first duel until the morrow. The women captives must have been party to Lancelot's arrival, for they had mortified themselves for the past three days in order for him to win—an interesting glimpse of female behavior.

Lancelot finds a good match in Meleagant. Each youthful champion is handsome, skilled, eager, and graceful. From a special window in the tower, a vantage place she had particularly requested, Queen Guinevere looks down upon the tilting ground, a very cramped, square area, or castle quadrangle. During the first hard-fought duel Lancelot hears a damsel call him by name. This detail signifies, for it helps to fit this adventure into the Lancelot annals, the damsel from "Maiden Land" (Caerlaverock) instructed to tell him his name only when he had fulfilled his life work, that is, had conquered Dodone. The deference with which Bademagus greeted Lancelot was duly proffered, then, as to a sovereign equal to the overlord, King Urien himself.

Queen Guinevere halted the first combat, at the urgent prayer of King Bademagus. Even then, Meleagant wounded Lancelot spitefully, under the cover of the truce.

Along with King Arthur's other prisoners, the queen is forthwith released from Gorre, Lancelot pledging to meet Meleagant again a year hence. Chrétien seizes this opportunity to recount a salacious episode between the queen and Lancelot, to the effect that he had intercourse with her, proved by blood on her bedding. Thus, the old marriage consummation of Pictish society, and the shadow of Brunhilde, persist long after the sense of it has been forgotten. The *Lanzelet* substitutes another chastity test of a telltale mantle that only Lancelot's Queen Yblis (Sybilla, Sebile), as the most pure, could wear. Thus, both tellings besmirch Queen Guinevere, whose guilt Chrétien gleefully extends to include all women.*

Still Lancelot continues to defend Queen Guinevere's reputation, which is probably a true reporting, since this took place prior to the typical clericalism and bitter antifeminism of the intellectual High Middle Ages. Lancelot fights a second, judicial combat on her behalf, but again King Bademagus intercedes in the nick of time to save his unrepentant son.

At this point a tournament, *recte* pitched battle, intervenes, Lancelot's supreme status having been recognized among the persons on the field, all of whom make the very earth shake when they tread. Chrétien says that when the King Herald recognized Lancelot, he crossed himself. He then announced him as the one contestant against whom the other young men could and would be judged. On the proverbial scale of one to ten, Lancelot obviously rated ten. At this point Chrétien's continuator, Godefroi de Leigni, picks up the narration, at around verse 5640.

Once more waylaid by dwarfs, who are not depicted as emissaries of King Urien of Gorre, Lancelot falls prisoner to Meleagant. Here precise details concerning the unnamed castle where Queen Guinevere had been held are provided. Where Arthur's castles in the romances are frequently named, this one castle with its weird bridges and position, for some arcane reason, remains shadowy and as if purposely concealed. Why?

It appears again that this castle really is in Gorre but also that it stands upon an island, or islet, as the earliest or Glastonbury abduction story had claimed. This island is separated from the shore by an arm of the sea. From the quarry there, which was at the very edge of the seashore, Meleagant had stones transported across a channel. His purpose was the construction of a round tower, or Pictish broch. It required fifty-seven days to build and had only one small window near its roof. In this tower, upon this island, he had Lancelot immured. Such a round tower upon an island, beside a small, ancient castle mound which has two approaches, or a tower overlooking a narrow arm of the sea, and a quadrangular tilting ground enclosed within might still be visible in aerial photographs.

Lancelot was to be starved, obliged to pull his daily ration of bread and dirty water up through the narrow aperture. Meanwhile at the home court of King Bademagus, which is situated at some distance from the island prison, Meleagant's sister suspects what has befallen Lancelot. She is the same Loathly Damsel for whom Lancelot once severed his challenger's head, she who rides the specially bred mule with the distinctive, swift gait. For a month she undertook a quest for Lancelot, whom she finally found. Here the author lapses, saying that the tower stood in a deserted area, alone by an arm of the sea. The damsel finds a stonemason's pick, with which Lan-

*v. 4760 ff.

celot chops through his prison wall. His amorous rescuer shelters him and nurses him back to health.

The third combat, formally witnessed because it was decisive, takes place on a plain beside this or another tower not on the island itself. The plain is described as "this side of Ireland" and as remarkably beautiful, none greener except in Ireland itself.* Over the spectators towered a giant syca-more tree. A spring flowed there in runnels of purest gold and silver. Ob-viously the author is talking about an opulent garden or plaisance. A valley stretched away into woods. King Arthur was seated at the place where the view was superb and unspoiled. The tree itself was not natural but the result of landscape architecture, having been planted during Abel's time, it was believed, or just after his parents left Eden.

The reference to Paradise is well taken. These precisions offer a first description of the shore facing the island, of which the medieval illustrator of the celebrated *Lancelot* knew nothing at all.

Thus, we now see that Lancelot would have approached the "sword bridge" after having passed from a forest into a valley. Furthermore, the judiciary combat occurring one year after the queen's first rescue by Lancelot takes place at some sacred site of amassed treasure and antiquity. It seems, in fact, to be the site of King Arthur's treasury, and at least one person in the Middle Ages had also heard of it. There Lancelot kills Meleagant, first amputating his right arm, then cutting his mouth, breaking off three of his teeth, and finally beheading him.

The *Prose Lancelot* adds several interesting bits of information. First, Lancelot duly awaited Queen Guinevere's signal at the end. It was she who ordered Meleagant beheaded. His severed head bounced on the ground in the direction away from Lancelot. As wronged defendant she meted out the cruel sentence. The final combat lasted three hours, until noon, at which time Meleagant was, characteristically of the Picts, bereft of his strength. Thus, he can now be identified as a Pictish prince. The truce had stipulated that the queen was to return to Gorre if Lancelot defaulted, which he did because of his incarceration. Thus, we are assured, the final combat took place there. When Lancelot had first released Queen Guinevere, she had led her party of forty persons to "Kamalot" in the Carlisle area. This number of freed prisoners suggests that the fort on the island was not large, as were the much later medieval, Norman French castles at Cardigan, Tintagel, or Conway. The *Prose Lancelot* further confirms that Lancelot was already an important ruler, since he is addressed in Old French both as "Sire" and "Monseigneur," titles accorded the king of France.

The Loathly Damsel here is herself named Jandree, and she too will become a queen, for she—and not Meleagant—inherits. The name *Jandree* is

*v. 7000 ff.

the same name as Wolfram's *Cundrie*, or Chrétien's, the initial consonant seemingly indicating only a regular change from Gaelic into Manx; one finds *j* replacing the velar *c* or *g* when a word comes into Manx, as *Cronk Guckley* (Broom Hill) into *Balla Juckley* (Broom Farm).

Jandree's behavior proved both her capability and her rank. After liberating Lancelot from his tower, the damsel herself rowed him to the opposite shore. This detail confirms Gawain's postern gate on the sea side. There was obviously no bridge or sword bridge at all over the narrow arm of the sea, but more likely a punt that a damsel could not operate. We learn something else of interest—that after she freed him Lancelot had to escort Jandree to the safest place on the coast, which turns out to be Geoffrey of Monmouth's Dumbarton, here called "Fort of the Welsh," or Galefort. Lancelot must have been put in his tower somewhere adjacent to the Firth of Clyde, and in that ocean and Firth he was again in home territory.

We turn again to the *Prose Lancelot* to test these conclusions. It clarifies for Arthur's day the rapidly changing realms: the Out Isles are the Hebrides and not the Scilly Isles off the tip of Cornwall. Here, F. Lot had located Lyonesse, not realizing it was Lothian. Most recently, Geoffrey Ashe followed Lot into wild improbabilities long ago shown to be in error by the linguist William J. Watson. By Norgalles was meant the Rhinns, or promontories, of Galloway and Lancelot's kingdom in the north. King Arthur's seat was at Carlisle, and not at Cardigan in modern Wales, as Loomis has so long argued. "Cardigan" was called Aber Teivi until the twelfth century. King Arthur's "Caradigan" is named over and again in the *Prose Lancelot* as the chief embarkation port for Ireland and located on the marches into Ireland.

Loomis was also wrong about the other or marches of Galore (Gorre). In *Wales and the Arthurian Legend* he reasoned correctly that that meant "Gadhelic shore," or shore of the ancient Welsh. The shore of the ancient Welsh was not in what is now Wales, or way in the south on the Gower peninsula of southern Wales, nor on the Severn estuary between Wales and England.

In *History of the Celtic Place-Names of Scotland* William J. Watson demonstrated that the "Gadhelic" shore is the Galloway shore of southern Scotland, just south of the Firth of Clyde. In fact, an ancient book corroborates: Jocelin's *Life of Saint Kentigern*, which plainly says that the original land of the Picts was called Galloway, or in Latin *Galweithia*. Lady Charlotte Guest corroborates this in the notes to her translation of the *Mabinogion*.*

The problem of King Arthur's chief port arises. Where did Lancelot take ship when leaving Galloway for Gorre and the island where the queen

*See "Gelli Wic," p. 103.

was being held? Watson offered an excellent solution, upheld by linguistic evidence. He looked to an ancient *Triad*, which gives the three thrones of ancient British monarchs: (1) at Gelliwig in Cornwall, (2) at Caerleon (we have decided it was Carlisle) where King Arthur was crowned, and at (3) Penrhyn Rhionydd "in the north"; King Arthur was "the chief lord of Penrionyd in the north." There is "no doubt," explained Watson, that what is indicated here was the Rhinns of Galloway, and specifically the promontory or the west side of Loch Ryan. "Rhionydd" means the very royal place, the "Port Rig," or King's Haven. King Arthur himself was the "ryon" or "rhion," the chief lord of that peninsula, and of that harbor. Stranraer City today remains as chief embarkation port for Ireland, precisely what the *Prose Lancelot* said about "Caradigan." "Celli Wig" too means Galloway.

Careful research in western Britain could hardly discover a more hidden or better protected port than inside Loch Ryan. Not only is it perfectly concealed from the Irish Sea by the long rhinn, or promontory, but the loch itself is long and narrow, a handy refuge for small craft in heavy weather. In addition, it is very close to Dumbarton and the Firth of Clyde, near to the Mull of Kintyre, close to Arran also, not far from the headland on the east coast of Islay that today is still named for King Arthur's son Lohot. McArthur's Head. Down this coast, from Glasgow to Loch Ryan, stands a long line of ancient fortresses: Kennedy, Culzean (where General Eisenhower was offered a home and refuge during World War II), Robert Louis Stevenson's Ballantrae, and others beside the Heads of Ayr.

Passage around the rhinn takes a ship into the Solway Firth and up to ancient Camelot and Carlisle. Loch Ryan is not only a northern port of importance today but an easy harbor to find even in fog because of Ailsa Crag standing so prominently in those waters, whether one looks from Ballentrae, from Ayr, or from the loch itself.

The problem of King Arthur's chief residences is, thanks to the new indexes of L. F. Flutre and G. D. West, no longer very difficult. By tabulation, modern scholarship today affords a considerable advantage over the heroic efforts of the medieval clerics, who were the romancers themselves and who tried in the years between 1136 and 1300 to situate King Arthur inside Britain.

In the Middle Ages denials and dismissals of the great King Arthur could and did provoke riots. Even in those days many refused to believe that Arthur was the stuff of myths and fairy tales. The best heads of western Europe, Geoffrey of Monmouth first and foremost, labored mightily to place King Arthur in reality and royalty.

Thirteen major sites harbor King Arthur throughout the European romances which, as they turned to a more voluminous prose in the thirteenth century, uncovered more and more elaborate accounts of his deeds.

1. Caerleon, Carlion (plus 8 variants) .... 35 mss.
2. Caradigan (plus 4 variants) .... 12 mss.
3. Carrehoi, Carreor, a locality .... 1 ms.
4. Quarrois, Roais, a fortress .... 1 ms.
5. Carduel, Cardoeil, Quaraduel, Charduel .... 70 + mss.
6. Camaalot (plus 18 widely divergent spellings) .... 15 mss.
7. Montagu(t), a dukedom of allies .... 8 mss.
8. Sinaudone, Isneldone, Dodone .... 6 + mss.
9. Dina(s)daron .... 3 mss.
   (Castle of the Church of Aaron: Caerleon or Carlisle),
10. Londres (London) .... 6 mss.
11. Orquenie .... 1 ms.
12. Pouret (Pomfret?) .... 1 ms.
13. Tintagel, Nantael, Cintagel (Watson says probably Dunn
    Dagel) .... 3 ss.

This evidence shows that the great majority of romancers recognized the border city of Carlisle as unquestionably King Arthur's chief seat. Carlisle seems also Geoffrey of Monmouth's nodal point, and it is frequently named by the writers of the romances, and given as a point of rendezvous by the questers themselves at an intersection of seven roads. The city of Carlisle dominates three regions: the Carlisle Plain, the Eden River Lowland, and the Cumbrian Dome. Carlisle sits at a crossroads into (1) Dumbarton and Glasgow to the northwest, (2) Edinburgh and Stirling to the north, (3) Newcastle via the Haltwhistle Gap to the east, (4) York by the Eden Gap to the southeast, (5) Cumbria and the Lake District to the west, (6) Penrith and Chester to the south, and (7) Galloway and the embarkation ports to Ireland to the west. Carlisle thus affords entrance to Northumbria, Yorkshire, and Lancastria and yet is strategic and defensible because it is separated from each area. There were no bridges to the west of Carlisle, and the city was flanked by two rivers, the Eden and the Caldew. In ancient times the mosses (marshes) stretched far away to the north above Carlisle.

Carlisle is King Arthur's chief residence and his chief city, with the seventy references added to the thirty-five that call it Caerleon, like Geoffrey of Monmouth. The references to "Caradigan" seem to mean his seaport at Loch Ryan. The names of Camelot cause more difficulty, but the author of the *Perlesvaus*, which was written at Glastonbury Abbey, tells us that there were two castles called Camelot, one near Carlisle and the other in the north on a cliff facing west—or that it was an alternate spelling for Arthur's Knot at Stirling, or even another of his fortresses at Stirling. Arthur's birthplace at Tintagel was Caerlaverock on the Solway Firth, but nobody seems to have known this original and Pictish name. The alternate spellings demonstrate the confusion.

Fortunately, one feature of King Arthur's castle at Carlisle can be visualized; this was a prominent object called the Stone of Honor, translated into French as the *perron*. Thus, the castle at Carlisle was called the *Château del Perron*. Various heroes sat upon this stone or were tested upon it, like Lancelot and Wigalois. Marie de France, who added that the stone was not striped but of marble, also claimed that it lay at Arthur's chief seat of government and was therefore adjacent to the lands of the Scots and Picts.

When Marie de France's superb damsel came to fetch her lover Lanval, she stood upon this stone. More will be said thereupon in the Perceval manuscripts, of course. Ancient kings of Scotland stood upon the Stone of Scone, one reads, but it was of red sandstone. Once built into the walls of Dunstaffnage Castle, it was thereafter reverently transported to Scone. That site in the High King of Alban's realm was the "sacred center of Pictland."

Chrétien's *Lancelot* makes a complete story in itself, but it is only one episode in the hero's life. In his telling of it, Chrétien was primarily concerned with narration, plot, human drama, and the fierce confrontation of two men at peak effort, when each transcended his daily life. For this, Chrétien needed no antecedents, even less to pay heed to Lancelot's conquests of Albania. Geographical precisions appear more frequently in his other romances, where he betrays more easily his knowledge of the history and the geography of Scotland. There he speaks openly of Scottish reigns between 1107 and 1185. His heroine Laudine de Landuc is obviously an eponymous queen of Lothian (in Latin, Laudonia), reflecting a real Queen Sibylla. Ulrich names her Yblis and has Lancelot wed her. The point is finally that Chrétien's *Lancelot* reads like one chapter highlighting the Lancelot-Meleagant duels and is therefore recounted from that vantage point.

Even so, it is impossible for Chrétien's reader not to strain constantly to return the Meleagant contests to some ancient historical context. When in the course of Lancelot's life and adventures did they occur? One keeps remembering that Lancelot appeared suddenly out of his childhood "Lake," which was probably not a lake in the modern meaning of that English word, where as a boy he had been unable to ride horseback because there were no horses there and because his teachers were sailors, men of the sea, of course, and not mermen.

His training and his mission had been to conquer three separate kingdoms, and especially Dodone, or Stirling. He was also to wed the greatest heiress of all, whose name was Yblis (or Sebile, or Sibylla), and then to learn his name. After this, a damsel would tell him that his was his grandfather's name, which was the name of a line of kings: Galahad and Lancelot. Their name in Latin would be Anguselus, precisely as the much maligned Geoffrey of Monmouth had it.

This elucidation of the situation occurs in three separate romances: Chrétien's *Lancelot*, Ulrich's *Lanzelet*, and the *Prose Lancelot*. Since the genealogy of Lancelot, repeated again and again in the Perceval manuscripts, is said to have been tremendously sacred throughout Britain, we shall have another opportunity to examine it as we study the last of the Grail Kings, Perceval himself.

During his early years, Lancelot defeated two kings, who were brothers and his uncles. One was Patrick of the Hill Fort, none other than King Loth of Lothian and Traprain Law, as described in Ulrich. Geoffrey had both kings attendant upon King Arthur at his coronation. He vanquished King Loth at a tournament, said Ulrich, but he did not kill him. He subsequently fought the second brother, whose name Ulrich gave as Valerin. This was most probably King Urien of Gorre. They met at Carlisle, at which time King Urien surrendered and gave pledges of good conduct. Lancelot fought this king named Urien a second time, at some unidentified castle in Gorre, and he killed him. (None of the Lancelot annalists doubles or confuses Lancelot with himself or with the third brother, King Anguselus, who also attended King Arthur's coronation.) To acquire domains in Scotland, Lancelot had to defeat the father of Yblis, supposedly a regent named Iweret.

One surmises that by the laws of Pictish succession Lancelot, even though a grandson and a son of a king, was bypassed at birth. This hypothesis seems to satisfy the records, but it presents an inescapable conclusion— that the King Anguselus who accompanied King Arthur on his Roman campaign, who, in fact, took the lead in advocating it, was the Lancelot of the French romances. The continental romancers never knew how Lancelot died or what really became of him. If Geoffrey of Monmouth knew for a fact what he claimed to have known, then he may have been truly the most trusted recipient of vital, private information concerning the history of ancient Scotland.

King Urien of Gorre, says Ulrich, appeared one day in Carlisle at King Arthur's court to lodge a formal complaint and institute proceedings of the gravest consequence. He claimed that he had been promised Queen Guinevere as his bride before she was of marriageable age. Lancelot immediately proved him a liar before everyone, in a judicial trial by combat. King Urien then pledged his word to cease and desist. He may have kept his word, but it is difficult not to suspect King Bademagus, who is King Urien's nephew, and Meleagant of being agents on behalf of their overlord.

So when he defeated Meleagant for the third time, Lancelot had only fought his way back to this hateful King Urien again. The other accounts put his adventures in perspective. Although Ulrich has the most information, he treats the general story as if it were entirely fabulous and relaunches the mode of the fairy tale.

After several intervening adventures, Ulrich finally picks up the story of Lancelot and the abduction of Queen Guinevere at the home fortress of King Urien. He calls this place "Das verwarrene tan," which seems to be his approximation of the castle Tanroc granted to King Urien by King Arthur. Then, to make matters more interesting, Ulrich's translator renders "Das verwarrene tan" as Tanglewood. So now Queen Guinevere has been kidnapped, we assume for the second time, and is being held in King Urien's fortified lair, which is Tanroc, Tangled Wood, or Tanglewood. In real terms it is described as a wooden fortress surrounded by a thorn hedge and a palisade, all of which rings true. These methods of fortification were common in the Dark Ages, and such a place is commonly called a Palisade or Peel Castle. The same stockades were characteristic of the American Old West and Old Russia.

King Urien abducted the queen in order to inherit her real property, for she is reputed to be immensely wealthy. Several authors repeat this interesting information, the *Merlin* adding that she also brought King Arthur the Round Table. They do not know what the Round Table was or is, or where it was or is located.

Queen Guinevere's desperate son Lohot arrives in haste to defend his mother. We only know that his head was interred with her in her grave.

In Ulrich's *Lanzelet*, then, we have come full circle to the fairy tale. King Urien's castle has once more fallen into fairyland, a place out of time and space where all slumber, surrounded by the poor, pitiful Brunhilde's thorn hedge. Enchantment reigns. However, since the fairy tale stems from the same original source as the medieval romances of Chrétien and Caradoc, we can't dismiss it but must look at it carefully.

> Queen Guinevere is attended by thirty maidens. King Arthur, Lancelot, Lohot, and Gawain arrive to storm Tanglewood. The war is long and bloody. Lohot dies. Through all this Queen Guinevere sleeps the sleep of . . . ?
>
> During this war the queen sleeps without waking in the bailey of the castle. She is surrounded by serpents, which guard her, and which forbid access to her. Tristan is there too; he and Gawain are captured at the next-to-last moment.
>
> King Arthur wins, however. He storms across into the bailey. . . .

The queen awakens? She rises to dispute the taking of Tristan and Gawain as hostages?

We may conclude that, first of all, King Urien's castle was not on the sea like the first or Bademagus castle in Chrétien where the queen underwent her first imprisonment. The *Lanzelet* account, we now understand, follows that of Chrétien, but goes on to give us the true ending of the whole affair.

What we have here is an alternate version of "Sleeping Beauty." It is touching to think that Queen Guinevere did not die among her serpents, bitten on the finger by a viper, it would seem, without being remembered forever as a favorite heroine.

Maligned by the medieval churchmen, who dwelled on female vice and adultery, the old British queen has sailed through centuries of authors who treasured the fairy tale as closer to reality than any other form of record. Charles Perrault's version "La Belle au bois dormant," which appeared first in Holland in 1696 in the collection called approximately *Contes de la Mère Oye* (Tales of the Mother Goose), provides an ending for the great queen's story. The fairy tale never admits the death of the beautiful and noble heroine, of course. In the tales of the Mother Goddess called "Goose," or in the tales of the Mother Isis from ancient Egypt, the princess always emerges safely as immortal.

The fairy tale insists upon its *true* record of the faraway past. Queen Guinevere is the lovely White Queen wedded to the noblest prince, who is King Arthur. The double of the queen is the hateful stepmother or Old Black Queen, Morgan le Fay. No matter that she was King Arthur's beloved sister. She reigns in the Island Fortress, where her son Gawain meets her in *Gawain and the Green Knight*. She hates him, for he had been born a twin and had thus threatened her life in more than one way.

In this telling King Arthur becomes the Young King wedded to the princess, and he will come to her rescue, as in Caradoc's Glastonbury account, which also was a fairy tale. The alternate hero is Lancelot of the Lake, who drops out after the first series of adventures. The Old King is King Urien of Gorre. Queen Guinevere's son in the Perrault version is called "Day," or "Jour." He is to be killed. In the Mother Goose or Goddess Diana version the queen also has a daughter called "Dawn," or "Aurore."

Just as the Welsh *Triads* claimed, the father of Queen Guinevere was an ogre from the land of Gorre. We have the same story in Mother Goose. Equally, we have the same reason for the wedding of the princess Sleeping Beauty; her king married her for her immense landed wealth.

King Urien's castle is called Tanglewood and is surrounded by a peel, or stockade and thorn hedge. The dwarf is a servant of the powers of darkness. Queen Guinevere slept like Sleeping Beauty and was awakened by the king.

Except that in real life Queen Guinevere was thrown into a snakepit. She died from the bite of a viper, it is now clear. Thus, as Caradoc says, there were two queens of King Arthur.

The fairy tale hates the real world. It insists upon a happy ending, claiming emphatically that Sleeping Beauty only pricked her finger and that she was merely asleep and not dead. Ulrich says the same. The fairy tale says that her ladies all slept beside her and that they too were not dead. A period of one hundred years passed (one year in Caradoc's account). The castle Tanroc (which King Arthur had bestowed upon King Urien) had been the original property of the King Ogre. Queen Guinevere had brought it to King Arthur in her dowry.

When Prince Charming penetrated the fortress, he entered the silent kingdom of the dead. It was the Old Queen who had prepared the snake pit filled with vipers and other snakes. The fairy tale wants to see her punished for this and causes her to commit suicide in her own snake pit. But we know that King Arthur's sister was in the real world the much honored queen who bore him away to her castle at Avalon. Now the hunt for Avalon is on because we now think that Queen Guinevere was bred and perhaps born there.

It is time to recapitulate our meager information about this chief actor, King Urien of Gorre. Something peculiar is happening to our accounts—a change in narrative focus. The narrator's point of view reveals from time to time a discriminatory attitude not only toward Queen Guinevere but toward King Arthur. Thus, some of these versions we have been poring over must come from the point of view of King Urien.

Geoffrey of Monmouth knew of this King Urien, that he ruled in "Moray," which was probably Murray, or western Scotland, in the "land of the Scots" or Irish immigrants to those shores. Thus, Geoffrey did not place him in modern Wales, as Loomis and Ashe have done, or anywhere off the southern coast of Cornwall. Nor does Geoffrey know of "Gorre," but we can assume from the many references to Ireland that Gorre has to lie somewhere within the radius of Irish territory. And yet Saint Patrick's injunction against serpents, if it was an injunction against death by venom, did not yet obtain in this mysterious land of Gorre.

Geoffrey omitted King Urien from the roster of King Arthur's commanders in his last or continental campaign. This is significant. King Urien is not mentioned at the battle against the "Romans" on the continent, or supposedly at Autun. Since King Urien was one of the kings conquered by King Arthur, he must have been dead by the time King Arthur left for the continent again, accompanied by Angusel (Lancelot), Gawain, King Loth of

Lothian, King Aschil, King Hoel (North Wales), and Cador, Guerin, and Boso.

Furthermore, King Urien's name does not occur among the roster of the slain on the continent: Kay, Bedevere, Holdin, Lodegan, Cursalem, and Galluc (*Historia*, book 10). Geoffrey also reports (book 11) that after the deaths of Gawain and of Angusel, both of which occurred inside Britain, King Urien's oldest son or older son named Urien and also Yvain (in French) acceded to the throne of King Angusel of Scotland. This could have been the Yvain (Owein) who died in 560 against the Angles of Bernicia, as reported in the *Anglo-Saxon Chronicle* concerning the Bernician King Ida.

What Geoffrey of Monmouth has reported here sits well with the information common to the European romancers, who also report that a King Urien had already been slain, by Lancelot, before King Arthur's departure from Britain. This King Urien, known to all, was a sacred ruler because he was a direct descendant of Saint Joseph of Arimathea.

Our Arthurian King Urien of Gorre should not be confused with his namesake, King Urien (Urian) Rheged. The latter ruled King Arthur's same old kingdom, from Carlisle, between the years 572 and 592, thirty to fifty years after the death of King Arthur. This last King Urien had three sons, who were named Owain, Pasgent, and Elphin. This king (fifteen variant spellings of his name are recorded) was the one who ruled not only Cumberland but also a part of modern Wales, or Carmarthen. He is probably the one whose castle is called Carreg-Cennan. This fortress ruin rises three hundred feet above the Cennan River in Carmarthen and crowns a conical outcrop. It has passages that plunge one hundred fifty feet through solid rock and windows cut into the rock itself.

Our King Urien of Gorre, whom Lancelot is said to have killed, doubtless left a stable of writers of his own. Much of the Arthurian material is hostile to King Arthur. As we know, the *lai* (short narrative poem) called *Yonec* by Marie de France continues the stories left off by Chréien, by Caradoc, and by Ulrich von Zatzikhoven. How else would Marie de France know what happened to King Urien of Lancelot's day, unless she had access to "Irish" material from Gorre?

A continuation of the story of Queen Guinevere's abduction and death follows Ulrich's finale in the *lai* called *Yonec* (Young Yvain, Young Urien) by Marie de France. One also supposes that it was composed for the court of King Henry II. Here Marie tells how King Urien of Gorre had a second son born out of wedlock. His name was also Urien, or Yvain the Bastard. When he grew to manhood, he avenged the death of his father. This account stems, then, from the enemy of King Arthur and of King Lancelot. What is of interest to us is the geographical precisions concerning the land of Gorre, especially of the small Island Fortress where Arthur's queen was initially held prisoner, and near where King Arthur witnessed the final duel between Lancelot and Meleagant.

After this duel and the departure of King Arthur for the continent Lancelot disappears from all the accounts. This is difficult to countenance. Once there were Annals of Lancelot, however, claims the *Prose Lancelot*. These were compiled and stored in Carlisle where they were found after the terrible carnage of Camlan and King Arthur's departure. Whoever found them destroyed the conclusion, or failed to write the conclusion to the "Life" of Lancelot. One could suppose that they were taken into Scotland with the new King Urien, who succeeded King Lancelot. What happens when the enemy succeeds the king? One also supposes that Chrétien and Geoffrey of Monmouth both and at the same time in the twelfth century had access to parts of these lost annals. The Carlisle material also found in Ulrich had to come from these annals too, since all three writers present their tellings from a point of view favorable to Lancelot, and as if he himself had told the original version.

Marie de France, on the other hand, sympathized with King Urien of Gorre and narrated from his point of view and from that of his line of kings. At the end of the affair her hero is the illegitimate son Yonec. Scholars have always claimed without proof that her material originated in a Breton French source and was translated from Breton into French. It would appear from the evidence of *Yonec* that they are wrong. Even if her source was ultimately Breton French, it was not originally P—Celtic but Q—Celtic, or Irish.

No author as yet has sympathized with Meleagant, but perhaps we should feel for him, so young, so rash, and so burdened with pressures. No author recorded his death from the standpoint of his own family. We should see in the passing of Meleagant, with his vanishing strength in the fading sunlight, the symbol of a vanishing, vanished race: the Picts.

The last recorded ruler of the Picts, some four hundred years after the death of Meleagant, fell in the year 839. He was slaughtered in battle by the invading Norman French as they swept over Britain. This last prince also bore what probably was Meleagant's real name: Prince Eoghann.

PART III

THE GRAIL KINGS

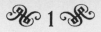

1

Perceval
among the Saints

As long as the writers of the twelfth century followed Geoffrey of Monmouth's revolutionary new material but treated Britain as a single realm composed of its greater parts, they rang out their words confidently enough. They failed to solve such troublesome smaller problems as the sites of King Arthur's battles and the city of his coronation. Over the centuries the same perplexing localities have so irritated modern scholars that the more confident among them have preferred skepticism to admissions of ignorance. Thus, aspersions have right and left been cast haughtily upon King Arthur and the Arthurian literature, until both have been perforce deemed fantastically fictional.

The most troublesome subject matter of all, unlike the battle sites and coronation city which were profusely documented, concerns the Holy Grail. No other area has for eight intervening centuries presented a greater challenge to readers of medieval literature. The old nagging questions of religion tantalize everyone alike.

Who were the Grail Kings? What was their function? What was their condition? Why were they terminally ill? What was this suppurating wound of the Grail King? Where was their realm? What sort of kingdom was it? Did a Grail Castle ever exist? If so, where? What was the Holy Grail? Must one abandon the search for truth here and abort the inquiry, close the books, and consider this matter fiction—Welsh myth, Irish myth, or Greek myth?

The wonder is how painstakingly the great admirers of King Arthur in the twelfth century, who are our chief authors, labored over their shadowy accounts. Searching through lengthy works, they coaxed gray imponderables from their ancient sources. From Arthur's court into the light of day, they said, the truly hardiest champions, those connected by birth both to saintliness and to royalty, actually came upon the Grail Castle once or twice. They were few and most privileged. After severe hardships these delegate youths actually stumbled across it, by chance.

Reverently the twelfth-century poets relate their stories, how King Arthur himself had cause to undertake such a pilgrimage to the Grail Castle, which proved to be, strangely enough, not far from Camelot or his other seats.

Notoriously, Lancelot of the Lake attempted the Grail Quest and failed to achieve it. This must have been due, theorized the romancers who were men of the cloth, to Lancelot's lack of celibacy, or even to his adultery. Certainly Lancelot appears in their accounts the very image of a proud, masculine, worldly king. The Lady of the Lake, who had raised him on an isle, had first assigned his life work: to conquer the Waste Land, as we have already learned, where once she herself reigned. A twelfth-century French writer concurs with Ulrich; Lancelot became, under the suzerainty of Arthur, king of Lothian. His marriages to heiresses established his rights to rule their property.

The great older warrior Gawain, who before Lancelot wielded Excalibur for Arthur and who also served the king on his continental campaign, himself attempted the Grail Quest. In all but one account, *Du Krône* (Two Kings) by Heinrich von dem Turlin, he too is said to have failed.

Both Gawain and Lancelot, dispatched by King Arthur upon the Grail Quest, were princes and the sons of reigning kings. Quite suitably, Gawain attempted the quest, for he was said to have been educated in the household of the Sulpicius who became an abbot or a pope. But there was no such pope at Rome in either the fifth or the sixth century. Gawain's Sulpicius must have been some great local dignitary in Britain only.

It seems to have been King Arthur who dispatched young Perceval on the Grail Quest. The youth was contacted when alone in the woods, alerted by messengers first, and then subsequently dispatched on his way. This youngest cousin of Gawain alone succeeded in completing the Grail Quest, remaining in the secret Grail Castle, probably crowned there as its wounded king. Thus, the problems surrounding the mysterious Grail are best approached through this other hero, Perceval.

Ten major accounts of Perceval began appearing during the last quarter of the twelfth century and exhaust the subject after about forty years, or until Malory revived it, albeit fragmentarily, in *Le Morte d'Arthur*. The primary or twelfth-century accounts deal with Perceval's early life and with a double series of adventures. Most authors tend to drop the subject somewhere in the middle, as being too hot to handle, no doubt. Perceval was born youngest of several sons, all agree, in the generation after King Arthur's. The Grail story itself continues on into the following generation, or through the deaths of King Lancelot's saintly son Galahad and Perceval's saintly son, the swan knight Lohengrin.

There seems no swifter access than that provided by the Holy Grail to the real but lost world of King Arthur. Here even the sovereign treads softly when he ventures to perceive the Holy Grail. The experience quite overwhelms him, and he is not more able than Perceval to utter a word, much less to state or repeat aloud what has happened.

Some hierophany reigned at this place, which Arthur and his contemporaries held utterly sacred. The place of worship was obviously set apart from profane sites by weird passageways, which are, of course, usual in ancient oracular centers of worship. Dense and unreal, sacred time either passed there or lapsed, or unrolled in depth, as it were, vertical in dimension.

The holy place glowed with white objects against gray shadows, bright firelight against dark stone, noted Chrétien. There were feminine beings of ineffable beauty and youth, familiar symbols, white vestments shining in processionals, solemn investitures, dead silences. Horns sounded, presumably to announce a solemnity, on the four corners of the castle, but they were replaced in later or Christian times, it seems, by bells. Sacraments were then performed. The Grail came in surrounded by a blinding white light.

Even nature participated, a sudden cyclone blasting Gawain as he left the sacred precinct and rode along the opposite shore. Lancelot too was severely bombarded, and perhaps he was there also.

Through some hermeneutic Perceval, however, grew to belong finally or to calm the winds and the waters or to fulfill the unknown criteria, satisfy the equation, and complete the prophecy. It is therefore essential to establish wherever possible what was authoritatively recorded concerning this noble prince Perceval, last of his generation, whose name to the French writers sounded like the three syllables: Per-ce-val.

As was the case with Lancelot, Perceval's story derives first from Chrétien de Troyes. His poem, composed from a source lent him by the count of Flanders, is entitled *Conte del graal* (Tale of the Grail), subtitled *Perceval*. Chrétien and his three continuators compiled, between 1174 and 1200, a huge unfinished work totaling 65,000 verses. Thus, they labored diligently to set those events which establish for all time the famous and much copied morphology, or Perceval's life:

1. His boyhood in the Waste Forest
2. His departure for King Arthur's court, and his initial adventures
3. His education at his uncles' several castles
4. The conquest of his future wife's castle
5. His first visit and stunning rejection at the Grail Castle

6. His dazed return toward King Arthur's court and his final adventures, such as the return, in final farewell, to his mother's castle in the Waste Forest

7. His induction at the Grail Castle

Succeeding authors might reverse the order of these seven parts or expand one at the expense of the others; but basically all their accounts fall somewhere into this pattern of chronological, developmental biography.

This most celebrated of Arthurian plots, that of the brave young warrior slowly made wise until he achieves such sanctity that he is mysteriously removed altogether from the cycle of worldly conquests, appears over the centuries in other literatures also, at various levels. It furnished a favorite subject for histories and romances, for the developmental prose novel *(Bildungsroman)*, and for the aristocratic fairy tale, as well as for folklore common to most European literatures. Since the story of Perceval runs its embroidered but familiar course down the centuries, passing from one culture to another, translated from tongue to tongue, the only way to recover the primitive facts of this hero's life is to collate the earliest versions.

Each version contains some of the same uresolved questions about Perceval's fate at the end. Supposedly he entered the Grail Castle permanently but of his own free will. Or was he disabled and purposely incapacitated, unable ever to leave? The reader never knows.

Chrétien and his continuators were followed within two decades by these greatest of the Perceval manuscripts:

1. Robert de Boron's version, called *Joseph of Arimathea* (c. 1190, revised c. 1215)

2. The anonymous French version referred to as *Didot-Perceval*, also written between 1190 and 1215

3. The *Perlesvaus*, wirtten in French prose at Glastonbury between 1191 and 1212 (also called the *Perceval li Gallois* or *The High History of the Holy Grail*)

4. *Parzival*, written in German by Wolfram von Eschenbach, also between 1198 and 1212. Wolfram erroneously situates Perceval's (Parzival's) family in the ancient French province of Poitou, which formed a part of the dowry of Eleanor of Aquitania to King Henry II of England. I believe he confused "Pictish" with the Latin designation for "Poitou," *Pictones* (a people of Gaul) for *Pictavensis* (the French *Poitevain*, a native of Poitou). He also mistook "moor" for "Moor," a native of Morocco.

5. *Sir Perceval of Galles*, an English verse version copied by a monk named Robert de Thornton from Yorkshire in the fifteenth century (called the Thornton Romance)

6. "Peredur," the Welsh prose version or *Mabinogi*, which forms a part of the collection of sacred tales entitled *Mabinogion*, of uncertain and disputed dates

In addition, two of the five books that compose the *Prose* or *Vulgate Lancelot* also contain relevant material. By the time of this compilation, however, Perceval had already been largely supplanted by his son Galahad. Both *The History of the Holy Grail* (originally called the *Grand Saint Graal*) of c. 1204 and *The Quest of the Holy Grail* of c. 1220 are sections containing material on Perceval.

The final important medieval manuscript, before Malory, of course, is the *Sone de Nansai,* an overlong Old French verse version. Here the real hero, called Sone, has replaced Perceval. Marvelously, however, this author, a careful realist, kept in his version a priceless and perfectly unique geography of the Grail Castle itself.

Perceval manuscripts, and those which carry the tradition on into the next generation of Galahad and Lohengrin, treat primarily the Quest of the Holy Grail. Since it was King Arthur who personally dispatched his best men, those who were closest to him by virtue of blood ties, upon this quest, one may reasonably view the Arthurian Age as one of Christian piety. It seems wiser to accept their Christianity rather than to dispute it with what Saint Augustine, sent from Rome into Britain to convert the Saxons, might have called a Christian heresy.

The twelfth-century writers could not have been more intrigued, or at the same time more baffled, by the religious practices at the Grail Castle. To them finally, as to Robert de Boron, who by 1190 had recovered from the shock of Chrétien's initial account of "a graal," the ceremony at the Grail Castle was accepted, if for no other reason than because King Arthur had sanctioned it and had actively participated. Now King Arthur ranks among, but *first* among, ancient Christian heroes, as we all know, and has done so for centuries. He is the oldest of the three Christian Worthies of the West: King Arthur of Britain, the emperor Charlemagne of the Franks, and Duke Geoffrey or Godfrey de Bouillon of Belgium, who in 1099 captured Jerusalem and made of the First Crusade a magnificent victory.

While the earliest proofs of Christianity in Britain are said to go back no farther than the year 120, when the emperor Hadrian erected his wall to keep the Scots and Picts from occupied Roman territory, or to 167, when King Lucius was converted, the religion was apparently flourishing by King Arthur's time. Saint Gildas, whose testimony supports Arthur (c. 475–542), was a brilliant Christian writer. If Saint Patrick died in 493, then his life also overlapped Arthur's. Powerful in its influence, then, was the "great monastery" built around 400 by Saint Ninian on the point of Galloway which faces, across the Solway Firth, the point of Ayr, and the northern tip of the Isle of Man. Called a "bishop of the nation of the Britons," this senior Saint Ninian of Scotland was certainly a Christian missionary and was said to have been trained in Rome. He built his foremost stone church in the territory of the Niduari, or Southern, Picts, just before 400, it is thought. His mission in the south of Scotland predates Saint Columba's mission in the north: to convert the Picts, and also to make peace between them and the Britons and Gaels. Called the White House (Candida Casa), Saint Ninian's chief community stood, then, on the Isle of Whithorn, on or close to the main route between King Arthur's chief seat at Carlisle and the seaports of the Gaels in western Galloway. Along this route Lancelot traveled, it seems likely, as he pursued the abducted Queen Guinevere. We shall see King Arthur worship here.

By the year 400 Britain had in an unfortunate way come to the attention of the orthodoxy on the continent. Heretical doctrines were being preached here as elsewhere, it was believed, by a famous Briton perhaps called Morgan, but known to this day as Pelagius. According to Bede's *Ecclesiastical History* (II, 2), the heresy propagated by this Pelagius was already rife in Britain by 429, for the Britons "preferred their own traditions before all the churches in the world." Such famous writers as Orosius and Prosper of Aquitaine on the continent, for example, attacked Pelagius and his Irish associate Celestius, calling the former a low scribbler, a cunning snake, a sinuous viper, and also a "sea-green Briton."

Obviously, King Arthur lived in stimulating times when far-flung intellectuals joined combat. In 429–30 and again in 448–49 Saints Germanus and Lupus were dispatched from Gaul to Britain to stamp out heresy. It was around 432–33 that Saint Germanus's protégé Saint Patrick returned from Rome and Gaul for his second residence in Ireland—approximately forty years.

In Gaul the great Christian bishops of the fifth century, Saints Mamert of Vienne, Germanus of Auxerre, Rémi of Reims, Perpet of Tours, and Lupus of Troyes, were designated *defensores civitatis,* defenders of the state, for they upheld both Roman administration and Christian charity. The Saint Lupus who visited Britain in the fifth century was, in fact, considered by Sidonius Appollinaris "the first pontiff of the world." Saint Ninian's bishopric, comprising Galloway and Strathclyde, likewise represented a civil and an ecclesiastical domain with a Romanized congregation, as evidenced by tombstones among the ruins there, of persons with Romanized Celtic names. His other church in Stirling, or in the Bannockburn Corridor, is considered one of the oldest in all Scotland.

While in Britain Saint Germanus commanded an army, it is told, which on an Easter Sunday joined in combat with bands of Saxons, Scots, and Picts. The saint had earlier that day baptized his followers and taught them to cry, "Hallelujah!" Their shouts so echoed from the hills that the enemy, overcome, one imagines, by the ancient Celtic fear that the sky was about to fall upon their heads, fled in terror from the battlefield. Given the fact that Celtic Christian churches were, prior to the eighth century, named for their founders, Saint Germanus may personally have dedicated a church on the west coast of the Isle of Man, at Peel Island. The ruins of a church bearing his name stand there prominently today, and the island bears the name of Saint Patrick.

Unquestionably, these saints and bishops remain the greatest individuals of King Arthur's day, persons of such stature that their few words and many deeds are still remembered. Despite the fact that no master calendar exists for the fifth and sixth centuries, there is no problem of actually identifying certain contemporaries of Arthur: Boethius, Saint Benedict of Nursia, Saint Germanus of Auxerre, Saint Brieux, Saint Rémi, Saint Medard, Saint Eleuthère, Saint Cesarius of Arles, and Saint Brachion. Nor are there doubts about King Arthur's counterpart in Gaul, King Clovis of France and Queen, or Saint, Clothilde, who died on June 3, 545.

Other contemporaries of Arthur possess only shadowy biographies and chronologies. Their names, like those of Arthur, Guinevere, Lancelot, and Perceval, exist, but differently, in many languages, which shows how widespread was their renown and how great the devotion to them. Both Saint Patrick and Saint Brigit are cases in point. Saint Geneviève of Paris (c. 422–512), who also received a visit from Saint Germanus, was a contemporary. The statue of this girl saint, who saved Paris from the Huns, is first before the queens of France in the Luxembourg Gardens of Paris. Even though these were times as calamitous as Cesarius of Arles said, they also were, perhaps for that reason, a great age of saints. From these times come the sainted chronicles of Perceval and of the Holy Grail. While today the problems the Dark Ages have almost lost significance, the personages who rose to meet them remain familiar names.

Many of these well-known saints could have met the warrior King Arthur: Brigit of Ireland (c. 450–c. 525); Briocus (d. 576 during an outbreak of the plague); Cadoc (d. 570), who was a friend of Saints David and Dubric whom Arthur protected and who died perhaps in 601 and 612 respectively; Saint Eleutherius (Eleuthère) of c. 456–c. 531; Saint Iltutus (Illtud), who was the learned nephew of Saint Germanus and who died in c. 540; the patron saint of Scotland, sometimes called Kentigern (527–612); Saint Padarn; Saint Radegundis (519–87); Saint Remigius (c. 457–530); Saint Samson (floruit c. 555–57), Saint Servanus (d. 540); and a cousin of Saint David named Saint Teilo.

If Arthur was born around 475 and Gawain a few years later, which seems at least possible, then their life spans coincided with this great leap of piety, scholarship, and theological activity in Britain. In *The Age of Arthur* John Morris connected the king to Saints Padarn, Cadoc, Gildas, and Illtud.

The twelfth-century rulers and monks, despite their obviously great faith, nonetheless hastened to disinter the bodies of many of these same personages: King Arthur, Queen Guinevere, Saint Brigit, Saint Patrick, Saint Columba, and Saint Dubric.

The body of Saint Kentigern, who continued the work of Saint Ninian, lies today entombed in the Glasgow Catholic Cathedral. It was to one of the stone churches that he built, Saint Asaph's in Flintshire, Wales, that Geoffrey of Monmouth was named bishop. Saint Kentigern's lovely church stands modestly to the side. We find all these persons in the *Lives of the British Saints* and/or in *Lives of the Cambro-British Saints*. Lives of Saints Cadoc, Padarn, and Carantoc, although less famous than those of Saints Columba and Gildas, were also composed during the early twelfth century.

The closed circle of these elite British or Cambro-British saints was surely broken when Pope Gregory (540–604) sent Saint Augustine into Britain. We find in R. H. Hodgkin's Anglo-Saxon history many pages on the early Celtic church. Supposedly, these primitive and resident Christian leaders had declined or "refused to propagate Christianity among the Anglo-Saxons." Furthermore, they maintained a "policy of aloofness," it is still alleged, which seems hardly an exaggeration if warfare was occurring between the old British and Pictish inhabitants and the new Irish and Anglo-Saxon immigrants. Into this turmoil and resettlement of populations King Arthur strode with power and authority. The redistribution of peoples and the resulting chaos lasted for three entire centuries, from the fourth century onward.

The immense prestige still granted these older saints stems from several reasons. There is the fact that many of them were born into the most exalted ranks of ancient society. Saint Brigit, who prepared Saint Patrick's winding sheet, was herself descended from the royal house of Leinster. Saint Cadoc, on the other hand, who was renowned for his maxims, founded the monastery of Llancarvan, which in Arthur's lifetime became an illustrious center of secular learning. It would be in no way unreasonable to suppose that Geoffrey of Monmouth could very well have recorded his history of King Arthur from one of the many little books originally written at Llancarfan or treasured there in the library and that illustrious school.

Saint Columba, or Columcille, which means Beloved Colum, was a prince of the blood royal of Ireland. Or his name was Colum Cille, which means Dove of the Church. His real name in Gaelic was Crimthann or Cremthann, which some say meant "fox." Others claim that his name translated into Greek was Peristera, or even that it was a Hebrew translation: "Iona." Others say Iona was the name of the island he chose for his religious settlement, a name that was a misreading for "Iova," as Columba's biographer Adamnan had originally spelled it. Saint Columba also founded colleges in Derry and Durrow before establishing his renowned school on the holy island of Iona in Scotland, where forty-eight Scottish, four Irish, and seven

Norwegian kings were both educated and later interred. Saint Columba personally transcribed three hundred copies of the Bible, it is said, plus the *Book of Durrow* and the *Book of Kells*.

In his person Saint Columba must have been like King Arthur himself, a man of tremendous presence. Saint Columba is renowned for his remarkable singing voice, which was piercing, and for his lovely, fervent prayers for Ireland. His voice is said to have carried over a distance of fifteen hundred paces. The Pictish King Brude at Inversess and his entourage were astonished—and their Druid priest was struck with terror—when Saint Columba burst into full voice outside their wooden hall, singing the Forty-fourth Psalm. In his celebrated *Life of Columba*, Adamnan, who was his successor, tells how the monks of Saint Columba's future settlement rowed from Ireland to Iona. The Glastonbury *Perlesvaus* speaks in much the same terms of the hero Perceval, who also rowed and sailed his coracle all by himself through the islands of the Irish Sea.

This early Christian culture in Britain seems not to have enforced celibacy among the lower orders of the clergy. Many of these saints appear to have fathered dynasties, as was perhaps the case with Perceval before he was inaugurated at the Grail Castle. There are cases of French saints who did not repudiate their wives until they became bishops. Most such personages spent their mature years in scholarship and in the training of those scholars most apt to continue their research. The Arthurian manuscripts speak often of books compiled at King Arthur's court also, although no other historiographer than Merlin is named.

The adventures of Lancelot, among others, were preserved in archives, claimed the *Prose Lancelot*, by Queen Guinevere herself. Such records, like the celebrated art treasures which the medieval writers stated were being housed in King Arthur's chief fortress, must have been widely known, if not precisely located. They were presumably destroyed overnight or during the rout following Camlan. The ones that survived, however, as we have already supposed, probably remained in the area of Strathclyde. For a long time after Arthur's death, that was the safest region. Its architectural ruins were visited a century later by King Ida's Northumbrian wife, Queen Bebba.

Most of these early British saints retired from the world, probably at the onset of old age, to become desert ascetics. After their deaths their sainted bodies were often laid on beds, then cast out to sea on small crafts. The holy body of Perceval's sister was disposed of in this way. When these bodies drifted ashore they were again pushed out to sea. In some cases the bones of the greatest saints, such as Saint Martin and Saint Gildas, were eventually recovered and treasured, divided among many Christian communities as most sacred and efficacious relics. Such may also have been the case with King Arthur's body; a small place on the road north from Carlisle is still called Arthuret, Arthur's head.

The possibility on the other hand that neither Arthur, Perceval, nor Galahad actually died in Britain is not too incredible. According to the romances only Gawain and Lancelot were buried in Britain.

In those days great personages were said to have afforded the pilgrimage to Jerusalem: the empress Helena Augusta, the king or emperor Arthur, and his kin Saint David, patron of Wales. Twelfth-century Perceval manuscripts assert that both Galahad and Perceval died in the Holy Land, at a place most often spelled "Sarras," which is probably Nazareth. One recalls Sir Walter Scott saying that in the Holy Land Christians were called Nazarenes.* Only their companion Bors survived the long return to Britain. From the fourth century, in fact, Gallo-Romans and Romano-Britons frequently made one such journey, which ensured them a consideration of divine mercy at the moment of death. Those doctrines of Hell and Purgatory, which would become orthodox, were being expressed and established during Arthur's lifetime. The emphasis in his day was, then, on the afterlife. Writing from Bethlehem (c. 347–419) Saint Jerome had said that the most illustrious men then alive in the world resided, like him, in the Holy Land.

The route to Jerusalem in Arthur's day was well traveled. Embarking either at (one of the) Berwick(s) on the east coast of north Britain, Berwick being a port often mentioned in the French romances, or at one of the ports of Galloway, which are often also alluded to, the pilgrims' route crossed the sea to Celtic Brittany. Thence the travelers proceeded usually via Tours and Lyons to the Mediterranean coast, either to Marseilles or to the older, royal, Roman city of Narbonne. From there they crossed to Carthage in North Africa. From that renowned Christian center the pilgrims took passage by ship to Alexandria, then crossed the Sinai to Joppa, with tours of the Christian churches at all the cities along the way.

The biggest attraction in the Western world was without a doubt Jerusalem, the Golden City. Illuminated manuscripts show its golden walls rising story above story behind lofty ramparts. Incomparable in its grandeur, say modern art historians, the city boasted in excellent condition the Rotunda of the Holy Sepulcher, the Anastasis Rotunda, and the Martyrium of Christ. The emperor Constantine and the empress Helena had intended it to be so, that nothing in the world should equal the splendor and golden magnificence of Holy Jerusalem. The lamps and candelabra there defied description, so intricate and brilliant was their light. In the Martyrium itself, says Emile Mâle, was kept an onyx chalice of the Last Supper, or the "Holy Grail."

Leaving Jerusalem, the itinerary led the devout pilgrims to Bethlehem, where through a polygonal opening they could gaze underground and see Jesus' *crèche*, or manger, displayed. They could also gaze upon King David's

---

*See *The Talisman*, chapter 1.

tomb. Leaving Bethlehem they journeyed north to Samaria, Galilee, Jericho, the Jordan River, Nazareth, and Mount Tabor (after which some say the Glastonbury Tor was named).

Fantastic, glittering mosaics—an Adoration of the Magi on the facade of the Church of Bethleem, a Visitation of the Virgin on the facade at Nazareth—entranced them. They probably saw the Grotto of the Nativity at Bethlehem, the baptismal church on the Jordan, the Calvary, the Holy Women depicted at the Tomb of Christ, the representation of the Ascension of the Mount of Olives, and the Descent of the Holy Ghost upon Mount Sion. This commemorative art, in Jerusalem especially, established an iconography not only for France, where written records of the Dark Ages were not virtually obliterated as in Britain, but for all Western churches.

Such background material supplied by historians from several areas of specialty goes far to establish a climate in which one may now read more sympathetically about the adventures of Perceval. Many scholars have also accused Robert de Boron of having falsified his sources in order to make Chrétien's original account Christian, which seems an unnecessary complication.

What if the symbols used at the Grail Castle—the chalice or grail, the sword, the lance, and the platter—were once pagan symbols? Educated youths in Arthur's day, and Perceval was educated enough to react responsibly and predictably, would have known, even as laymen, that the cup from which Christ drank at the Last Supper, or a replica thereof, must be a relic of inestimable value, price, and sanctity. So would be a chalice that had caught His blood or that had held wine representing that blood for the sacrament of communion. He would have known that a sword signified the cross, that a lance had pierced Christ's side, and that the wicked Salome had held the head of John the Baptist upon a platter.

After long reflection, doubtless, each of our twelfth- and thirteenth-century authors, some of whom had received the benefit of advice and religious counsel from fellow scholars in their own congregation at home and abroad, made his own decision as to what the "graal" or Holy Grail really was. Some called it a cup or chalice; some thought it was a platter, or a monstrance, or a brilliant gemstone. All associated it with dazzling white light and with a secret ceremony involving both men and women in the hidden Grail Castle, in the presence of the immobile, wounded Grail King.

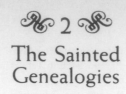

2

The Sainted Genealogies

In view of the attacks against the Arthurian material, assaults that commenced at the moment of King Arthur's defeat at the final Battle of Camlan, it is a wonder that any statistics such as genealogies survived. The fact that genealogies for King Arthur, Lancelot, and Perceval did survive attests to their sacred importance to future rulers of Britain. In Arthur's day such documents and verbatim knowledge were of the utmost significance; it may even have been necessary to recite them in order for Arthur, Lancelot, and Perceval to look forward to receiving crowns. In order to rise in the ancient orders of learning and religion men were obliged to prove their ancestry and their descent from nine generations of free men.

King Arthur vanished from the face of the earth, as it were, leaving memories and but a few physical objects that were carefully hidden. As king, he owned no land of his own, and no other real estate. In ancient days it was understood that kings should remain landless so that they would not be tempted by greed. At the moment of King Arthur's wounding, said a later chronicler in Scotland, he was bearing into Scotland for interment there the body of Lancelot. It would be almost certain that no member of King Arthur's retinue would have survived him, that being the natural law and established custom.

So far as we know, a single trace of King Arthur turned up once in the twelfth century, at Jerusalem. In that city, newly reconstituted as a Crusader State after its conquest by Godfrey de Bouillon and Tancred in 1099, King Richard Coeur de Lion handed King Arthur's sword Excalibur to a Tancred as a gift and reward for heroism. The Tancred in question was not the same as the deliverer of Jerusalem but probably the popular Tancred of Lecce, king of Sicily. This Tancred died only five years before King Richard. After the capture of Richard the treasures of Britain were exhausted in the rigorous effort to scrape up enough gold and jewels to purchase the king's freedom. Into that pile of valuables probably went the rest of King Arthur's treasures.

The story that Bedevere or someone else threw Excalibur into the water or into the sea is certainly apocryphal. No member of King Arthur's household would have survived him, and above all, none of the Round Table knights. That the Lady of the Lake came to bear Arthur away and that she took the sword Excalibur into safekeeping in Avalon, on the other hand, seems not only logical but correct according to ancient protocol.

The death of King Arthur left his realm adrift and his memory prey to religious and political revisions. The Synod of Whitby in 664 cut Scotland off from Ireland, severing the Celtic realm anew. In Ireland itself the new saints, along with Saint Columba, continued the burning of ancient records that Saint Patrick had commenced earlier.

When he dedicated the *History of the Kings of Britain* to King Stephen around 1136, Geoffrey of Monmouth walked right into that controversy which would soon erupt into the wars between England and Scotland. In the terrible slaughters that continued through the reigns of Henry II, Edward I, Edward II, and Edward III, the name of King Arthur and especially of Merlin caused political mayhem. In his book of prophecy Geoffrey of Monmouth had Merlin say to Vortigern, among other inflammatory predictions:

> Scotland shall be moved to rage and calling all men to her Lion's banner shall look only for blood. . . . A new conqueror in Scotland shall be named and crowned Lion. . . . London shall feel the Northwind's blast and mourn the deaths of twenty thousand. . . . The three Islands of Britain shall feel the Lion in his wrath, roaring, swollen with the blood of men. . . . The Lion shall hold the Balance and stretch his palm over Scotland. . . . The Chariot of the Moon shall disturb the Zodiac. . . . The planets shall turn their faces away from men caught in the wrath of the stars.

It would have been difficult not to see William Wallace and Robert the Bruce in such dire predictions of new lions. But the old lion of Arthur's day, also slaked with blood, was Lancelot:

> *Then the moon shall rise in the northwest*
> *In a cloud as black as the bill of a crow;*
> *Then shall the Lion be loose, the boldest and best*
> *That ever was in Britain seen in Arthur's day.*

Like Lancelot before him, William Wallace won a resounding victory at Stirling Bridge. Like Lancelot before him, Robert the Bruce came suddenly into the leadership of Scotland out of his western isle, in 1307. And like Lancelot before him, Robert defeated his foes at Bannockburn, the most severe combat taking place around Saint Ninians Church, where, we have theorized, Lancelot first saw the tomb of his grandfather.

But when Glastonbury began claiming King Arthur for itself and saying that it was there that Lancelot visited the tomb of Queen Guinevere and there that she had been abducted, Scotland let go of both Arthur and Lancelot. In the same way, Scotland let go of Excalibur, buying its freedom from Richard Coeur de Lion.

Moving farther and farther away from Britain, the Scots veered toward the French and fought beside them in the Hundred Years' War, and in death lay beside them in Holy Cross Cathedral dedicated at Orléans to Saint Joan of Arc. But, curiously enough, it was the Norman French and then notably Geoffrey of Monmouth who resurrected both King Arthur and Lancelot and put them where they belonged—not in Glastonbury but in the border area of Edinburgh, Dumbarton, Stirling, and Loch Lomond. And Arthur's name still graces, as he wished, the volcanic mountain in Edinburgh, and the Celtic people say the dead haunt the high hills near where once they lived.

The Renaissance included King Arthur and especially Lancelot in its anathemas against all that was Gothic and medieval. Its scholars and teachers fulminated against the medieval world of the twelfth century that had resurrected these kings from the Dark Ages. The famous English classical scholar, teacher, tutor, and diplomat Roger Ascham detested the Lancelot stories, which, he said, rested upon two points: open manslaughter and "bold bawdrye." Murder and adultery could no longer be condoned in literature. On the continent François de La Noue, a noted Calvinist, condemned the Lancelot book for the same reasons. The Protestant theologian of Geneva, Denis de Rougemont, whose book *Love in the Western World* was edited by T. S. Eliot, has blamed the high divorce rate in the Western world upon the triangular myths of adultery in Arthurian literature.

The facts seem otherwise, the Arthurian literature being an exaltation of the ancient Celtic church, and even Lancelot's adultery nothing more than an assumption.

Yet in spite of all this the pedigrees of Lancelot, King Arthur, and Perceval were treasured and saved. They are called not only royal but sacred. The Welsh archives agree, stating that there were three sacred and holy families inside Britain: the families of Cunedda, Brychan, and Caw. The first includes King Arthur, the second includes the Tudors, and the third also includes King Arthur and Geraint of the *Mabinogion*. Perceval is an ancestor of Godfrey de Bouillon and, thus, of the same Belgian princes who freed Jerusalem in 1099.

The sacred pedigree of King Arthur, monarch of Britain, can be traced through the Dark Ages to the prehistoric Brute, original settler of that realm. From King Arthur it descends, verified by many genealogists, in doubled royal lines through the kings of Wales and Scotland. Their two kingdoms are eventually united again under King Arthur's descendant James I, king of Great Britain. Thus, the Tudor and Stuart rights to that throne have been carefully researched and are well known and formally established.

For its part twelfth-century Arthurian literature took pride in offering two other royal and saintly pedigrees, those of Lancelot and Perceval. They reigned, like Arthur and James I, in an unbroken succession, their subjects perhaps equally comfortable "in clarity and kingly order." In fact, even the medieval writers of romances in Old French understood the importance of recording for their readers certain sacred pedigrees. From the death of Brute and the division of his realm among his three sons, authors and archivists watched over the pedigrees of these three lands: Logria (England), Cambria (Wales), and Albania (Scotland). In addition, King Arthur conquered at least some part of Ireland and then maintained peace over what has been regarded as a united Britain. In the major romances his realm comprised Logres (the French spelling), at least as far west and east as Carlisle and York, perhaps to Chester in the south. For most ancient times, said Nennius, and despite the mutability of wartime, Britain was divided into three parts—Logria, Cambria, and Albania—plus three islands: Inisgueith (Wight), Eubonia or Manau (Man), and beyond the Picts, Orc (Orkneys). The second island, called Man, was said to be located at the navel of the sea.

At the time of King Arthur's death in the sixth century, Britain was largely Christian, so such pedigrees as these three were also kept by the church, particularly because, as with Saint Kentigern of Scotland, by whose time and because of whose ministry Glasgow had become the religious center of that land, the Arthurian nobles had become or had fathered great religious leaders. Saint Kentigern's father is said to have been King Arthur's knight of the Round Table Sir Yvain (or Owain). He is Chrétien's Yvain, the Knight of the Lion. Practically speaking, Chrétien probably saw in his material that Yvain was from Lothian (Lyonesse) and substituted "lion," for thereby hung a tale. Owain's corrected pedigree, offered by Lady Charlotte Guest in *The Red Book of Hergest*, shows the three brothers who attended King Arthur's coronation and that of his queen, Guinevere:

The Welsh pedigrees of the saints of Britain (Bonedd y Seint Ynys Prydain) establish Saint Kentigern's lineage as follows:

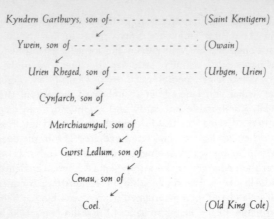

Kyndern Garthwys, son of- - - - - - - - - - - (Saint Kentigern)

Ywein, son of - - - - - - - - - - - - - - - - (Owain)

Urien Rheged, son of - - - - - - - - - - - (Urbgen, Urien)

Cynfarch, son of

Meirchiawngul, son of

Gwrst Ledlum, son of

Cenau, son of

Coel.   (Old King Cole)

Saint Kentigern, who is also called Saint Mungo, was known by his Welsh or Cymric name, *Kindyern,* which means "head chief." Thus, in Welsh he is called Prince. *Mungo,* as we have already seen, probably means "beloved."

J. R. R. Tolkein observed that Owain, according to the Welsh bard Taliesin, killed the Anglian king Ida of Bernicia, a death recorded in the *Anglo-Saxon Chronicle* for the year 560. According to Nennius (Tolkein also called it to our attention), Owain's father Urien warred against Ida's son Theodoric. King Urien died either in 572—for King Redderch (Rydderch) Hael ascended the throne of Rheged in 573—or in 592. King Ridderch Hael ruled the expanded British kingdom of Strathclyde after the Battle of Arthuret (Ardderyd), or Arthur's Head, fought in 573. Rheged, or Cumbria, was absorbed into this larger Strathclyde kingdom extending from Carlisle on the south to Dumbarton and the Clyde River on the north.

Thus, the pedigree, fragmentary though it is, attests to the historical King Urien and to the political situation after King Arthur's day. In his *Life of Saint Mungo* (Kentigern), Alexander Gits, S.J., states:*

> In the beginning of the sixth century Scotland south of the Clyde and Forth was still inhabited by the ancient Britons, who were bound together in a loose confederation known as the kingdom of Alclyde, or Strathclyde, as it was called in later times. Their military leader or Guledig, Arthur, in a series of battles between the two Roman walls of Tyne (Hadrian's Wall) and Forth (Antonine Wall), had temporarily crippled the power of the invading Saxons.

*A booklet (Glasgow, 1967, 1975, 1977) of 31 pages available at the Glasgow Cathedral, page 5).

If according to the major thrust of modern scholarship in the twentieth century, Arthur was only a legend drawn from Welsh or Irish fairy tales, the patron saint of Scotland was also, as the Historiographer Royal for Scotland P. Hume Brown admitted in 1911, legendary and not historical. If the North Britons, say the modern historians Myles Dillon and Nora Chadwick, could have consolidated and held a united kingdom in the north of Britain after Arthur's death, they could have withstood both the Picts in the north and the Angles (Saxons) from Bernicia, or Northumberland, to the south. As it was, eastern Scotland was overrun by the Angles in the seventh century, but not for long.

Unfortunately, the records of King Arthur's reign have been lost, so we must turn to the romances to learn that the King Urien who attended King Arthur's coronation was killed by Lancelot before King Arthur left for the continent. Otherwise, Arthur would have drafted him. No commander would have turned his back on his worst enemy and faced yet another enemy. Dillon and Chadwick theorized that these records and those of the reign of King Urien Rheged, following Arthur's death, were kept in some northern *scriptorium*, such as Carlisle. What remain are their fortresses or their emplacements—Old Carlisle (not the present city, which is the medieval one), and Dumbarton on the Clyde, Stirling on the Forth, Aberlady, and Dunpelder (Traprain Law). The ancient military road across Scotland still leads from Dumbarton due north four miles to the southern shore of Loch Lomond, then along Route A811, which cuts directly east, south of the Fords of Frew in ancient times, to Stirling Castle itself. This Dumbarton-Stirling line runs horizontally into the estuary of the Forth River, which separates the Edinburgh-Glasgow area of Scotland from the Highlands. Two more stunning sights than these vast fortresses of Dumbarton and Stirling, high upon giant mountains, would be hard to find. Thus, at eastern and at western sea, they massively anchor the line.

One would not expect King Arthur to be mentioned in connection with Glasgow, since that city as a religious capital dates from the second generation after him. One would expect King Arthur to be mentioned in connection with Dumbarton and Loch Lomond and also Stirling, and Geoffrey notably situated him at the first two sites. As we have seen, the writers of French romances place him predominantly at Carlisle. The ruins of Carlisle Castle in the present city of Carlisle date from 1092, when William Rufus laid their foundations. Marc Alexander's *Legendary Castles of the Border* mentions them and King Arthur's connection with a Northumbrian border tower of Sewingshields, as we have seen.* It is no longer standing.

The historian H. Munro Chadwick gave a clear picture of Britain in Arthur's day. Chadwick placed King Arthur and his heirs in what he desig-

---

*A pamphlet (Cumbria, undated).

nated the Heroic Age (500–650), which was a period of contending states. Then princes called "Gwallawg," who were the king named Urien and his descendants and clan, fought the Northumbrians, by whom they were eventually defeated (572–593). The former British princes reigned at Dumbarton, high on the red volcanic rock of Clyde, where Geoffrey often placed Arthur. Saint Columba later told King Rodercus at Dumbarton that he would die peacefully at home, and this "Rex Rederech," if he is the one who died at the Battle of Arthuret (573), was the "Erec" of Chrétien's romance *Erec et Enide*. The more stable states during King Arthur's lifetime would have been Rheged (Strathclyde), Dalriada, and Pictland north of the Antonine Wall.

The areas of shifting power would have been Lothian (middle Scotland), East Lothian (from Berwick to Edinburgh), and Northumbria where Logria begins. These are precisely the areas, as we have already seen in the *Lanzelet*, that Lancelot reconquered.

There have to be good reasons why the genealogy of Lancelot is the one most proudly preserved in the *Prose* or *Vulgate Lancelot*. Obviously, the work is about him. And obviously he has conquered territories in Scotland, which makes him a great king. But that is not all, for the genealogy of Perceval is also treasured. Could it be that behind the account of Lancelot and that of Perceval there lies a war for territory and for revenge? Do they represent two contending states?

There was a certain king named Claudas, goes the French narrative, whose kingdom is not named directly, only periphrastically as "la terre deserte" or the "waste londes." King Claudas waged a war against the father of Lancelot, whose name was Ban of "Benoïc."

Now that Lancelot has been placed fairly safely in Scotland, we may offer in support the Scottish metrical romance called *Lancelot du Lak*, for there Lancelot's father is called "Bane . . . king of Albanak."* Therefore Lancelot was, as we have guessed, probably born at Berwick, on the border of what was or was soon to be Northumbria. It would therefore follow that he began his campaign of reconquest, after an initial victory for the essential equipment and supplies, in his native East Lothian. For that reason we would expect him to be associated with Bamborough, called "Joyous Garde" by the French. As an infant he had to be sent away, which Adamnan says was a custom of the Picts; they sent their children to Islay or some western isle for fostering and for protection. If his life's goal was to reconquer his father's domains, then he conquered "Snowdon" or Stirling, known to the French as the Waste Land, less than two decades after the death of his father.

Alternate possibilities occurred, of course, to the busy French compilators across the Straits of Dover; and in the Pseudo-Map Cycle of the *Prose Lancelot*, they concocted the story that Lancelot was a Norman. Of course,

*v. 202

Lancelot died centuries before the Normans or Vikings even arrived in Normandie. To them, obviously nothing daunted, Benoïc became Saumur, the "waste land" became Berry, one of the most fertile regions in a fertile France, and the Lady of the Lake became the prioress of Fontevrault Abbey near Chinon, a royal establishment and royal necropolis. King Ban then became King Henry II buried in Fontevrault, and Lancelot became William Marshal, earl of Pembroke (d. 1219). By another leap, the Lady of the Lake became Queen Eleanor, devoted to her son King Richard I, who became King Claudas. Arthur of Brittany fitted in there somewhere, too. J. Neale Carman in *A Study of the Pseudo-Map Cycle of Arthurian Romance* has explained this further complication.

The genealogy of Lancelot, seen by him in a vision (*Quest of the Holy Grail*), traces his lineage to an apocryphal saint named Joseph of Arimathea, and therein lies another controversy. According to the Gospel of Nicodemus, the *Prose Lancelot*, and other Arthurian lore, a noble Jew named Joseph of Arimathea received the body of Christ from the cross and entombed it. He was later imprisoned in Jerusalem, but he escaped and traveled to Britain. As a premier missionary and disciple of Christ there, he converted kings and lesser persons to Christianity. In the Holy Land Joseph and his son Josephes had already converted two kings, Evelac and Seraphe, who then took the names of Mordrains and Nasciens. From Nasciens's son Celidoine (Caledonian?) were descended the nine original kings of Scotland. Now the Arthurian lore has derived Celidoine (Caledonian) as the first king of Scotland, a considerable feat. Moreover, before Merlin he knew the names of the planets and the courses of the stars. After him reigned eight rulers:

1. Warpus
2. Chrestiens
3. Alain li Gros
4. Helyas
5. Jonaans (who migrated to Wales)
6. Lancelot I (who married the king of Ireland's daughter)
7. Ban of Benoïc
8. Lancelot II (who sired a son by the Fisher King's daughter)

We now have a whole cast of new characters, the last of whom achieved the Quest of the Holy Grail.

This can be verified in *The Lost Books of the Bible and the Forgotten Books of Eden*. The William Smith *Dictionary of the Bible* gives Joseph of Arimathea, mentioned by both Mark and Luke, as probably a member of the Sanhedrin, who with Nicodemus received the body of Christ and entombed it. On the other hand, the Reverend Sabine Baring-Gould in *Lives of the British Saints*, calls the "legends . . . wholly worthless" and adds, "they must be passed over."

The authoritative Perceval manuscripts disagree. There was a Fisher King named Brons, who dwelled in the isles of Ireland. He was the father of Alain li Gros, called the great-grandson of Celidoine, according to Lancelot's genealogy. Alain's son was Perceval and was called "le Gallois," which refers him to ancient "Galles" in eastern Scotland and not to modern Wales. It was Perceval, not Galahad, says the *Didot-Perceval*, who achieved the Quest for the Holy Grail, who ended the perilous times, and who released the wounded King Brons to those angels who bore him aloft to heaven. After this victory, Merlin withdrew from the world. In these descriptions lies the first hint that the warring parties behind the Lancelot and the Perceval histories are these two houses, the only ones whose genealogies figure inside the twelfth- and thirteenth-century romances.

A second time, in the *Grand-Saint-Graal*, *The History of the Holy Grail*, the genealogy of Lancelot, now called the "rolette" of Celidone, is given in substantially similar terms:

1. Narpus
2. Nasciens
3. Elyan the grete
4. Ysayes
5. Jonaanz
6. Lawnceloz
7. Bans
8. Lawncelot, "who was a sinner, like a hound"
9. Galath, "like a flood" (who achieved the Grail)

This same manuscript acknowledges a person named Bron(s), who was the second Grail Keeper after Joseph of Arimathea and who was, in fact, the father of an "Alein," twelfth among his twelve sons. Chapter 55 of the *Grand-Saint-Graal* gives the succession of Grail Kings as follows:

Joseph of Arimathea
Josephes, his son
Alein
Josue
Aminadappe
Catheloys
Mangel (or Manaal)
Lanbar

Pellean
Pelles, whose daughter Pelle (?) bore the son to Lancelot
Galahad

These two books of the *Prose Lancelot* manage early in the thirteenth century to supplant Perceval with Galahad, to oust Perceval's line from among the most sainted, and to establish Lancelot's son as the most perfect of all King Arthur's companions of the Round Table. Perceval's aunt, identified as queen of the Waste Land, explains that there have been three great fellowships: (1) the table of Christ, (2) the table of the Holy Grail, which Joseph of Arimathea brought into Britain, and (3) Merlin's Round Table of King Arthur and his companions, which was a secret military order.

Although altogether there are five Galahads in Arthurian literature, only three concern the Grail. The first is a son of Joseph of Arimathea. The second is Lancelot himself, called Galahad at baptism and Lancelot when kinged. The third is his "perfectly good" son, borne by the Fisher King's daughter, perhaps named Pelle or else Elaine, and ninth in descent from the first king of Scotland. The name *Galahad* is from the Bible, where it designates three different persons and a place.

The first Perceval telling, the *Conte del graal*, which Chrétien, according to his habit, left unfinished in the last decades of the twelfth century, explains that Perceval's father had been killed and that his last surviving child was raised by his mother in the Waste Forest, five days distant from Arthur's court at Carlisle. Setting out upon his adventures, Perceval killed King Clamadex and wedded the princess Blanchefleur, whom Clamadex was persecuting, at her castle and kingdom of Beau-Repaire. Before this, he had already killed the Red Knight, who had stolen golden cups from Arthur's Carlisle. Perceval's adventure at the Grail Castle is cut short by Gawain's adventure on the same quest.

As if it were an intentional correction of the Chrétien version, the English or Thornton manuscript called *Sir Perceval of Galles* not only clarifies but rectifies the situation. Sir Percyvelle the Galayse (or "de Galays") was their youngest son. Thus, just as with Lancelot, more than one hero albeit lineal descendants, bears the same noble and family name. King Arthur's sister, Sir Percyvelle's mother, was named, we are now informed, not Blanchefleur but Achefleur.

Percyvelle wedded Lufamour, whose castle is the same Caerlaverock, called also Castle of Maidens (a corruption of *maidan*, or place of assembly) and Maydene-lande. Her enemy was a "sowdane" or "Sarazene," or a club-wielding Pictish warrior. (Savage warriors wielding clubs figure as supporters on several armorial bearings of Scotland.) His name was Golrotherame. In this version also Perceval had previously killed the Red Knight, and for the same reason: five golden cups. Here too Perceval became king of Lufamour's lands. Thence he returned home to visit his mother, but he ultimately died in the Holy Land.

While there is no Gawain or secondary parallel track, the reader learns that Gawain and Perceval are first cousins, sisters' sons. Therefore King Arthur had two sisters, at least, both of whom married kings, Loth and Percyvelle. The latter seems originally to have been king of the Waste Land, although only his widow, Perceval's mother, and Perceval's aunt are so designated, as former queens, or both dispossessed queens of the Waste Land. Such a queen, according to Malory, also accompanied King Arthur to Avalon, after the fateful Battle of Camlan.

Through the study of the younger Perceval the chronology of King Arthur's reign, as established by Geoffrey of Monmouth, is glimpsed again. The adventures of Perceval seem to occupy a period of roughly seven years, and they end the "enchantments" of Britain. At the time when Perceval first arrives at his royal uncle's court, the king has just completed the conquest of the western isles. Seven or so years later, Perceval is inaugurated as Grail King, or Grail Keeper, if the two offices are identical, which seems the case. At this installation the Quest of the Round Table is ended. The thirteenth seat at Table is mended and occupied. At this time, then, King Arthur leaves for his continental campaign.

The *Perlesvaus* or Glastonbury manuscript now proves invaluable, for in its branch 1 the author carefully established further data concerning the lineage of Perceval (here called Perlesvax). Perceval's paternal ancestor was a "Nichodemus" *of the Valleys of Camelot.* He owned fifteen castles, most prominent among which was the renowned Camelot. These domains occupied a broad, fertile area called the Vale or Valleys of Camelot, from the chief seat, which stood on a promontory, at the head of the valleys. The next heir was Gais li Gros of Hermit's Cross, whose son was the Alain li Gros who appears among the ancestors of Lancelot.

Alain li Gros married Yglais, who was a niece of Joseph of Arimathea. By this time the family holdings had dwindled to the chief seat, Camelot. This most dstinguished bride of Alain li Gros had three powerful brothers: (1) King Fisherman of the Grail Castle, (2) King Pelles, also called King Hermit, whose son slew his mother, and (3) the King of Castle Mortal. Thus, the lineage of a father and a son who were both named Perceval creates a puzzle for the reader and one that will not be solved easily. By one account Perceval is King Arthur's nephew. By another, he is considered the nephew of Joseph of Arimathea, and this despite the chronological discrepancy of several hundred years.

Perceval's story takes its departure among the declining fortunes of a once very great line of kings, but the hero's maternal connections are even more illustrious because, through Arthur and through Joseph of Arimathea, he is connected closely to some secret fellowship and to a most highly revered position at the Grail Castle. Perceval's sister here is named Dindrane.

Sir Thomas Malory understood that King Arthur had at least two sisters. One was named Margawse, and she married King Loth and bore him four sons, the oldest of whom was Gawain. She, or another sister, alleges Malory, bore Modred to King Arthur. Another of Arthur's sisters was called Morgan (Morgana, Anna), and she married King Urien of Gorre, whose sons were named Urien. Marie de France knew that they were cousins of Gawain.

Wolfram von Eschenbach worked out for Parzival, whose name reproduces the English spelling of *Percyvelle,* the most complicated genealogy. Essentially it differs little, still giving Perceval's mother's descent from two Grail Kings (Frimutel and Titurel), with two brothers, one of whom is the Grail King Anfortas. On his father's side Parzival descends from the same common ancestor as King Arthur, and his cousins are Gawain, Cundrie, and Gareth. His wife's name is Condwiramurs, also similar to the English spelling, and here he has a half brother and two sons, one of whom is Lohengrin.

One of Chrétien's continuators has Perceval say, as Lancelot himself declared his birthplace: "There at 'Sinadon' (Snowdon) I was born." Thus, one has again a name, and the same name for the chief fortress of that kingdom, the Waste Land; and that name now is Stirling.

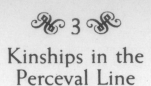

3

Kinships in the
Perceval Line

The famous Perceval story unfolds against a bright middle ground of relatives, the hero himself silhouetted dark and unfathomable before their colorful persons. Not content to transmit Perceval's story as they had it, however, the medieval narrators grasped at exotic details in order to waft them all off into fairyland. For instance, Perceval's enemy in his home territory is the Lord of the Moors, from which the German version derives the mistaken idea that the hero's brother is a black man. Second, Perceval and his mother, having escaped slaughter in the Waste Land, are hiding in the "foret soutaine," which prosaically designates their Lower Woodland. The German text gives this an exotic twist by mistaking the adjective for some nonexistent Arab country called "Soltane." Perceval's brutality, which is quite consistent with the age, is generally not honestly presented as ancient savagery but as clumsy, lovable, and boyish stupidity.

In branch 15 of *Perlesvaus* the brutal red hero Perceval shows his true colors as he finally kills his mother's predator, the Lord of the Moors, by disarming him and then suspending him head down in a vat filled with the blood of his eleven vassals. In branch 18 Perceval's uncle, who is the King of Castle Mortal, has reconquered the Grail Castle, relapsed, and returned to whatever his former religion had been. Perceval has hastened there to salvage the Grail Castle's treasures and reconvert the inhabitants to Christianity. At the approach of this terribly cruel nephew, the old king pierces himself with his sword and leaps from the castle wall into the sea, which runs swift and deep there.

Among such frightful pictures Perceval's blond and aged father eludes us still. The German version calls him an Angevin, which is simply a compliment to King Henry II. The Welsh *Peredur* recalls him as an earl from the north named Efrawg or York, and again York, which is nearer, has been mistaken for the distant Stirling. The French manuscripts consistently name Perceval's father Alain li Gros.

Her great connections prompted most early narrators to visualize the loud-voiced but illustrious mother of Perceval against such a family arrangement:

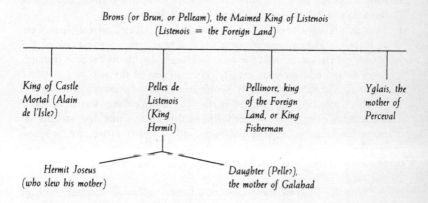

Brons (or Brun, or Pelleam), the Maimed King of Listenois
(Listenois = the Foreign Land)

| King of Castle Mortal (Alain de l'Isle?) | Pelles de Listenois (King Hermit) | Pellinore, king of the Foreign Land, or King Fisherman | Yglais, the mother of Perceval |

Hermit Joseus (who slew his mother)

Daughter (Pelle?), the mother of Galahad

Although dispossessed of her realm, Perceval's mother is always deferentially saluted as the Widow Lady of Camelot. There in one of her demesnal forests, she has sought refuge for herself and her last surviving son. The French manuscripts give Perceval a brother named Agloval, identified as king of Escavalon. Leaving aside the interpreters, who fancied Perceval some analphabetic Tarzan emerging from the trees, the story says he encountered a party of mounted warriors traveling on King Arthur's business. Whether or not the men came expressly to summon Perceval, now that he was of age to bear arms, they traveled a road through his parents' realm, like ordinary mortals presumably. This information, plus various other clues, begins to provide a real location and the following preliminary conclusions:

1. The Waste Forest (Chrétien vv. 75, 296, 390, 2953) is near a pass or strait, defined as a narrow defile in the mountains near the Widow Lady's chief seat. It is called "li destroit de Valdone" or "li destroit desnaudone." "Dodone," Lancelot's kingdom by conquest, is mentioned prominently again. This was the same realm, then, as Perceval's Valleys of Dodone, where, by his own testimony about his birthplace, he was born: "in Snowdon."

   R. L. Graeme Ritchie, who in *Chrétien de Troyes and Scotland* made the first real progress in Arthurian literature by identifying Caerlaverock, believed that Perceval's realm was in western Scotland, perhaps in the Valley of the Doon in Galloway, between Ayr and Dumfries. For his part, Roger Sherman Loomis concluded and maintained unreasonably that Perceval was born on the nearly barren crags of Mount Snowdon in Wales. The Widow Lady's holdings formed one of the chief and richest realms of her day, however, and included the splendid seat where Lancelot was crowned king.

2. King Arthur's castle in Carlisle is five days from this fortress and site of Snowdon, a distance of about one hundred fifty miles.

3. Snowdon is mentioned as standing near fertile valleys, where there were as many as fifteen separate domains, such as that of the Lord of the Moors. There are extensive moors, or mosses, beside this realm. It stands upon an exceedingly wide estuary, once an arm of the sea.

4. Perceval's sword was forged at "Cotovatre," which by common consent is "Scots' Water," of the Firth of Forth. The smith's name was Trebuchet. There have been immense ironworks in that area to this day, at Carron.

5. Perceval's kingdom adjoins Galloway with its ports in western Scotland serving the Irish Sea.

6. Snowdon is the chief seat of the Valleys of Camelot and/or the name of the castle.

Thus, the Lord of the Moors could very well have dwelled south of the Forth River, in the fertile clay estuary that was crossed then as now by the old Roman road from the south. Passing Bannockburn, the road continued to Stirling on its cliff and then crossed the Forth by a narrow defile in the hills, where, as the *Prose Lancelot* also confirms, the men had to pass single file. This was the only, single crossing of the Forth, or the celebrated Fords of Frew. The manuscript in French calls it the Straits of Snowdon. Hence the Roman road continued into the far north. Since this was the only road to cross the Vale of Menteith, or the only road north from King Arthur's realm, it is reasonable to expect that it should have been mentioned. And furthermore, the Fords of Frew, what Chrétien calls the gorges of Dodone, were long considered one of the wonders of Scotland. These precisions seem to confirm Ritchie's belief that Chrétien de Troyes had received privileged information about Scotland.

7. Perceval's maternal relatives came from the isles of the Irish Sea, and there he was bound to fight for "Beau Repaire" castle and his fiancée. (The French kingdom of "Beau Repaire" becomes "Brobarz" in the German, and even "Pelrapaire.")

8. One of King Arthur's castles at Carlisle was not inland but on the seacoast, namely, the Solway Firth, says the Chrétien text. Thus, such a fortress is also, as the *Peredur* gave it, *Caer Llion,* which is Welsh for Castle of the Waves. Geoffrey of Monmouth's Caerleon is probably this "Caerleon" in the Carlisle area itself.

9. A final piece of information corroborates the site of the kingdom called the Waste Land. In the "Quest" section of the *Prose Lancelot* Perceval finds himself stranded on an island and subject to hallucinations. Here he receives the visit of a damsel in exile, whose home is the Waste Land. In the course of their conversation she mentions the fact that this kingdom is the one bisected by a wide river called, not by its Latin name *Forth*, but by the name *Moss Water*, "l'eau Marçoise." In Scotland the word *Moss* still designates distinctively the peat marshes on either side of the Forth River. Therefore from the damsel's words one can assume that as a child Perceval lived somewhere south of the River Forth, in what would reasonably have been called the "Lower Woodland" or "Forest" of that extensive kingdom.

As he departs into the world from his mother's Waste Land, the castle of Snowdon, the Forth estuary, and the Valleys of Camelot, then, Perceval follows a route that can now be traced. First, he descends the Roman road from the Firth of Forth south toward Carlisle, a journey of five days. King Arthur is the first of the many "uncles" upon whom the youth calls. He receives young Perceval warmly, shelters him, instructs him, and sends him on his way. Since his way is well understood to have been directed toward the service of the Holy Grail at the Grail Castle, whenever he shall have merited reception there, then King Arthur may have been, as chief lord of the Round Table, a prominent member, if not head of the secret Grail brotherhood. What that fellowship was and how it functioned can only be learned from a study of the Perceval manuscripts, especially when they are authenticated by other Arthurian texts.

Departing Arthur's seacoast castle of Caer Llion, or Carlisle, Perceval immediately crosses a plain, or the Eden River estuary, along a very large body of water with many tributaries, that is, the Solway Firth. There he presents himself at his second sponsor's castle, that of his tutor Gorneman de Gorhaut. This second noble "uncle" instructs Perceval in military matters, or makes of him a trained warrior, or "ordained him a knight," said the medieval modernizers. This succession of male sponsors characterizes Perceval's story more than any other single feature, and sets it quite apart from Gawain's long series of military victories or Lancelot's lightning territorial conquests. Perceval visits their fortresses, seemingly presenting himself for inspection and vouching for his birthright, and demanding compensation and endorsement from these "uncles," or collateral affinities.

By ancient British law, it is said, relatives through the ninth degree were affected in any serious legal process, such as the murder of a father or the reiving of such a domain as Camelot. Those closest to the plaintiff owed the greatest portion of the damages. Perceval's visits read as if he were simultaneously being indemnified for some past losses, private and real, and

recognized by right of birth, heir nominated to the Grail kingship and kingdom. In each case, young Perceval gives proof of his savage, unleashed
strength and his purpose—that of a furious avenger.

Despite its logic and order, the Chrétien manuscript fails at the precise
point where it failed for Lancelot: it omits directions from the second to the
third castle. Perceval appears next at Blanchefleur's "virtually dead city" of
Beau-Repaire, which is located in another kingdom. There the earth has
been laid bare, the houses have been demolished, the abbeys for monks and
nuns stand deserted. The poor damsel is beset by a club-wielding giant, a
ravisher of the isles. According to Chrétien, Perceval does not instantly con-
summate his marriage, but other sources believed that he fathered sons there.
Neither case would invalidate his claim to sanctity later, at the Grail Castle,
where he could, according to primitive Christianity, repudiate his wife at
some future date.

The most interesting fact, repeated several times, is this: the Grail
Castle lies within a day's journey from Beau-Repaire, Pelrapaire, or *Maydene*
Land. In fact, it is sometimes possible to hear the bells of the Grail Castle
toll when one is in "Maiden" Land. Presumably, then, this "Maiden" Land is
not Caerlaverock but is to the east of the Grail Castle, whence the prevail-
ing winds in Britain would be more apt to carry the sound. Second, the
name of Beau-Repaire suggests that it was some sort of convent for women,
and for maidens a refuge from the world. The English translation *Maiden
Land* reinforces the suspicion. Third, the pious Blanchefleur later dowered
the chapel of Aaron at King Arthur's Carlisle, referred to here as Dinasdaron, City of Aaron.

Thus, we can see that Geoffrey of Monmouth's churches of Julius and
Aaron probably were at Carlisle. The new heroine Blanchefleur sounds like
Saints Bridget, Radegunde, and Clothilde, other contemporary princesses
who had sought refuge in convents.

Fourth, we now know that the Grail Castle is in the "Foreign Land,"
which informs us that the people there speak a foreign tongue and live under
their own sovereign, not necessarily or not always under King Arthur. The
Didot-Perceval adds that this kingdom is in the western isles, which lie across
from or facing Ireland.

The one "uncle" whom Perceval usually visits twice, which visits correspond to his two visits to the Grail Castle, is the King Hermit. At the first
visit the hero usually swears to his innocence. The second visit directly
precedes his inauguration at the Grail Castle and his withdrawal from the
secular world. At that instant the King Hermit, who in *Parzival* is called
Trevrizent, instructs him more fully in Christianity, answers his objections,
and tells him more about the Holy Grail. No man can accede to the Grail
kingdom unless he has been called to it, is known in heaven for his good

deeds, and has been called by his own private and sacred name. Thus, the moment when Perceval first knows his name is a high point in each telling.

Since it was apparently King Arthur who first summoned Perceval, who in the English manuscript burst into tears at the sight of him, and who presumably must first have nominated him for the Grail lordship, it is interesting to observe their second meeting. The hero has returned to the vicinity of the uncle's castle, which stands near the sea at Carlisle. It has snowed recently, and an entranced Perceval stands looking at the red blood from a black bird on the white snow.

The scene is very famous, and justly so, for red, white, and black are the three sacred colors of religion. We are being told that the sacrifice of Perceval is drawing near. Only his cousin Gawain can revive Perceval or draw him safely from his meditation.

Now, King Arthur left Carlisle expressly to meet his nephew on this snowy plain, and he returned that same night. Why else did he trouble, if not to check on Perceval's progress toward holiness?

The Perceval narrators usually identify this hero by a second, similar, and related tale of a circular meadow, which is his world, bisected by a river (the Forth) over which sheep are jumping. As they jump, they change color, from white (Christian) to black (Pictish) and vice versa. As we know, the Forth separated Lothian from northern Pictland.

Such incidents, the insistence upon a black and white symbolism, and the open use of the words *Templar* and *Knights Templar* in *Parzival*, have related Perceval, and the Round Table also, to this twelfth century crusading order and to Beau-séant, their argent-and-sable banner. The Knights Templar, it should be recalled, were established under a Benedictine rule, c. 1118. Members wore white mantles over their armor, and squires wore black mantles. At the request of Saint Bernard they wore on these mantles the red cross of the Crusades. They were quartered in or near Solomon's Temple in Jerusalem. Doubtless, Perceval and his story were favorites with these doughty warriors.

The *Perlesvaus* gives Perceval a total of fifteen male instructors or sponsors, or "uncles," and this number is certainly significant. First was Joseph of Arimathea, the hero's great-uncle. Then come King Fisherman at the Grail Castle, King Hermit, and the King of Castle Mortal, plus the eleven brothers of his father Alain li Gros (even though all twelve are dead by the time of Perceval's birth). *Sir Perceval* adds King Arthur to this list of fifteen. The other French and the German manuscripts corroborate the King Hermit, more often called the Fisher King, Chrétien adding the grandfather Bron, who is the third, the old King or Maimed King. The Welsh *Peredur* mentions only the Maimed or Lame King and the Grail King, the *Prose Lancelot* insisting upon the former. The *Sir Perceval* points out, lest it be forgotten, that

King Loth was also Perceval's uncle, and so, of course, both Lancelot and Gawain were his cousins.

The *Didot-Perceval* version gives Perceval two last teachers of extraordinary power and goodness: Merlin and the grandfather Bron. Perceval learned from Merlin the directions to the Grail Castle all over again. Merlin had come from Northumberland, says the text, and *dressed like a reaper wore a scythe about his neck.* He told Perceval that his quest for the Grail would end within the year, and that his adventures were being recorded by Merlin's "master" Blayse, who would eventually join the new king at the Grail Castle. By having him meet the Grim Reaper, authors warned their readers that *Perceval's end was to be death,* or a death in life, for at the Grail Castle he would quit the world. If in his turn he became a castrated king or Maimed King, in a ceremony that Robert Graves says in *The White Goddess* was a ritual wounding of the ancient kings, then the meeting with Merlin was doubly dire and doubly appropriate.

In certain versions dire warnings are multiplied whenever Perceval sojourns at the fearsome Chessboard Castle. There in some horrible ritual, which comes into Irish and Arthurian literature from ancient Egypt, it seems, the hero plays chess with Death for his life. In *The Wandering of the Soul* Alexandre Piankoff tells how the Egyptian game of draughts played on a thirty-square board represented the gaming for one's soul—a legend that can be found spread all over the world. His examples commence with well-known Irish legends, "The Wooing of Etain" and "Dairmaid and Grainne," and the Arthurian Tristan-Isolde story. There it was King Mark who played and lost. After Perceval loses the game three times in a row, he attempts to throw the pieces into the water and deny this omen. The third ominous portent concerns one of his trials, a search for a white stag's head. In another weird episode he must combat the Black Knight of the Tomb. The Welsh version gives him frightful tasks against the Black Worm of the Barrow near a collective burial site called the Dolorous Mound. The idea seems to be that during this long period of harried and initiatory adventures he must constantly display unqualified courage, redress wrongs, earn credits for himself, and then seek absolution for all his crimes on earth so that, having put several earthly kingdoms to rights as best he can, Perceval may then be forgiven and be consecrated only to the service of God.

Quite a new, surprising view of women in the Dark Ages is eventually forced upon that reader who perseveres in comparing the kinships in the various Perceval tellings. Many of his teachers, and those most critical of him, were not men but outspoken women. Chrétien introduces the first such learned person as Perceval's cousin. The same girl enters three times in Wolfram's *Parzival,* where her name is given as Sigune. A second learned princess to scold and instruct, in this case not only Perceval but the whole Grail company assembled at his inauguration, is Gawain's brilliant sister Cundrie. She seems to have inherited Merlin's lore, for at her final appearance she delivers a set oration in the course of which she charts the planets. In the Glastonbury *Perlesvaus* the hero's sister Dandrane (or Dindrane) reproaches her brother much as Sigune did. In this case, however, her own spiritual progress becomes more the focus of the author's interest. This same sister, never named, appears in the *Didot-Perceval*, as both saintly and learned. In the Welsh *Peredur* she is portrayed differently—cursing Perceval—and described as handsome and auburn-haired (the reddish hair color then much admired). The "Quest" section of the *Prose Lancelot* tells a pitiful story of this sister's sacrifice of her life too.

When Perceval first meets his female cousin in Chrétien's early account, he has just visited the Grail Castle for the first time. He now learns from her what he did not know before—that he has failed the test. From this cousin he hears the major points of his life:

1. He departs abruptly from Camelot, which caused his mother's death;
2. He stupidly neglects to ask questions at the Grail Castle when he is permitted to see the service, the processional, and the hallowed objects used in the sacrament.
3. When his cousin asks him if he realizes who the Fisher King is and he thoughtlessly replies that he was one of the men seen the previous evening fishing from a boat rowed by another man.

Shocked at this lack of intelligence, Perceval's cousin explains who this personage was: the Maimed King who suffers cruelly from an old wound and is unable to use his legs. This Fisher King had actually deigned to shelter the unworthy Perceval overnight. Had stupid Perceval seen the hallows: the lance, the Grail, the candles, and the silver platter? What were they? He saw them, he replies, but he did not inquire. Angrily she calls him a name!

4. Suddenly Perceval knows his name and who he really is. Before leaving his cousin, he also learns where his sword was forged and where it can be repaired: near his home castle in Camelot.

This same exchange, now between Perceval and Sigune in *Parzival*, takes place in the forest of Brizlan, or Broceliande, which has over the centuries been stubbornly sought in Brittany, France. According to Wolfram also, it lies not more than two days from the Forth estuary, and on the main road to Carlisle. Thus, Broceliande Forest must be in the southern Uplands, probably what is the Ettrick Forest, or the Kershope. The word *Broceliande* is less likely to be French than to represent a clumsy translation from some

Celtic language, such as from *bro* (land) and *llan* (temple), or land of the temple.* Just south of Perceval here, or on the next day's journey, he would be passing through the Kershope Forest, where modern geographers of Britain continue today to indicate on their road maps King Arthur's campsites and staging center. Those would be, then, just a few miles north of Hadrian's Wall.

The splendidly auburn-haired Sigune in Wolfram begins by informing her cousin Perceval of his name, helpfully, of course, for he had not yet even arrived at King Arthur's court, to say nothing of the Grail Castle. When she meets him a second time, she explains to him the origin of his sword and where it can be mended. Now he has just come from the Grail Castle, and Sigune can berate him soundly. He saw the bleeding lance, the Grail, the maidens wreathed in flowers, the candlesticks, a great hall with one hundred couches and yet unbelievably asked not a single question? The saddest part is, as Perceval now realizes, that the castle can only be found by chance. And chances are he will never come across it again.

Perceval lives to see his cousin Sigune one last time, when she has withdrawn from the world into a tiny cell, in which rigid sequestration she soon expires. Even at her death hour Sigune still attempts to assist Perceval. It seems that Gawain's sister Cundrie, she who rides the ambling mule, brings Sigune her food once a week. Since she has just now left the hermitage, she can perhaps be overtaken. Although Perceval hastens after Cundrie, he loses her track. Now one suspects that Cundrie is the same Grail Messenger who led the frantic Lancelot during his pursuit of the captive Queen Guinevere.

Gawain's sister Cundrie, as she is portrayed in Wolfram, is also King Loth's daughter and the sister of an ugly dwarf called Malcreatiure. It was he who earlier drove Lancelot in the cart, and he was not a gnome but a real person. Wolfram describes the Loathly Damsel, who is nicknamed "the Witch": blue silk gown, hat trimmed with peacock feathers, black braided hair and eyebrows, hairy face, pug nose, with big teeth and ears. She had let her fingernails grow into claws, and she carried a jeweled whip and rode her mule jauntily, one leg over the animal's neck. After having scolded King Arthur, Cundrie eloquently chastised Perceval, cursing his "pretty face and handsome thighs." Before bursting into tears, she has driven him to action, told him his lineage, and predicted both his future and the history of the Arthurian realm.

No person in the Arthurian literature surpasses the weird Cundrie for learning, style, and nobility. She and Sigune are perfect opposites: the former an aggressive, fearless, and worldly noblewoman, the latter an other-

---

*The English manuscript *Of Arthour and of Merlin* (EETS, 1973) understands the Welsh phonetics and calls it "Brocklond."

worldly nun. After Perceval's inauguration, everyone will be once more obliged to listen to Cundrie's final harangue.

Four other authors present briefer glimpses of Perceval's sister, but only the *Perlesvaus* names her Dandrane. Were the "Quest" section author a modern novelist he would have called her the damsel of the silken tent or the temptress of the desert island.

When Perceval first met Dandrane on his road and accompanied her back to Camelot, the two showed affection for and trust in each other. During Perceval's absence Gawain had guaranteed the safety of his mother and her daughter for a year, but now Perceval has returned to kill the Lord of the Moors. Meanwhile, his sister stops at the Graveyard Perilous for a holy relic, a piece of Christ's shroud from the Holy Sepulcher at Jerusalem. Dandrane impresses upon her brother how urgently he must search for the Grail Castle because of the King of Castle Mortal and his wars against it, and furthermore because King Pelles has left the world to become a hermit. During the occupation of the Grail Castle by the King of Castle Mortal, all the hallows have remained safely hidden, and the Grail company has apparently dispersed. As Perceval rides forth from the forest, he stops in the shade of a tree to admire the splendid view of Camelot in the distance, laved by its river. His mother has him pay his respects at the chapel of the four marble columns, which stands between the forest and the castle, where Joseph of Arimathea lies buried. Here Lancelot learned his name and was told that he would fail to advance in the hierarchy of the Grail Castle.

Perceval advances, however, and meets his sister on the road out of Stirling three years after his initial departure from Camelot. By this time his mother has already died, a loss with which Perceval is bitterly reproached.

His sister conducts Perceval to their uncle's hermitage, but here the author has sadly confused Perceval's lineage. He does report the tradition, however, that Joseph of Arimathea had the Grail, which was the vessel containing the blood of the crucified Christ. According to his uncle-hermit, it was Christ who prophesied the advent of Perceval as Grail Keeper and who decreed that the young hero would eventually find the Grail, after much seeking, of course. The present Fisher King is Perceval's grandfather Bron, he says, and he cannot be healed until he transmits his charge to his grandson. The hermit urges Perceval to avoid murder and sin, for Christ so loved his lineage that He gave to them the care of His flesh and blood. His sister took pride in Perceval, felt joy to be with him then, and wept when he left after a few hours. Four years later he returned to see her tomb.

In the *Quest of the Holy Grail* Perceval's sister establishes the Grail achievement for three youths: Bors, Perceval, and Galahad. The most complete and the latest of all tellings, this text seems to follow learned theologians into the doctrine of transubstantiation, established in 1215 at the Fourth

Lateran Council, whereby substances of the Eucharist become divine. In the course of her instruction she also tells the origin of the two kingdoms known as the Waste Land. Grain crops failed there, fruit trees bore no fruit, and fish were not to be found in the waters because of a terrible duel between a pagan king and the missionaries from the Holy Land, who were ancestors of Perceval and Galahad. The damsel also establishes for us the same location of the Grail Castle: on an island, facing Ireland.

The death of Perceval's sister occurs in the Waste Land, at a castle where a damsel is afflicted with leprosy. Any virgin passing by is forced to donate a basin full of blood as a cure for the damsel, but if that maiden is a king's daughter and a queen's, then her blood will surely cure the sick girl. Perceval's sister volunteers. Before her arm is cut, she makes her will. She asks to be placed in a ship and allowed to float to the holy city of Sarras, where her body will eventually lie beside those of Perceval and Galahad in the Holy Land. Her dying words urged Perceval and his companions to continue searching for the Grail Castle.

Perhaps only Perceval's aunt speaks with more authority than this sister, for she was more able to develop the theology underlying the three fellowships: Christ and the Apostles, Joseph of Arimathea and the Grail, and King Arthur and the Round Table. That last fellowship was designed by Merlin to represent the earth and the orbits of the planets and of the stars.

In Geoffrey of Monmouth's beautiful Latin poem the *Vita Merlini* (Life of Merlin), Merlin was both observer of the heavens and prophetic poet. He asked for an observatory in the forest, with seventy doors and windows (v. 555 ff.), and learning from the stars and planets he prophesied that Dumbarton would fall and not be rebuilt, and that Scotland would fall.

Merlin also foresaw (v. 614) that Carlisle would stand without a shepherd after Arthur's passing. Geoffrey had certainly written his poem by 1150, or seventy years before the French *Quest* was composed.

These learned kinswomen of Perceval are plainly members of the Grail community, but it still is not clear how or in what capacity. It is true, of course, that through the time of Saint Augustine of Hippo (354–430), women such as the oracles and sibyls were accepted into the company of Christian theologians and were honored like them.

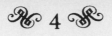

4

Directions
to the
Grail Castle

Itt is not Camelot but the Grail Cas-
tle that is the most important place inside the kingdom of King Arthur. We
know that here King Arthur will be interred and that here his Queen Guinevere
was preparing at her own expense a lavish and splendid tomb for the king.
We also know that Arthur was royally transported to the Grail Castle after
his fatal wounding at the Battle of Camlan.

The Grail Castle is also the residence of Merlin in his function as
recorder of the events of that kingdom and in his role as the Grim Reaper.

During its relapse into paganism and its rule by King Urien and his
deputy the magician or Druid Bademagus, the site of the future Grail Castle,
as King Arthur and Queen Guinevere would build it, was coveted by warring
factions. To them it must have been a site of inestimable holiness, like Notre-
Dame-de-Paris or Delphi in Greece or Mont-Saint-Michel in France.

What we need in order to dispel the theories almost universally held
for centuries that King Arthur and the Grail Castle were legends only are
directions to the Grail Castle.

To date most writers have called the Grail, the Grail kingship, and
the Grail Castle a pagan legend. In this conclusion they have followed such
leaders as Jessie L. Weston, Dorothy Kempe, and Alfred Nutt. The latest
expression of this school of thought comes from Richard Cavendish's *King
Arthur of the Grail*. Here the Grail itself is said to have been derived from
several religions: Christianity, Celtic paganism, classical mysteries, and Byzantine, Persian, Jewish, and Islamic traditions plus the Gnostic heresy or
Catharism. The resultant manuscripts are here labeled "fragments of a coherent pagan myth, muddled up by medieval story-tellers." What is worse,
says Cavendish, is that the Grail hero wins his kingship outside the channels

of the church. The hero is not instructed by churchmen but "taught by a hermit, an unauthorized maverick" in his solitary retreat, outside the church.

And yet in Britain there was no organized church supervised by Rome and therefore no orthodoxy of undisputed authority. It is true that Perceval wins his kingship largely by right of birth, which means that in those days the priesthood was still at least partially hereditary. The Grail Castle was not only a legend in its time and in ours but a real place. Its last kings, Perceval and Galahad, were real men.

Thus far, the study of a real Perceval has established his starting point on the Quest of the Holy Grail as Snowdon, which is Stirling in the Forth estuary. Thence he moves southward to King Arthur's principal seat at Carlisle. His wife, or affianced bride, resides one step from the end of the quest, at a site whence the bells of the Grail Castle can sometimes be heard. Between Carlisle and the Grail Castle, presumably, reside Perceval's various teachers and relatives. Through this middle, unknown area Perceval, his sister, his cousin, his foes, and the other Grail questers travel to and fro. The other questors are the two unsuccessful heroes, Lancelot and Gawain, and the successful seeker, Lancelot's son Galahad. King Arthur also makes this same round-trip journey from Carlisle to the Grail Castle.

Introducing his famous Grail Quest book, the *Grand-Saint-Graal* of around 1200, the anonymous author refers us to the year 717. This is of utmost importance. Nobody can say that this anonymous churchman invented his *Grand-Saint-Graal*. The work to which he refers us is attested by two of the most important churchmen of that era: Helinand de Froidmont (c. 1170–1230) and Vincent de Beauvais (c. 1190–1264). Both men, who were not only churchmen of impeccable reputation but also historians and chroniclers of renown, bear witness to the fact that the Grail material descended to them from the Dark Ages, and the year 717 (see Appendix).

In his *Chronicle of Helinandus* the monk of Froidmont tells us that the Holy Grail was the dish from which Christ partook of the Last Supper. The *Grand-Saint-Graal* begins with this allusion to Vincent de Beauvais and to Helinand de Froidmont. We recall that Chrétien found his Lancelot manuscript at Beauvais, whose clerymen had assisted King David I of Scotland to rebuild his abbeys and churches.

The anonymous author of the *Grand-Saint-Graal*, which is known in English as the *Quest for the Book of the Holy Grail*, begins his book as if he had just seen a vision of 717. In that vision he saw Christ Himself. Christ gave to a monk inside White Britain (Scotland or Albion), a wonderful book that He, Christ Himself, had written. It was a small book, small enough to fit into the palm of a hand. This book of Christ consisted of four parts: (1) lineage, (2) Holy Grail, (3) the terrors to come, and (4) the commencement of marvels. Because the monk doubted the words of Christ, he lost or misplaced the little holy book. In his vision of this incident, however, the anonymous author of the *Grand-Saint-Graal* learned where it had gone and how it could be recovered. For this reason, he undertook the arduous writing of his book, determined to reveal the secrets that the book of Christ contained.

Most curiously, the quest of Perceval duplicates the quest of our own author. We seem therefore to be dealing with a ritual quest preliminary to the refusing, or admitting and inauguration, of a new Grail King at the Grail Castle of unknown whereabouts.

We read the *Grand-Saint-Graal* with a sense of mounting excitement, as if it were a future Grail King speaking to us. He begins his journey at the same spot from which Perceval began his, the plains around the Valley of Scotland ("es plains de walescog"). Thence he proceeded to the junction of the seven roads, near Carlisle.

We really are at Carlisle, and nowhere else, because of what follows next: details about the sacred stone (*perron*). Here was a sacred stone called "anvil," from which the boy Arthur had drawn the sword prior to his recognition as the future battle chieftain. We have another testimony, now from Marie de France, that this same stone was a mounting stage upon which passengers to Avalon stepped. We have a third confirmation from *Wigalois*, that it was called the Seat of Dread, or of Honor. Lancelot had sat upon it. Nearby were a pillar stone, a memorial, and the Forest of the Three Stones (*perrons*). King Arthur's Camelot stood nearby, on the Solway shore. It was a port of embarkation for Ireland—perhaps even the Roman site now called Port Carlisle.

Here Lancelot joins us in his pursuit of Queen Guinevere, for Perceval and the monk author of the *Grand-Saint-Graal*, we now suspect, are following one and the same itinerary to the Grail Castle. Two holy sites intervene, both fountains of repute and of memory. One is near a famous pine tree, also a memorial to a dead hero, according to known, ancient custom.

The last two steps on the quest route are also familiar. The first designates a convent that must have stood beside a great meadow. Both were near a river but also upon the shore of the "Queen's Lake." If one continues, firm in the belief that Britain is not such an impossibly large landmass geographically but a smallish area carefully mapped by ancient and by modern ordnance surveyors, and furthermore that there are too many precisions given here for these similar texts to be dismissed as either coincidental or fantastic, then one may proceed one step along the road to locating this next-to-last place. As was suspected earlier in the Perceval texts, the affianced bride of the son Perceval resided, like many princesses of that age, in a convent for women. The French text called it Beau-Repaire, the English text Maiden Land. The convent in question—not to be confused with the sister institution where King Arthur's mother resided, in Caerlaverock—stood alongside a great meadow. Authors insisted upon the prominence of this impressive geographical feature.

Now, great meadows in the Dark Ages, as during the Middle Ages, were used for two purposes other than agriculture—as battlegrounds and as tilting grounds, sites for tournaments and fairs. Therefore Blanchefleur's convent, or the ancient site thereof, should most logically stand near the runways of a modern airport, which are invariably built on large meadows. The ruins of old monastic foundations probably still lie nearby. The meadow we seek is also near a river.

The Perceval texts have already stated several times that the Grail Castle stood on the shore of "Alain's Lake," the body of water named for the father of one of the Percevals, "Alein's stagne." The convent for women stood upon the Queen's Lake; the "queen" was probably the distinguished aunt of young Perceval, the former queen of the Waste land and one of the exalted queens who after the Battle of Camlan accompanied the wounded King Arthur to Avalon.

It would then follow that *Maiden Land* designated the convent ruled by the queen of the Waste Land when she resided in Maiden Land. While a queen regnant in the world, she had resided in Snowdon. Therefore she raised Lancelot, if she was also the Lady of the Lake, to reconquer Snowdon, which was the Waste Land. To her convent Perceval naturally came, then, for final assistance. The limits of King Arthur's world gradually come closer and closer together, more like those of a human kingdom than the far-flung fairy ramparts of the antipodes to which medieval comedians relegated King Arthur. (In such details the debasement of the legend of Perceval can be traced down through the Middle Ages into the *Mabinogion*. The author of *Peredur* could think no nobler thought than that Perceval as a grown man assassinated his women teachers, lately called "witches.")

Finally, since Perceval delivered his fiancée's estates from a conqueror, one should consider whether or not the convent in which she resided beside the river, meadow, and seashore lay adjacent to a castle of the same name. Thus, one should search for an area similar to a county or shire of modern and medieval Britain. This largish enclave should probably touch that of the Grail Castle. And over such ancient, holy places there should have been bishops ruling even in modern times.

After Lancelot decided to wed, or at least to reside with the Grail King's daughter and not to kill her, which had been his first reaction to the girl's unsolicited presence in his bedchamber at night, he remained with her for several years. The island upon which they dwelled during this period was called "Isle de Joie," Joy Island. By the time Lancelot was summoned from his holiday, his son Galahad was fifteen years of age, ready to assume arms and the same Grail Quest that his father had failed to complete. From this isle Lancelot said he could see the coast of Logres (England). He was, therefore, looking toward the west coast of Britain, a shoreline so elevated into promontories and huge cliffs as to be visible from a distance of twenty or thirty miles.

With so much evidence—and even without the priceless additional criteria that will be supplied by the *Sone de Nansai* manuscript, minutiae that will put the Grail Castle on the map of Britain—a real and increasingly familiar geography begins to emerge from the ancient sources. One has become convinced that a partial concealment was practiced so successfully that no person outside the Grail company could have given directions to their sacred castle. This taboo applied because King Arthur's treasury probably stood alongside.

Since not only Perceval and Lancelot but also Queen Guinevere, says the *Prose Lancelot,* knew the way to the Lady of the Lake's castle, which could be reached by wading across shallows *if* a person knew the right way, one may suppose that King Arthur's queen had been educated in the Grail Castle or in Maiden Land. This hypothesis receives some support from an unexpected quarter, Wolfram von Eschenbach's *Parzival.* There we learn that the insignia, or ancient heraldic bearing, of the Grail company was the turtledove. Geoffrey of Monmouth, it will be recalled, had Queen Guinevere preceded by her especial cognizance, four turtledoves, at her coronation.

In book 9 of *Parzival* Wolfram makes several astounding elaborations (v. 495 ff.) concerning the uses and customs of the Grail fellowship. It was a secret order, he says, like Rabelais's Abbey of Thélème, for both men and women. From this company certain men, who had been carefully educated and prepared for kingship, were dispatched to become rulers of realms left ungoverned. Three such examples from Arthurian literature come immediately to mind: King Arthur, Lancelot, and the younger Perceval. Why have these replacements, all three of more or less uncertain parentage, never declared themselves delegates from their order? Because, explains Wolfram, the male candidates always set out secretly, never openly revealing their origins, and never at the outset able to declare either their names or their genealogies. One might suspect Wolfram of either delirium or prevarication, were there not another independent, anterior source that substantiated this statement.

In her poem called *Lanval* (Launfal) Marie de France corroborates Wolfram's further information to the effect that the Grail maidens went out openly upon their mission to bear children for the Grail fellowship. Thus, Lancelot was as an infant taken to some nursery just as the *Prose Lancelot* recalls so tenderly, there to be nurtured in a sunny climate, fostered, reared, tutored, and prepared mentally and physically for kingship. In the same way King Arthur, like Galahad at age fifteen, suddenly appeared out of nowhere, full-fledged, confident, and able effortlessly to draw the flaming sword from the

stone anvil. On the other hand, the system was about to collapse when the
boy Perceval was suddenly drawn from his forest and substituted. His long
story of teachers and tutors represents an emergency measure.

Once, when King Arthur was wearing his crown at Carlisle—it was at
Pentecost in the month of May, says Marie de France, and petitions for
adventures were being entertained—a beautiful maiden appeared from the
enchanting isle of Avalon. The damsel wooed the hero Lanval, called him
to her upon the *perron*, and leaped off, as it were, on her horse (sea horse,
or ship) in the direction of Avalon. Similarly, the Grail King's daughter,
whose name was probably Pelle (and not Helen, Ellen, or Elen, since *ellan*
is the Manx word for island), seduced Lancelot in order to bear Galahad.
This childbearing mission may perhaps also explain why there exist so many
reports of two or three Guineveres, a situation that has caused some writers
to censure King Arthur unjustly. It may also explain Arthur's reputed son
Modred, whose mother according to some was either his sister Morgan, who
was King Loth's wife, or the wife of King Urien of Gorre. Perceval's cousins,
sister, and aunt were probably Grail maidens, as were those who brought
fresh weapons to Lancelot at various points in his career.

According to the monk whose vision of 717 sent him on the quest for
Christ's Book of the Holy Grail, the journey from Albania (Albion) to the
Grail Castle, not counting the sea crossing, took upwards of four days. After
leaving the convent he came at last to a chapel, which stood upon a rocky
and conical island.

He had arrived at the Grail Castle! There upon the high altar he found
Christ's lost book, and there he received a letter in which the "Grand Master" announced to him the completion of the quest. After this introduction,
the monk commences his Arthurian work the *Grand-Saint-Graal*, which fortunately informs the reader further about the Grail Castle.

It stands in the Foreign Land, as we had decided, or in the "land of
Foreygne." It had been built by the new Grail shepherd Alain, presumably
one of Perceval's forefathers. Since his father is dead before the last Perceval
commences his quest, that block of time constitutes an interregnum during
which, as was the custom, the king's chair, perhaps called the Seat of Dread
or Perilous Seat or Seat of Honor, remained vacant. The last Perceval, last
of his line to rule, will eventually occupy this Perilous Seat.

Both Robert de Boron's *Joseph of Arimathea* and the *Prose Lancelot* believe
that the original tabernacle of the Grail had been Galafort, or Dumbarton
Rock, where according to Geoffrey of Monmouth King Arthur attended his
wounded relative and ally. In those days the Grail Keeper was a Joseph,
whom Boron calls Brons. The Grail was moved thence, farther away from
the ravages of sea raiders, to the isolated foreign land. There a new chapel

and a new castle had been constructed to house it. One assumes therefore that the new castle could be reached conveniently by sailing from the Clyde estuary past Arran, south past the coast of Ayrshire, the port in Loch Ryan, and out into the Irish Sea.

The name most commonly applied to the new site is either Corbenie or Corbenic. It will be the new repository for the Holy Grail, sometimes called the "Holy Vessel" when it fed the Grail company. If and when it was a vessel, the Grail stood upon a table of silver. In its presence one heard the sounds of birds' wings. Then it vanished. Sometimes the castle vanished too. Over the centuries these occurrences presented such thorny problems that scholars gave up solving them and in exasperation consigned the Perceval manuscripts to a largely Irish never-never land.

In the course of his vision of 717, the monk elucidates:

> *thus sone thanne vppon A watyr side,*
> *A castel he Ordeyned that Ilke tyde,*
> *that strong & merveillous it was to se,*
> *With a ful fair paleys certeinle;*
> *And Manye Riche howses there weren dyht,*
> *Ful Riche And Ryal to Alle Mennes syht.*
>
> . . . . . .
>
> *And vppon the tonzate In that sted*
> *they fownden lettres wreten with Red;*
>
> . . . . . .
>
> *that this Castel scholde ben Clepid Corbenie;*
> *And in Caldev was this scripture . . .* *

Here, one is told, the new island was large enough to hold several houses plus a royal palace and the chapel. It was not fantastic but in plain sight of such men as stood before it. As far as its name was concerned, *Corbenic* is as reasonable as any of the variant spellings: *Cornebic, Corbenic, Torbenic, Cambenic, Lambenic, Bellic, Corbierc, Corbiere.*

The best derivation of *Corbenic* seems to be Watson's in 1926.† While he found it very difficult to be certain of the first syllable, he opted for *caer* (castle) rather than for *coire* (cauldron), *carr* (rocky ledge), or *carn* (cairn). Thus, the place name adheres not to Chaldean but to the usual large series of native Celtic names beginning with this syllable and almost always associated with water or with places situated near water. The second syllable probably derives from *benn* (horn), Watson thought, or from one of its compounds such as *beannach* (horned). This etymology contains its own conse-

*Grand-Saint-Graal, vol. 2, v. 55, p. 331.
†p. 366

quence, however, if one searches Britain for the emplacement of the ancient Grail Castle; for "castle in a horned bay" adds another criterion that must be satisfied.

A key word that orients the reader as the quests unroll and assures the hero that he is on the right road is *perilous*. Various dire adventures occur at these several places:

1. A Perilous Cemetery, sometimes called Ascalon's or interpreted as being a Devil's castle underground where Gawain stole Satan's whore, a site sometimes thought of as Glastonbury

2. A Perilous Bridge, or "sword bridge," sometimes also called Pontparles at Glastonbury

3. A Perilous Chapel, or "chapelle Morgain," visited by Gawain, Eliduc's maiden (*Yonec* and *Eliduc* by Marie de France), and Yvain's Lunette (Chrétien's *Yvain*)

4. A Perilous Castle, where Nimue rescued King Arthur, which Malory called "Avilion" (Avalon)

5. A Perilous Fountain, which boiled, was guarded by lions, and would be calmed by Galahad (near Merlin's *Perron*, where the tomb of King Lancelot I oozed healing blood, which was guarded by two lions until Lancelot of the Lake killed them)

6. The Perilous Forest (Malory 1:97, 321)

7. The Perilous Ford or leap near the Solway, as in the *Didot-Perceval* and in *Parzival*, where it is Gawain who must leap a chasm for a (holly?) wreath

8. The Perilous Gates into an underground barrow, as in *Yonec, Guingamor,* and the Tannhaüser stories

9. The Perilous Port on the island where the second Grail Castle was built, where Evalac(h) traveled in the *Grand-Saint-Graal*

10. The Perilous River (*Guingamor*)

11. The Perilous Seat, to be occupied 454 years after Christ, by Lancelot's son Galahad

(In Chrétien there is also a perilous mountain or "Mont Dolereus," thought to be Old Melrose Abbey in Scotland.)

Several of the above-named places are linked to the Grail Castle and its immediate vicinity: the bridge (no. 2), the chapel (no. 3), the castle (no. 4), the seat (no. 11), and the harbor (no. 9). Two others appear to be the same or fairly close to each other: the cemetery (no. 1) and its underground barrow (no. 8). More than one river flows near Carlisle, and there is one at the Grail Castle, and another at the convent. The perilous forest, fountain, ford, and leap are all on the mainland, north and west of Carlisle. Caerlaverock, called "Roche de Champguin" (*Perceval,* v. 8478), figures in Gawain's quest. It belongs to King Arthur's thrice-wed mother Ygerne, who must have been a Grail maiden because her castle contains the test of the Marvelous Bed, undergone successfully by both Gawain and Lancelot (*Perceval*, vv. 8005, 8409, 8737). These perilous places remind the reader that the road between the convent and the Grail Castle should pass alongside an ancient underground or community burial place on the order of the chambered tomb at West Kennet, Wiltshire, or of Silbury Hill, or of any one of the dolmens called "King Arthur's Graves" inside Britain.

Another problem intimately linked to the Grail Castle is the title of its king, always called in Old French "Riche," which means "noble," but also designated as "Fisher." That second word has, of course, delighted the mythologists, both modern and twelfth-century, who have thrilled to echoes of Poseidon with its concomitants of horses, floods, tridents, arks, towers, sea gods, and fish gods. Even better, it evokes Irish stories of King Lear, Manannan mac Llyr, swans, sea horses, and Lohengrin. Understandably, with all this poetry subjacent, the Grail literature has proved irresistible.

Above that level is life on earth and kingdoms for whose people a great Fisher King would be infinitely appealing. Two of our authors, quite separated by time and distance, Marie de France and the clerk Branque who in Cyprus translated the *Sone de Nansai* text, vouched for a certain other detail: that the Fisher King dwelled in a British port serving one of the richest fishing grounds in that realm. There were, said they, over three hundred ships in the fleet that sailed from the Grail Castle's horned bay to fish.

Tallying this information, it would appear that the Grail Castle was situated on the west side of an island, facing Ireland. From the neighborhood of a convent one could see the mainland, which Saint Columba, who sailed these waters in Lancelot's days, so aptly called "Alba of the beetling brows." This sets the queen of the Waste Land's abbey on the eastern side of that same island. Therefore Alain's Lake and her lake must be what we now call the Irish Sea. If the questers embarked at Port Carlisle, or if they crossed the Rhinns of Galloway to take ship at Loch Ryan, then King Arthur, Lancelot, Gawain, and Perceval landed at some harbor on the eastern coast of this same island.

Here at the Grail Castle were witnessed what Christ's Grail book had predicted: terrors to come and the commencement of marvels. As for the secrets of the Grail ceremony, one can only hope now to gain a dim sense of them.

5

The Grail Ceremony

Now that we are at the crucial point in our journey to the Grail Castle, with Perceval about to come upon it, we must proceed with caution. Will Chrétien de Troyes again pull the "sword bridge" out of his hat?

Fortunately, no. Here his two most authoritative *Perceval* manuscripts check out (B. N. MS. fr. 794; and Mons 1866, vv. 2977 ff., and v. 3047 ff., respectively). They agree as to the following account:

> Perceval skirted the curtain wall of the Grail Castle precinct, until he was stopped by a river. He found no crossing, neither by punt, bridge, nor ford. He stood there perplexed. Then he saw two men in a boat, one of whom was fishing for gudgeons with a hook and line. Perceval hailed them.
>
> The men told Perceval there was no boat larger than what could carry five men, thus, no transportation for his horse on this river. They added that he should go back upstream along the rocky defile until he came to the head of the valley. From there, he could cross over and retrace his steps down the other side of this V-shaped valley.
>
> Turning around as they suggested, Perceval went back uphill. Shortly he came out on the top of a conical hill.
>
> From the summit of this hill, Perceval could see nothing below him, however. No descending valley at all was at once visible. All around him was nothing but sky and bald earth.
>
> Still persevering, however, Perceval began the descent from the (north?) side of the steep defile. He soon discovered that there was a castle below him. It was not entirely screened from view by trees and

by the sharp drop of the land. Soon he could also make out its square donjon, and beyond that, a chief tower flanked by double turrets. It was the Castle of the Holy Grail.

Before the main gate was a swing-bridge. [In other words, Chrétien has already forgotten his "sword bridge" translation. In *Crestomathie* Karl Bartsch and Leo Wiese have it right: "un pont torneiz—ein Drehbrucke equals a swing-bridge." It was this contraption that Lancelot earlier had to manage by himself.]

Before Perceval the route lay open. It happened that the bridge was turned and let down. Easily, then, he entered the actual castle enclosure.

Here for the first time we have the significant details concerning the opposite shore: valley, river, sharp defile, conical hill, height of the land. When King Arthur witnessed the first duel between Lancelot and Meleagant, he sat on an eminence so that he could look down into the castle quadrant. From his seat at that height, he also had a marvelous view. Unfortunately, Perceval was made of other stuff and had no taste for seascapes.

Chrétien de Troyes, it would appear, did not connect the two castles: (1) the castle surrounded by the sea, to which Queen Guinevere was abducted by Meleagant, and (2) the Castle of the Holy Grail, which Lancelot, Gawain, Perceval, and Galahad all sought. The latter is Corbenic and Avalon.

To us, even this early in our collation of accounts, the two seem one and the same. We have been directed to a small island surrounded by the sea, on a dangerous coast facing Ireland. The small island is to the west of a larger island and has a conical hill overlooking it. Along the side of the conical hill runs a river, which must flow into the sea between the two islands. This would explain the dreaded currents and dangerous waters. Somewhere near here a fishing fleet of three hundred ships is anchored. They are apparently all small craft, so we are not to look for a deep sea harbor like the later, modern Liverpool. It is true that Gawain in *Gawain and the Green Knight*, as we have read it, descended into the Liverpool area and then turned up next on an island in the sea.

When Gawain approached the Grail Castle in *Perlesvaus* (5), he took a different route from that of Perceval. Then he passed through the Perilous Cemetery, which led directly into the narrow descent to the Grail Castle. Instead of the bridge that Perceval crossed, Gawain encountered three bridges, or we have an augmented account, for Gawain passed over three separate waterways: the "Needle Bridge," the "Ice Bridge," and the "Bridge with the Marble Columns." When later in the same telling Perceval in his turn passed the very real Perilous Cemetery, he heard a voice announcing the death of King Fisherman and his own accession to the kingship of the Grail Castle.

Both Gawain and Perceval saw the same Maimed King, or King Fisherman, moreover, but only Perceval arrived at his fortress at dusk. The latter conversed with the Maimed King in his hall, where four hundred men could have warmed themselves before the fireplace, says Chrétien. Gawain must have been confused, for the four columns he saw were not on the bridge but on the king's fireplace, and, to discredit Gawain further as a narrator, they were not of marble but of brass. The Maimed King was carried into the hall upon a bed or litter upheld at its four corners by valets. The several accounts agree that King Fisherman was lavishly garbed in purple and sable but was unable to sit upright or to walk. In Chrétien, he presented Perceval with the jeweled sword forged for the youth near the Firth of Forth.

The ensuing ceremony in Chrétien consists of the passage before the fire and through the hall of the following:

1. A shining lance from the point of which falls one drop of blood and which is grasped at midpoint by a valet
2. Two valets bearing gold candelabra burning at least ten candles each
3. A remarkably beautiful, elegant, and noble damsel holding between her hands a "grail," and escorted by valets
4. A damsel bearing a silver platter

The light from the Grail was so blinding that the candlelight was eclipsed as if by the direct rays of the sun or moon. These four constitute the famous four hallows of the Grail Castle.

The Grail itself* was made of the "purest, most unalloyed gold," Chrétien added. It was set all over with precious gems, all of which were rarities. No other work of art could compare to the blinding Grail. The cortege bearing it passed silently through the castle, from one apartment to another. No one spoke.

On tables gleaming with white cloths a splendid dinner was served to Perceval, followed by nightcaps, delicacies, and sweets, after which he was escorted to his chamber and prepared for sleep. When he awoke the following morning, he found himself alone in a deserted castle. As he rode across the swing bridge, it closed so fast that his horse was almost trapped. He saw nobody until he met his angry cousin in the forest. From her he learned

---

*The Antioch Chalice, so called because it was unearthed from a garden in Antioch (1910), is now at the Metropolitan Museum of Art in New York. Many persons consider it to be the Grail. This Chalice is an ovoid silver goblet 7½" tall and 6" in diameter consisting of a silver inner cup, a silver-gilt outer container, and a silver base. Some have said it was buried in 361–63; if that is so, then it was not the Grail. Furthermore, the chased and appliquéd figures on this Chalice do not relate to any Arthurian iconography. See a summary of the question to date in "The Holy Grail" by Michael Glenny, Colin Simpson, and Jeffrey Schaire (*Art & Antiques,* May 1985, pp. 41–48). The Chalice is photographed also in *National Geographic,* vol. 164, #6, December 1983, p. 733.

where he had been, whom he had seen, in what ceremony he had unwittingly participated, and why he had supposedly failed. That was specifically because he had not requested an explanation of the Grail. His excuses were unacceptable.

Most readers of Arthurian literature have seen at once that these objects were unquestionably four hallows implicit in the Grail ceremony: a Grail, which was probably a cup, plus a lance, a sword, and a dish, and that these four correspond to any number of sets of four, such as the Tarot and other playing cards: hearts, diamonds, spades, and clubs. Students of Irish mythology, however, have silenced most other readers, having seen it in the pagan Irish symbols of the ancient ancestors of Ireland called the Tuatha de Danaan, noble children of the goddess Dana: Tara's stone of destiny, the sword, the spear, and the Grail as a caldron of plenty. The Italian scholar Leonardo Olschki argued that this Grail ceremony could not have been Christian because there was no mention of cross, clergyman, blessing, church, or liturgy. According to him, the Grail ceremony was Gnostic rather than Christian, medieval and Catharist rather than ancient.

While it is true that the new surge of Grail literature beginning with Chrétien about 1174 falls into the period of intense interest in eastern Christianity, this curiosity followed the Second Crusade preached by Saint Bernard after the fall of Edessa to the Turks in 1144. Nothing here proves Gnostic influences in Britain. On the other hand, the ancient Christianity of Britain may have involved practices that today seem foreign and bizarre to us. It is furthermore not true that no church was mentioned in the Grail texts, as Olschki claimed. Every text mentions confession at a hermitage prior to entry and the Grail chapel where the sacred objects repose. Nor is it true that no liturgy is recognizable, for the idea of the Grail healing and feeding the faithful or multitude recalls the life of Christ, the Last Supper, and the sacrament of the Eucharist. More than such specifics, however, the manuscripts suggest that the Holy Grail, as the French theologian Etienne Gilson understood it, represented the Grace of the Holy Spirit. The cup or Grail was the spirit of love, which fed the Christian soul. From the arguments of these two modern scholars, Olschki and Gilson, one understands how easy it is to proceed from meager evidence to diametrically opposed conclusions.

Arguments for the pagan nature of the Grail Castle are no longer so easy to make. Nowadays they fall afoul of such modern art historians as Ronald Sheridan and Anne Ross, who in their book *Gargoyles and Grotesques: Paganism in the Medieval Church* give several specific examples of paganism and pagan worship. The first example of paganism cited is the Green Man, whose head was represented entwined with foliage and crowned with leaves. Other images are extremely obscene, such as the hag represented at Saint Michael's Church, Oxford, and at Kilpeck, Herefordshire, as in many Irish churches.

Just as occurs to the Green Knight in *Gawain and the Green Knight*, whose story contains no mention of the Grail ceremony, so the "sexual old hag," who becomes beautiful when the king weds her, as Sheridan and Ross explain (pp. 31, 64, 66, etc.), probably once represented Morgan le Fay, the goddess, in the former work, as in Chaucer's "The Wife of Bath's Tale." This goddess surely is none other than King Arthur's noble sister, who was once a queen. Medieval copyists of *mirabilia* (marvels) were well aware of this pagan heritage, so King Arthur was by certain among them equated with the mallet god Sucellos with his attributes of hammer, patera, and dog. Certain popular medieval authors, like Gervase of Tilbury and Walter Map, specialized in mythology and connected King Arthur to such amusing trifles as dwarfs, giants, caves in Sicily, and the far antipodes. Their works were purposely comic, debunking for political reasons, ridiculing King Arthur and relegating him to fairyland. When modern critics find such mythologizing in medieval literature, they find leads planted maliciously by medieval writers, who upheld the pagan theory and promoted it with their own droll wit and skepticism.

Gawain's first visit to the Grail Castle in *Perlesvaus* (5, 6) recalls Lancelot's arrival in Gorre where Chrétien had him cross a "sword bridge." Gawain's first bridge is a needle bridge (v. 2296), which the English translator Sebastian Evans mistook for an "eel" bridge, having read *anguille* for *aguille*. The second bridge is of ice, which shows how baffled was the medieval author with his source, until he decided that the whole story must have been meant as a descent into the endless realms of ice, the underground Hell of the Middle Ages.

In the castle Gawain meets a Joseus of the lineage of Joseph of Arimathea and learns that Joseus slew his mother after a dispute over property. Such a small detail crops up again and again, alerting the reader that a hero has arrived at the Grail Castle. Sone de Nansai is told that Joseus killed his mother because she had relapsed into paganism, a likelier tale. Gawain too sees a lion chained at the gate, which Lancelot thought he saw in Gorre. Despite the fact that he presented King Fisherman with an inestimably valuable relic, the sword that had beheaded John the Baptist, Gawain is still adjudged to have failed the quest and is curtly ordered to leave. A storm sweeps him along the opposite shore of the river as he departs, or he leaves by the alternate route. Such details go far to help us visualize the Grail Castle in its peculiar geography and furthermore to persuade us that real places form the distant basis of this stunning literature.

Parzival's first approach to the Grail Castle in Wolfram von Eschenbach's German version occurs also after a ride of a full day from Pelrapeire (book 5). The last part of his journey was hard going through fallen trees and the marsh that Chrétien had already located in Gorre, directly in front of the castle of Bademagus and Meleagant, where Queen Guinevere was held hostage. He came at dusk not to a river, as Chrétien said, but to the shore of a "lake." The discrepancy involving water here might well have stemmed from a Latin source again, for the word *lacus* in poetic or literary Latin meant "lake," "pool," "mere," "river," "spring," or "stream." Similarly, the Latin word *stagnum* as used in the Old French *Alain's stagne*, by itself failed to differentiate between "pool," "pond," "swamp," "fen," "the sea," and "waters" generally.

Parzival rode up to the shore whence he could hail fishermen riding at anchor, says Wolfram. The one passenger was royal, since he wore peacock feathers on his hat. There was no habitation within twenty leagues, as in Chrétien. Parzival's directions are: turn right at the end of the cliff, ascend the (conical) hill, advance to the moat, ask for the drawbridge to be lowered. Wolfram has not explained how the moat comes to be on the hilltop, or he has not visualized the site as carefully as did Chrétien, whom he is at some pains to criticize.

Wolfram's castle contains the same oriental luxuries as that of Chrétien, but its hall holds one hundred chandeliers, one hundred couches, and one hundred coverlets. There are three fireplaces, not of brass but of Gawain's marble. The fire burned hot in order to warm the Maimed King, and because of his illness he wore furs.

The ceremony differs in that blood gushed from the lance. The persons present then wept loudly. A running squire rushed past bearing the lance. Second, two noble damsels wearing circlets of flowers bore candles, followed by ladies bearing ivory stools. Then eight ladies carried a tabletop carved from a gem. Then came six more bearing dining utensils. They were followed by the virgin queen holding aloft the marvel ("Wunsch"), or Grail, which was preceded by lights and incense. The *same* dinner just as Chrétien recorded, on white tablecloths was served, but the Grail here provides delicacies in abundance. Parzival received the jeweled sword, retired, and was served the same delicious nightcaps and sweetmeats. King Fisherman was also borne on a litter. Upon awakening, Parzival found the castle deserted, and as he departed, the bridge almost knocked down his horse. Thus, one sees how Wolfram has embroidered but agreed with Chrétien.

Meeting Sigune along his way, Parzival next learns that the castle can only be found by chance, that it is called not Corbenic, but Munsalvaesche, Mountain or Land of Salvation, and that he is called Parzival. He has failed the quest, as we knew.

Returning four-and-a-half years later, Parzival learns from his hermit uncle (9) that the Grail is a stone engraved with the names of the Grail fellows and maidens who had entered that service as children, who were summoned to leave their families and do service there. As adults they constitute a noble brotherhood unknown to those who had never been summoned there. Until Parzival can become Lord of the Grail, the Maimed

King must suffer untold agony from his wound, and Parzival cannot release him until of his own wit he discovers the solution and asks the correct questions. Meanwhile, the sight of the Grail keeps the Maimed King alive until Parzival's second coming, at the proper point in their orbits of Mars and Jupiter.

Cundrie's speech in book 15 gives an astrological schematism:

The Seven Planets of Parzival

Planet	Day	Tree	Letter	Zodiac	Hero	Deity
Sun	Sunday	Birch	B(eithe)	Pisces	Perceval	Quirinus Vishnu Oannes Attis/Adonis
Moon	Monday	Willow	S(ail)	Cancer	Morgan	Diana Matrona Demeter
Mars	Tuesday	Holly	T(inne)	Aries	Gawain	Cuchulain Amon-Ra Marduk Ares Tiw
Mercury	Wednesday	Ash	N(ion)	Gemini	Gwydion	Woden/Wotan Odin Nabu
Jupiter	Thursday	Oak	D(uir)	Leo	Lancelot	Thor Baal Helios Shamash
Venus	Friday	Apple	Q(ert)	Virgo	Guinevere	Freia Isis Eve
Saturn	Saturday	Alder	F(earn)	Sagittarius	{ Arthur { Bran	Iao Cronus Chiron Allfadur

Parzival's wife, brother, and two sons are reunited with him at the Grail Castle after a separation of five years. The text gives us Good Friday and then Easter Sunday. Wolfram finds the Grail ceremony at Parzival's inauguration, including the baptism of his half brother, entirely Christian. He congratulates himself that he has, through the use of a Provençal source, improved upon Chrétien's version, which was completed by continuators, all much inferior to both Chrétien and to Wolfram. The very great personal virtues of Wolfram, which include his love of God, his admiration for women, his appreciation of medieval chivalry, and his general kindliness and goodness of heart, are unfortunately not characteristics that advance very far the search for lost knowledge concerning King Arthur and the Holy Grail.

Another briefer view of the Grail Castle comes from the "Quest" section of the *Prose Lancelot*. The quester Lancelot arrives in a boat in which he has been sailing for a month. It is midnight when he floats into the lee of a great castle that has two main entrances, just as in Chrétien's *Lancelot*, one on the land side guarded by two lions, and one on the seaward side that was open to approach by small craft such as that in which King Fisherman fished by day. Lancelot moored his boat and walked around the island to the main portal, passed unscathed between the lions, mounted the steps and street to the donjon and keep, and entered the hall. It was Corbenic Castle, so bright that it seemed the sun's very dwelling, in the far sunset west of Britain. After this other failure to complete the quest, the gallant Lancelot lay near death for a long time.

By far the greatest effort and resources of poetry, theology, and imagination are displayed by the anonymous Benedictine monk who wrote the *Perlesvaus*, or *High History of the Holy Grail*. He wrote at the abbey-church in Glastonbury about the time when that distinguished abbot Henry de Sully exhumed what the monks of Glastonbury said were the bodies of King Arthur and Queen Guinevere. Before Geoffrey of Monmouth wrote his *Historia*, which defiantly placed King Arthur in Dumbarton and Loch Lomond, Scotland, William of Malmesbury had already declared, or his text had been so tampered with that it seemed to have declared, that Arthur was English and the Avalon was Glastonbury: *De antiquitate Glastoniensis ecclesiae*, 1129–34. In 1160 he was reinforced by the *Vita Gildae* composed in Britain, which, as we have seen, placed the site of Guinevere's abduction at Glastonbury, or which repeated that Avalon surely was Glastonbury.

It was alleged that the bodies of Arthur and Guinevere were recovered in 1191 from the floor of the Lady Chapel at Glastonbury, which had burned along with the abbey in 1184. It had been rebuilt in 1186. That reconstruction, again, is very important here, for *in 1186 a lead roof replaced the old wooden one*, which had burned. The bodies were then removed to the main church, after the witnessing ceremony. Some four hundred years later, the whole foundation was destroyed by order of King Henry VIII. At that time the evidence was irrevocably lost.

Nobody today seriously believes that the monks really discovered King Arthur's body or that of the queen. The *Perlesvaus* author believed that she was initially interred at Avalon, which is no proof that Glastonbury is or was Avalon. While the bones of Saint Columba were transported in a reliquary carried before the Scottish army as it marched into the Battle, of Bannockburn, there never was, says the Welsh *Triad*, any grave for King Arthur.

But Arthur went to Avalon for treatment of his wounds, and Queen Guinevere was once interred there.

The author of *Perlesvaus* has placed the story in historical perspective such as no previous author had thought to do, seeing it as a period of the Christianization of the western isles. Then the world existed in three movements, he said, each one struggling for converts and for supremacy, as Shakespeare recalled in the three caskets between which Portia's suitors had to choose: gold signifying the New Testament or Christianity, silver signifying Judaism or the Old Law, and lead signifying the infidels or "Saracens" (*Perlesvaus*, vv. 2170–73.) Thus, the King of Castle Mortal, who was the one evil pagan in Perceval's line, relapsed, conquered the Grail Castle from King Fisherman, and renamed it with its old pagan name: the Turning Castle.

The *Perlesvaus* author rearranges the same elements that each author found in his source. Since the castle was associated with *horn* or *elephants' horns*, he called the now pagan island *Isle of Oliphants*. Those were the battle horns made of elephants' tusks, such as the famous one that Roland finally blew at Roncevalles. The walls of the Turning Castle were high and surrounded by swift water. The whole castle, not just the bridge, swung round, so that in its whirling it defended itself by presenting to the enemy the side that had no gates. Thus, it resembled the castle of Curoi mac Daire, the Irish storm god in Munster.

Even so, Perceval overcame all obstacles, valiantly defeating the dragon warrior—Beowulf's feat—and then attacking the copper bull upon his altar within the temple. Passing the Perilous Gates, he killed fifteen hundred and converted thirteen. His evil uncle committed suicide, after which Perceval restored the sacred Christian relics to the sanctuary. It is an interpretation that makes much good sense.

The *Perlesvaus* confirms Ulrich in the matter of Lohot's death and then that of his mother, Queen Guinevere. Both deaths are connected here to Arthur's many wars against "Briens of the Isles." Ulrich names him correctly King Urien of Gorre, who twice broke the truce and who kidnapped the queen because he said she had been promised to him. The news of the queen's death is brought to King Arthur at the Grail Castle, and there he takes formal possession of her crown. We now learn that he had left the queen in command of his forces at Carlisle while he went to the Grail Castle in pilgrimage at the death of his son Lohot.

The same author of *Perlesvaus* (v. 7567 ff.) recounts now how Lancelot rode to Avalon to see the queen's tomb, which also held the head of her son. Yet the monks of Glastonbury, who claimed to have found her body, which was so well preserved that before the air destroyed it they saw her golden hair, made no mention of a separate, male skull. They made no mention, furthermore, of the interment on an island completely surrounded by water at all times. The *Perlesvaus* says nothing of Lancelot's passage or passages over water to reach her sarcophagus. Clearly, then, the author has substituted the geography of Glastonbury for that of the Grail Castle, as it was in Arthur's day. The *Perlesvaus* gives us an island location, such as Glastonbury with its chalice well, its dairy farms, and apple orchards. From Lancelot's route, in fact, the chapel where the queen lies seems to have been, in the author's mind, located on the summit of the Glastonbury Tor, and not in the Lady Chapel at the foot of the hill.

Lancelot in *Perlesvaus* is said to have climbed a hill so steep that he could not ride to the summit. There is no other hill or even hillock within thirty or so miles of Glastonbury. Only the Glastonbury Tor rises out of the marshy land. The *Perlesvaus* makes no mention of Lancelot crossing water or of ferrying his horse.

Then the Glastonbury author makes his great mistake, which invalidates his account altogether regarding this incident: Lancelot saw the lead roof. Unfortunately the lead roof was that of the Norman chapel built in 1185.

Compounding this disastrous error, the author then has Lancelot go directly from Avalon to nearby Carlisle and its Castle of the *Perron*. Glastonbury is many hundreds of miles distant. Finally the author regains control and follows his source when he returns to the subject of the Grail Castle.

The Grail Castle, he says, is both Avalon and Corbenic. It has water running around it, indeed, sparkling sea water, swift, blue, and very deep. It is called moreover by at least three other names, all most appropriate given its manifold functions: Eden, Castle of Joy, and Castle of Souls.

King Arthur presented Queen Guinevere's golden crown to the Grail Castle and there prayed and sorrowed at the sepulcher of this "valiant" warrior queen.

The words that King Arthur speaks to his knights in the "Quest" (*Prose Lancelot*), as they solemnly dedicate themselves to the Quest of the Holy Grail, mention his grief and loss at their departure but, more important, place him for better and for worse, but without a doubt, as the Christian king of Britain.

His education completed, Perceval becomes another king of Britain at the Grail Castle, Corbenic, and Avalon. One of his most important first acts is to move the sacred bodies of his ancestors away from the invaders, who are coming closer and closer. Lancelot has already done as much. King Arthur's body, one feels sure, was not found and will not be found.

The Perceval accounts have revealed that the Grail Castle was the religious center of King Arthur's kingdom and that it was a secret place. Before it was finally Christianized, it had been a pagan holy site of great renown.

We have also accumulated fairly concrete directions to that ancient site.

The frequent dates in the Perceval stories, counting backward to King Arthur's departure for his continental campaign, indicate that we are drawing to the close of his reign.

Perceval has been left in charge at the Grail Castle, as the king, Lancelot, King Loth, Gawain, and the rest depart Britain for the continent. There at Avalon Perceval will supervise the religious ceremonies, the royal necropolis, and the royal nursery. Lancelot has killed King Urien of Gorre, and Gawain has killed King Bademagus, Perceval's predecessor. A queen or queens are resident on enclaves adjacent to the Grail Castle.

Before King Arthur departed for the European continent, he bade farewell to his dead Queen Guinevere at Avalon. Lancelot also bade farewell to his liege lady. The reference to the twelfth-century lead roof at Glastonbury, which the *Perlesvaus* says Lancelot saw at the queen's tomb, is erroneous.

We now know that Queen Guinevere was already dead before King Arthur departed for this continental European campaign. The story of Modred's alleged treachery must be a different story. Therefore we must still scrutinize the information concerning the Battle of Camlan. The late accounts, such as that of Sir Thomas Malory, are incorrect here, beautiful as they are.

Historically speaking, after the death of King Arthur and the dissolution of his realm, which happens within the hour of his wounding, Avalon will not have long to go as a religious center. The Grail Castle also will soon disappear.

Saint Columba and Rome will replace this early Christianity. Iona will presumably replace Avalon. The Clyde River will be dredged far upstream of Dumbarton Rock, and Glasgow will replace them all as the next religious center of the north.

Nowadays the Celtic Christian Church of King Arthur is re-classified as a mystery religion,* in the sense of having practiced a religious service, or *ministerium*, of an arcane nature.

Various Arthurian personages, King Arthur, Lancelot, Gawain, and Perceval notably, worship at the Grail Castle shrine. Perceval enters most

---

*See *Mystery Religions in the Ancient World*, by Joscelyn Godwin (London, 1981), p. 91.

memorably when the *sanctum sanctorum* lies in almost total darkness, on Good Friday evening. Perceval is mystified by the service which features flares of light so brilliant they dazzle his senses. He is stunned by the sight of gold candelabra (very like those, lodged today in museums, which were originally household furnishings made for and used by multimillionaire Roman Emperors). Such a lighting apparatus as the Holy Grail might have resembled these Roman art objects for size, beauty, richness, and complexity. The text allows us to assume some flaming, jeweled, gold bowl (similar in size to the Gundestrup Cauldron from North Jutland, Denmark).* Or it resembled, only in solid gold, the incised brass lamps set with plastic jewels which are sold in the Istanbul bazaar today. Even these globes cast pretty colored rays about them. But the lighting apparatuses belonging to kings like Arthur conceivably also incorporated horn lanterns, lampstands with massive gold chains, laminae of horn and glass, even diamonds, and were capable of casting bursts of white fire up in the air, just as modern magicians do.

After the *ministerium* Perceval is so plied with such sweets and potions that he still suffers a memory loss on the following morning. Then, uncomprehendingly, he finds no trace of the shrine, or of the service. Even weeks later, he can not clearly reconstruct what took place within the shrine.

On the Easter morning when Perceval, clad in red, is consecrated Grail King, blinding light again announces the joyous news of the Resurrection of Christ, and of the bodily restoration of the Old Grail King whom Perceval replaced. The texts are correct in their theology: Knowledge was the wing whereby Perceval too would fly to heaven.

We are still wondering about these uses of light in the Celtic Church, just as we still ponder Arthur's feats of drawing the sword from the stone, and lighting the King's fire, presumably by friction or percussion. The use of glass, or rock crystal, also poses its riddle. We remember Caer Wydr, the Castle of Glass, or Grail. We recall the cryptic words of Taliesin, that there is in the ocean a holy sanctuary, a deep crystal cup. And Geoffrey of Monmouth's even more mysterious words that there lies in the ocean a holy sanctuary, the gate of which is a hard diamond, an unconquerable adamant, gem of the daylight, and, adds Harold Bayley, the diamond forms the base of the Cross of Light.

---

*See Anne Ross's *Pagan Celtic Britain*, Fig. 190. A man on the cauldron is drowning his foe as Perceval did. Ross observed the resemblance of the symbols on the cauldron to Pictish art.

PART IV

❧❦❧

THE
PASSING
OF
KING
ARTHUR

1

The Battle
of Camlan

The Battle of Camlan is so well remembered that the phrase itself has become a common noun in the Welsh language, meaning a rout or terrible carnage. The Welsh say it happened on a Thursday. Modred divided his men into six battalions; Arthur divided his into nine. Only seven men survived, some for strength, some for speed or the speed of their mounts, and one for his holiness.

The question has always been whom to blame. The two most popular culprits have been Queen Guinevere and Modred.

Local tradition has had its word too, although nobody has believed it. The local people in the environs of Hadrian's Wall say that Arthur died there at Camlan and that his body was laid temporarily in a castle crypt in that area, awaiting transport.

There remain other mysteries. Where for certain was or is the battleground? What does *Camlan* mean (besides "crooked enclosure")? Where were Lancelot and Gawain that day and why were they so lamentably absent? Where did Arthur disembark upon his return from Europe? Was it on the east coast or on the west coast? In what direction did he then proceed?

We know that the battlefield was at a distance of three days from the port of disembarkation. If Arthur was in Brittany or returning from northern Europe, he could still have landed on the western coast. We know that none of his retinue, the elite guard of the Round Table knights, survived the king's death. By all the laws of warfare in the Dark Ages, they must have preceded him into death. The contrary would have been inconceivable. We also know that here Geoffrey of Monmouth is unreliable, his Aube River more probably the northern Elbe River; but he has both the name of the battle and the date correct.

All texts are silent concerning the last summer that King Arthur spent in Britain, between his crown-wearing in the spring and his rendezvous in August prior to military action upon the continent. Geoffrey of Monmouth has the king preparing that summer for an eventual and improbable autumn advance into the land of the Allobroges, who dwelled, when Julius Caesar met and defeated them, between the Rhône and Isère rivers, or deep in southeastern Gaul. For their parts the French romancers had totally lost track of events and, like Sir Thomas Malory, who perhaps pored over their now lost pages, swam in unlikely conjectures of final dooms. The last major events between Whitsuntide and that last August were perhaps those reported last by the romances. Then befell the king, they said, a rebellion by King Urien of Gorre, lord of western Scotland and the isles.

This sudden reversal of attitude, this withdrawal of a major king from King Arthur, either brings with it or results from two determinative catastrophes. They signal, along with the departure of some Round Table heroes upon the Grail Quest, the collapse of King Arthur's realm.

First, King Arthur and Queen Guinevere lost their son Lohot, whose severed head was delivered to them. Thus the question of succession must have been raised. Surely the king would, before leaving Britain, have to pronounce upon a matter of such weight.

Second, Queen Guinevere is defeated and then captured by King Urien, whose vassal King Bademagus had previously released her to the invincible Lancelot. Following this second capture comes a rescue mission, says the *Lanzelet,* at a fortress surrounded by a stockade or, as such structures are commonly called throughout northern Britain, a peel castle. (The Latin *palus,* or stake, gives the doublets *palisade* and *peel.*) This mission may coincide with Perceval's liberation of the Grail Castle. In any event, the heroic rescue mission avails only partially, for the queen is not saved or does not long survive. The popular version hesitates to accept that she died, great warrior queens, or even warrior maids like Joan of Arc, rarely lie quiet in death. Rumor still has it that King Lancelot's successor stole the queen away into Angus, where she languished in solitary confinement the rest of her days. Modern guidebooks tell tourists not to tread upon her accursed tomb for fear of being made barren. Thus, whatever good Queen Guinevere had was interred with her bones, too.

Consequent upon these grave calamities, King Arthur conceivably undertook, as *Perlesvaus* says, a pilgrimage to the Grail Castle. He presented Guinevere's golden crown to the treasury there, and he prayed for her soul and for that of his murdered son, whose head lay at rest in her coffin. There King Lancelot, as befitted King Arthur's most important ally and vassal— Lancelot had been crowned king of Albania—paid his respects at this tomb and wept for these royal dead.

At King Arthur's court, when the decision was made to undertake a continental campaign, Geoffrey's King Anguselus of Albania (Scotland) spoke first in response to King Arthur's request for counsel. His words of support appear not in the romances but in Geoffrey's *Historia*, and they are certainly not what King Lancelot would have said or what King Anguselus would have said, even were the two not one and the same person. In other words, the speech of the king of Scotland, the revered Rí Alban, rings particularly false in Geoffrey's text.

The chief subject of Arthur began by saying how glad he was in his heart for the war: "tanta leticia animo meo." In fact, he thrilled for the blood of Romans and Germans (i.e., Saxons): "romani & germani." Oh, he cried, shall I never see that great day dawn (when I can drink their blood?): "O si illam lucem videbo?" Then my wounds will be sweet: "quam dulcia erunt vulnera!" That great death which I shall suffer then and there *will also be sweet to me:* "Illa etiam more dulcis erit." Hopefully, he concluded, we shall enjoy our victory, and I therefore pledge two thousand horsemen.

King Arthur was about to wage a continental campaign with the Rí Alban as his second in command and principal supporter. If such a distinguished king were lost, King Arthur might need similar words when explaining and excusing himself in Scotland thereafter. One remembers how hard pressed Charlemagne was to explain the young Roland's death to his fiancée Aude. No warrior and brave man in any case would make such a speech. Such bloody words are dreamed up by scholars and other cloistered persons little acquainted with a world of military men. Reading such words and longings for a hero's death, one may suspect that King Anguselus/Lancelot will not long survive. He will probably not live to see Albania again.

Aside from Sir Thomas Malory's brilliant, wonderful, and moving accounts of the deaths of Queen Guinevere, Sir Gawain, and Sir Lancelot in the last chapters of *Le Morte d'Arthur*, and they are heartbreaking pages unequaled in medieval prose, the story of Queen Guinevere's adultery has proven in the long run a poor solution to the problem of lost knowledge. The careers of great kings and great queens are not, according to history, based upon such lamentable vices as uncontrolled sexuality. Such accusations emerge from the life experiences of distant authors, long centuries after the events, removed from them in land and custom. They show unfamiliarity with Britain, lack of sympathy with British royalty, and lack of knowledge of that or of any other ancient warrior ethos. Thus, aside from Malory's well intentioned and romantic sentiments, which demonstrate a sad disillusionment with women on his part, there exists no death at all or passing account for the beloved Lancelot.

How could the young Lancelot, at the height of his glory, disappear so suddenly? How could he have become a faithless turncoat at the particular moment when he was most needed? How could he have vanished without a trace in the prime of his life?

The king who volunteered first to support King Arthur in his continental campaign, to furnish the heaviest contingent, and to command one of the two wings of the battle line was Lancelot, King Anguselus of Scotland. The *Lanzelet* text told how this youth rose by his own efforts to eminence and how he assisted King Arthur against King Urien of Dalriada, the same who had a legitimate and an illegitimate son named Urien.

The one king who according to Geoffrey did not volunteer and who failed to accompany King Arthur to the continent was this same King Urien. Geoffrey lists eight major commanders in order of rank:

1. Anguselus, king of Albania, commander of the left wing (the Welsh translation calls Anguselus "Aron, son of Kynvarch," and nowhere connects him to Lancelot; however, Lancelot is not a Welsh hero, his name in Welsh being "Lawnslot," an approximation of English phonetics)
2. Cador, duke of "Cornubie," of Cornwall
3. "Aschil, rex dacorum," king of the Dacians, or Danes in Britain
4. "Loth, rex norgueigensium," King Loth of the northerners
5. "Hoelus, dux armoricum," or Duke Hoel of the Britons
6. Kay
7. Bedevere
8. "Gualguainus, nepos regis," or Gawain, the king's nephew

Aside from King Urien and his two sons, who are notably absent, the full roster of army commanders tallies with the royal personages present at King Arthur's Whitsuntide crown wearing.

Geoffrey adds one interesting fact—that the six island rulers could provide only foot soldiers, the use of the horse in war not having been introduced to them. This repeats what Chrétien established in his *Lancelot*, that the boy had not learned how to ride at the time when he arrived as a young champion on the mainland of Britain. Educated near Stirling, Perceval had as a youth already acquired this skill. The Irish tell another story, also collected by Lady Augusta Gregory, of how King Arthur introduced the horse into Ireland.

Geoffrey's reconstruction of King Arthur's expedition to the continent appears to be a scholarly attempt to imagine such a campaign. Aside from the bare facts, Geoffrey attempted a prose epic in five parts, the fourth section being the war against the Romans. While one admires his writing for its poetic qualities, one must look upon the European geography with some dismay.

King Arthur was said by Geoffrey to have assigned as his place of rendezvous on the French coast the estuary of a "Barbe" river, specifically named, "ad portum barbe fluuii" (to the harbor of the Barbe River) and "in portu barbe fluuii" (in the harbor of the Barbe River). Translating Geoffrey, Sebastian Evans suggested Barfleur on the Cotentin peninsula near Cherbourg, despite the anachronisms involved in using Norman place names and despite the lack of a Barbe River. Geoffrey then rashly launches into King Arthur killing a giant at Mont-Saint-Michel, where he further mistakes the French word for "rock" (*tombe*) for the English word *tomb*. Thence the British allies proceed the impossibly long distance overland to the Burgundian city of Autun, Geoffrey insisting on Langres and Chinon. Arthur's victory near Autun actually borrowed and followed the rapid conquests of King Clovis between 486–511. Geoffrey's reference to the "White River" led him perhaps to the Aube near Autun so that one wonders again whether or not he should have chosen the Elbe, another White River in the territory then disputed with the Vandals, and landed in Cuxhaven-Hamburg.

Geoffrey and his translator-adapters have all erred badly again in their reconstruction of King Arthur's return to Britain. They had him come ashore at the worst possible place, in the port of Dover, under the eye of the old Roman Pharos, where the ancient Roman emperors came ashore into Britain. Precedent argued with Geoffrey here, but erroneously. The port of Dover had been in Saxon hands even before King Arthur was born, or from c. 450. Even nearby Pevensey had fallen to the Saxons by 491. So where did Arthur come ashore?

At his departure for the continent the king was said, erroneously, to have appointed Modred and Queen Guinevere as joint regents; King Arthur returned to dispute the realm with Modred. In any case Modred had entrenched himself in King Arthur's kingdom, governed at Carlisle, with its chief port at Loch Ryan (the present city of Stranraer). Archaeologists have found ancient craft there, as a matter of fact, which are very fine and which are neither Roman nor Viking.

The king fought two engagements against Modred, we know, one at the port where he attempted to disembark, and the second at Camlan, three days distant from that port.

Geoffrey of Monmouth called the first engagement "in rutupi portu," which is Richborough or Dover, and the second "ad fluuium camblan," or on the River Camblan. The latter is usually spelled "Camlan." Old prophetic verses from Scotland claimed, concurrently with Geoffrey, that King Arthur ruled all the "fair south," in fact, "fra Dunbartone to Dover." We cannot, then, reasonably blame Geoffrey.

Modred awaited King Arthur in his own kingdom, thus, and either at Stranraer, which was the King's Port, or at Carlisle itself, that is, at Port Carlisle and the Castle of the *Perron*. We remember that King Arthur had two fortresses at Carlisle and that one of them lay on the edge of the Solway Firth.

Most persons have rejected Geoffrey of Monmouth's ending and his explanation of those two engagements which decided the future of the kingdom. Some writers have delighted at the "treachery" of Modred, and others have enjoyed the "treachery and adultery" of poor Queen Guinevere, who was long dead by this time. Others have resented the allegations of treachery on Modred's part. Allegations of this sort spawn all sorts of charges and countercharges as lesser authors treat the material down the centuries. Those who thought poorly of kings besmirched King Arthur, and those who thought poorly of women sought personal revenge by charging the long-dead queen.

The view proposed by Geoffrey of Monmouth, that Modred was a tyrant and a traitor and that he usurped his uncle's throne, was resented by a certain group of men representing a body of opinion transmitted from the fourteenth century through the sixteenth. These men were the chroniclers of Scotland, such as John of Fordun who composed (c. 1385) a Chronicle of the Scots, and John Major, who published in Aberdeen in 1527 a history of the Scots. Their works, which can't be found in the United Sates, step in and purport to elucidate the question of Modred and King Arthur. It is clearly high time that someone spoke for Scotland.

Generally speaking, and despite the disfavor in which these protohistorians are still held both in Scotland and elsewhere, the chroniclers of this ilk assert that both King Loth and his son Modred were Scottish heroes and not traitors. They maintain furthermore that when King Arthur named Modred regent during his absence abroad, he also appointed him heir apparent to his throne. King Loth was a king of the Scots or of the Picts, they say, not of the Norwegians or of the Orkneys, as often supposed in the nineteenth century, and he had married the sister of Aurelius, and was hostile to the Britons.

The war between King Arthur and Modred pitted Britons against Picts because the king had accepted the Pictish Modred as his heir, pronounced it, and then repudiated him. The Alliterative Morte Arthure repeats a part of this theory, that Modred, the Picts, and Lancelot fought King Arthur at Camlan. How quickly Queen Guinevere fled to a convent, or how skillfully she must be defended, as the Victorian poet William Morris did on the grounds that women are normally immoral, cannot concern the reader further. Nor can the equally monstrous and insulting theory that Lancelot joined Modred in this last war, or that he slew Gawain.

Both Gawain and Anguselus, king of Albania, were most tragically lost at the first battle, where Modred attempted to stop King Arthur from disembarking. It was a scene of terrible carnage before the forces of Modred were put to flight and the landing effected.

Why did King Arthur subsequently consent to meet Modred in pitched battle three days later? The chronicles of Scotland have that answer, too:

because Modred then blocked the way as King Arthur attempted to convey the body of the slain king of Albania to his people in Scotland.

Since King Lancelot, whose Latin name was Anguselus, was crowned at Stirling Castle, known far and wide as the "key to Scotland," then the Battle of Camlan was fought between Carlisle, or between Loch Ryan, and Stirling, three days distant from one or the other harbor.

Now that we understand the story behind the Battle of Camlan, we see how Geoffrey of Monmouth's oration put into the mouth of Anguselus fits the case. He was to die soon.

Charlemagne had Roland's body sewn in a deerskin and coveyed in all honor into Toulouse. King Henry IV had the body of King Richard II encased in lead and displayed, only the face remaining bare, throughout England, as the French envoys saw and reported. If Gawain's body was buried in a harbor, so that he lay in death face to the foe, then Gawain was buried not on the beach at Dover but either at Carlisle or at Loch Ryan. There is a cairn at Loch Ryan.

The burial services for Lancelot/Anguselus were held, after Camlan, doubtless, at the Old Abbey adjacent to Stirling Castle, where Lancelot learned his name.

The first real victor, to whom fell the spoils of this war, was one of the sons of the old King Urien of Gorre. The manuscript called *Brut*, or Chronicle of England (MS Rawlinson, B. 171), also reports that both bodies, those of Gawain and of Lancelot/Anguselus, were borne into Scotland for burial, after the disaster of Camlan.

The tenth-century *Annals of Wales* (Harley 3859) made one of the most authoritative statements concerning the Battle of Camlan, which Geoffrey of Monmouth two centuries later dated in 542:

> 537   Gueith Camlann, in qua Arthur et Medraut corruerunt, et mortalitas in Brittania et in Hibernia fuit.
> [537. The Battle of Camlan in which Arthur and Modred fell together, and there was death in Britain and in Ireland.]

The date of Camlan, argued P. K. Johnstone in *Antiquity*, was more probably closer than 537 to Geoffrey's 542, at least by two years. The death or mortality referred to was the plague that broke out in 539. Summarizing modern theories, O. G. S. Crawford had concluded in *Antiquity* as follows:

1. Arthur was the successor of Aurelius Ambrosius, who flourished c. 445–467 (as Geoffrey of Monmouth claimed).
2. The historian Roger of Wendover confirms this reasoning.
3. Arthur's twelve battles occurred between 467 and 516, after which Arthur lived another twenty-one years.
4. Arthur died sometime after 537.

In his major article, "Arthur and His Battles," Crawford concluded that King Arthur, in fact, died at the Battle of Camlan. The death there of Modred has not been questioned. Crawford pointed out that there is no place called "Camlan," despite a possible Old Celtic derivation from *camb(o)* = curved, and *Landa* = enclosure. The word was probably not Celtic but Latin. If it was Latin, then it would originally have been spelled "Camboglanna." There is such a place, and it is a prominent one at that—a visible antiquity.

Crawford also supposed that fragments of the *Annals of Wales*, which Geoffrey consulted in writing his *History*, were possibly transcribed in Scotland, as we have surmised throughout this book. They were perhaps drawn up at Saint Kentigern's Glasgow, or in Old Melrose Abbey, or in Carlisle, or at Saint Ninians Whithorn in southern Galloway. That these records were preserved in such authentic forms was probably due to the prestige and influence of King Urien's family and those of his heirs, who benefited most from the deaths of King Arthur and of King Anguselus. As we have seen, Ritchie theorized along the same line, wondering how Chrétien de Troyes, so far away in France, came to possess such privileged personal, and geographical information about Scotland, if not through ecclesiastical dignitaries sitting in closed sessions during Chrétien's lifetime, when the life and works of Saint Kentigern were formally reevaluated by the church.

F. T. Wainwright has also pointed out that there were learned men among the Picts, who took their new king from the family of Gwynedd. They too may have recorded what was for them the disastrous Battle of Camlan. The king of North Wales, the infamous Maelgwn Gwynedd, excoriated by Saint Gildas for his sins, is said to have survived the Battle of Camlan and to have died finally from the plague that recurred then. He died in Anglesey in 547 or 549, but his son Brude mac Maelchon became King Bridei of the Northern Picts at Inverness, where he ruled from c. 554 to 584. Thus, this line also profited in the aftermath of Camlan.

While the area and farmlands east of Tintagel Castle in Cornwall, England, particularly the farmhouses along the Camel River, justly claim a very great antiquity, and while medieval churchmen on holiday and on business of the church visited the area like modern tourists out of respect and veneration for King Arthur, the material found in Chrétien de Troyes and Ulrich's *Lanzelet*, not to mention other romancers on the continent, generally supports the conclusion of modern scholars like Crawford and Johnstone that King Arthur's last battle was fought close to Hadrian's Wall.

The great defensive fortification called Hadrian's Wall was built after 122 and was repaired and maintained as an offensive military network until some time in the fourth century. The wall consists of a stone rampart ten feet high in spots, running seventy-three miles across Britain from Wallsend on the east to what was once the fortress of Bowness on the Solway Firth at its western end, passing directly through the present city of Carlisle. On either side of the wall are ditches and mounds or steep earthworks. In addition, this chain of fortifications included turrets, milecastles, temples, towns, supply depots, barracks, luxurious officers' quarters, bridges, and three very large forts, which are, from east to west, Chesters, Housesteads, and Birdoswald. The first two have been fully excavated and are open to the public.

King Arthur's Camlan would have been fought at the large, westernmost fortress on Hadrian's Wall, the one now called Birdoswald. On road maps such as "Carlisle and the Solway," published by John Bartholomew and Sons, Ltd., Edinburgh, it is called Birdoswald and "CAMBOGLANNA ROMAN FORT."*

In 1979 this fort, which had not been fully excavated at that date, was open to the public by invitation of the dairy farmer who owned the land and charged admission.

The Camboglanna Fort stands on high, rolling land overlooked ten miles away in the northwest by Chamot Hill. That hill and two other adjacent hills are called on the map Arthur's Seats. They were once his staging areas. Access to these sites, in what is now the Kershope Forest, was forbidden in 1979. They can almost be reached by Routes A7, B6357, and B6318, from the junction of the M6 and A7 outside Carlisle. By car they are not more than twenty miles from Carlisle City.

The terrain of Camboglanna and vicinity persuades one that Modred awaited King Arthur there at this extensively fortified hill fort of the Romans, which barred the king's route into the Edinburgh and Stirling areas, or at least, the route from Carlisle to his main camps at and around Chamot Hill, the highest point in the area.

The death of King Arthur and of so many powerful personages is also remembered in this area, at and around what is today only the crumbling ruins of Sewingshields Castle, once a border tower on Hadrian's Wall a short distance to the east of Camboglanna Fort. Folklore and local history both attest to this site as being where, in an underground crypt, the body of King Arthur was once laid. Beside him were put his sword, his garter, and his bugle horn.

In a hallucination a shepherd of that area once fell down into the tomb, where he saw before his dazzled eyes the beloved King Arthur awaken. This same memory, or folktale, is so common to Arthurian tradition that it may actually be a real memory transmitted over the generations.

*National map series no. 38.

2

King Arthur's
Castles

Now that we have agreed with the conclusion of O.G.S. Crawford that the Camboglanna Fortress on Hadrian's Wall was the site of Arthur's terrible last battle in the west, "sore Camlan," we can see where the king's life probably drew to a close. Camlan also lay inside the Border Country, between Scotland and England, as historians and Sir Walter Scott have already supposed.

The next task should be to consider again the thirteen residences of King Arthur as they appear throughout the works of the High Middle Ages. By resuming the accumulated evidence to date, we can draw our own final conclusions about their actuality and their probable locations.

We delimited King Arthur's kingdom at its four corners: Dumbarton (NW), Carlisle (SW), Stirling (NE), and Berwick (SE). These are key centers today, with the possible exception of the seaport of Berwick, where Lancelot most probably was born, which was largely destroyed during the subsequent wars between Scotland and England.

King Arthur's first holy site seems to have stood upon or near what is today Holyrood in Edinburgh, a war memorial inherited from Aurelius Ambrosius, who had erected there or near there his monument to the dead of those wars fought before Arthur was born. His ancient site probably stood close to the modern memorials to the dead on Calton (or Caledonian) Hill, raised there recently by the citizens of modern Edinburgh. What was then the Mount of Ambrosius, referred to in Nennius, became in Arthur's lifetime, one has supposed, Arthur's Seat. One also sees no reason why the Arthurian name for Edinburgh (Teneboc, Tenebroc) could not have derived from this same volcano: *Etna (Attuna)* + *broch* (defensive tower).

Looking east from Calton Hill one sees the ancient hill forts called

Berwick Law and Traprain Law rising easily above the near horizon. The latter was once a residence of King Loth and still houses a prominent family of Scotland. Looking north across the Firth of Forth, one can see the castle hill of Stirling. Looking down the Royal Mile into Edinburgh City one can see the castle hill of Edinburgh. Looking across Holyrood, according to the commands of Sir Walter Scott, one can see the nose and faint profile of King Arthur on the Salisbury Crags.

Moving south from Edinburgh, the main road winds at once into the steep valleys toward King Arthur's staging areas above the Camboglanna Fortress on Hadrian's Wall. This is the famous mountainous country, always a battleground, now called the Border Country, between Scotland and England. These bald hills, now being reforested with conifers, are known as the Tweed River Uplands. They have always been the home of great poets, "this big purple heather country of broken stones," wrote Kipling. It is no wonder, then, that King Arthur lives on in literature that rapidly diffused, as if by capillary action, from ancient Scotland over large parts of the world.

These Uplands were the home of the renowned Taliesin of the White Brow, of Aneirin of the *Gododdin*, of "Marvelous" Merlin of prophecy, and of Thomas the Rhymer. They were also the preferred abode of Sir Walter Scott, whose verses come to mind whenever these localities occur in medieval accounts of King Arthur, Lancelot, Perceval, Gawain, and Merlin:

> *Full fifteen years and more were sped,*
> *Each brought new wreaths to Arthur's head.*
> *Twelve bloody fields with glory fought,*
> *The Saxons to subjection brought:*
> *Rython, the mighty giant, slain*
> *By his good brand, relieved Bretagne:*
> *The Pictish Gillamore in fight*
> *And the Roman Lucius owned his might;*
> *And wide were through the world renowned*
> *The glories of the Table Round.*
>
> . . .
>
> *Seemed in this dismal hour that Fate*
> *Would Camlan's ruin antedate,*
>   *And spare dark Modred's crime,*
> *Already gasping on the ground*
> *Lie twenty of the Table Round,*
>   *Of chivalry the prime.*
>   (25)(*The Bridal of Triermain*, II)

Place after place brings to mind the poets' verses and their explanations for its fame:

The mightiest chiefs of British song
Scorned not such legends to prolong.
They gleam through Spenser's elfin dream,
And mix with Milton's heavenly theme;
And Dryden, in immortal strain,
Had raised the Table Round again.
                              (*Marmion*, canto 1)

The towns here are very ancient. Peebles gets its name from the Roman commanders' flaming tents, so like winged butterflies, called "pavillions" in Latin, hence, Peebles. The Forest of Caledon, where Arthur cut down the trees in order to surround the foes, was then a dense growth of birches and hazels. It also sheltered Merlin, the "lone haunter" of that wood. Thomas the Rhymer says Merlin was buried not on the hillside at Drummelzier, where there are ruins of an ancient fortress, but down in the valley, at Drummelzier Kirk, where "Tweed and Pausayl meet."

The sites of the abbeys here are also ancient, newly reconstituted by King David I of Scotland. Sir Walter Scott had Turner come there to paint the old site of Melrose Abbey. The name of Dryburgh Abbey comes from the Celtic *Darach Bruach*, formerly an "oak tree grove," or Druid shrine, before Arthur's Christian day. From 522 it was inhabited by an Irish hermit. No trace of his shrine remains, nor could it be expected to. The ruins we see of Melrose Abbey are the towering, pink ruins of the later, medieval installations.

Characteristically, in frontier areas such as this border land between Hadrian's Wall and the Antonine Wall, the only ancient remains still visible, mostly from the air, would be of a military nature: walls and fortifications, peel castles, roads, and Roman camps. Along the journeys of Lancelot, King Arthur, and Perceval there are sites only, such as the swampy site and overgrown mound of the castle from the Dark Ages at Caerlaverock. At Lancelot's "old abbey" stands the ancient parish and the modern church of Saint Ninians, still curiously round and surrounded by a round wall at about eye level. Of that famous center of worship and learning at Whithorn there remain only a few cut stones. The immense Clachmabenstane near Gretna Green remains to show where one of the meeting places was from time immemorial. If Lancelot posted along the road from Carlisle to Dumfries, a stretch of thirty miles, he passed close by this ancient stone, which was a meeting place for the warriors of his time. It was still used during the wars of the beloved William Wallace and of the warrior Robert the Bruce.

The memory of Lancelot, Merlin, and the warrior Arthur may very well be what modern writers such as Lawrence and Yeats call "the spirit of place." The very stones seem haunted by such poetic memories, which form the common property of poets through the ages. The poet and prophet

Thomas of Erceldoune, born, like Lancelot, in Berwickshire, seems in his occult verses to be speaking of that invincible warrior Lancelot when he says:

> *Then the moon shall rise in the northwest*
> *In a cloud as black as the bill of a crow;*
> *Then shall the lion be loose, the boldest and best*
> *That ever was in Britain seen in Arthur's day.*

For those who think of King Arthur as historical, the chief problem in this talk of landmarks must be the emplacements of King Arthur's castles. Camelot must remain most important of all, not only because of its renown but also because it was "painted" (Pictish) or it housed murals and frescoes painted by Lancelot himself. At one time it is likely that it housed the king's treasures.

The well-known encyclopedist Lambert de Saint-Omer, who was until his death canon of the Collegial Church of Saint-Omer, France, reported these treasures. Thus, they were known and considered factual across the Channel from Dover, and before 1120. In his reference book called *Liber floridus*, which antedated Goeffrey of Monmouth by more than a decade, Lambert reported:

> Est palatium in Britannia, in terra Pictorum, Arturi militis, arte mirabili et varietate fundatum, in quo factorum bellorumque ejus omnia gesta sculpta videntur.

The *Liber floridus* may be found today in the library of the University of Gand. "There is a palace," said Lambert, "in Britain, in the land of the Picts, of the warrior Arthur, built with marvelous art and variety, in which all the epic deeds of his conquests and of his wars are to be seen sculpted." The Welsh *Mabinogion* confirms this residence, as "fair and many-roomed." The *Prose Lancelot* adds that Lancelot himself was the artist: B.N., MS. fr. 112, vol. 3, fol. 193. Lambert continues his reference by listing the twelve battles of Arthur as given in the Nennius documents. The thirteen royal residences attributed to King Arthur in the texts that followed Lambert and Geoffrey are:

1. *Caerleon (Carlion)* and 8 variants in 35 MSS, plus Geoffrey of Monmouth; residence of Arthur and place of his coronation.
2. *Camaalot (Camaaloth)* in 15 MSS, including the Chrétien *Lancelot,* the *Prose Lancelot,* the Chrétien *Perceval,* and the *Perlesvaus* from Glastonbury.
   The variants are so interesting that they must be looked at in alphabetical order. They suggest that the medieval authors were stumped by this or by these place names. However, when they are listed, as in the new

indexes of Flutre and West, they show a remarkable similarity. They seem to be compounds of the word for castle *(caer)* plus the name of that particular castle:

> Ca + *maaloit*
> *maelot*
> *mabalot*
> *mabelot*
> *mala(b)ot(b)*
> *maloc*
> *mal(l)ot*
> *maloth*
> *mellot*
> *melot(b)*
> *mellot*
> *melot(b)*

In addition, the following forms appear also:

> *Kamaalot*
> *Cramalot*
> *Quamaalot(b)*
> *Chamaalot*
> *Gamalot*

Camelot has been identified as the following places inside England (which does not take into account the works of Lambert, Geoffrey, or the writers who followed them in the High Middle Ages): Colchester, Cadbury, and Winchester. John Morris, Wendelin Foerster, and Roger Sherman Loomis have insisted on these sites; but Loomis finally concluded that Camelot was not the name of any place in Britain.*

3. *Caradigan*, a castle   12 MSS
4. *Cardueil, Cardoeil*, capital city of the kingdom called
   "Galles"   over 70 MSS
   > (Variants *Quaraduel* [Chrétien's *Erec*], and *Charduel*
   > [Béroul's *Tristan*, and *Fergus*] are considered regu-
   > lar; since *c* regularly becomes *ch* as it comes into
   > French from Latin).
5. *Carreboi, Carreor*, a residence   1 MS
   > (*Prose Tristan*)
6. *Quarrois, Roais*, a castle   1 MS
   > (*Erec*)

Arthurian Tradition, pp. 480–81.

7. *Dinasdaron*, a castle of refuge   3 MSS
8. *Londres*, a capital city (including the *Prose Lancelot*, with its added or slavishly complimentary emphasis upon King Henry II)   6 MSS
9. *Montagu, Montagut*, castle and dukedom   8 MSS

   This is sometimes the castle and dukedom of King Arthur's allies—King Loth, King Marc, and King Bademagus. Or it is the city called in error *Chastel aux Pucelles* (Castle of Maidens in *Perceforest*). Generally it is referred to as a Mount, as in

   Montagu = Steep Mount,
   Mont Doloreus = Mount of Dolor, 4 MSS
   Mont Agned = Geoffrey of Monmouth's Edinburgh,
   Mont Perilleux = *Perceval*.

   By Castle of Maidens is meant Edinburgh in the 15 MSS. It should have been instead Castle of Assembly.
10. *Orquenie, Orcanie*, city and residence   1 MS *(Perceval)*
11. *Pouret*, castle   1 MS *(Yder)*
12. *Sinaudone, Senaudone, Isneldone, Dodone*, residence and kingdom of importance: Town of the queen of Galles *(Le Bel inconnu)*, the Gaste Cité, or the Waste Land: Arthur's castle *(Béroul's Tristan)*; Lancelot's conquest *(Lanzelet)*; The Gaste Forêt, the Waste Forest *(Perceval)*   11 MSS
13. *Tintagel, Nantael, Cintagel*, residence of Arthur or of King Marc   3 MSS

   (Prose Lancelot, Perlesvaus, Prose Tristan)

Several names among the thirteen can be eliminated at once:

Nos. 3 and 12 (Caradigan and Tintagel) because they are attempts to relocate the Arthurian legend in the south of Britain, and anachronistically in Norman French castles of the twelfth century.

Nos. 9 and 10 (Edinburgh and Orquenie) because they do not claim to be King Arthur's castles but those of his vassals, such as Erec and King Loth. The word *Orquenie* does not indicate, in any case, the Orkney Islands, as has often been thought. The Orkneys are *Ynysoedd Erch*, and there is no phonetic resemblance.

Nos. 5 and 6 (Carrehoi and Quarrois) because the reading is corrupt, meaning only "castle of the king" (?).

No. 11 (Pouret) because it is a lone, late MS and from southern Wales and Cornwall, without authentication.

No. 8 (Londres) because that capital city was mistaken for Edinburgh, Glasgow, or Arthur's capital city at Stirling or for the other chief or capital city at Carlisle. The first came about because of the "West," which Malory took for Westminster and Church of Saint Stephen. At Carlisle it was Saints Julius and Aaron.

No. 7 (Dinasdaron) because this indicates Carlisle and should be added to the more than 70 MSS naming King Arthur's chief city. *Dinas* = castle + Aron = Aaron, the martyred saint. King Arthur was crowned here, at Carlisle, the most heavily fortified place in all the Border area.

Loomis thought, but without evidence, that *Dinasdaron* indicated Dinas Bran, which is on the access route from Chester to the Snowdon Mountains in North Wales. However, the Welsh name for Snowdon is *Yr Wyddfa*; Snowdonia is *Eryri*. It is true that Dinas Bran is a tiny Dark Age fortress of unforgettable access and aspect, atop the crown of a spectacular conical hill overlooking the Dee Valley and the town of Llangollen. The climb to it is vertiginous by any Alpinist's standards. Turner included the fortress as background to his painting of Valle Crucis Abbey.

The real authority in matters concerning Dinas Bran is C. A. Raleigh Radford, who makes no mention of it in connection with King Arthur, and rightly so.

In conclusion, then, no. 13 among our castles, or Tintagel, should be our "Castle of the White Field," now Caerlaverock, the birthplace of King Arthur, because it was his mother's castle.

The eleven manuscripts referring to Sinaudone, or Snowdon in its English form, are probably separate from the Camelot of King Arthur but in the same vicinity. Snowdon is King Lancelot's castle, after having been the domain of the Widow Lady of the Waste Land, Perceval's mother.

This leaves very impressive grand totals:

Carlisle			Camaalot		
1. *Caerleon:*	35	MSS	2. *Camaalot:*	15 MSS
4. *Cardueil:*	70+	MSS	8. *Londres:*	6 MSS
7. *Dinasdaron:*	3	MSS		
	108	MSS		21 MSS

Clearly Carlisle is indicated as King Arthur's principal castle, and we know that he claimed two in that immediate area, the one on the water's edge called the Castle of the Rock (Perron).* We also know that the above names

---

Perron = *perhen* = large △ of stone, at least twenty feet high. A Perron Round = a stone circle.

refer truly to Carlisle because they are often qualified in some way, such as "near the land of the Scots and Picts," for instance.

The harder question of Camelot has challenged the best of the English scholars, like Howard Maynardier in 1907 and Vida D. Scudder in 1921, both of whom studied King Arthur in relation to the poets and Malory in relation to his sources. Camelot, we know, has long been considered fictitious.

One of the most able poets to write of it was Tennyson, whose verses in "Gareth and Lynette" (*Idylls of the King*) are so beautiful:

> *So when their feet were planted on the plain*
> *That broaden'd toward the base of Camelot,*
> *Far off they saw the silver-misty morn*
> *Rolling her smoke about the royal mount,*
> *That rose between the forest and the field.*
> *At times the spires and turrets halfway down*
> *Prick'd thro' the mist; at times the great gate shone*
> *Only, that open'd on the field below;*
> *Anon, the whole fair city had disappear'd.*

And Scott celebrates Stirling in "The Lord of the Isles":

> *Old Stirling's towers arose in light,*
> *And twined in links of silver bright,*
> *Her winding river lay.*
> (6)
> *Through Ninian's church these torches shone. . . .*
> (19)

The verses of Tennyson are unwittingly accurate. From the eastern side of this castle rock, as one gazes out toward the mouth of the Forth River and the North Sea, the gray cliff drops abruptly and steeply down to the loops of the Forth River. That river winds directly under the castle cliff on that eastern side, so that standing on the ledge of rock one looks down upon the river snaking far below. The bridge, which once led to Cambuskenneth Abbey curled inside a loop of the river, is still there though the abbey is not. It would have been possible for Lancelot and Queen Guinevere to have looked down and seen the barge of Elaine, the Lily Maid of Astolat, floating toward the open sea.

On the western side, where the cliff face is steepest, the plain below it stretches flat except for the castle mound called Arthur's Knot. Tennyson has his gate, or castle entrance, on the side of the plain when, in fact, it probably lay as it does today on the eastern side, at the sloping or entrance side of the fortress. The most ancient engravings also show it there. And in any case, the traditional and mythological entrance to all castles lies only on the eastern side, just as the altars of all churches stand on their eastern sides.

Tennyson's major source for this, Sir Thomas Malory, saw Camelot as "many-towered," a medieval capital of a land of dreams. Malory knew more Arthurian material and lore than any author before him or since; he should not be dismissed simply because he generally thought that he was writing tragical fiction.

Camelot in Malory often seems to mean King Arthur's castle at Carlisle, but not only the *Château del Perron*, the one beside the sea, or Solway Firth. Queen Guinevere is at Camelot, for instance, when Gawain arrives to serve her. There Tristan is received into the Round Table. Lancelot also waits there after the departure of the knights on the Quest of the Holy Grail and there hears tragic news concerning Perceval and Galahad. This Camelot squares with what *Gawain and the Green Knight* claims—that it was King Arthur's official court at the holy Christmas time. The earliest reference to "Camaalot" occurs in Chrétien's *Lancelot*, where it is similarly King Arthur's ceremonial court at Pentecost, another Christian holy time. The prestige and authority of these three texts argue against the hasty relegation of Camelot to fiction, or feigning.

In Sir Thomas Malory there occurs quite another Camelot, however, and it is a great castle beside a river, but high above it, so high that from its windows a craft floating downstream can be plainly seen. Such a panorama, viewed from a height, happens not once but twice in isolated instances in the *Morte d'Arthur*.* First, the sword of Balin comes down to Camelot upon a floating stone (ark). Then Elaine from Astolat, which Sir John Rhys thought was Dumbarton, lying on her funeral barge like Perceval's sister after her phlebotomy, floats down the river to her beloved Lancelot. Again, this is specifically Camelot, where and when Queen Guinevere herself is formally in residence. In each case cited, Malory carefully identified Camelot as the capital of Britain *in his day*, which is to say, as London, and the river as the Thames. In these ascriptions, however, he followed the *Prose Lancelot* and made no change or took no initiative by himself.

From the beautiful pages of Malory, then, the perception begins to intrude upon the reader that *Camelot* refers not so much to any one geographic spot that can be pinpointed upon a map as to King Arthur's castle, wherever he is in residence. When he was in residence, probably some pennant flew from the tower, just as it does from Windsor Castle today. One

---

*Book 2, chap. 19, p. 70; book 18, chap. 20, p. 304.

would then do well to look again at the word *Camelot* to see if a solution lies there after all.

In the word *Camelot* the variants consistently present, after the initial first syllable indicated by the velars *K* or *G* (the French *K* or *Ch*) the word for castle (*caer*), another invariably two-syllable word. The second two-syllable word consistently breaks down, however, into *m* followed by a vowel, which, true to form, becomes long and open before the liquid *l*. The *l* appears rather to be *ll*, which increases the duration of the preceding vowel, until it frequently becomes, as regularly in Old French, a diphthong. *M-a-e* and *maha* are fronted into the sound of *e*, as *m* + open *e* where the vowel is opened because of its length and its position in the mouth. Even the *m-e-l* becomes in other instances *m-e-ll*. Now, the fronting phenomenon in Old French characterizes the speech patterns of Celtic Gaul, as the inhabitants there came into contact with spoken Latin. Thus, regularly, a Latin word beginning with the sound of *k* becomes *ch*, as *Camelot>Chamelot*. Second, the Latin vowel *a* becomes diphthongized, as *mal>mael* and as fronted, the Latin phonemes always pronounced farther to the front of the mouth, as *mall>mell*.

After looking at *Camelot* phonetically, one concludes that it is made of two words: *Caer* + a Latin word originally spelled *malleus* = hammer, and/or its derivatives. *malleator* = a hammerer, and *malleatus* = armed with a hammer. The English diminutive form became *mallet*, the suffix being virtually identical with the last syllable generally in the word *Camelot*, *Ca* + *mallot*. Those writers who heard the suffix *oc* instead of the Latin-French regular diminutive *ot* in the masculine, pronounced "o" as in *Lancelot* ("lanseló") and *Camelot* ("kameló"), were probably Anglo-Saxon speakers, who assimilated the Anglo-Saxon suffix, as in *mattock*.

Camelot probably indicates, as Malory seems to have been inclined to believe, King Arthur's castle when the king was in residence there, at whatever site that may have been. It seems to mean "Castle of the Hammerer," King Arthur having been called by the Nennius glossator in the tenth century and thereafter "malleus ferreus," the Iron Hammer(er). In later heraldry, the clawed hammer crowned actually became the symbol of a duke, *Arturus dux*.

The *Perlesvaus* text comes in here to explain furthermore that there were two Camelots.

The former Camelot, which belonged to the Widow Lady, stood at the head of the most savage isle of Gales [Wales], near the sea, inclined toward the west [*devers Occident*]. The only things there were the fortress itself, and the (Waste) Forest, and the water all around.

The other Camelot sat at the entrance to the kingdom of Logres, and this was a populated area, and was the chief seat of the king's

domains due to the fact that there he held dominion over all the lands
of that part of the country that adjoined his own holdings. (*Perlesvaus*
10, vv. 7280–87)

Thus, there were probably two chief seats called "Camelot." One was
at Carlisle, and the other was at the King's Knot below the western-facing
cliff at Stirling.

Had Sir Thomas Malory adopted the reading of *Perlesvaus*, he would
have seen corroborated his hunch that there was more than one place named
Camelot—or that Camelot indicated no one particular site and castle of
King Arthur but the castle of King Arthur, the sovereign in residence at that
time. But Sir Thomas Malory followed, for long periods of time as he composed the *Morte d'Arthur*, the composite authors of the *Prose Lancelot*. These
persons were intent upon flattering their patron, and particularly King Henry
II of the Angevin Empire. Thus, they made their story come out so that
King Arthur was King Henry II, King Lancelot was William Marshal, first
earl of Pembroke, and the Lady of the Lake was Queen Eleanor of Aquitania. Had Malory followed the English *Perlesvaus*, he would have found confirmation for his own hunch concerning Camelot. In *Perlesvaus* occurs a host
of precisions that open the eyes upon the real world of history in the Dark
Ages.

Perlesvaus gives first of all the long explanation about the several Valleys
of Camelot, where once there were fifteen domains and castles. In that large
estuary stalked the fierce Lord of the Moors, more properly, Mosses. A
paved Roman road cut this valley in half, running into the far north, in the
direction of the Moray Firth, along a most remarkable geographical feature.
This was a strait or defile, actually the only crossing of the swampy, un-
drained Forth River estuary, and below it the Romans had stretched the
Antonine Wall, at the Roman fort of Camelon.

This passage or strait was called the "steep defile," in Old French, the
"Gaut Destroit." Along this chasm, one abreast, warriors could ride down to
the unique Ford of Valdone, stipulated Chrétien in *Perceval*. The *Perlesvaus*
complements him, mentioning river, castle, moors, high road, strait and
stipulating that this was the east-west cutoff line into the great north. South
of this Forth-Clyde line were the Picts of Alba; to their north were the seven
provinces of the Northern Picts, whose military capital was Inverness.

This topography places one in the unmistakable Camelon-Stirling Battle Corridor, the Cockpit of Scotland. Whether in the Dark Ages or today,
one can stand at the Stirling Gap, beside the lofty Campsie-Gargunnock
Hills to the west and the Forth estuary to the east. The north-south corridor, famous for many battles but especially for Bannockburn in 1314, is ten
miles long and four miles wide. It leads to Camelot, identified by O.G.S.
Crawford as Stirling Castle and the "key to Scotland."

The prehistoric fort sat, like the modern fortress and barracks still in use today, upon the "great impregnable" wall, looking down its precipitious cliffs toward Dumbarton on the west. Stirling Castle commanded the "Gaut Destroit" of the French romancers, the only and very narrow crossing of the flooded Forth River estuary. At peak flood the Forth stretched one mile wide across flatlands. To the west the military road to Loch Lomond and Dumbarton still cuts deeply into the peat mosses across the Vale of Menteith, and outflanks the Stirling crossing. The Gaelic word for the path descending the narrow cleft to the Ford of Kildean was *Bealach-(na)-gaig.*

O.G.S. Crawford arrived at this conclusion—that King Arthur's castle was probably Stirling—from his familiarity with the geography of Scotland and from his readings in the British and Roman histories and geographers. Several French romances, especially Chrétien's *Perceval* and the Glastonbury *Perlesvaus,* support his original and daring conclusion.

Standing beside the castle and looking down the west cliffs of Stirling, one can plainly see on the meadowlands below the "King's Knot." This is an octagonal mound, now more like a formal garden, but whose name means "castle mound," the mound upon which the wooden palisaded castles were built in ancient times. Upon this mound once stood King Arthur's Camelot. It is now called "knot" from the Gaelic *cnoc,* but there is no doubt that the meaning is "castle mound."

There at his castle at Stirling King Arthur chaired the Round Table. A fourteenth-century testimony assured O.G.S. Crawford of it: there was a "round table below the castle" of Stirling. William of Worcester (1415–82?) added a final piece to the puzzle: King Arthur "custodiebat le round-table in Castro de Styrling, aliter, snowdon west castell" ("King Arthur presided over the Round Table in the military fort of Stirling, otherwise known as Snowdon West Castle").

It may have been this same reference to a "west castell" that caused Sir Thomas Malory to write and to think of "Westminster," ergo London. Jean Froissart, the very accurate and most distinguished French chronicler of King Richard II in the fourteenth century, said very much the same, that Stirling was known in French as "Sinaudon."

An alternate view, which has dominated Arthurian studies for a considerable time in our century, was that proposed by Roger Sherman Loomis. He contended vigorously for his prior conclusion, that Snowdon was the Roman fortress of Segontium of North Wales, never acknowledging that Snowdon in Welsh is *Eryri,* or *Yr Wyddfa.* As Basil Clarke says, Segontium stirred the medieval imagination because of its impressive ruins, and thus passed into Nennius and into the *Mabinogion.* The most respected Arthurian scholars always opposed Loomis and opted for Stirling as Snowdon.*

*A. Ewert, E. Brugger, and others.

Five writers of French romances told interesting stories about romantic Snowdon: that it was a renowned kingdom, that the queen of Gales, or Wales, whose name was the Blonde Esmeree, lived there, that it was called alternately the Waste City (Gaste Cité) and Waste Land because of the treachery of a villain named Mabon (*Le Bel inconnu*). The early and authoritative *Tristan* of Béroul put King Arthur's chief seat and residence there. Chrétien placed the youth Perceval in the Waste Forest there, beside the castle ruled by a sister of King Arthur. She was the vocal Widow Lady of Camelot. Chrétien had Perceval's sword forged there, at *Cotouatre*, or *Scottewatre*, or the Firth of Forth. He called the strait above Stirling *Valdone*. Ulrich's *Lanzelet* took that other hero on a line of conquest from Limors, probably the Lammermoors made famous by Sir Walter Scott, to Beforet Castle on the Calder River, which has seemed to designate Edinburgh, thence to the great, rich fortress of Dodone on its cliff near the sea, but well enough inland to withstand pirates, only a day's distance from Edinburgh. Thus, *Valdone* and *Dodone* seem to be the same Snowdon, or Stirling.

To Stirling the sword of Balin returned, floating downstream to its cradle, to the same smith and anvil that had forged it. This is one Camelot, then, standing near what the *Perlesvaus* said was an "uttermost headland," that formed the "wildest island" of the estuary. The author of *Perlesvaus* had learned from someone or from some text that it was a feast for the eyes, one mountain almost alone in the expanse of flatlands. Stirling seen from the Antonine Wall is an even more impressive mass than the red lava Rock of Clyde standing beside the broad Clyde River, as the road from Stirling turns south at Loch Lomond and dips down to sea level.

Chrétien wrote in *Perceval*:

> Et cil dit: "Sire, ore esgardez
> Cel plus haut bois que vos veez,
> Qui cele montainge avironne:
> La sont li destroit de Valdone . . ."
>
> (*v.* 298)
>
> [And he said: "Sire, now look at the highest
> trees that you see, which surround that mountain:
> there are the Straits of Valdone."]

And Perceval said, "A Sinadon la fu jo nes: . . . ." [At Snowdon, there was I born: . . .].

All things considered, King Arthur probably first housed his treasures and paid his sculptors and architects and gardeners first at the fertile loops of the Forth at Stirling, rather than in volcanic Edinburgh also flooded then by the North Loch, or in devastated Roman Carlisle. The Border Country around Carlisle constituted over the centuries the most dangerous territory in Britain, overrun by legions and other Romans and by raiding Picts. Edinburgh itself stood in another borderland, between the Hadrian and Antonine walls, vulnerable on the west from the Clyde River, despite Dumbarton, and on the east open to raiders crossing the Firth of Forth.

Stirling brooded alone on its mountain ten miles north of the second wall, the Antonine, above a marshy crossroads whence one could leap across into the hills and mountains of the Highlands and seek safety far from alarms that called men instantly to wars. Thus, the majesty of Stirling and the relic of King Arthur, the King's Knot, keep close company, there where "a loop of the Forth is worth an earldom in the north."

3

The Round Table

Ever since the middle of the twelfth century, when, so far as is known, the phrase "the Round Table" was coined, the world has been intrigued: What was it? Several major theories have tried to answer this. Nobody seems to have got as far as a second question: Where was it?

The first and most commonly held theory explains that the Round Table was a table. This is a pragmatical answer. Like other tables of our experience, it was used when eating. The Welsh still have a tune called "Gorleg yr Halen," sung, they say, when the salt cellar was placed upon the table before King Arthur. But was this "Prelude of the Salt" played when the salt cellar was placed upon the Round Table? Probably not.

According to this first and strictly utilitarian theory, the table was round so that no person took precedence over any other vassal of King Arthur, which is preposterous because Lancelot took precedence over all and sat at the same level as the king himself.

When we start totting up the figures, we see immediately that nobody, including medieval artists, knew how many men were supposed to have been seated at the round dinner table. The *Prose Lancelot* claims that two hundred fifty knights sat at it during an August session of King Arthur's court. Before that, it claims that ninety knights, brought into King Arthur's service by the queen as a part of her dowry, sat at it. Malory ventures to claim that the queen brought to her husband one hundred knights for the Round Table. Geoffrey of Monmouth's translator/adapter Layamon earlier claimed that Arthur had a carpenter in Cornwall make him the Round Table, which could seat a full complement of sixteen hundred knights at a meal.

Earlier in the century Chrétien de Troyes had started to make a reasonable statement about the number of knights in the Round Table; he counted up to ten then lost count and added another twenty-one or so. It seems clear that nobody knew positively the number of actual eaters or members. And yet membership it was, and a membership not all that casual, for Lancelot was "elected" to that "fellowship" on an All Saints' Day after he had by means of a severe ordeal proven himself worthy. Wace, who first had broached the subject and who had coined the phrase "the Round Table," made no attempt to discuss the logistics of board feet and lumber from Cornwall or elsewhere or to venture a guess as to the number of sitters or members. He thought it was a "fair fellowship," known far and wide for errant deeds, and "gestes," which are errant deeds in French, and/or poems about those deeds. He made no association between "table" and "board."

The possibility that we are dealing here with King Arthur's chosen honor guard, or special retinue, must also, alas, be discounted. Chrétien gives the names of the first four members, whom we recognize, as Gawain, Erec (who was crowned at Edinburgh), Lancelot, and "Gonemanz de Goort." This last person is no youngster dedicated to serving King Arthur but an older man and one of the much esteemed tutors and uncles of Perceval. He neither attends Arthur nor subsequently serves him abroad. Furthermore, the members of King Arthur's retinue are called servants, the word *Gilla* in their names or titles indicating their functions: Henchman, Sword Bearer, Bard, Piper, Piper's Servant, Porter (who carried the king over water), Equerry (who led the king's horse over difficult terrain), and so on. These persons are recognizable among the attendants upon the king at his coronation, as detailed in Geoffrey of Monmouth. They are much lesser dignitaries than the aristocratic Lancelot, Erec, Gawain, and Perceval's uncle.

The only writers throughout the Middle Ages who maintain the same story are those affiliated with the Judeo-Christian theory about King Arthur and his knights. Queen Morgan at the Grail Castle, who is King Arthur's sister, represents this intellectual point of view when she declares that there have been by her time three Christian fellowships: the Disciples of Christ at His Last Supper, the members of the Holy Grail, and the members of the Round Table. The numbers in each case were, of course, twelve plus one, or thirteen. Both she and her learned daughter, who seems to be one of the Loathly Damsels, then launch forth into erudite discourses upon astronomy. Thus, we have another recurrent association with "the Round Table."

Robert de Boron's *Merlin* says that the Round Table was originally built for Uther Pendragon by Merlin. This sort of information also continues on its own separate track through the Middle Ages and on into the sixteenth century, where it is insistently repeated in the Chronicle of Ihon Hardyng (1543).

When other authors repeat the interesting fact that the Round Table was brought to King Arthur as part of the dowry of his Queen Guinevere, they take it literally: that she or her attendants actually shouldered a table, which was big and round, and physically transported it to the wedding. As we can surmise, this fact hangs upon the use and meaning of the word *brought*.

Merlin raised Arthur, and he arranged for Arthur to show his prowess by drawing the sword from the flint anvil stone (lighting the torch) where Merlin had placed it. Merlin built the war memorial or monument for Aurelius Ambrosius from stones taken out of Ireland. They were used there as part of a temple and set under the jurisdiction of an Irish king called Gillomanus, according to Geoffrey of Monmouth. Now, the Arthurian scholar Laura Hibbard Loomis tells us that *Gillomanus* means "Servant of the Stones," or pagan priest. Rethinking this information, we are prone to think that when Merlin built the Round Table for Uther, it was of stone and not of wood. Nor was it for any such prosaic use as dinner; Mrs. Loomis concludes, in fact, that megalithic folklore from around 2000 B.C. continues to gleam occasionally through the Arthurian literature. It was hardly Geoffrey of Monmouth's fault that he leaped to the erroneous conclusion that Merlin built Stonehenge, since olden stones and Stonehenge lurk subjacent in the actions of Aurelius Ambrosius.

Stuart Piggott came to the defense of this ancient material underlying the Arthurian literature, noting the pronounced archaism of the entire Arthurian tradition. Sanctuaries open to the sky, ritual enclosures, the cult of the severed head, the massive hill forts such as the one at the northernmost Eildon Hill, where or near which Uther suffered his defeat and which was even in 500 B.C. some forty acres in area—all point to megalithic, or huge stone, constructions. Even in Arthur's day the king seems to have been able to muster unbelievably large numbers of skilled craftsmen for stonework and metallurgy. Copper nails were discovered in the ancient ship found at Stranraer, and there were fancy columns of copper at the Grail Castle. The three-tubed, vertically held war trumpets employed in ancient times may be seen in museums or reproduced on coins. Swords, spoked-wheel chariots, gold torques and crowns, underground tombs surrounded with flame, three hundred ships in the harbor of the Grail Castle, silver hoards, and alveolate walls for the storing of the bodies of heroes after death (and Lancelot was shown the cell for his own body) give some hint of a society technically more advanced than had been thought.

This ancient culture of King Arthur, said Stuart Piggott, demonstrated a remarkable continuity, and it was a common, Celtic culture. Thus, alveolate walls similar to the ones shown Lancelot are to be seen today in a porch in Provence. In Provence they were miniature because they were used to store severed heads, not entire bodies. The Ulster cycle of tales, the Arthurian cycle, and Homer's *Iliad* all depict the same warrior ethos and much of the same personalities and behavior traits. Perceval resembles Agamemnon, Lancelot resembles Achilles, Gawain resembles Hector, and Arthur has always been seen to resemble Hercules. All were savages in battle. All showed the same contempt for pain, for death, and yet the same reverence for the dead. They rushed to combat at the first flash of the beacon or heliograph. One after another each raised the war cry, which was called "Hubub" in Welsh and "Slogan" among the ancient Caledonians. Like Perceval, these warriors could run with the speed of a wild deer or a galloping horse. The last person to arrive at the assembly, once the Slogan sounded, was put to death—publicly and ignominiously. It is no wonder Lancelot caused horses to founder.

The art historians study some symbols, albeit in vain, for the sense of them more often than not escapes the scholar, to wit the carnyx (war trumpet), the comb, the horn of the Grail Castle (or the horned bay), the masted ship, the golden torque, the boar ensign, and the harp. Ancient Celtic art is powerful and enigmatic. The Celts continued to be great builders in stone, whether we can find proof of it or whether their stones have long since been hauled away and used to build dams, or purposely cracked into pieces.

The question we will ask, for the first time, it would seem, is: Should we look for some sort of stone building somewhere in the vicinity of Edinburgh and/or Stirling? Have we been on the wrong track all these centuries looking for round dining tables and measuring odd board feet?

Lancelot went to an old abbey, which was a stone building, and descended into the crypt to see his grandfather's tomb surrounded by flames. The *Perlesvaus* manuscript talks about a chapel and a tomb in which a body and other relics were housed. That sort of building would be called a martyrium. In the years 425–50 Galla Placidia was erecting in Italy a mausoleum for herself and for the emperor; Queen Guinevere was at the same time erecting a mausoleum for herself and for King Arthur at the newly conquered Grail Castle. In the years between 468 and 483, during the lifetime of King Arthur, the martyrium of San Stefano Rotondo was being constructed; it was built on a table or has an entablature instead of an arcade level. One begins to suspect Wace and his careless, laconic way of launching the troublesome phrase "Round Table."

In 1720 the Reverend Dr. William Stukeley published a pamphlet on an ancient building that he had found in Stirlingshire, actually on the Carron River bank, near Falkirk, and thus a few miles south of Stirling Castle. The prominent and strange stone building sat on the main Roman roadside from the south into Stirling. The local residents habitually termed it "Arthur's O'on." They thought it was an oven for baking the bread of an army or that it was a huge, outdoor furnace. From the outside it looked exactly like an enormous stone beehive.

Fortunately for the world, Dr. Stukeley sat down immediately and made a careful drawing. He is the same Stukeley who first discovered at Stonehenge, astonishingly, that this structure was aligned to the midsummer sunrise, and he was the first person to compute its date (c. 1750 B.C.) as long before Christ. He also was first to have discovered the Avenue at Stonehenge and also the Cursus. Copies of his drawings can be viewed and purchased at the Avebury Museum, near Stonehenge. They are marvelous to behold and are treasures worth acquiring. The eminent contemporary archaeologist R. J. C. Atkinson of University College, Cardiff, informs us that Stukeley was much in advance of his age and that the megalithic monument of Avebury was hardly known at all to the general public until the year 1743, when Stukeley published his book called *Abury*.

The same is true for Arthur's O'on. Without the knowledge, effort, talent, and the perseverance of Stukeley, Arthur's O'on would have been lost to the world, irrevocably and utterly. Twenty-three years after Stukeley drew his picture of Arthur's O'on, the building was demolished and its stones carted away to make a dam. Now all that remains are Stukeley's invaluable pamphlet, his correspondence, and his drawing of Arthur's O'on. The contemporary French authority Fernand Niel also assures us that Stukeley's drawings of megalithic stone monuments are astonishingly accurate, to within inches, in every case.*

The structure that local residents commonly called "Arthur's O'on" thus far has been considered by scholars to have been a war memorial developed from the Roman custom of displaying battle standards and conquered arms on a tree trunk. In later days a stone column might replace the clumsy tree trunk. This perfunctory sort of memorial of a Roman victory was called a *tropaeum*, hence our word *trophy*. An alternate scholarly theory was advanced, however, that the Arthurian structure might have been an early Roman temple to the god Terminus, god of boundaries. According to this second theory, the edifice would have been a territorial marker, then, not far from the Antonine Wall, and built along with it.

Neither theory takes sufficiently into account, however, the nature of the architecturally complex structure itself, which is well documented and recognizable. Nor does either theory take into account the reference to the famous "chapel" that Perceval knew was near Stirling Castle, his own mother's residence and castle, where he stopped to worship, to pay his respects, and to view once more the holy relics.

*Two of Stukeley's drawings were reprinted in the pages of *Antiquity* 48 (1974): 283–87; Alain G. Brown's article " 'Gothicism, ignorance, and bad taste': the destruction of Arthur's O'on."

The question to ask now is this: What sort of building was used or erected in the fifth century for the purpose of housing a valuable relic? The answer: a rotunda, also called a *martyrion*. The Holy Land was full of them.

Arthur's O'on was not an impromptu trophy but an architectural marvel, an unattached circular, beehive-type structure, built of forty courses of ashlar blocks, according to Stukeley. These blocks of hewn stone were set without mortar upon an elevated, square stone platform. The stone platform itself seems to have been set upon an earthen mound. The worshiper entered the edifice by means of an unroofed portico of two stone slabs, a smaller upon a larger, the width of the doorway. The door opening was enclosed by a true arch constructed of voussoirs, wedge-shaped blocks pointing toward the center or top of the arch. Above that was a stepped-mountain symbol in stone, probably for the donor's name or for the name of the temple. Nothing at all is visible upon the smooth stone in Stukeley's painstaking drawing.

The relative size of both platform and building can be inferred from a mounted horseman carefully drawn in Stukeley's architectural rendering to the left and below the temple. Even without that, one could infer its size from a comparison with the well-preserved and thus better-known rotundas from Arthur's day.

Although Arthur's O'on was clearly built in imitation of the renowned Treasury of Atreus, this building was not used for such a mundane purpose in the fifth century. Nor would it have represented anything so worldly as a military victory, when the similar rotunda in Jerusalem housed the very body of Christ. Furthermore, a wordly monument to the goddess Victory would hardly have taken the form of a commemorative rotunda, or a most holy martyrion. Such buildings were all the rage since the days of the convert Constantine and his passion for Christian building in Eternal Rome and in Golden Jerusalem.

Art historians have demonstrated that all round buildings in the ancient world, especially since Constantine's building of the Martyrion of the Holy Sepulcher in the Holy Land, followed a similar plan. They trace these round buildings back to the *tholos* of Aesculapius in the fourth century B.C., and then forward to the temple of the Tiburtine Sibyl, to the Pantheon at Rome, and to Constantine's Mausoleum of Santa Costanza (c. A.D. 330), to the Lateran Baptistery (c. 430), and thence to the Martyrion of the Holy Sepulcher. That complex rotunda and cross shape was used everywhere in the Christian world from 350 or 380. As we have already seen, this prototype furnished an iconography for western Europe.

King Arthur's O'on was in his lifetime a round, domed temple used, like those of Jerusalem, to shelter and to display a tomb and holy relics. Like the Pantheon it had a circular opening at the top. This opening, called the crown of the dome, furnished illumination in the structure in Scotland and the one in Rome. It was left open in Rome, but it is not certain that it was left open in Jerusalem. Perhaps there it was covered with a dome of timber construction. In Arthur's edifice the crown terminates in this opening, technically termed an *opaion*, encircled by one course of voussoirs, or it is finished open at the crown, as such. In such structures, and in Arthur's building, the diameter usually equaled the elevation. The original Constantinian Martyrion was one hundred feet in diameter, with a conical dome and central eye. Arthur's O'on terminated, so far as one can discover from studying the drawing, in a flat crown and open eye. Stukeley drew a square opening over the doorway, but in such a way as to show that it had been made at some later date, by the removal of the stones, observed Arthur D. Stevens. Such buildings were often encircled by columns, but one sees no trace of such nor of their emplacements in Stukeley's drawing.

It is very important now to search Arthurian literature for a trace of this structure called King Arthur's O'on, for linguistic evidence plainly shows that it may have been the origin of what writers through the centuries have called the Round Table.

After the first mention of "the Round Table," which occurs in Wace's adaptation of Geoffrey of Monmouth, the more daring writers of Arthurian literature plunged headlong into deeper waters. None understood or even stopped to consider what Wace meant by the phrase. Nobody asked where Wace found it—certainly not in Geoffrey's text. The *Merlin* thought it a place where King Arthur sat in state four times yearly—at Christmas, Easter, Pentecost, and Saint John's Day—or that the Round Table was the round hill fort of Camelot, that is, Stirling's King's Knot. *Le Roy Artus* thought it seated two hundred fifty warriors, which Layamon built into a carpenter's nightmare. The *Grand-Saint-Graal* also considered it a table with a thirteenth seat, the Seat of Dread, it was located at the Grail Castle, Corbenic, the Foreign Land. Wolfram in *Parzival* solved the problem of logistics by having a picnic cloth laid around a meadow, dinner served al fresco, and no table built at all.

Laura Hibbard Loomis suggested that the Round Table might once have referred to Christ, whose table of the Last Supper was by medieval accounts not rectangular but round, a *mensa* (table) *rotunda* (round) *Christi* (of Christ). In the Romance languages, as here in Latin, the routine order of words is noun followed by modifiers. Mrs. Loomis has given us an idea, by calling us back to Wace's wording of the phrase.

It is important to see exactly what Wace said: "Fist Artus la Roönde Table" (*Brut*, v. 9747). "Arthur made (or built) a tabled rotunda," a rotunda upon a platform or foundation. In Old French the noun should be the word *roönde* (Latin *rotunda*), not the word *table* (the Latin word for table is *mensa*). We know that *rotunda* also refers to Virgil's tomb, which was a concave dome, or sepulcher. Thus, Arthur's *O'on* probably represented the Old French and Scottish corruption of the original Latin word *rotonda/rotunda*.

Fortunately, the art historian M.J.T. Lewis studied the question carefully in his work *Temples in Roman Britain*, concluding that Arthur's O'on had been a monument absolutely unique, without any parallel, in fact, in the entire Roman world, unlike any of their many free-standing monuments. He believed its dimensions were twenty feet (interior diameter), twenty-one feet (height), and twenty-eight feet (outer diameter). These precisions recall Stukeley and the topographical antiquarian A. Gordon, who is said in 1726 to have measured and drawn the monument. In his *History of Scotland* (1873) John Hill Burton resumed the question as of that date.* Lewis for his part granted the fact of a huge stone block inside the monument, a statue base or altar. He accepted the date of Stukeley as of c. A.D. 290–93, and the Nennius gloss, as follows:

> Carutius . . . domum rotundam politis lapidibus super ripam Ca-
> run . . . fornicem in victoriae memoriam erigens construxit.

> [Carausius built on the bank of the Carron River (just south of Stirling, and near the Roman fortress of Camelon) a round house of hewn stones, erecting a monument in memory of his victory.]

Thus, the matter rested there, leaving unsolved the question of Nennius versus Wace: either Carausius built Arthur's O'on, or Arthur's father and Merlin built it.

Lewis also recalled what J.C. Bruce in his *Handbook to the Roman Wall* defined as the "Sculptured Fragment from Rose Hill, Gilsland, at Rockcliffe, Cumberland," or from Hadrian's Wall, which shows a round, domed building with a high door standing under a tree; but this building, which is closed at the top, and is comparatively higher and narrower than Arthur's O'on, moreover, cannot help us find the Arthurian construction on the Antonine Wall. Otherwise the Nennius gloss refers to what Nennius called the Carausius construction, which was on the Antonine Wall, and which was perhaps what was later called Arthur's O'on.

Lewis also pointed to William of Malmesbury's *Gesta Pontificum Anglorum* 3:99 (Rolls ed.), as follows:

> . . . videas mira Romanorum artifitia; ut est in Lugubalia civitate triclinium lapideis fornicibus concameratum, quod nulla umquam tempesta-

---

*The reader will find the masterful summary and conclusions of Maitland in the Appendix.

tum contumelia, quin etiam appositis ex industria lignis et succensis, valuit labefactari . . . scripturaque legitur in fronte triclinii: "Marii Victoriae."

[. . . that you may see the marvelous works of the Romans; as there is in Carlisle, the (Roman) city-state, a vaulted seat built of hewn stones, which no buffeting of storms, nay even when wood was industriously heaped up against it and set afire, could cause to totter . . . and written on the outside of the seat: "To the Victory of Marius."]

Interesting as this is, the words of Malmesbury do not describe the rotunda, Arthur's O'on.

Chapel 1

If Arthur's O'on was a rotunda used by the members of King Arthur's secret fellowship, then it should have been mentioned in Arthurian literature as a temple, a chapel, or some other place of worship. Let us return, then, to the *Perlesvaus* telling, where there are several chapels, each one distinguished from the others. First, King Arthur sets out from Carlisle, on the first night arriving at a chapel containing the body of a dead hermit. Here occurs an intervention on Arthur's behalf by the Mother of God.

Chapel 2

On the second day Arthur comes at nightfall to the chapel of a Saint Augustin, where the hermit recognizes him as King Arthur, son of "Uter," or of "Pandragon." A ride of two days might have taken Arthur west to Whithorn, or in Latin "Witerna," on the Rhinns of Galloway. Has the author of *Perlesvaus* mistaken "Augustin" or "Augustinian" for the forgotten, ancient, Scottish (Saint) Ninian?

That soon appears to be the case (ll. 282–328), when the story unfolds there. During celebration of the Mass the Christ Child in person appears, is transformed into the crucified Christ, then vanishes in flames. King Arthur meanwhile has been required to remain outside the chapel so that in a sense he witnesses this, while unable actually to see it. The king is said to be aged forty now, ten years into his reign, and therefore in a period of peace.

This dramatic and memorable scene is important for another reason, however. It is not fictional or original with the *Perlesvaus* author at Glastonbury. This is, in fact, the longest section from the eighth-century poem on Saint Ninian as reported by Wilhelm Levison in *Antiquity*. There it is the wafer that becomes the Christ Child, then Christ embraced by the priest, and Christ who then becomes the sacrificial bread.

In the light of this discovery the chapels in the *Perlesvaus* become authentic and therefore merit a new consideration. One suspects that King Arthur is "going right," making a religious pilgrimage and a righthand circuit of his realm.

Chapel 3

With Perceval's sister as his holy guide, King Arthur then visits a chapel distinguished from other shrines by its being small and built upon four columns of marble (l. 467 ff.), and its having within a sarcophagus containing a body and writing on the slab to the effect that it would open only before "the best knight in the world, when he came."

As a child Perceval (here called Pelles-vax and so named for the *vax* or valleys of "Kamaalot," of which inheritance he had been despoiled) had once asked his father, Alain, whose body lay there in this same chapel. Alain replied that the chapel was truly ancient, built before his own grandfather's time. This would give us a date of not later than 440, accurate for the lifetime of Saint Ninian. This third chapel also had a wooden roof. Furthermore, it stood beside a well-traveled road; when Arthur inquires of the damsel if many knights have stopped to worship there, he is told, "Yes."

The same third chapel is also described, seen, and visited by Gawain (l. 1028 ff.), and we learn that it is actually within sight of the fortress of Camelot, that it lies open, not within a fenced enclosure, and separated from the Stirling cliff by a river. At this time Perceval has been absent from home for seven years.

The high point of the narrative (l. 5208 ff.) depicts his return, his seeing from the distance the great, high fortress on its cliff, surrounded by loops of the river, and as he drew nearer, the same small chapel on its four columns, standing between the forest and the fortress. Then the sarcophagus opens for Perceval, and it is marvelously discovered to hold the body of Joseph of Arimathea.

After consulting the Ordnance Survey Maps of Ancient Britain, one sees that this third chapel that Arthur visited was probably situated on the main Roman road as it came into Stirling from the south, where W. Douglas Simpson, historian of Stirlingshire, located the ancient parish and royal church of Saint Ninians.

A final reference to this chapel and to the coffin that Perceval is finally obliged to remove elsewhere for safekeeping, for all about him Arthur's realm is dissolving, discloses the significant statement that the Widow Lady of Camelot, who is King Arthur's sister, caused this chapel of the marble columns either to be "constructed" (Sebastian Evans's translation), or to be "installed" (according to Nitze and Jenkins), or to be restored ("estoree"), as I prefer to read it. At the least this information implies and has been assumed to mean that construction in stone actually occurred during King Arthur's reign, and rotundas only became fashionable in the fourth century, rather than in the third century with Carausius.

Chapel 4

With such thoughts in mind, one turns for another examination of a fourth chapel called "Gaste" (l. 5025 ff.), the Waste Chapel. This building is also small and ancient. It stood within an enclosure, the unforgettable Graveyard Perilous. The Waste Chapel contained an altar draped with the shroud of Christ, which covered Him at His Resurrection. This cloth was not in the Holy Sepulcher, as Sebastian Evans read it, but in "el saint monument" (l. 5035), our fourth chapel.

In this awesome spot Perceval's pious sister must spend a night in solitary vigil. Furthermore, such being the custom of the place, she must remain there alone and unprotected. Surrounded by the noise of clashing swords and warring ghosts, the damsel bravely passed beside the Holy Rood. This Rood was an immense cross that towered over the entrance to the temple enclosure. She entered the precinct, which was a military cemetery dating back to the first settlement of the land. The necropolis was personally blessed by Saint Andrew.

Now, Saint Andrew is the patron saint of Scotland, which seems to mean that her vigil celebrated his martyrdom on the X-shaped cross and that her worship in honor of the war dead fell not long after an All Saints' Day, for Saint Andrew's feast day also falls at the end of November (l. 5072 ff.). However that may be, the *Perlesvaus* author was much interested in the details of her lone vigil. In fact, he was terrified.

The dark night spent by Perceval's sister in the cold military cemetery grips the modern reader too. During her vigil several most peculiar phenomena occur, all striking the reader as fearsome and incomprehensible. As if the wind were lifting it, the altar cloth rises before her eyes into the night air. Second, it is black night all around outside the chapel but light within the building, even though it is not illuminated. She can apparently sometimes grasp the cloth as it rises, but once it rises so high, floating above her head, that she cannot even touch it. (This transpires within a small temple!) Finally a voice speaks to her from overhead, from above the temple.

What easier conclusion than that the maiden is spending her vigil inside Arthur's O'on, a chapel without a roof, one that was open to the skies? That might explain the precious altar cloth rising above her head. It would also explain light falling inside the chapel from the night sky, moon, or planet, and the voice from above. Since the voice foretells the death of King Fisherman, it (or Merlin) knows that Perceval and his pious sister Dandrane are of his sacred lineage and come from Camelot. In short, Dandrane has not far to go from this sacred necropolis to her home in the fortress of Camelot.

When Lancelot arrives there, he too sees the chapel inside its sacred precinct, within the enclosure of a military burial ground. The whole is said then to be surrounded by a forest, with a huge cross towering over the gateway. He sees an extensive valley around it, doubtless the Carron River valley near Falkirk. Perceval's sword was forged near there, he knows, and the Carron ironworks were once the largest in the world.

The following day, as he rides away from the Waste Chapel surrounded by its thorn hedge—for Lancelot is the best observer—he comes to what he calls a vast, antique, deserted city. We know now, because of the work of the historian Simpson on Stirlingshire, that what Lancelot thought in his day was the ruins of a lost "city" was more probably the ruins of the rectangular Roman fortress of Camelon. We even know its dimensions: two thousand feet on east and west, seven hundred fifty feet on the north and south sides. Its main or southern gate acceded directly to the Antonine Wall, by passing through four trenches and two ramparts, so strongly was the fortress defended by earthworks. On its north and east sides three ramparts curved protectingly about the fort, which had only two other entrances, smaller ones to the west. The Roman Camelon—although Lancelot does not report that it was Roman—was, thus, somewhat larger than the modern fortress of Stirling Castle as we see it today.

Any remaining doubt as to the antiquity and veracity of the Arthurian romances should be dispelled by what follows. Lancelot was amazed to see such a sight, what to his mind had once been an "entire city." In other words, as the English historian Hodgkin observed, most of the Britons within one generation had forgotten the Roman occupation. Lancelot, without inquiring further, sees a place

> v. 2863 ff. empty of people, and he sees the great palaces torn down and laid waste, and finds the markets and the money exchanges all empty, and sees the great cemeteries full of sarcophagi and the churches all laid waste. He rides down the wide streets and finds one great palace which seemed in better condition and less gutted than the others.

We in the twentieth century should be willing at last to credit this narrative, indeed, knowing from the study of British history how short memory is and how it must have felt to Lancelot to live among the vast ruins of the five-hundred-year Roman occupation of Britain.

Both chapels (3 and 4) stood in the Bannockburn Corridor, then, a logical site for an ancient military cemetery, a battlefield for centuries. Lancelot's Camelon, then a crumbling ruin, had once controlled, for how long no one could say then or now, the passage north into the Highlands of Scotland. There the main Roman road crossed what the Scots traditionally called Graham's Dike, what the Romans knew as the wall of Antoninus Pius, at Camelon. The fortress had been built just a few hundred feet to the north of Falkirk, fortress 14 among the 17 forts of this wall.

The third chapel, the one on the marble columns, was called "An Eaglais," one of the Eccles Churches. Its name resembles that of Perceval's mother, who was said to have had something to do with its construction: Yglais. Her daughter Dandrane kept her holy vigil, there seems little doubt about it, in the rotonda/rotunda called King Arthur's O'on. Whether he built it or not, Arthur, too, spent many hours in solemn worship there, and so it was later associated with his Order of the Round Table. The Christian symbol of a beehive still commonly represents the prototype of which Arthur's rotunda was once an outstanding example, a real architectural wonder of the ancient world.

If light entered the structure from the open eye of the dome, then this light implied knowledge of the recurrence of celestial phenomena. If the light was very bright, it may have come from the full moon shining down upon the interior of the temple, probably not from Venus, which would have been too low on the horizon. The building also represented an ancient observatory, the *cava cortina*, a hollow caldron of the circumpolar constellations as they appear from the earth. As an inverted kettle the building mimicked the dome of the heavens, with the North Star at the center of the open eye, whirling like the space between earth and sky in the Northern Hemisphere. After rising at sunset the full moon would have traveled across the sky so that it shone directly into the open eye of the temple sometime in the middle of the night. We know from Geoffrey's *Life of Merlin* that the prophet wished to have his own observatory, and that his wish came true.

Twelve knights probably sat in solemn worship inside this Round Table with King Arthur as president of their military order. Above this order was that of the Holy Grail, immensely more prestigious and an even more guarded secret. They all awaited the coming of Galahad, which they knew would signal the expiration of King Arthur's tenure on earth.

❧ 4 ❧

The Isle
of Avalon

That the glorious King Arthur was gravely wounded (at the battle of "Camblan") and furthermore that he was borne to the island of Avalon for the healing of his wounds comes first from Geoffrey of Monmouth's *History*. Geoffrey wrote only a few succinct words to that effect: "inclitus ille rex arturus letaliter uulneratus est qui illuc ad sananda uulnera sua in insulam avallonis euectus." The Welsh tradition embroiders and corrects Geoffrey's words, saying that he was taken out from the "middle of the battle" and that he went to "ynys Avallach" to be healed. The Welsh correction consists of substituting the island of Avallach for the island named Avalon. This cunning alteration relates Geoffrey's words to the later Grail literature and to Perceval, the *Grand-Saint-Graal* having told at some length of an unknown king named Avallach/Evelake of Sarras (Nazareth?), who after long instruction from Joseph of Arimathea became converted to Christianity under the baptismal name of Mordreins, meaning Slow of Belief. Years later, long after he had emigrated to Britain, Mordreins (or Mordrains) was blinded in war. He prayed that he might live until the ninth generation, to witness the coming of Galahad. After the building of Corbenic the invalid Mordreins lay in an abbey where he remained until Perceval and Galahad had achieved the Quest of the Holy Grail. Corbenic Castle in the (foreign) land of "Foreygne" was his final resting place. This castle served, then, as a repository for the Grail, a place of coronation for the Grail Kings, and a hospital where "sleeping knights died."

The Maimed King Mordreins, whose body was reported to have remained alive for nine generations, resembles Saint Spirido, who is much revered in the Greek island of Corfu, whose body is taken from its tomb every August and kissed, and who is considered to be alive in death. Thus, such a custom is not unknown. So Corbenic Castle probably was Avallach's Isle, a name that became Avalon.

When Geoffrey of Monmouth wrote his *Life of Merlin*, he returned another time to embroider the sober words that he had written fifteen or so years before. This time, he had the half-mythical Celtic bard Taliesin, that renowned poet, report that Arthur was taken to the "insula pomorum" (island of apples), which is called "Fortunata" or Fortunate, because of its profuse vegetation and the longevity of its inhabitants. These qualifications appear commonly in medieval encyclopedists. The healer "Morgan" and her nine sisters ruled there, Geoffrey added. The pilot of Arthur's ship was Saint Brendan's Barinthus, or another Barinthus, claimed Taliesin, and Arthur still lived on there in Avalon. Then Merlin took up the story, agreeing that Arthur had been "mortally" wounded at Camlan, that he was borne *over the sea* to a palace of nymphs, not to any real place like a nunnery.

Fortunately for the modern reader of Arthurian literature, several scholars, notably Sir John Rhys, saw through Geoffrey's attempts to keep up with King Arthur's rapidly growing legend or to exculpate himself, if that was his intent. Rhys demonstrated how the original connection between the Welsh word for "apple tree" (*afall*) and *Avalon* was mistakenly made by William of Malmesbury—Geoffrey's peer, as the world then judged. This great prelate, who was already official historian to Glastonbury Abbey, connected all three to Glastonbury; because he was an imposing man, he weightily imposed his mistaken opinion upon the world, and probably upon Geoffrey.

After the theory that Glastonbury was Avalon is cast aside as invalid, there remains principally what Geoffrey reported: *Avalon* is a name for the island of the famous living dead, or wounded, king. If Geoffrey found an alternate name such as *po + more* and if he thought it Latin, he might have declined it in the genitive plural as island *pomorum* ("of apples"). If the word he heard or read was German, on the other hand, and not Latin, perhaps it already meant "by the sea" (*Pomerania*). Also, the island was known for its verdure and its marvelous fertility. Here Geoffrey seems to agree.

Scholars have argued that they did not necessarily need to seek an island Avalon since the word *island* often indicated a religious foundation like the Glastonbury Abbey of Benedictines or the Isle of Whithorn, the Isle of Ely, the Ile-de-France, or the Abbey of Westminster called the "Isle of Thorney." Others have diligently tried to show how Glastonbury was once an isle, probably surrounded by the sea, in the Dark Ages. These arguments fail to convince, however, because they ignore Geoffrey's words that King Arthur was "euectus," transported on a ship, not across coastal waters only but across the deep sea to Avalon. His oceangoing pilot was named Barinthus, after the ancient pilot of Saint Brendan who took that saint and his companions in their coracle from Ireland to the New World via the Stepping

Stone route. Geoffrey insisted upon an ocean voyage, during which the craft would therefore have either to be out of sight of land, navigating in difficult waters, or sailing into some dangerous harbor—cases where a pilot is usually not only wanted but required.

Sir John Rhys obliged by drawing up a list of ten British islands, any one of which, he held, might have been this Avalon. By the time that he drew up his list, one should in fairness add, he had gone over to the mythologists, believing that *Avalon* did not mean any one real island where a historical King Arthur was really borne to be treated, but that any number of real islands were mythical isles of the dead. The ancient dead, he said, were buried on such far islands out to sea, for water prevented their returning to haunt the living. Here he too failed to credit Geoffrey, who had for his part twice stipulated that Arthur was only gravely wounded, not dead, even when Taliesin and/or Merlin were discussing his eventual return to his realm. The *Didot-Perceval* says that Arthur's subjects waited in Carlisle for forty years for the king to return to them, to no avail.

Sir John Rhys listed the following islands:

1. Glastonbury
2. Gower
3. Aberystwyth
4. Gresholm
5. Scilly Isles
6. Bardsey
7. Puffin Island
8. Man
9. Tory Island
10. Anglesey

The elimination of most of them can be made easily. Glastonbury is not a true island seagirt; its association with Avalon was fortuitous. Neither is Aberystwyth an island, except at high tide. Gower is not an island but a peninsula in southern Wales. Gresholm and Bardsey, the latter a celebrated burial place of ancient Druid priests and priestesses, are small rocky isles and therefore too small and infertile. The same is true of Tory Island off the northwest coast of Ireland. The Scilly Isles are too far from the theater of action and furthermore constitute an archipelago, not an isolated true island.

Thus, only Man and Angelsey remain in serious contention. The Welsh *Triads* afford some measure of hope that this elimination stands, for they say that only three islands were originally adjacent to Britain: Wight, Orkney, and Man. Orkney became a multitude of islands, and Anglesey became an island after the first two. Wight is too distant to be considered and too well known by writers and navigators, Romans, Britons, and Gauls, not to be recognized and called by its name Vectis (Wight), names that over the centuries have remained unaltered.

It would have been unthinkable to deposit King Arthur on some rocky islet, or on some island less important, less opulent than Man or Anglesey and expect him to recover his health there. If one considers King Arthur a wounded king of Britain in need of therapy, no inhospitable crag standing out to sea will do. Man and Anglesey must be gravely weighed and considered.

In Anglesey, after a Brythonic conquest of the early fifth century, a Goidelic (Irish) population gradually settled on the island, eventually ruled by the stable and powerful Welsh dynasty of Maelgwn Gwynedd, who reportedly survived the Battle of Camlan, and whose descendants reigned in Anglesey for eight hundred years after him, or until 1282. A royal rival like King Arthur might not have been welcomed there, however.

On the other hand, the island of Anglesey fulfills Geoffrey's criterion of fertility, for in ancient times it was called "Môn" and "mam Cymru," granary of Wales. To reach it from the mainland, however, King Arthur and the queens would not have needed either pilot or ship, for even then there was a ferry across the narrow Menai Straits.

Its capital of Aberffraw had seen royal feasting in the *Mabinogion*, and its Holyhead boasted the impressive ramparts of an ancient Roman fort. Despite the fact that in the ninth century Anglesey became a center of culture—and thus a source for modern knowledge of the Heroic Age in North Britain—no mention of King Arthur having sought medical attention there survives.

The huge island of Anglesey lies low in the straits, without mountains or tableland, always densely populated because of its rich agricultural land. It has always been well known, certainly to the Romans, and a landmark for mariners sailing up and down the Irish Sea. Its massive, low coast cannot be hidden or mistaken.

But the Avalon we seek was a disappearing island, remote from the mainland, easily lost and difficult to find, as the Grail questers knew. Anglesey was settled and governed by the Romans, who called it by its old name of Mona. The name Anglesey postdates King Arthur's day and belongs to the following conquest of the isles by Norway, and means in Norwegian "Angles' Isle." No connection between Arthur and Anglesey has been reported to date, however, which casts more doubt upon the possibility that Anglesey might have been Avalon.

The Welsh connection to Arthur had been declared tenuous by Lloyd, and then thoroughly explored by another distinguished Arthurian scholar and predecessor of Sir John Rhys, Sir Edmund K. Chambers in 1927. In his masterful treatment *Arthur of Britain*, he pointed out the many entertaining references to Arthur and to his contemporaries in comical Welsh fiction and delightful folklore, then moved on to the Latin lives of South Welsh saints. There he found a valid connection, but not between King Arthur and the dynasty of North Wales, which was certainly hostile to him and which had profited from the slaughter at Camlan, but between King Arthur and the Isle of Man.

There King Arthur was reported to have gone, declared Chambers, and once there he slew the brother of Saint Gildas, who was born near Dumbarton on the Clyde. Gildas later gave Arthur a penance for his slaying of Hueil and after that forgave him with the kiss of peace. Hence an early connection between King Arthur and the Isle of Man.

The ancient Welsh text, *Black Book of Carmarthen* suggested to Chambers that the "Gorre" of the French romances, notably Chrétien's *Lancelot*, was a duplicate name for Avalon, realm of the dead.

The theory that Gorre was Gower, accepted by Loomis and Sir John Rhys, is an error. It has depended, unfortunately, upon a mistaken understanding of the phonetics not only of Old French but of French poetry of any period. Rhys and Loomis supposed that the French *Gorre* was pronounced "Gore," as it would be said in spoken French. That might have led them to suggest the peninsula of Gower in southern Wales.

In French poetry the word *Gorre* is always pronounced "Gor-rə," which removes it from any close phonetic resemblance to the Welsh *Gower*, in southern Wales spelled in Welsh *Gwyr*. Furthermore, this correction also moves King Urien and his Queen Morgan away from that southern area of Wales and back to the western isles, where they more probably reigned. Gorre, which may be Avalon or which may contain Avalon among its isles, may be, as Rhys theorized, the isle Brittia of the Byzantine historian Procopius, an isle found dropping below the western horizon. If that were the case, then it must have contained a hill or mound for the burial of illustrious dead and a hospital where the ill hoped to regain their health.

Although Geoffrey of Monmouth had set himself to speak about this island called Avalon and had come back to the subject years later in his *Life of Merlin*, he still earned for himself a less than full consideration. Scholars shrugged at his alleged ignorance of islands previously mentioned in his narrative. In listing King Arthur's coronation guests Geoffrey had mentioned six islands of Britain: Ireland (Hibernia), Iceland (Hislandie), Gothland (Gudlandie), Orkneys (Orcadum), Denmark (Dacorum, Dacia), and Norway (Norguegie). In his paraphrase of Geoffrey twenty years after the *Historia* appeared, Wace busily corrected—or thought he corrected—this list of conquered islands by omitting Norway and Denmark and fussily adding "Finland."

In 1929 Geoffrey's sympathetic readers and editors Griscom and Jones finally explained that what Geoffrey intended by his "Gothland," "Norway," and "Denmark" was most probably Scotland; the territories and isles of Scotland occupied by blond Norwegians (the Finn-Gall); and the parts of Scotland, notably Caithness, Sutherland, and Ross, that were in Arthur's time settled by the dark Danes (the Dubh-Gall).

Inasmuch as Geoffrey's credibility has been somewhat refurbished in matters of geography, the harsher criticisms, notably Wace's alterations of text and Edmond Faral's indictment of his "chimerical precision (but we knew what to expect from such an invented scenario!)" now permit the reader to hear Geoffrey's voice clearly again.

Geoffrey said Avalon was an island; thus, the town of Avalon in the Yonne, France, fails to meet his criterion. The hunt must continue elsewhere. There still remain in favor of Geoffrey, however, two other independent but supporting statements, both from contemporaries of high credibility: Chrétien de Troyes and Marie de France. In the former's *Erec et Enide* King Arthur attended the young hero's wedding in Edinburgh, but also came

> . . . Guingamors . . .
> de l'isle d'Avalons fu sire:
> de cestui avons oï dire
> qu'il fu amis Morgant la fee. (v. 1904)

> [Guingamors, . . . who was lord of the
> isle of Avalon, of whom we have heard
> that he was the lover of Morgan la Fée.]

Here Chrétien corroborated Geoffrey around 1170.

In her poem titled *Lanval*, before 1189, Marie de France spoke of King Arthur as holding court at his castle at Carlisle, near "the Scots and Picts," who were raiding his lands (v. 5 ff.). To his court came the beautiful foreign queen who took the hero Lanval with her upon the *perron*, whence both leaped off to Avalon, which, Marie adds, was a beautiful and enchanting isle:

> Od li s'en vait en Avalun . . .
>
> . . . . . .
>
> En un isle qui mut est beaus . . .
>
>   (v. 640)

> [With her he went off to Avalon,
>
> . . . . . .
>
> Into an isle that is very lovely.]

The second text by Marie de France to bear directly on the problem is *Yonec*, named for the hero Yonec (or Yvain in French, Urien in English). This young hero is the illegitimate son of King Urien of Gorre, enemy of King Arthur and twice abductor of the queen. This king's palace, says Marie, is at "Carwent" on the "Duëlas" (Douglas) River, and there King Urien took the disguise of a bird to woo a lady whose husband had kept her seven years immured. By the time the lovers were discovered (v. 332 ff.), the lady was pregnant. Her royal lover Urien was shot as he leaped out her chamber window, which was a drop of twenty feet, but he was already mortally wounded (by Lancelot). As he fled, the lover was followed by the frantic lady. What she saw along the trail of his blood and the route she followed seem without question a description of another arrival at Corbenic Castle in Avalon.

The lady followed a road until she came to a hollow hill, which she entered. Inside the hill the road ran straight through to the exit. She came out into a beautiful meadow (v. 356) where beyond it, but not far distant, stood a citadel ("une cité") enclosed by a wall. Not a house, hall, or tower of it did not gleam silvered over, so rich and so splendid was it. Toward the town was marshland and woods and a peel stockade. On the other side, toward the keep, water ran around the brilliant fortress. Into that dangerous channel came ships, and more than three hundred of them were moored in the roadstead. The gate toward the upstream or land side was unbarred; through it the poor lady passed, then ran between the houses and up to the citadel ("al chastel"—v. 374). No person was about—Perceval's experience upon awakening at the Grail Castle. She heard not a word. She came along the mosaic floor to the central palace ("al paleis"—v. 377) and into a fine chamber where she found a knight asleep. Another lay asleep as she ran through the first and into a second chamber. In the third chamber she finally found her lover, surrounded by such royal luxury, such white linens, such candles and candelabra burning night and day, and bedposts of such shimmering gold that they alone equaled the value of an entire city.

These precisions almost duplicate Chrétien's Perceval arriving at the Grail Castle.

Her lover, the wounded king, gave the lady a talisman to keep as proof of their love and begged her to leave, for he would soon die. Their son Yonec, or the Bastard Urien—King Urien fathered two sons named Urien (or Yonec or Yvain)—in time and after he had avenged his father's murder became king in Caerwent-Douglas. We infer that this younger Urien eventually killed Lancelot. Urien's older brother, as reported by Geoffrey, became king at Lancelot's Stirling Castle after the Battle of Camlan. Marie reports (v. 467 ff.) that the old king, whom one now recognizes and clearly identifies as King Urien of Gorre, was buried at Carlisle in the (coronation) Chapel of Aaron.

Marie de France in *Lanval* and in *Yonec* has told King Urien's side of the same story of which Ulrich's *Lanzelet* recounts King Arthur's version of the same broil between these foes, Arthur and Urien. From such various Arthurian manuscripts the picture of the island of Avalon becomes clearer and clearer; but to connect these details from the Grail versions, from Chrétien, and from Marie to Sir John Rhys's one remaining island, the Isle of Man, poses a far graver problem.

Whereas Mona, now Anglesey, was named and governed by the Romans, the Isle of Man, to the north, remained isolated and unconquered. Julius Caesar also called it Mona. There are, however, no Roman records of it, and even its name has been so variously reported as to make of it an elusive island. It has been called Falga, Manna, Manau, Manavia, Monapia, Inis-Manann, Moenig, Dun Scáith, and Eubonia. Nennius calls it "Menavia vel Mevania" and also Eubonia, adding the cryptic remark that as Eubonia it stands in the sea's navel—"in umbilico maris." This list we have made of the names of Man does not exhaust them.

To call any geographical place a navel, such as Jerusalem, is to equate it with Delphi in Greece, another of the world's oldest known oracular and holy sites. To be thought of as standing in the navel of the earth, like Jerusalem, or of the sea, like Man, makes the latter an image of utter holiness in ancient days. This unavoidable suspicion of holiness associated with the Isle of Man in prehistoric times now dawns upon us, reinforced by the Manx emblem of three legs within a wheel. Its flag bears this emblem.

Three legs in Greek and in Latin make a "tripod," the meaning and use of which at Delphi, the navel of the earth in Greece, is unknown. To students of religion the tripod symbolizes holy things: trinity, triad, the three legs of the sun (rising, zenith, setting), the three hours in a medieval day after prime (terce, none, vespers), the three Fates, and the mystical phrase *three in one* ("ter unus"). Such a designation, and such familiar, sacred symbols combine to make the Isle of Man eminently worth looking at as a possible site of the ancient and very sacred Castle of the Holy Grail.

Man, or Ellan Vannin, which is its name in the Manx language, is an island of two hundred twenty-one square miles, lying roughly northeast-southwest, thirty-three miles long, and twelve miles at its widest part. The island is bisected by a road from its chief city of Douglas on the east to its chief medieval ruin of Peel Castle off its western coast. The island lies on a line, approximately, with the center of Britain and in the northern part of the Irish Sea. From many spots on Man the coasts of England, Ireland, Scotland, and Wales are visible. One immediately recalls the *Prose Lancelot* where Lancelot says that from the Isle of Joy, where he and the Grail King's daughter raised Galahad, he could see five lands. This is true of Man, and today its people say it proudly to everybody. The fifth land is Man, of course. In 1979 the Manx people and their visitors celebrated in the pres-

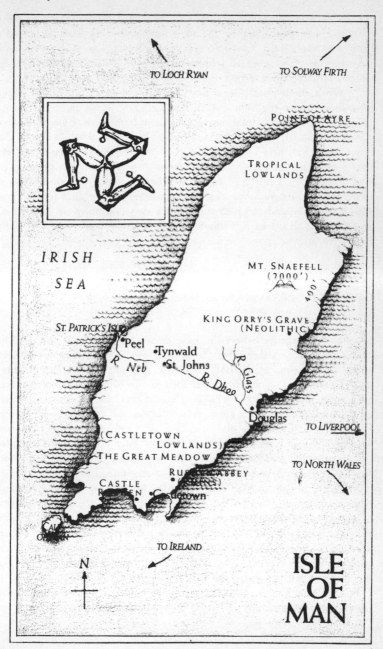

TO LOCH RYAN

TO SOLWAY FIRTH

POINT OF AYRE

TROPICAL
LOWLANDS

IRISH

SEA

MT. SNAEFELL
(2000')

400'

KING ORRY'S GRAVE
(NEOLITHIC)

ST. PATRICK'S ISLE

•Peel
•Tynwald
•St Johns

R. Neb

R. Glass

R. Dhoo

Douglas

TO LIVERPOOL

(CASTLETOWN
LOWLANDS)
THE GREAT MEADOW

TO NORTH WALES

RUSHEN ABBEY
(RUINS)

CASTLE
RUSHEN •Castletown

CALF
OF MAN

TO IRELAND

N

**ISLE
OF
MAN**

ence of the king of Norway the one thousandth year of autonomous government, a celebration falling on the old Midsummer Day, long dedicated to Saint John the Baptist. One now recalls Gawain's gift to the Grail King of the sword that had beheaded John the Baptist. One also recalls the precious and mysterious platter carried in the Grail processional.

While the records of Anglesey survive—the island fell to the Vikings for a short time in the Middle Ages, and soon after came under the dynasty of North Wales—no written records of ancient times exist in any form whatsoever for the Isle of Man. Thus, although historical times in Britain date from the arrival there of Julius Caesar in 55 B.C., history begins for Man only during the last years of the lifetime of King Arthur, that shadowy period called "Early Christian," 450–800. There exist for the Isle of Man no earlier regnal lists, no chronologies, no writing of any kind for the years 450–800, at the end of which the Vikings swooped down on Man, began superimposing their own rich culture, and became the resident peoples. Cried an ancient poet:

> *Bitter is the wind to-night,*
> *it tosses the ocean's white hair:*
> *To-night I fear not the fierce warriors of Norway*
> *Coursing on the Irish Sea.* *

The Vikings are believed to have destroyed Peel Castle in the eighth century, and it was there that the ancient peoples had their first church, where Saint Germanus probably preached, and where Saint Patrick also is said to have preached in 444. In the fifth century the little island must have been an important center of religion if Saint Germanus was dispatched there by the pope, and if such a great prelate traveled, all the way from Auxerre, France—to such a remote place. Since Saint Germanus was sent to stamp out the Pelagian heresy and succeeded, the later ceremony of the Holy Grail, supposing that Peel Island off the west coast of the Isle of Man was Avalon, seems to have been acceptable and recognized as Christian.

Since the Isle of Man was not ceded by Norway until 1266, it was Norwegian during Geoffrey of Monmouth's lifetime—thus, his mysterious island called "Norway." Its ruler was one of the kings of Man who attended King Arthur's coronation, King Urien. Furthermore, Marie's city of Caerwent-on-Douglas further indicates the present port of Douglas on the east coast of Man, where the Dhoo (Black) and the Glass (Green) rivers flow together before passing into the port of Douglas.

Another startling geographical feature characteristic of Man is the mild climate, in which subtropical plants grow without protection. For this rea-

---

* *Selections from Ancient Irish Poetry Translated by Kuno Meyer* (Edinburgh, 1911), p. 101.

son, but more especially for the stark western cliffs, the serene farmlands, the profusion of fruits and flowers, and the extreme and startling beauty of this dazzlingly bright island, its sea unbelievably blue and its clouds rosy and yellow, the Isle of Man is a prime vacation spot for the British today.

Man seems very like what Lancelot himself would have called "Joy Island." In all its sparkle, sudden storms, and mists Man is still truly the "necromancer's island," over which the ancient sea god of Ireland, Manannan mac Llyr, often cast the "Lengel," or veil of concealment. Thus, the island fulfills the other criterion, as the Grail questers' disappearing island.

Manx fairy tales tell how Man was always considered paradise on earth, if one believes in the spirit of place, and also that it was called in Manx "Ellen Sheaynt," Isle of Peace. Thus, Man was originally home to the chief deities of the Celtic world, says the historian of Man R. H. Kinvig: to the sun god Lugh, from whom Lancelot has often been mythologically derived; to Llyr, the god of the wind, storm, and fog; and to his son, the sea god Manannan. Heroes came to Man to seek magic weapons from secret smiths at hidden forges, and it was, to be sure, upon leaving the Grail Castle that Perceval received his sword forged at the Firth of Forth.

The mythology of Ireland believes that the gods were raised in the peace and beauty of Man, far from the quarrels at the courts and fortresses. Thus, there in safety the sun god Lugh, that hero so often taken for Modred, was fostered. Then, as it now seems possible, both Lancelot and his son Galahad were raised there by the "mariners" of Man. To the young Irish hero Cuchulain, whose story that of Gawain resembles, Man represented the quiet island in the stormy "lake."

It was the land that dropped beneath the waves to ancient Irish poets, from whose vantage its western cliffs seemingly sheer as glass rose sometimes from the dark blue deep.

Lady Augusta Gregory collected many such poetic stories of Man, of its glass tower on an islet, its castle beside an arm of the sea, and its apple-eating mermaids. In the same vein Nennius had told a droll Latin tale, how the visiting Saint Germanus ate the calf of man only to find it alive the next day, the Calf of Man being a sea-beaten rocky islet beyond the dangerous strait and off the southwest tip of Man.

On Man very probably the Arthurian material received at least that valuable contribution which distinguishes it as literature—its underlay of uniquely Irish mythology. Scholars like Roger Sherman Loomis and Charles Squire have over the years compiled lists of correspondences between Arthurian heroes and heroes of ancient Ireland. On Man, the British material from Carlisle, or from Whithorn, Glasgow, Melrose, and Stirling, met that almost pristine ancient mythology of Ireland. It is, we know, one of the most original, brilliant, and extensive bodies of mythology in the world. When *Perlesvaus* tells how Arthur looked out over his shoulder at the sea and drew his gray mantle about his shoulders, the reader can be fairly sure the king is meant to be looking over the dangerous waters west of Man, wearing old Manannan's veil of concealment.

When the wounded Arthur was seen in his splendid palace, lying upon a regal bed like that of King Urien, Yonec's father, that palace was not in Stirling but in Avalon. King Arthur therefore had three large establishments—the one, Camelot, at Stirling, the second at Carlisle, and the third well hidden on the west coast of Man, opposite the islet upon which stood the Grail Castle. We know that this third and last site was constructed in Arthur's lifetime, after Dumbarton had been won back and pacified and Arthur's realm stabilized. Gervase of Tilbury painted King Arthur in a royal establishment, claiming that the palace was in the three-sided, three-legged island of Sicily. How Arthur came to be there is not too difficult to grasp if Gervase outsmarted himself, not thinking of the British island symbolized by a tripod but jumping to the conclusion that his source meant the more famous, triangular Sicily. Gervase redeemed himself somewhat by adding that Arthur's wounds, received in battle with Modred, were healing anyway day by day. Thus, he at least avoided contradicting Geoffrey of Monmouth.

Most experts in the field of folklore and Irish mythology have attempted valiantly, but with little success to date, to derive the Holy Grail from earlier magic caldrons of Irish inspiration, King Cormac's quest for the golden cup of truth, or the Manx farmer's discovery in an underground barrow of the silver cup that was long kept at Rushen Church on the Isle of Man but reputedly sent finally to London. The usual injunctions against eating and drinking while in the underground barrow obtain in these tales, of course. In fact, says another Manx fairy tale, the Isle of Man was created during a war between the Irish giants and the red-haired giants of Scotland. One wonders whether this is a folk memory of King Arthur's war against Dalriada.

> Later the island was known as Ellen Sheaynt, the Isle of Peace, or the Holy Island. It was a place where there was always sunshine, and the singing of birds, the scent of sweet flowers, and apple-trees blossoming the whole year round. [Here we see that the Manx point of view corresponds to that in Arthurian literature.]*

The cultural anthropologist Margaret Killip, author of *The Folklore of the Isle of Man*, studied the possible relationship between the many Manx legends of sleeping giants and King Arthur's sleep in Avalon. She even mentioned a possible connection between the Isle of Man and Perceval. According to her

---

*"The Making of Man" and "The Silver Cup" from *Manx Fairy Tales*, ed. L. Morrison (Peel, Isle of Man, 1929), and here pp. 18–19.

research, a "folklorist . . . Lewis Spence considers the story as it is found in the Isle of Man to be even more basic, and adds to these the maimed king of the Grail Legend. p. 153." Killip dismissed this opinion from Spence, however, allowing no possible connection between Man and the Grail and without mentioning Lewis Spence's other learned books, such as *Boudicea*, or his work on Druidism, whose aim and scholarship are impressive. Spence (who was native to Scotland) believed that King Arthur was closely linked to the Isle of Man. He also came to believe that there King Arthur slept like the Greek Cronos before him, and he believed that the Isle of Man was a tremendously ancient holy site and "that Arthur was a god of the culture-hero type is obvious enough." Thus, Spence finally endorsed the school of mythological thought formulated in England and Wales by Chambers and Rhys in the decade 1920–30 and later expanded by the Loomis family in the United States.

Since the study of Manx folklore brings inconclusive and rather disappointing results, and since it fails to prove any real survival of King Arthur on the island, one turns to history to discover what can be found there. Kinvig, the historian of Man, has considerable information about the Norse kings of Man between the years 800 and 1266, when they gave up the island. The *Orkneyingersaga* tells how the Vikings fared home to Man each winter, from the eighth century on. Their great king named Godred Crovan, who reigned from 1079 to 1095, and who is recorded in the *Chronicle of Man and the Sudreys*, was also raised from childhood on Man. He was and is still called King Orry, says the history, or called in Gaelic King "Gorry." Thus, in the history of Man we can make progress.

"Gorry" is the name and the very pronunciation that we have been looking for ever since first reading "Gorre" in Chrétien's *Lancelot*. We can therefore hardly believe now that the original King Gorry was Godred Crovan, when King Gorry's Grave is a Neolithic site on the east coast of Man, and not far inland from that coast. The "Gorree" or "Orrye" of Manx tradition can hardly be the same as a king who died in 1095 and who was defeated by King Harold of England at Stamford Bridge in 1066. The original King Gorry must have been an eponymous founder of Man, for he is buried in a Neolithic grave there, a site well documented in Man as elsewhere in Britain.

The kingdom of Gorry, and the Old French Gorre, seems to have named the Isle of Man itself, then, where King Gorry's Grave has always been such a major landmark. Or the Isle of Man, from its administrative center at Douglas, where King Urien's chief seat was located, formed a central part of that kingdom.

Another important part of Gorre would have been Castletown, probably near the present airport, the large meadow, and the domain where Perceval's bride once lived. Her realm probably included Castle Rushen and perhaps also the old monastic site that became Rushen Abbey in the Middle Ages. These sites adjoined a third part of Gorre, the land and castle on and around Peel Island, off the west coast of Man, given to the regency of King Bademagus by his uncle, King Urien of Gorre.

Gorre seems thus far to name the Manx land, where King Arthur built the second castle to house the Holy Grail. Here Corbenic Castle was built after the original conquest and submission of King Urien of Gorre, in this land and island of Gorre. At the time of his second rebellion and repudiation of his promise, King Urien abducted Queen Guinevere again, and this time she succumbed, as the cryptic remarks about her having slept through the storming of the Tanglewood Castle seem to indicate. The palace of King Arthur seems to have been across the narrow channel from the Grail Castle, or on the mainland of Man, where the town of Peel is today.

Such preliminary discoveries and deductions now prompt a further ransacking through the archaeological data concerning Man as documented by the Manx Museum and National Trust in 1973. A second find is truly astonishing. It corroborates Marie de France's *Yonec*, or life of King Urien of Gorre and the birth of his son Yonec (Urien).

Among the ancient monuments of Man we find what is called the Giant's Grave. This is a Bronze Age burial mound centrally situated at Saint John's Church, on the main east-west road from Douglas to Peel. The giant's burial mound is thirty yards north of the famous parliament or Tynwald Hill, thus, a short distance from Peel Castle and Island. Madly following her wounded lover, Marie's heroine had run the distance from King Urien's fortress at Caerwent, supposedly at the modern Douglas on the east side of the island. Then she passed through a tunnel. It was the Giant's Grave at Saint John's, which is "the central cist of an early Bronze Age burial mound, long exposed in side of road cutting, passing through the original mound. About 1500 B.C."* This modern substantiation of Marie de France of a poem written by this unknown lady in the Anglo-Norman language before 1189 is astonishing. She said that Yonec's mother ran along a road, which went directly through a burial mound ("une hoge . . . cele hoge"—vv. 346–47, 355) and then led her to a walled town and a palisaded or "Peel" Castle. She said this poor lady also passed by King Arthur's citadel, which was all silvered over and magnificent in its lovely opulence.

Such a second discovery prompts the reader of Arthurian texts in Old French to look upon these manuscripts with new respect—not as fabrications and fictions only, but perhaps as the only written sources concerning the history of remote, lesser known parts of Britain, like the Isle of Man. Returning to R. H. Kinvig's *History of the Isle of Man*, one learns that King Godred II reigned there from 1153 to 1187, the very years when Marie de

---

* *The Ancient and Historic Monuments of the Isle of Man* (Douglas, 1973).

France was writing and when the best of the Arthurian romances were being commissioned, composed, and read throughout western Europe.

Kinvig's map (his Figure 24) shows that during the lifetime of King Godred II, as the result of a costly expedition into Ulster and a naval defeat at Colonsay (1156), the king of Man was forced to fall back for protection upon King Henry II of England. Now, King Henry II notoriously offered British lands to any Norman adventurer who would take them. A number of Norman writers, specialists in Arthurian lore, including both Wace and Marie de France, depended personally upon King Henry II and upon his Queen Eleanor for patronage. Did they also depend upon such persons for suggestions, if not for subject matter?

King Godred II had a son-in-law, said Kinvig, named Jean de Courci. This Jean was a special favorite of King Henry II. This is the same Jean who took part in the bloody conquest of Ulster. At this point the student of medieval literature in Old French begins to feel himself on very familiar ground. He also begins to sense the onset of a great discovery.

Consulted next, the *Atlas of Irish History* confirms that a Norman French nobleman of that name, Jean de Courci, led a small force into Ulster in 1176–77, where he defeated the local Irish king and seized territory up to the Bann (?) River. He subsequently ruled in Ireland for twenty-seven years. The famous newswriter of King Henry II, Gerald of Wales, could not have missed recounting in his book on the conquest of Ireland such an adventure by one of his own famous and very successful contemporaries.

Effectively, corroborates Gerald of Wales, a "Iohan de Courcy," by successfully invading Ulster, fulfilled a dire prophecy of Saint Columba, plus another by Merlin, and on the Irish strand he waded in Irish blood up to his knees. This same victorious adventurer *also had all his martial deeds, his "stalwarth gestes," written in Irish in a chronicle!* This Iohan or Jean de Courci then married the king of Man's daughter, the daughter of King Godred II.*

The book of deeds, that the Iohan de Courcy caused to be written exists in Old French as the romance we have been calling *Sone de Nansai.* Now we shall see Arthurian literature set down on the Isle of Man.

---

*See *Expugnatio Hiberniae*, ed. F. J. Furnival, as the *English Conquest of Ireland*, EETS, no. 107, p. 114 ff., from MS Trinity College Dublin E. 2. 31 (c. 1425) and MS Rawlinson, B 490, Bodleian (c. 1440).

5

New Evidence: Perceval's Inauguration

The *Sone de Nansai* manuscript contains not only new evidence about the Grail ceremony but twelve or so geographical precisions about the Grail Castle's whereabouts. And we find an entire scene that was altogether missing from the Arthurian texts: an eyewitness account of Perceval's wedding and inauguration as king at the Grail Castle.

The Old French text called *Sone de Nansai* presents a complicated maze. Supposedly it has been known to the world since it was edited in Germany by Moritz Goldschmidt under the German title *Sone von Nausay*. So far, it has been accepted unquestionably—all 31,321 verses of it—as authentic and Arthurian. Now that assumption appears more than likely to be false.

The *Sone de Nansai* text is not Arthurian but almost entirely spurious. Most of this hoax did not originate in the Dark Ages but in the Middle Ages—more precisely, in the twelfth century, which discovered King Arthur. Only a small part of the text is authentic, and Arthurian.

An examination of the French hero's un-French and very odd name of Sone, which ought to be but is not French, provides the first inkling that something is strangely amiss. The Old French approximation of *Sone* appears to be an equivalent for John and Iohan, which, had it originally been Irish and/or Q-Celtic, would have been spelled *Sean*, though pronounced something like "Sone." If the hero had been originally French (he was born in France and was therefore supposed to be French) his name would have been some form of *Jean*.

This hero called "Sone" set about in his early manhood to marry the king of Man's daughter and to conquer a part of northern Ireland. According to the text, he did it in Arthur's day.

However, we know very well that it was King Arthur who conquered a part of Irish territory and the Isle of Man, where he killed the brother of Saint Gildas. The fortress and harbor on the eastern side of the Isle of Man is at the estuary of the "Douglas River," a probable site of one of the king's twelve battles (and the present city of Douglas).

Did anybody else conquer the Isle of Man and a part of Ulster in the Middle Ages, perhaps? Was it a French nobleman named Jean who did this? The history of Ireland has answered in the affirmative. The noble conquerer was French, was named Jean, and lived very prominently in the twelfth century. He was well known in England and France. He also married the daughter of the king of the Isle of Man.

The French conqueror of Man and Ireland in the twelfth century was a man called Jean de Courci, a French nobleman. He was both confidant and protégé of King Henry II of England, as we have learned from both English and Irish history, and he conquered Man and a part of Ulster with the permission, approval, and blessing of King Henry II. And he also had access, on the Isle of Man and again at the court of King Henry II, to Arthurian manuscripts.

Then, bursting with pride in himself, King Jean de Courci paid somebody on Man or in Ireland to write a long, laudatory, pseudo-Arthurian text recounting ad nauseam his "great" adventures or "gestes." So the text was composed in Q-Celtic; this point is important.

As a matter of known fact, Jean de Courci looked around him and decided that he was fully as worthy as Perceval and Lancelot of celebration. He had trod, he pointed out to his writer, in their very footsteps there at Man. Queen Guinevere had been imprisoned there, not once but probably twice. Yonec had been born there, after the death of King Urien. Jean de Courci too had married the king of Man's daughter in a royal ceremony. So why not have himself crowned king of the Grail Castle? This original "geste" in Q-Celtic has been lost since the twelfth century.

The only extant manuscript, which is called *Sone de Nansai,* is, by admission of the translator a hundred years later, a translation into Old French of the Irish text commissioned by King Jean de Courci. The self-glorification of King Jean de Courci must have prompted little real interest in its readers, one concludes, for nobody has seen this amusing complication. It would seem that scholars have read only the first half—the language is peculiar and often difficult, in its spelling particularly, and in its unfamiliar wording. Had they persevered, however, they would have seen that there are very good reasons why no French nobleman in the twelfth century could have had himself crowned king of King Arthur's Grail Castle.

In the midst of this mawkish tale, the reader suddenly stumbles into another time. It is not the world of Jean de Courci and his boring adventures, but King Arthur's lost world. We know it positively, for there are whole passages that could not have applied to Jean de Courci in the twelfth century. The text is ancient, about places that in Courci's time no longer existed. We are most definitely not reading about the inauguration of Jean de Courci at the Grail Castle. The Grail Castle had not been there for hundreds of years. Jean de Courci could not have seen it, much less have stood in it to be inaugurated.

Perceval was the last of the Grail Kings, not Jean de Courci seven hundred years later. The site and the Grail Castle were totally destroyed around the year 800. There was no Grail fellowship in the twelfth century, for Roman Christianity had ruled for hundreds of years by that time. Sone de Nansai was never inaugurated as Grail King, any more than was Jean de Courci.

What we have is a lost text from the Dark Ages that was copied, and incorporated into the adventures of Jean de Courci. The latter is a stand-in for Perceval, and Perceval's inauguration has been grafted onto Courci's real conquest of Ireland. Jean de Courci attempted, in other words, to ride into immortality on the shoulders of Perceval, last king of King Arthur's Grail Castle and Grail Fellowship.

In its present Old French form, the *Sone de Nansai* manuscript is an endless biography of the French hero Sone, conqueror of Ireland. The hero incontestably leads a successful expedition into Ireland from the Isle of Man, dull episode in a dull career, which supposedly established him and his French family in positions of eminence in Europe. Sone is first presented to the reader as a vulgar copy and pallid successor to Lancelot, extolled for silvery beauty and strength.

The later Old French translator/author took his revenge by focusing more and more passionately upon the geography of the original Irish or Manx account. Thus he becomes in medieval letters a veritable treasure of information and a passionate geographer—a rarity. Maps of the continent show how carefully he checked it and calculated time and distance from one Burgundian castle to another, where Sone spent his youth. The author/translator must have revered topographical exactitude, for he names castles, times, routes, guests, notables, and nobles all the way from Ireland into Jerusalem. In chronology he took no pains—no doubt a function of his being an author at the end of the thirteenth century writing the adventures, principally the martial deeds, of a real European nobleman at the end of the twelfth century, whose ancestors are made out to be the same remote swan knights, ancestors of the illustrious Godfrey de Bouillon, who first captured Jerusalem in 1099, ending the First Crusade, the only successful one.

The translator must have known that the coronation of Sone at the Castle of the Holy Grail was wholly anachronistic but that the inauguration itself was authentic and corresponded closely, though in much greater detail, to other Arthurian texts by Marie de France and Chrétien de Troyes. He may even have seen clearly that this was not Sone's coronation at all, but that of someone in King Arthur's court, probably Perceval. The manuscript demonstrates, with such blocks of ancient material, that it follows an ancient source, albeit unsteadily. *Sone de Nansai* is therefore of inestimable value.

The appended prose section reveals who "commanded this work of my clerk": "the Lady Baruch, a Chastellaine of Cyprus." The clerk or secretary says, in an appended prose section:

> I the clerk Branque, aged one hundred five years, undertake this work, have served the lady for forty years. Here is the genealogy of our matter [the subject matter of our romance].

Sone was translated into Old French during the reign of the Lusignan dynasty in Cyprus—although that name is never mentioned in the text—between 1192 and 1489. They had received Cyprus from King Richard I of England.

Branque gives the first interesting genealogy of Sone's family as treated in his Irish text:

> Sone went to England, Scotland, and Ireland and in Ireland married the [first] queen, who bore him a son. This child grew up to become king of Sicily and of "Ireland in Norway" [i.e., Ulster]. Then Sone married the daughter of the king of Norway ["Norouweghe"] v. 2915 ff.

(We know from history books that Jean de Courci actually married the daughter of King Godred II of the Isle of Man.)

By his second wife Sone fathered three sons:
1. Houdourans, crowned emperor at the age of a year and a half, married Matabrunne.
2. Oriant married Elouse, who bore the famous triplets born with golden chains about their necks; when the evil stepmother turned them into swans, they swam to the Arthurian castle called Galoches.
3. Elias [Lohengrin] married Biautris, asked the fatal question, which caused him to blow the horn and summon the swan.

While Irish stories of the sea god Llyr had made it clear that his children turned into swans and swam the cold sea, they had not said that the Swan Knight was Perceval's son Lohengrin. Nor had they specified that these swans inhabited the Isle of Man. To be sure, Llyr's son Manannan mac Llyr was supposed to have been the first king of Man, who gave the island its name.

Even this mythological genealogy suggests that a considerable part of medieval Arthurian lore came from Man, which, aside from Lewis Spence's hypothesis about King Arthur and the Isle of Man, has otherwise been unsuspected. *Sone* has also made it clear from the beginning of the text that Geoffrey of Monmouth's "Norway" was known elsewhere as an island, for there Sone arrived and there he met King Alain (vv. 3160, 4249, 4862 et passim).

Now, the king whom Jean de Courci met was Godred II. The king whom he met in the text was therefore Perceval's father Alain, the Grail King. From about the middle of *Sone* the text abruptly duplicates the life of Perceval and modernizes it, attributing Perceval's deeds to Sone.

Alerted to the importance of the *Sone* text by Jessie L. Weston, Roger Sherman Loomis devoted seven pages to it in his *Celtic Myth and Arthurian Romance.* He understood none of this complication but only concluded that the whole manuscript was "authentic," not suspecting its origin, its intent, or its historicity. He declared it authentic (p. 206) because the author knew Chrétien's romances, the several romances of voyages, the *Perlesvaus* (and, one must add now, the *Grand-Saint-Graal*). Loomis decided, erroneously, that the manuscript was "Welsh" in origin, "a document of the highest value for the recovery of the Welsh Grail tradition" (p. 207). He apparently thought that the Irish spoke Welsh (P-Celtic) and not Gaelic or Manx (Q-Celtic).

By now we are so familiar with King Arthur's world that we can let the manuscript speak for itself. We shall thrill to see the Grail Castle rise out of the sea mist, and we shall have confirmation of and a closer look at King Arthur's famed palace, which the French medieval encyclopedist Lambert de Saint-Omer so carefully detailed in his compendium of world knowledge.

Summaries and a partial translation from the *Sone de Nansai* text follow:

> As soon as he arrived at the island of Norway, which lay between England and Ireland, Sone joined the forces of King Alain of Norway, whose army was drawn up on the Great Meadow, adjacent to the great castle.

The poem has placed Sone in the vicinity of what is now the airport of Man, near the southeastern coast of the island. This center is still called Castletown because of its crumbling, ancient ruins. Along the south shore is Castle Rushen, the "great castle" mentioned. In the ensuing battle ten thousand men are slain, including the two sons of the King of Norway, and the King of Ulster also is slain. Thus, Sone is able to wed his widow in Ulster. Sone's career at first reminds one of Lancelot's (whom the author never mentions). From the battle scene to the next high point of the narrative, the author/translator Branque is able to satisfy his love of geography. A range of high hills separates Castletown from Peel and Peel Castle on the rugged west coast of Man. Sone accompanies the King of Norway across a range of mountains where strange creatures (v. 4285) are to be seen. They come to a creek and two rocks. There two monks prepare to convey them in their ancient-style craft (v. 4331). Here we have had Lancelot's arrival at the arm of the sea, Perceval's arrival at the two rocks—the same place seen by Gawain and by Yonec's mother. The author will get to the ferry or punts later.

> Sone and King Alain were then transported across deep water to
> a beautiful palace, surrounded by a curtain wall, standing out in the sea
> v. 4370 ff.

Now follows the first complete description of the Grail Castle on the Isle of Avalon.

> It was so marvelously constructed upon bedrock and so far from
> shore that neither siege machinery nor catapults could damage it a whit,
> and the sea beat against it all around [v. 4378]. The curtain walls had
> been laid upon the bedrock with four towers, the highest of which was
> the donjon, or palace. In the great hall the fireplace was set upon four
> pillars with copper flues. The place was so luxuriously appointed, so
> sculpted, so overlaid with gold, so superbly furnished that a person
> would think that he was in paradise, just to be there and see all that
> wealth [v. 4412].

At this point there seems to have been a break in the text, for the next paragraph is written from another vantage. Here the observer seems to be on the mainland part of the island, looking out upon the smaller islet.

> The table for dinner was set in a plaisançe overlooking the sea
> scape, enclosed within walls of carved marble showing all the rare birds
> and fishes, and over them weathervanes turned and rang in the wind,
> each one its own tune and rhythm. On one side was the sea and on the
> other a forest of elders, cypress, almond trees, olives, and sycamores,
> where deer browsed, coming and going freely. At that place fresh water
> and salt water flowed together, but the whole was so situated that from
> the land one could hardly ever, or never come upon this site and hidden
> islet, and castle upon it [v. 4498].

After Sone's confession is heard by the abbot of a nearby abbey, he learns the history of the castle, which corresponds more or less to that in the *Grand-Saint-Graal*. As we know, Joseph of Arimathea founded the Grail Castle to house the vessel known as the Holy Grail, which was light-bearing, food-producing, and sweet with Holy Balm (v. 4619 ff.).

> He had had the castle built safely in isolated waters teeming with
> fish, and he fished them to forget his distress, and he was the first Fisher
> King [v. 4823]. His castle cannot be stormed, cannot even be approached from the sea by a hostile force because of the rocks all around
> it.

After the benediction the abbot opened an ivory reliquary carved with many stories and showed Sone the Holy Grail ["le saint grëal", v. 4905], at which the whole land lit up [v. 4906], and the monks wept and sang "Te deum laudamus." The Grail was then placed upon the altar, near the cross. Then Sone saw the white spear with its marvel, a drop of red blood at the point [v. 4919], and the sarcophagi ["fiertres"; v. 4921], of Joseph of Arimathea and his older son. His younger son was Josephus, first bishop to be ordained [v. 4926].

In his love for order and detail the author went so far as to describe the departure from Galoches, opposite Avalon, of Sone and of the king named Alain (v. 4958).

Here our original theory of Lancelot's craft is confirmed from Chrétien, for leaving the islet they went to the ferry ("bac"), which was waiting for them. The men went on one scow, the horses on the other. The crossing was quickly accomplished, so the channel must have been very narrow. Using the abbot's precious sword (which was the sacred object given by Gawain to the Grail King, to be used here as a talisman borne before the army), Sone conquered Ulster.

Subsequently he refused to be crowned at the Grail citadel or to wed the king of Man's daughter (v. 7893). No reason is given, but the text has specified that he was already married to the queen of Ulster. Further, we know that Jean de Courci, unlike Lancelot, did not live in Pictish times and under Pictish customs. The kingdom of Norway was, by inheritance, the realm of the king of Norway's daughter. Thus, this was once an ancient Pictish realm, where matrilinear succession obtained in Arthur's day. Sone returns to Burgundy, landing on the continent at Bruges.

In case there is any further doubt as to the site of the Grail Castle, the author/geographer left in his translation (v. 8211 ff.) the detailed route that Sone followed from Galoches to Bruges:

1. He sailed north along the coast of "Galles," with that coast on his right hand.
2. He then sailed along the coastal waters of Scotland.
3. He approached Denmark, where there were rich fishing grounds for salmon and sturgeon.
4. He then entered Finnelaye, passing Denmark, and treacherous rocks.
5. Finally, he came to Logarde and went thence to Bruges.

Sone's story contains another and final visit to the Grail Castle, however, which took place after he received word that King Alain had died.

Leaving the Isle of Man, Sone went north to the Mull of Galloway, past the entrance to the Firth of Clyde, up the North Channel into the Gulf of the Hebrides. Then his oarsmen rowed him into the Little Minch, the North Minch, past Cape Wrath, which was the Vikings' point of no return, and into the Pentland Firth between Caithness and the Orkneys. After that came the long passage over the deep water of the German Ocean. They came at last to the Great Fisher Bank in the latitudes between the Moray Firth and the Firth of Forth, at three-fifths of the distance from Scotland to the Jutland peninsula. Then the route lay south along the Jutland Bank, the Eastern Grounds, Heligoland, the Friesian Islands, and the Low Plain of Holland, in sight of the coast all the way to "Logarde" (probably Leewarden), Antwerp, and Bruges. The rich fishing grounds were seemingly the Dogger Bank, a broad shoal about halfway between England and Denmark, or the Well Bank south of that.

Leaving the emperor at Cologne, Sone again embarked from Bruges to complete the round trip to Galoches. There three hundred fishing boats met him in the harbor, the same number reported by Marie de France in *Yonec* and at the same roadstead, Avalon.

A galley had preceded Sone to announce the bridegroom's arrival, its crew of monks having rowed day and night to prepare for his ceremonious arrival ashore. The final approach to their abbey was difficult because of the rocks (v. 16,806). Queen Odee, daughter of the late king of Norway, ordered all her barons to participate in welcoming her bridegroom Sone, whether in small crafts, which could land passengers when larger crafts had to stand well out to sea because of the heavy waves breaking on the rocks (v. 16,859), or by land (v. 16,866) following the coast (v. 16,875). The river and sea provided lavishly for all, as did the hawking.

What follows can only apply to Perceval as he became Grail King:

> The abbot at the nearby abbey informs Sone that as king he will have custody of the spear that pierced Christ's side, of the Holy Grail ["saint gr ël", v. 16,941], as of the kingdom. The abbot then climbed upon a scaffolding to show Sone the Laws of Christ, which Joseph of Arimathea received directly from Saint Peter.
>
> Sone then leaves the abbey, enters a galley, and is rowed with his barons to Galoches. Arriving there, they then climb up to the castle [v. 17,017]. There an archbishop, assisted by three bishops, celebrate mass and the wedding of Sone and Queen Odee.
>
> The Grail then appeared and the candelabra, which were borne uncovered before the face of the king. The Grail was then returned to its reliquary.
>
> Several vessels then transported the wedding party.

The second description of the Grail Castle, or of Avalon, as it was in King Arthur's day and Perceval's follows.

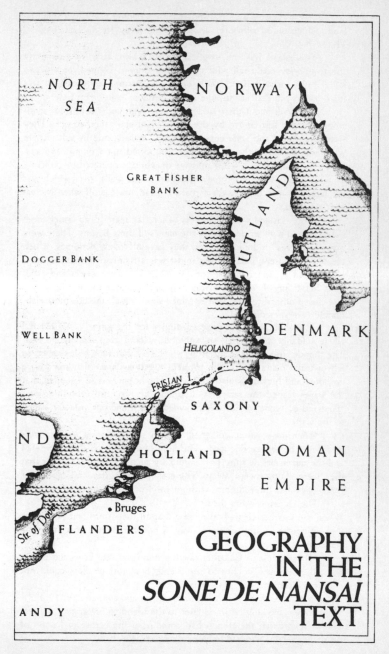

NORTH
SEA

NORWAY

GREAT FISHER
BANK

JUTLAND

DOGGER BANK

DENMARK

WELL BANK

HELIGOLAND

FRISIAN I.

SAXONY

ND

HOLLAND

ROMAN

EMPIRE

• Bruges

Str. of Dover

FLANDERS

GEOGRAPHY
IN THE
SONE DE NANSAI
TEXT

ANDY

Several vessels then transported the wedding party to a small island, which stood offshore, about a mile away [from Galoches; v. 17,155 ff.] . . .

This island was the loveliest in the world. It was so perfectly square nobody could tell which side was longest. Named for a pagan King Tadus, who built its walls before he became converted, it was ruled by his son Bademagus, the most courteous man of his time.

The walls about the island were very high and cut of [red] sandstone, entirely surrounded by the sea but laid upon the bedrock. They were crenellated and wide enough for two chariots side by side. There were four towers at the four corners supported upon pilings and sustained by vaults. There was a massive drawbridge operated by pulleys.

An arm of the sea came almost up to the walls, over which was the famous sword bridge where many a head was cut off when Meleagant was lord.

On the island was a cemetery where lay many dead under tomb slabs covered with writing giving the names of these barons. There were many rare trees on the island, and they gave off lovely perfumes, which pleased immensely, and in their midst was a fountain where the water issued from a copper horn ["cor"; v. 17,203]. It was sweet and cold, none better anywhere. There was only one entrance to the isle, which was closed otherwise, and that entrance was through the one most elaborately constructed portal.

The abbot had just ordered dinner for the king [v. 17,231 ff.] when suddenly the heavens split. Nobody could even see anyone else. The thunder followed the lightning so closely that each bolt seemed to fall on each man's head. The torment raged so fierce that trees were uprooted and hurled against the walls. The ocean was so whipped that the waves leaped the ramparts, flooding the isle until everything was afloat and everyone would have drowned if each had not instantly leaped to the walls.

Then the weather worsened, causing such suffering as our ancestors never before experienced. The king huddled upon the stone wall and the queen beside him, both struck by such floods of sea water that they were almost swept away. There they clung, day and night, for three days and three nights, without food or drink, or sleep, or rest. . . . The Queen Mother died.

When the weather cleared, they saw that all their ships had been lost. . . . When the waters drained away, a horrible stench arose from the cemetery.

Those across in Galoches saw the storm and sent boats and barges and galleys from Galoches to the island, but most of them could not endure the stench (v. 17,315 ff.)

Survivors of the storm hid in the forest and ate game (v. 17,423).

When the king returned later to the island to investigate, he was able to report that the stench had come from the corpse of Joseph of Arimathea's wife. She had been pagan (v. 17,453 ff.).

The *Sone von Nausay* text corroborates details concerning the Grail Castle from Chrétien de Troyes, Marie de France, *Perlesvaus*, and the *Grand-Saint-Graal* section of the *Prose Lancelot*. All six of them support several key statements made earlier by Geoffrey of Monmouth:

> Avalon was the Isle of Man. There King Arthur at some time kept his treasures. There he resided in one of his sculpted palaces, the one named Galoches. It stood in a former land of the Picts. There he retired wounded from the Battle of Camlan.

No trace of this treasure, of this Arthurian palace of Galoches, or of the Grail Castle remains today, nor has any memory of this survived at these locations. And yet the evidence has accumulated: that Avalon or Avallach's Isle, across the slender channel from Galoches on the mainland of Man, was the islet famous in Arthurian literature. This islet is today called Saint Patrick's Isle. On it now stands Peel Castle, which is a massive red ruin, cut off from Man by an arm of the deep sea.

From one source to another, the descriptions of Saint Patricks' Isle, of the River Neb, which there flows into the Irish Sea, the quarry on the opposite shore, the roadstead for fishing boats, of the sandstone curtain wall, the dangerous waters offshore, the surrounding rocks and cliffs of the shore, and the frequent cyclonic storms all tally with the written evidence.

The two accurate and complete descriptions in *Sone* of the smaller, adjacent island, where now stand the derelict Peel Castle and the Church of Saint Germanus, are not eyewitness accounts written for Jean de Courci and preserved by his descendants. These two accounts, including the coronation scene in *Sone*, are literary borrowings from a source written before the Viking destructions of c. 800. After that the wide curtain walls, palace, castle, sword bridge, portal, chambers for wounded companions of the Grail, and gold and silver and trees simply did not exist there. Had they been written originally by Jean de Courci or his clerk, these accounts would have mentioned Saint Patrick's Church and the Round Tower, both standing in ruins today on the highest point of the small island. They date from the tenth century, according to the Manx archaeologists.

It is very strange that Chrétien told how Lancelot was so long imprisoned by Meleagant in just such a tower, at just such a place, or in this same location. Another red tower dominates the ruins of Peel Castle today.

The *Sone* manuscript fails to mention King Arthur, Lancelot, Perceval, Gawain, and King Urien. Perhaps Branque, in describing Sone's coronation, borrowed from his ancient source but failed to acknowledge it in order to make the narrative of Sone seem more authentic. If so, he succeeded, for Loomis read only enough of *Sone* to decide it was "authentic." Certainly, Sone's coronation and his wedding were in no way authentic, for when Sone

became the king of Ulster, even if he was inaugurated on Man, there were
no Grail, no Grail Castle, no sword, no light, and no candelabra. All had
disappeared three or four hundred years earlier.

On the other hand, one cannot say that Branque's topographical description of the Grail Castle site was not authentic, for it is there today, just
as described.

Whose arrival and inauguration and wedding were borrowed from King
Arthur's annals and rewritten as Jean de Courci's? It was not Lancelot's, for
he was crowned at Stirling, according to Ulrich's information, which has
been confirmed. Branque made one telltale slip that betrays his ancient source.
He said that the new king followed the death, not of King Godred II of
Man, but of King Alain, who was Perceval's father. Therefore it was probably Perceval's inauguration from some lost but beautifully detailed account
that Branque had the good taste to preserve intact in at least two passages.
Thus, his testimony concerning the Holy Grail and the Grail ceremony is
not only invaluable but priceless.

The *Sone* testimony supports the earlier evidence, such as that brought
by the English *Sir Percyvelle*, that Perceval's fiancée resided to the east of the
Grail Castle, whence the bells could sometimes be heard. This places her
either at Saint John's or in Douglas. Perhaps she was another Grail King's
daughter, a noble girl raised by the Grail company, through whom Perceval
acquired domains, according to Pictish custom.

The *Sone* text suffers from the disarray characteristic of Arthurian manuscripts written in Old French. Chrétien's lacunae in the lives of Lancelot
and Perceval match those in *Sone*. From his vantage point in distant Cyprus,
the author cannot decide precisely what the geography of his islands really
is. He frankly does not know whether the magnificent, golden palace that
he calls Galoches stood on the mainland facing what is now Saint Patrick's
Isle, or whether the abbey stood there close to the shore and the two rocks.
Or perhaps the abbey stood farther inland, where the Tynwald and Saint
John's stand today. Both are close to Marie de France's barrow, through
which the main road from Douglas to Peel runs. The road from Saint John's
descends steeply to the beach, along the River Neb, close to the conical
hill. (We knew that from the Perceval texts.) One still emerges abruptly on
the pale beach before the open sea, and one sees across the arm of the
brilliant, dark blue channel ruins reminiscent of the Grail Castle, upon the
red-walled islet.

When King Arthur watched Lancelot's duel with Meleagant, he seems
to have been on the mainland. From the conical hill opposite the islet the
king would have had an excellent view down onto the tilting ground of Peel
Castle.

Perceval, Lancelot, and Gawain had trouble finding the road that led
them down beside the conical hill and the river and brought them suddenly

"Peel Castle as it doth appeare from the East"

(Copy of Peel Castle, Print by Chaloner, c. 1650)

A. The hill yt is farr hier than the Castle.

B. The sea that comes round about the Castle. When the tide is at highest the greatest shipps may runne about it and come into ye harbour, and when ye tide is out maie goe drie to the Castle.

C. The Rocks.

D. The Hill with-in the Castle.

E. The Wall aboute the Castle.

F. The Cathedrall Church.

G. Two other chappells. The rest are lodgings. The hills are the landskipp of Wale and Ireland.

to the beach from which they gazed at the islet, the towers rosy against the light. Is there such a valley today? Was there such a valley and descent to what was perhaps King Arthur's castle, called Galoches? The answer furnishes a surprise. There again Chrétien was correct.

In 1656 this road and approach to the castle was called "King's Vale-

Royall." On that date a French artist named Chaloner visited the Isle of Man and drew a picture of the ruins of Peel Castle. He stood on top of the conical hill as he drew and was able, like King Arthur watching Lancelot, to look down into the quadrangle of the ruins of Peel Castle. R. H. Kinvig reproduced this drawing in his book on the history of Man. Therefore all erred who said there never was evidence of King Arthur on Man.

Furthermore, the *Sone* text confirms the information reported first by Geoffrey of Monmouth, that his island called "Norway" existed and that it was conquered by King Arthur. Since Lancelot's "sword bridge," Perceval's drawbridge or swing-bridge, Marie's palace and infirmary, Gawain's water bridge—even today there is a slip where small boats can be anchored temporarily at the windward side of Peel Island, near the Sally Port where Gawain probably fell into the trap (which is also there today, cut into the bedrock)—even Meleagant's tower, or a Pictish broch just like it, and the clear spring of water known in Manx as Saint Patrick's Spring (Chibbir Pherick) were described at the Grail Castle in Gorre, Gorre and Man are one and the same.

Gorry probably named for the Giant's Grave called King Gorry's or King Orry's, was the Isle of Man and its islet. The stone quarry still stands across the arm of the sea, where Meleagant's sister with the Manx name Jandree rowed Lancelot to safety. *Sone*'s cemetery and graves on the small Peel Island show plainly in aerial photographs of Man and are clearly visible on the postcards sold today on the island.

The Isle of Man contains other geographical features such as a "Great Meadow," where ancient armies were massed and evidence of medieval nunneries that may have continued through the centuries at the same locations. One such is at Douglas, where Perceval's affianced bride probably resided. Perceval conquered this beautiful property for her and made her safe from attack.

Until very recently boys were educated at Castletown. Ruins of Dark Age and medieval churches dedicated to ancient eremites—Bridget, Patrick, and Germanus, to name three—dot the landscape.

Until recently the herring fleet of Peel Harbor, where the medieval romancers put it, numbered three hundred ships, exactly the number recorded by both Marie de France and the clerk Branque for the chastellaine of Cyprus in *Sone de Nansai.*

That author of the *Prose Lancelot* who wrote the moving passages concerning the childhood and fostering of Lancelot never tired of describing the beauties of the place where Lancelot was taught. He raved about the tropical climate, the invigorating winds, and the nonpareil scenery. The Isle of Man, and especially Peel Castle on its breaker-whipped red rocks, have often been called one of the wonders of the world. These have been known for nine hundred years, but the Arthurian manuscripts push their greatest glory back another five hundred years.

On these islands King Arthur and his Queen Guinevere built several truly marvelous structures, including the Grail Castle where Guinevere and Lohot would lie in death. To this refuge Lancelot and Perceval moved the bodies of their honored ancestors. That Queen Morgan conveyed King Arthur here and tended his wounds on this island, one can believe. It would have been only right and fitting.

6

Conclusion:
Arthur the Patrician
and Kid Conqueror

Even though he found King Arthur "elusive" both as ruler and as conqueror, still John Morris included him in his history *The Age of Arthur*. This book broke new ground, because until that time historians had limited themselves to examining the meager historical evidence and had concluded that King Arthur was largely legendary. Or they shook their heads, dubiously averring that since Arthur was demonstrably neither Welsh, English, nor Cornish, he was not historical.

The major Arthurian scholars such as Chambers, Rhys, and Loomis, who had dominated the field for a hundred years or so, also examined a great deal of evidence, particularly that of Gildas and Nennius, before concluding that King Arthur was mythical and legendary. To them he seemed a bear god, a plough god, or a nature god of some sort. In every case, they had concluded before Leslie Alcock that the evidence was too meager; as Alcock pointed out in 1974, there was in Arthur's case neither inscription, seat, nor site that could prove his historicity. That was his opinion.

A literary scholar like Loomis could have argued that much of the world's great literature is mythological but at the same time historical. The best modern example is the *Iliad* of Homer, proven historical when it led to the discovery of Troy.

Therefore in *The Age of Arthur* John Morris made history, resolutely turning his face away from the mythologists and including King Arthur in his history of the Dark Ages.

The Age of Arthur, far from closing the door, invited a more exhaustive search through the Arthurian material, which I have presented in this book. The major conclusion is that King Arthur and his kingdom should be sought in the Border area between what is now Scotland and what is now England. His twelve battles were for the most part fought there, and his camps were there. He was in all likelihood born around there, raised there, married there, and fatally wounded there. His still unsituated battle said to have been waged on the "Dubglas" River was probably fought at Douglas, on the river of that name, on the east coast of the Isle of Man. His last treasure house was most probably near Avalon, now called Saint Patrick's Isle, adjacent to the Isle of Man, or on Man's western coast facing Ireland. For this good reason the mythology of Ireland and references to a Patrick, either the saint or the later abbot, have crept into the Arthurian material or were always native to it.

This is the first book to have explored very minutely and in the original languages both the historical and the literary material concerning King Arthur. The initial breakthrough came in the geography, a branch of study that could also have served John Morris better as a most useful adjunct to history. The history and the literature both lead directly to real places in the Border area between the ancient realm of the Picts and an England already conquered and settled by Angles and Saxons during the lifetime of King Arthur. Since he won his battles, he obviously did not fight them in England, as historians of the Anglo-Saxons have been saying for centuries.

The search for King Arthur and the major personages in the fiction written about him and about them in the High Middle Ages was carried on for two reasons: (1) because fiction is also true and (2) because the writers of the Arthurian literature used historical documents long lost to the world. Saint Gildas knew, in Arthur's day, that certain archives or *Northern Annals* had already been lost. Nennius knew that they had been lost. Gaimar, one of the Norman or French translator/adapters of Geoffrey of Monmouth, also admitted that they had been lost.

At the Battle of Camlan King Arthur's elite guard and the members of the Round Table died before the king died. There was nobody to safeguard his archives from that moment. His body was taken, alive or dead, to the Isle of Avalon. It in turn fell to Viking raiders. All was destroyed, burned, and hauled away. Nothing remained.

Throughout the literature of centuries, however, the memory of King Arthur survived. A person or persons saw his tomb in an underground chamber, perhaps, they said, on the Isle of Man. Remember how Don Quixote fell into the Cave of Montesinos and how he too saw unforgettably the slumbering knights on their tombs. Victor Hugo wrote at some length in *Notre-Dame de Paris* (The Hunchback of Notre Dame) how literature is the most indestructible force in the whole world. Books cannot be destroyed. Pieces and bits turn up. Copies and translations are preserved. This is how the lost archives are little by little reconstructed. The search will not end here.

The search began with *The History of the Kings of Britain* by Geoffrey of Monmouth, a churchman and scholar at Oxford, a sincere, honest man with strong ties to Wales who may have been a graduate of the University of Paris. His work was examined minutely in order to determine whether this book was worth the candle. Geoffrey's account of King Arthur's life, early battles, and coronation held up rather better than previously thought in light of the knowledge that has accumulated about the Dark Ages over the past few decades. Geoffrey knew that King Arthur had lived in the ancient world, not in the Middle Ages. He saw that the king had come to the rescue of Britain at the collapse of Rome and soon after the withdrawal of Roman occupying forces from that island. King Arthur attempted to halt the spread of Anglo-Saxon settlement beyond Northumbria. He succeeded, many persons believe, in largely maintaining a Celtic realm there in the north of Britain. Geoffrey also knew that King Arthur was Christian, but I would say he was a member of the Celtic church, which was about to be replaced by Roman Catholicism. Thus, in this instance also, sources were lost, for ancient practices were not only sternly outlawed but forbidden. Even the holiest men of Arthur's day were soon discarded in favor of others in Rome. But Saint Patrick had founded the Bishopric of Man before Arthur's lifetime, in the year 447.

The method utilized throughout this search was to collate the various texts so that the best minds could tell their stories and be compared to each other. Their accounts, like Geoffrey, were held up to history, geography, linguistics, prehistory, archaeology, and architecture. Each discipline was asked to assist in making a biography of King Arthur, a chronology for his life, an explanation of the theology of his day, and information on the architecture of the fifth and sixth centuries.

Once Geoffrey of Monmouth seemed to have placed King Arthur correctly in Scotland and on the Isle of Man, which in Geoffrey's day was ruled by Norway and thus called "Norway," his successors were in their turns admitted into court. The search was extended to Chrétien de Troyes to see what could be salvaged from his many texts, and then to Marie de France to see what could be added. Astonishment grew as the former also placed King Arthur in Scotland and the latter placed his foe King Urien of Gorre on the Isle of Man, and even closer yet, on the very Saint Patrick's Isle where once upon a time the dead heroes really lay on their tombs.

Their texts were held up to noted recent scholars in related disciplines. Recourse to maps became increasingly necessary, and that knowledge was confirmed by correspondence with scholars in Britain and in the United

States, by borrowings from libraries here and abroad, and by almost annual trips to Britain.

The present inquiry has run its course from literary truth to physical reality—from the words of Geoffrey of Monmouth and Chrétien de Troyes, notably, to standing on the shores of the Firth of Forth and looking, as Lancelot did, across the waters to Stirling Castle, and to standing, as Perceval did, on the conical hill and looking down upon the site of the Grail Castle across its arm of the sea. The day I stood there they were unloading stone at Peel Castle, just as the *Sone de Nansai* manuscript described it, from the quarry across the arm of the sea. The bright sunlight danced upon the dark blue waters between there and Ireland, as Chrétien said. Ten minutes later, after the small punt had brought us to the isle itself, a sudden squall drove the rain in stinging runnels across our faces and forced us to shelter under the castle tower. A little harder and it would have driven the waves over the crumbling yellow walls, as it did on the day Sone (Perceval) was married there and tried to sit down at his wedding feast. Just as suddenly it ceased, and the sun came out across the rosy, golden sky in the direction of faraway blue Ireland just emerging from the mist. The other pilgrims on the isle felt as I did—as if they were on holy ground—and bent down and touched the small grasses and pink flowers on the rocky sward.

This investigation has proceeded from faith to evidence, given the honesty and integrity of the masters of literature and the fact that the study of the past ennobles the present and emblazons the future. Geoffrey of Monmouth on the witness stand led us to one discovery after another. We saw the truth of his place names, the sense of his understanding of those events, the strength of his admiration for King Arthur and for Queen Guinevere and for the unknown King Anguselus of Scotland, who turned out to be Lancelot of the Lake. Ultimately, Geoffrey gave us King Arthur.

Through the same kind of argument we could see that Chrétien de Troyes was a Scot native to that area or had access to the most privileged information. In any case the count of Flanders, who commissioned Chrétien to write the Perceval manuscript, had just returned to Flanders from Scotland, so we know that Chrétien had it on good authority.

The Arthurian material falls into five major categories: (1) the hero story of King Arthur, (2) the prophet story of Merlin, (3) the adventure stories of Lancelot and of Gawain, (4) the quest stories of Perceval and of Galahad, and (5) the love story of Tristan and Iseut. We have neglected the last as not likely right away to advance the other, major categories.

The heroical material about Arthur moves from his lost childhood accounts to his dukedom in the defense of Britain, conquest of the western isles, twelve terrible battles, sweeps off the seacoast, possible continental campaign in northern Europe, establishment of his treasury and necropolis on the Isle of Man, inauguration as king of Britain, and long rule from Carlisle, from Stirling, and from Dumbarton Rock on the Clyde River near Glasgow today. The 108 references to Carlisle as his chief seat seem to end the speculation about that matter.

Like a true epic, this first story ends with the death of the hero. Arthur's passing occurred after the disastrous Battle of Camlan on Hadrian's Wall, near his own mustering site of Chamot Hill in what is today the Kershope Forest, and his transportation overseas to the Isle of Man or Avalon. Virtually everyone who was anything to him was dead, including his queen, Guinevere. Other queens—so revered that they could walk freely upon the field of carnage unscathed—survived to bear away his body. Arthur's body was probably taken from Carlisle to Douglas on the east coast of the Isle of Man, whence the main road still cuts across the isle at low level to the descent into Peel Castle. That route was secret, as was the Round Table fellowship, as was and is King Arthur's function at the Round Table.

Arthur, Uther Pendragon, and Perceval met and knew Merlin, who, due also to Geoffrey of Monmouth, remains remembered and revered by Scots even today. Merlin built the necropolis for Aurelius Ambrosius on Calton (Caledonian) Hill, or on Arthur's Seat in the city of Edinburgh. Merlin also supervised the childhood and education of King Arthur, arranged for his test of merit by having him draw the sword or cross from the flint stone anvil at Carlisle, helped in the choice of his bride, presided at the Round Table at some time, recorded the history of King Arthur's reign, functioned as court astronomer, and survived the death of Arthur. He was not the Archdruid of the North, but was said to have reported on the Isle of Iona to that dignitary. While the graphic arts have not yielded Arthur, so far as is known, they have offered us Merlin—in the pictures of Father Time. He has a high domed forehead, a long white beard, and white hair. He carries a golden sickle. He wears a long white robe that falls to the ground. His eyes are blue, the familiar lentoid eye of Celtic art; and they are hooded, set deep in his head. Father Time is always said to rule the sacred Isle of Joy where the dead are laid to rest. The three feet inside the Manx logo or Wheel of Time represent their light footsteps.

The adventure stories of Lancelot and Gawain present the younger generation of heroes, Arthur's field officers who bore the sword Excalibur in Arthur's name, or as the symbol of their power from him, like the Roman *imperium*. Gawain aged during the course of his adventures, becoming scarfaced, and he was superseded by the fiery Lancelot, a much younger man. Like avenging, dark angels both were sacrificial victims to the arts of war. Gawain was raised in and associated with Galloway, it appears, but his tutor called "Pope" Sulpicius Severus has too common a name for us to trace him in that century. The much more brilliant Lancelot gave us less trouble, once we began to believe in Geoffrey of Monmouth.

The successful quester Perceval antedated by his royal priesthood the later royal priesthood of Saint Columba of Ireland. The folktale still says that the Great Fool (Perceval) slowly grew so wise that he finally married the daughter of the King of Ireland. His Grail Castle was in Irish territory, where Q-Celtic, the Manx language, was spoken. Perceval moved to holiness among the ancient Celtic shrines of the Border or of the Tweed Uplands, his progress forcing us to admire the ancient practices of Celtic paganism and Celtic Christianity. Thus, as Edward Gibbon saw it also, those ancient practices took their placid and quiet revenge after a long and bitter oppression. Saint Kentigern is of Perceval's ilk. The Swan Prince who liberated Jerusalem in the First Crusade was his descendant.

It is comforting to know that the exaltation of the Celtic church that one finds throughout the Arthurian material sat upon the solid rock of the Grail Castle at Avalon. There Saints Joseph and Gildas were venerated, the one with his box of ointment, his thorn tree, his thirteen wattled huts, and his budding thorn staff from the first century, the other with his bell, his staff, and the new spring of water at his feet. Saint Ninian, who was taller than any other man of his day, also saw a living fountain spring to life at his feet, perhaps the one where Queen Guinevere and her captors rested overnight on their way to the Grail Castle. Such are today Christian symbols, most of which evolved between the years 72 and 410 A.D. When it was said that King Arthur worshiped at the shrine, which we identified as that of Saint Ninian in the Rhinns of Galloway, the king was said to have remained out of doors and not to have attended the service inside the chapel. Such a detail authenticated the text, for in those ancient times the worshiper customarily remained out of doors.

The Grail Castle at the navel of the sea reminds us of Jerusalem and of Delphi; all three are ancient and oracular sites. It also reminds us, with its aura of holiness, its atmosphere of dream vision, and its line of temporal and spiritual rulers, of other such sites and other such places reputed to be paradise. Nowadays Tibetan guidebooks are being scanned for the physical site of holy Shambhala, said to be surrounded by two concentric rings of snowy mountain peaks. There scholars are seeking a distinctive natural site, a warrior like Arthur, a winner of fabulous battles, like that of Mount Badon. In both cases, the hidden sanctuaries are concealed by archaic place names; but both lie beyond a wasteland and desert area. Each historical site is swept with storms, hard to find, protected as they are by misdirections (the Arthurian lapse of a sea crossing) but recognizable finally because of its geographical uniqueness. Thus, Lancelot's "sword bridge," Gawain's "water bridge," Perceval's "swing-bridge," and what was probably then as now, a punt. The directions to Avalon consist almost of a litany: sea crossing, arm of the sea, three hundred ships in the harbor, the Fisher King, the descent from the conical hill, the stone quarry on the opposite shore, the tropical plants and flowers, the spring in runnels of silver. The key to the puzzle apparently was the mention of "Ireland": the stormiest sea opposite Ireland, for instance.

The *Chronicle* of Ihon Hardyng (1543) informs us that Galahad was the last Grail Lord to appoint twelve Fellows to the Order of the "saynt Graall."

Avalon was in the land of King Gorry, pronounced as such, and the surname *Gorry* is presently listed among the "distinctive Manx" names. The descent to Avalon from the Tynwald Hill and Saint John's goes along the "King's Vale-Royall," as one would have hoped. If one stands today and looks at the site of the ancient Avalon, many questions concerning King Arthur seem to resolve themselves.

We have answered the question about the extent of his kingdom: it is the Border Country of Scotland, with Berwick, Carlisle, Dumbarton, and Stirling marking its four corners. We have also answered questions about the kind of warfare Arthur launched in such a poor and mountainous terrain. Arthur fought pitched battles, then withdrew to regroup and waged war by attrition, by delaying actions, and by varieties of psychological terror such as night attacks. He laid waste enemies' lands, burned stockades to pen his foes like livestock, or lay in ambush for them. He threatened, cajoled, entreated, promised, and thus led men and fleets.

The king could always fall back upon the two anchor fortresses in the Carlisle area, where among the marshes of the Eden estuary he was safe from pursuit, and from which he could hasten to the islands. His four corner fortresses, all seaports, functioned as depots for arms and as rallying centers. The Britons under Arthur could easily disperse, slip quietly away to live off the Tweed Uplands, or hide deep in their ravines and steep valleys. From all over warriors poured in to serve under this most renowned of warrior kings, some, like Gawain and Lancelot, remaining with him until death. Arthur won all of his engagements, as everyone acknowledged, until Camlan.

We have addressed questions about the diverse roles of women in that savage society. We have located hill forts and Arthur's chief embarkation port of Loch Ryan and sought the magical Camelot. We have suggested that Arthur was born in his mother's seaside castle at Caerlaverock on the shore of the Solway Firth, not in southwestern England at a monastery, later Tintagel Castle.

The hardest puzzles have been the Round Table, the identity of Lancelot, the location of the Perilous Ford, the meaning of Merlin's sword bridge, the site of the necropolis and monument also built by Merlin for Aurelius Ambrosius, and the problem of the Picts (called swarthy dwarfs and dark, Loathly Damsels, as most conquered peoples are called by their superior, blond conquerors). We have seen that the Middle River bisecting their old territory was the Forth, which at the Fords of Frew separated the Pictish Highlands from the Lowlands of Scotland.

We have rejected the theories that the Round Table was constructed of wood, and that it might have been the turf condominiums or multiple dwellings visible today as flat, round surfaces at Penrith and on the Isle of Man. The Round Table was, I believe, in its heyday a temple of stone.

But two final puzzles still confront us as we approach a theoretical and provisional ending. Why, when he vanished so completely, and when the annals of his reign were lost so suddenly, could a king have continued, as King Arthur did, to grip the imagination from the year 542 until Geoffrey of Monmouth's rediscovery of him in the twelfth century? We know that the very memory of King Arthur so terrorized King Henry II in the twelfth century that this strong, efficient ruler took steps with his relative, the abbot of Glastonbury, to have Arthur's tomb uncovered there and his so-called remains reinterred once and for all. What was it that after six centuries so frightened King Henry II? Could it have been the prophecies of Merlin that in the intervening centuries had kept Arthur alive?

Perhaps we have not yet taken into account sufficiently the one survivor of the Battle of Camlan who was not an enemy but Arthur's prime mover, as it were. He was King Arthur's guardian and protector, this "Marvelous" Merlin of so many talents, an ally and expert handler.

Thus, King Arthur appears so many centuries later as "elusive" and yet vivid, real. We think of him in poetic images, and this despite the fact that, unlike Merlin's, there seems to be no artistic tradition as to Arthur's physiognomy. We cannot for an instant think that he resembled the pallid blond of the Heroes Tapestries.* The other artistic representations of Arthur differ completely. Only the Gustave Doré likenesses made for the *Idylls of the King* somewhat resemble the king's profile that can still be seen faintly on the Salisbury Crags, above Holyrood Castle, in the city of Edinburgh.

Very probably much of this subliminal recalling of Arthur, and much of the poetic symbolism that enfolds him, comes from the prophet called in Scotland "Marvelous Merlin." Today in Scotland the name *Arthur* falls upon deaf ears, which leads to a last question: Why does Scotland not remember King Arthur with something of the same veneration, or even with some of the same affection, felt there for Merlin but also felt for Arthur in other areas of Britain? The answer seems connected to the talent, the career, and the active promoting of King Arthur by the poet and prophet Merlin. The *Prose Lancelot* tells us that Merlin's time of prophecy was 1,690 weeks, or

*At the Cloisters Museum, New York City

thirty-two and a half years. He reigned inside the Wheel of Time at the Grail Castle, or Avalon. It was he who attributed to King Arthur in Malory, in Geoffrey, and elsewhere the cryptic suggestion that the king revolved also inside the Wheel of Fortune or Time, sometimes up and sometimes "upso-down."

Like the dawn, Merlin foretold, King Arthur would arise to come again from his mysterious retreat on the island, out from the dark cave where, wounded, he had been laid.

Meanwhile the stars would turn away from men, Geoffrey has Merlin say, and face away from them and alter their wonted courses across the ecliptic. In their wrath the very stars would wither the standing fields of grain and forbid the rain to fall from heaven.

Beware, Merlin warned, of the Bear loosing his muzzle for war:

> *The Beare his musal shal vpbinde,*
> *And neuer after bund shal be.*
> *Away the other shal waxe with winde*
> *And as they come so shall they flee.*

Such cryptic verses we have inherited from Merlin made great mischief throughout the Middle Ages and on into the terrible wars between England and Scotland.

Another brief example of Merlin's power comes from the old English chronicle by Peter de Langtoft, as adapted and enlarged by Robert de Brunne:

1. ". . . the clerk Merlyn sais certeyn,   Vol. 1
   That Bretons at the last salle haf this land agayne, . . ."*

Those are terrible and very dangerous words, emphatic and fearsome.

2. "Right as Merlyn spak had Edward the Kyng   Vol. 1
   Scotland, als Albanack had at the be gynnyng."
3. Men everywhere swear witness "of Merlyn mouth."   Vol. 2
4. "Gestes that er olde writen of many man, thritti reames men tolde, that Kyng Arthur wan. He parted his wynnyng tille his men largely, that nouther erle ne kyng wille withsitte his cry. they were at his wille, were he neuer sohie, Bothe of gode & ille at alle his nede redie."

What of King Arthur? asked Peter de Langtoft. Say men who read of him in Merlin, he was ever in the middle of the battle. Morning and evening he was sober and honest. Felons who grieved him, or enemies who stirred

---

*The word "clerk" meant educated person.

up broils were judged worthily by him, inclined by neither prayers nor presents. At council and in need he was a skillful king. There was never a prince more praised. There was nobody in all Christendom as he was in his time. How do we know all this? From Merlin.

The later, medieval seers and prophets of Scotland, such as Thomas of Erceldoune, were given to dire predictions that King Arthur would come to life again, regain his "thirty realms," and conquer all England, from Dumbarton Rock in Glasgow to Dover on the Straits. Such prophets tell how Arthur was chosen to be king, how he rode over Scotland, how he was then crowned king, how his legions laid waste the south, and (sadly for Britain) how he came to rule all Britain. It was on this claim that bloody wars flared up again and that England claimed Scotland. Arthur shall conquer and hold all Britain, says another old prophecy of the Scots:

> Yet this wicked World shall last but a while,
> While a chiftane unchosen choose forth himself,
> And rode over the Region, and for Roy holden;
> Then his scutifers shall skail all the fair South,
> Fra Dumbartone to Dover, and deil all the lande,
> He shall be kid conqueror, for he is kinde Lorde,
> Of all Bretaine that bounds to the broad Sea,
> The conquessing shall be keeped and never conquest after.

Thus, the ancient prophets in Scotland remembered the dead King Arthur, as the "kid conqueror" who would come again, conquer, and hold all Britain. Geoffrey must have had his Merlin Prophecies from them.

Our last question appears answered. A Scottish textual scholar named James A. Murray admitted in 1872 that "the Arthur legends had been allowed to die out in this their original birthland, on account of the unpalatable support which they gave to the English claim over Scotland." King Arthur was let go from Scotland, then, for in his name that land had again and again been laid waste.

Beware of Arthur, the unmuzzled grizzly Bear, warned the old buzzing prophets, remembering Merlin's words. In heraldry the fearsome Bear is now shown muzzled, and often chained. But Arthur's standard probably was the Bear's Gamb (paw) with its fierce claws extended. The hammer with its claws is called a hammer ducally crowned. Since the boy Arthur was named "dux" or duke, this too may have been his cognizance in the days before heraldry was a science. Nowadays, say some authorities, his armorial insignia is the Rouge Dragon, and Lancelot's is the three white lions on a blue field.

At the end of the Middle Ages the question of King Arthur rested very uneasily upon prophecy and faith. In 1544 John Leland argued that Arthur was the "patrician" and "emperor" of all the lands that could be seen and surveyed. But to the oracles he was still the fabled "kid conqueror" and victor of Mount Badon. Or he was temporarily interred at Glastonbury and not really dead, or he reposed under the great A of all the dolmens in Wales. Or, unmuzzled he would come again. Hard questions that were not even raised until the dawn of modern scholarship.

In 1801 Owen Jones opened a door on a new world. He had just finished editing the first ancient texts from the Dark Ages, *The Myrvyrian Archaiology*, which was published at two of the most ancient learned centers of the Celtic peoples, Edinburgh and Cardiff.

Not to be outdone, in England, where Geoffrey of Monmouth had first introduced King Arthur to the world, Matthew Arnold lectured on the beauties of Celtic literature in 1866. What scholars were witnessing, said Arnold, was the gradual unveiling of a whole new world, one that was both British and ancient. The question should be approached positively, he urged, rather than leaving the whole matter of King Arthur at any "lame and impotent conclusion . . . because the one interesting, fruitful question here is not in what instances the internal evidence opposes the claims of these poems to a sixth-century origin, but in what instances it supports them, and what these sixth-century remains, thus established, signify."

Taking his words to heart and shunning a retrogressive and negative scholarship founded upon contempt for ancient and medieval authors, I approached it positively and maintained faith, which faith in the possibilities of discovery has led me to offer King Arthur a kingdom.

APPENDIXES

🎀 1 🎀
Ancient Sources:
King Arthur

Area of Origin	Author	Date	Title of Work
Scotland	Gildas	c. 500	De excidio et conquestu Britanniae (The Epistle of Gildas)
Scotland	Aneirin	c. 600	"Gododdin" from Canu Aneirin (The Book of Aneirin)
Wales	Nennius	c. 800	Historia Britonum (History of the Britons). B.M. Harleian 3859 contains: The Six Ages of the World, Roman Britain, Origins of Britain, History (Vortigern, Vortimer), Lives (Patrick, Germanus) Arthur's Battles Genealogies 28 Cities of Britain Marvels of Britain Annals of Wales (447–954)
Wales	Poems and Tales	?	The Mabinogion The Black Book of Carmarthen

Area of Origin	Author	Date	Title of Work
Wales	Poems and Tales	?	The Red Book of Hergest See also *The Myvyrian Archaiology of Wales* for the poem "Preiddeu Annwfn" (The Harrying of Hades), ante 1100; and see the *mabinogi* (tale) "Culhwch and Olwen."
North Britain, perhaps Carlisle	?	?	*Northern Annals* A major work, lost since the thirteenth century.
Flanders	Lambert de Saint-Omer	1120	*Liber floridus*
Britain and the Continent	Cambro-British saints, among whom: Cadocus of Llancarvan (Llancarfan) David of Menevia and Caerleon Dubricius of Caerleon Eleutherius of Tournai Iltutus of Llantwit Major Kentigern of Glasgow Paternus of Llanbadarn Fawr		contemporaries of Arthur *Lives (Vitae)*

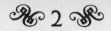

Major Arthurian Texts
of the
High Middle Ages

Vol. 1, "L'Estoire del Saint Graal"
Vol. 2, "L'Estoire de Merlin"
Vol. 3, "Li Livre de Lancelot del Lac"
Vol. 4, cont.
Vol. 5, cont.
Vol. 6, "Les Aventures, ou La Quest del Saint
Graal" "La Mort le Roi Artus"
Vol. 7, "Le Livre d'Artus"

18. Anon . . . . *Sone von Nausay* . . . . c. 1250
(Sone de Nansai)

❧ 3 ❧
Major Arthurian Texts
of the Late
English Middle Ages

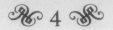

4

Geoffrey of
Monmouth

The only life of King Arthur was written by Geoffrey (1136) in his *Historia Regum Britanniae*, translated originally by Sebastian Evans as *History of the Kings of Britain* (1912). In English translation the material on King Arthur is divided into books 7–12 and into chapters, but in Geoffrey's original Latin, it was divided into paragraphs only. About half the history, or books 1–6, deals with Britain from the time of the Trojan War to the antecedents of King Arthur. Book 7 consists of the cryptic ten or so pages of the Prophecies or Vaticinations of Merlin. These most famous of Geoffrey's famous pages became so tremendously successful that the (handwritten) copies of the work were in great demand.

The remaining five books on Arthur take up about half the entire history, or some one hundred pages. Geoffrey worked on for another twelve years revising his text, so successful was it, and he allowed the first authorized translation, into Welsh.

Since 1929 we have at hand an excellent, reliable edition of Geoffrey's text, *The Historia Regum Britanniae of Geoffrey of Monmouth with Contributions to the Study of Place in Early British History*, which was established from the four best manuscripts collated by Acton Griscom and Robert Ellis Jones of Columbia University. In this edition the Welsh text is put at the bottom of each page of the Latin it translates. Most important, this edition is the first one sympathetic to Geoffrey of Monmouth. It therefore marks an important date not only in medieval scholarship but also in Arthurian studies.

"Merlin's Book of Prophecy" is Geoffrey of Monmouth's first book, these some ten pages that remain in the *History* as book 7 of the English-language editions. His third and last book was the life of Merlin, *Vita Merlini* (c. 1150), which is a Latin poem of 1,529 verses telling about Merlin surviving in the wilderness while Arthur was reputedly being healed of his wounds in Avalon. The life of King Arthur, in the translations from Latin, forms books 8–11 of the *History*. Geoffrey died in 1154. The great number of Latin manuscripts of the *History* that have survived, 190 copies in 49 libraries in eleven different countries of Europe, bear witness to the immense popularity of Geoffrey's work of history. He apparently attracted medieval readers from all over Europe, who suddenly had access to the Arthurian material in elegant Latin, which was universally read. Edmond Faral declared in 1929 in France that the international renown of "Geoffrey Arthur," as he was known during his lifetime, was simply staggering. Sebastian Evans, who is Geoffrey's best-known English translator, has said as much.

The two royal or presentation copies of the *History* are also extant: MS Cambridge 1706 and Codex Bernensis no. 568. They were offered to Robert of Gloucester, Count Waleran of Mellent, and King Stephen of England, who reigned from 1135–54. Geoffrey had offered the earlier and separate edition of the Merlin prophecy to Alexander, Bishop of Lincoln.

Best known of Geoffrey's translators and adapters are the Anglo-Norman Wace, who was commissioned by King Henry II of England, and the Anglo-Saxon Layamon. Both Wace and Layamon understand that what Geoffrey wrote about Arthur was epic in character and should be altered and rewritten as such. Of course, they are of little assistance to anyone who wishes now to read the material as history rather than epic, the latter usually having little to do with the former. Wace largely retransforms Geoffrey's already muddled geography into French terms, visualizing Arthur at the castle of Chinon. Layamon, who visualized Arthur as a George Washington, placed him in the Severn estuary, which was his own home, or around the area of Bristol and Gloucester. Had Arthur the benefit of wings he might have flown down from Dumbarton to the Severn for the renewal of yesterday's battle!

By the time of Geoffrey's death it had been well established among a certain group of authors that King Arthur should be sought in the Glastonbury region, and this for the reasons of tradition. Thus, a writer known as Caradoc of Llancarvan (or Llancarfan) wrote a biography of Saint Gildas around the 1130s, in which he told a scandalous story of King Arthur's Queen Guinevere having been abducted to the swamps around Glastonbury. It was there that King Arthur rode finally to her rescue. This sort of allegation, which in fact debunks King Arthur, does not occur anywhere in the pages of Geoffrey of Monmouth. He writes of the queen with respect, making much of her coronation and saying little else. As a matter of fact, Geoffrey of Monmouth displays the typical Englishman's respect for queens.

One reason for the scorn heaped upon Geoffrey probably stems from his ignoring the Glastonbury traditions. The reason for his unpopularity in Scotland is more complex. An example of the indignation Geoffrey drew there may be seen in William Maitland's introduction to his *History and Antiquities of Scotland from the Earliest Accounts of Time to the Death of James the First, Anno 1437*, where he calls Geoffrey a "wicked author"

> [who] has probably done the island of Britain more mischief than all the books that ever were, or, it is to be hoped, ever will be writ in it. For, on that legend [of King Arthur], Edward I, King of England, founded his pretended sovreignty over the kingdom of Scotland, . . . which occasioned those long and bloody wars which had almost ended in the destruction of both nations.

More likely, Geoffrey has been blamed for a firmly held Welsh tradition of history. The Arthurian story furnishes only one part of what must have been a vast body of literature called "history" (*ystorya*), including the Irish records (*seanchus*). The oldest stratum of this material is represented in the Welsh *Triads*, to which Geoffrey had no access; in his time they were restricted information. The *Triads* and the Welsh *Mabinogi* or *Mabinogion* harked back to the more ancient days when the Celtic peoples ruled all Britain. The story of King Arthur supported this belief and national consciousness. Thus did King Arthur become a spiritual king, as well as providing the memory of a real king for the Welsh. And for those across the Channel and the Irish Sea, he became the "Breton Hope."

Geoffrey apparently committed various errors in church history, for which he is still castigated. Christopher Brooke's article in *Studies in the Early British Church*, edited by the famous medieval historian Nora K. Chadwick, states that though a churchman himself, Geoffrey erroneously placed an archbishop in Canterbury in Arthur's lifetime and an archbishop at Caerleon. And yet as late as 1842 the noted church historian Edward Stillingfleet considered Geoffrey correct in such allegations.

The textual scholar Rachel Bromwich of the University of Cardiff, realizing that Geoffrey had no access to secret Welsh lore, approaches the matter of his accuracy in church matters with more understanding. Thus, she considers him a Norman, a Breton, or, at any rate, a continental churchman, not a native Welshman of bardic stock. The errors that Edward Stillingfleet made in his *Origines Britannicae*, seven hundred years later than Geoffrey, are equally shocking. He translated as follows:

> *Cilurnum* = Silchester
> *Vindolan(d)a* = Winchester
> *Amboglana* = Ambleside in Westmorland

Since the discovery of the Rudge Cup and the Amiens patera (see Bibliography) we know the names of the forts on the Hadrianic Wall:

> *Cilurnum* = Silchester in Muro, or Chesters
> *Vindolanda* = Chesterholm, also on the Wall
> *Camboglana* = Birdoswald on the Wall

Birdoswald is now thought to be the site of Camlan, which Geoffrey more correctly called "Camblan," where King Arthur was fatally wounded in his last great battle in the west. The correction of such errors encourages us to continue with Geoffrey's geography.

❧ 5 ❧

Medieval Chronicles
and Chroniclers

Alanus de Insulis (c. 1128–c. 1202)
Andreas Capellanus (1174–86)
Anglo-Saxon Chronicles (60 B.C.–1154)
Bede (c. 673–c. 735)
Caradoc of Llancarvan (1129–60)
Etienne de Rouen (c. 1167)
Geoffrey of Monmouth (c. 1136)
Gervase of Tilbury (c. 1211)
Gildas (c. 540)
Giraldus Cambrensis, or Gerald of Wales (c. 1147–c. 1223)
Guillaume de Rennes (c. 1235)
Hector Boece (c. 1465–c. 1536)
Helinand de Froidmont (c. 1170–1230)
Henry of Huntington (c. 1154)
John of Fordun, cont. Walter Bower (c. 1360)
Lambert de Saint-Omer (c. 1120)
Nennius (c. 800)
Ralph Higden (1300–1363)
Richard of Cirencester (d. c. 1401)
Robert de Torigny (c. 1152)
Roger of Wendover, cont. Matthew Paris (d. 1236)
Saxo Grammaticus (c. 1188–1201)
Vincent de Beauvais (c. 1190–1264)
Walter Map (c. 1190)
William of Malmesbury (c. 1125)

Note: A single date refers to the completion of a work.

❦ 6 ❦
Antecedents
and Contemporaries
of King Arthur

Dongardus.

To Eugene succeeded his brother Dongard, anno 452. This prince, according to Boece, must have been of a martial disposition; for he fought and defeated the Britons, under their king Constantine, on the banks of the Humber, in which battle he was killed, with the loss of fourteen thousand of his men, and that of sixteen thousand Britons. But by Buchanan we are told, that Dongard being a quiet and peaceable prince, nothing remarkable happened in his time; and that, after a reign of five years, he died in peace anno 457.

Constantinus I.

After the demise of Dongard, Constantine his youngest brother came to the crown, in the year 457, who, if Boece may be believed, was a very wicked man, his chief pleasure being to deflower virgins, ravish matrons, and encourage detraction; and, instead of frequenting the company of his nobles, assorted himself with common fiddlers, songsters, and other such vagrants. Buchanan follows Boece in this infamous character; but as Fordun had as good an opportunity of knowing him as either of them, his silence, to me, is a greater proof of his innocence than their bare assertions. Constantine must, at the discretion of the reader, either stand condemned, or be acquitted of the heavy charge brought against him. Be that as it will, we are told by the said writers, that Constantine, persevering in his wicked course of life, was slain by a nobleman of the Isles, for deflowering his daughter, in the twenty-second year of his reign, anno 479.

From W. Maitland, *The History and Antiquities of Scotland,* vol. 1, pp. 280–81 (London, 1757). See the Bibliography for Maitland's sources: John of Fordun, Hector Boece, the Venerable Bede, and George Buchanan.

Congallus I.

After the death of Constantine, Congal his nephew, son of Dongard, acceded to the throne, anno 479; and, being of a pacifick disposition, employed himself in reforming his people to a greater degree of politeness; and, to prevent a war with the Britons, renewed the treaty concluded between them and Constantine. But, according to Boece, the Scots and Picts having invaded Britain, Vortigern sent an army against them, under the command of Gwytell, prince of Cambria; and a battle ensuing, the Britons were defeated, with the loss of their general and twenty thousand men; whereas that of the Scots scarcely amount to four thousand. And by Buchanan we are told, that Congal carried on a skirmishing war against the Saxons during the whole course of his reign, which he finished after a course of twenty-two years, anno 501.

Goranus.

To Congal succeeded his brother Goran, anno 501, who governed his people with great piety and justice. He prevailed on the Picts to break their alliance with the Saxons, and to enter into a confederacy with the Scots and Britons against the Saxons, and, by making it a common cause, to endeavour to expel them the island: by whole assistance Arthur, king of the Britons, is said to have obtained divers victories. But Goran, having deviated from his first principles, encouraged Toncet, his justiciary, to fleece his subjects; which enraged his people to such a degree, that a conspiracy was formed against him, which ended in the destruction both of him and his iniquitous chief justice, in the thirty-fourth year of his reign, anno 535.

Eugenius II.

Eugene II, son of Congal, succeeded Goran in the year 535. He assisted Modred king of the Picts, and Arthur king of the Britons, against the Saxons; and sent out many parties to make incursions, but never fought a field battle; and, after a reign of twenty-three years, died anno 558.

Convallus, or Conal.

After the death of Eugene, Conval his brother came to the crown, anno 558, who, being a religious and pacifick prince, governed his people in great tranquillity. He assisted the Britons against the Saxons, without being a principal in the war; and, after a short but happy reign of ten years, died in the year 568.

Kinnatellus.

Kinnatel succeeded his brother Conal, anno 568; but being of a valetudinary constitution, only reigned fourteen or fifteen months, without anything memorable happening in his short reign, and died in the year 570.

Aidanus.

Kinnatel having resigned the crown in favour of Aidan, son of the late King Goran, he no sooner ascended the throne, in the year 570, then he suppressed divers bands of robbers in the province of Galloway; and held three conventions of the states in that country, Lochaber, and Caithness. But a tumult happening at a hunting match soon after, much blood was spilt, and the king's officers cruelly beaten, for endeavouring to apprehend the aggressors; who, for their security, fled to Brudeus, king of the Picts, in the country of Lothian; to whom ambassadors were sent by Aidan, to demand their being delivered up to justice, according to treaty; which being refused by Brudeus, a war ensued between the two nations, which proved not of long duration; for matters were happily accommodated by the interposition and good offices of Columba.

Some time after, Ethelfrid and Brude, kings of the Northumbrians and Picts, being in an alliance against the Scots and Britons, invaded the British or Welsh dominions with a powerful army; to whose assistance Ceulin, king of the West-Saxons, being on his march with a considerable army to reinforce Ethelfrid and Brude, the Scots and Britons attacked and broke the front of his army; but having soon after joined Ethelfrid, the united armies attacked and put to flight the joint power of the Scots and Britons. In this engagement Ethelfrid lost an eye, Brude was carried off the field sorely wounded, and Griffin and Brendin, two Scotish noblemen, were slain.

The occasion of this war is related by Bede in a different manner; for he tells us that Ethelfrid, king of Northumberland, having subdued and taken divers large territories from the Britons, he either made them tributary, or planted them with his own people. Aidan, king of the Scots, jealous of his increasing power, invaded Northumberland; and a battle ensuing at Degsastan, or Degstan, Theobald, brother to Ethelfrid, was killed, and that part of the army commanded by him routed: but Aidan's army being defeated and put to flight, his loss, according to my author, was so great, that the Scots, from that period to the time he wrote his history, which was above one hundred years after, did not perfume to invade England.

7

Arthur's Oven

This effectually destroys Buchanan's conjectures of these duns being either erected as trophies or sepulchres for great men, to perpetuate their memory to posterity; and as to their being built in imitation of his Templum Termini, or Arthur's Oven, near the river of Carron in Stirlingshire, there will, on comparing the draught of the one with the remains of the others, appear no other resemblance than that of rotundity: for, by their different manner of construction, the former, both by their name and appearance, shew themselves to have been fortresses; whereas the latter seems to have been erected for some domestick office, and for none, I think more likely than that of a cold bath, though by different writers it has been appropriated to a diversity of uses. And as to its construction, it was only a single-walled building, arched as it were at top, by stones projecting inwards, with an aperture in the uppermost part; which I take to have been casual, and not built so at first, as has by many been thought; for had it been at first so erected, there had been no occasion for so very large and lofty a doorway of ten feet six inches in height, and six feet four inches in breadth, with a window over the frame about three feet three inches square, in so small a building as this, which was only nineteen feet and six inches in the internal diameter. Besides, instead of having a coping thereon, the uppermost stones, which were of the same form with those of the common layers, composed only about half a layer; yet though the rest, through accidents and the inclemency of the weather, are gone, they nevertheless plainly shew that this was not the uppermost layer: wherefore we may justly conclude, that the layers formerly above this are lost and perished by the like contingencies.

Now as the construction of the abovementioned Dunaliscaigh is so widely different from that of Arthur's Oven, by its having divers rooms therein, with a large open area in the middle, never said to be close at top, and without a window on the outside, we cannot suppose that it, with the numerous edifices of the same kind

From W. Maitland, *The History and Antiquities of Scotland*, vol. 1, London, 1757. pp. 207–213.

throughout the kingdom, were any other than fortesses; for those duns or castles, both by their situation and construction, appear to have been very strong. And I imagine they were erected by the ancient Scotish and Pictish nobility and gentry, who formerly, without regard to the king, entered into alliances, and formed confederacies amongst themselves, against their neighbours: and being continually at war in one part or other of the kingdom, it was necessary for them to have places of strength to retire to, for the security of their persons, in case of a defeat; for those duns, by their small dimensions, were only fit for the reception of a family, and not for an army to retreat to, in case of an overthrow. And as to those duns being by some said to have been hunting-houses, that seems to be a notion as wild as that of the castle at Durness, in the county of Strathnaver, being erected by the fabulous king Dornadil.

REMARK. Although foreign to my present undertaking, I shall observe, that had I known the ancient Gaelick or Scotish language as well when I wrote the History of London, as I do at present, I would have declared it to be my opinion, that the city of London owes both its origin and name to our ancestors the Gael, and not to the Romans. The reason for my opinion is, that the appellation London, for aught I can learn, has not the least affinity with the Latin tongue: whereas in our ancient language it appears to be a Gaelick compound of Lon and Dun: the former part, Lon, signifying a plain, and the latter, Dun.

Notwithstanding of the above appearances of art, I am of opinion that this mount, by its huge dimensions, is not wholly artificial, being about ninety feet in height, in diameter at the foot about two hundred and forty, and in circumference at the same place about seven hundred feet. Were this hill artificial, it would have been attended with an immense expence of labour and money in the erection; and as, in the neighbourhood, no places appear whence such a prodigious quantity of earth could be taken as this mount contains, I am of opinion that the said mount at first must have been natural, and by art formed into the shape it at present puts on. Therefore I imagine that Buchanan never saw the said hills; if he had, I am persuaded he would not have converted them into Duni-pacis; for Dunie-pass, the genuine name of the said hills in the Gaelick language, imports the steep hills, as I was informed by Macfarlane of That-ilk, a great master and critick in that tongue. Besides, had Buchanan been at Dunie-pass, he might have observed a number of hills fitter for his purpose, by their greater resemblance of art than nature; but their names not corresponding with Duni-pacis would not have answered his design.

Gordon, in his account of the said hills, is as much mistaken as Buchanan, by telling us, that those mounts were erected by Agricola for exploratory castles; and in the next breath says, that one of the said hills is artificial, and the other supposed to be natural. But, instead of those mounts being erected on the account of peace, or for exploratory castles, I am of opinion, as already hinted, that the one is entirely natural; and the other, partly so, was a tom-moid or courthill, whereon were heard and determined causes both civil and criminal, which every where abounded in our country, and are still to be seen in many parts of Scotland, of the same form with the most eastern of the said hills of Dunie-pass.

About two miles north-eastward from Dunie-pass, a mile and a half benorth Falkirk, and about three hundred yards from the northern bank of the river Caron, on the eastern side of the road leading to the mansion-house of Stanners, at the

south-western corner of its park, on the gentle descent of a small eminence, stood
the noted and remarkable edifice called Arthur's Oven, from the manner of its construction.

This building, including the base or foundation, which consisted of four rows
of rough field stones, of the height of about four feet and six inches, (which, by the
ground's being worn away, were to be seen on the declivity at the fourth-western
side) was in altitude twenty-six feet and eleven inches. Above the foundation, on the
outside, the body of the fabrick consisted of twenty-four layers and a half (the other
half of the uppermost layer being wanting, shews that the upper part of the building
must either have been taken down, or, by decay of the edifice, fallen down) of dry
stone ashler, without cement; and the body of the work on the inside consisted of
twenty-three layers and a half, of the same manner of construction: whereas Gordon,
in his draught of this fabrick, only makes them twenty-three in number! The internal
diameter of the building was nineteen feet and six inches, the thickness of the wall
at the base four feet three inches, and at the spring of the arch three feet seven
inches: the exterior part of the house-wall was smooth; and on the interior were two
projections, the lowermost whereof, which was about four feet above the floor, extended eleven inches inwards; as was the uppermost, whereon the arched roof rested,
of the same dimensions.

In the eastern side of the edifice was a large door-way of the height of nine
feet, and breadth of six feet four inches. But as to what we are told by Buchanan, of
a Roman eagle and ensigns being engraven on a stone over the arch of the door on
the inside, I could not discover the least remains thereof: nor could I perceive the
letters I. A. M. P. M. P. T. said by sir Robert Sibbald to be cut on a stone in the
innerside of the wall. However, as we are told by Buchanan that in his time the first
were plainly to be seen, without doubt the part of the body of an eagle, and that of
one of its wings, which Gordon says were faintly discerned by him, were the fame
with those of Buchanan; though to me they were both invisible.

At the height of eight feet above the door-way was a window of three feet
two inches in height, three feet two inches in breadth at the lower part, and at the
upper part two feet six inches, and from the upper part of the said window to the
aperture at top (which was eleven feet and six inches in diameter) was above two
feet three inches.

This edifice, which was greatly decayed on the south-western side by the
weather, which had honeycombed the stones to a considerable depth, I take at first
to have been built upon a flat, some distance from the declivity on the south; but
the ground whereon it stood being a sandy clay, it was on the southern and southwestern sides so greatly impaired and diminished by the weather, that the foundation
of rough field stones abovementioned was laid open and the fabrick endangered,
insomuch that, without a proper reparation, it might in a few years have fallen down,
without waiting for its destruction by an enemy to antiquity, as quickly will appear.

Various are the opinions of writers concerning the origin, manner of construction, and use of this building. Nennius, a British or Welsh writer, tells us it was
erected by Caraufius, who assumed the purple in Britain, from whom the river Caron
was denominated, and to whose honour a triumphal arch was built in this neighbourhood. But as it does not appear, by any Roman writer, that Caraufius ever was
in the northern parts of Britain, these relations are justly regarded as fabulous.

John Major says this edifice was built by Julius Caesar, and from him denominated Julius's hoss. This is an invention equally absurd as gross, and deserves no other answer than to acquaint the reader, that by Caesar's accounts of his expeditions into Britain, he could have advanced but a short way in this island, which, by the most judicious and faithful writers, is agreed to have been no farther than the colony of Verulam, in the neighbourhood of St. Alban's in the county of Hertford, twenty miles benorth London.

Hector Boece says, that this fabrick was built by Vespasian in honour of the emperor Claudius, to whom and the goddess Victory he likewise erected statues; and that the remains of Aulus Plautius, who died in Camelon, (by him falsily called Camelodunum) were interred in Arthur's Oven. But as Boece is justly noted for the most fabulous of all our writers, little credit is due to him, especially in the case before us: for by Tacitus it appears that Julius Agricola, many years after Plautius, was the first Roman general that entered the country now called Scotland; whereby it is manifest, that Arthur's Oven could not be built by Vespasian, nor the ashes of Plautius buried therein.

Buchanan seems to have been of opinion, that this structure was erected for a temple to the god Terminus. This is contradicted by a modern writer, who says that the Romans, instead of building temples to Terminus, only set up stones or square posts in the ground, as a land-mark to direct travellers on the road.

REMARK. Whether the Romans built temples to Terminus, I shall not take upon me to determine: but that a land-mark or boundary should be set up to direct travellers on the road, is certainly a mistake; for countries or lands are bounded by limits or marches, and not by roads for the convenience of travellers.

However, though Buchanan at first seems to have been doubtful in respect to the use of Arthur's Oven, by there being in the northern parts of Scotland certain edifices resembling it; yet elsewhere, in speaking of it, he says, "for aught we can conjecture, it was erected to "the god Terminus." Be that as it will, had Buchanan seen the edifices in the county of Ross, and those in the island mentioned by him, he might have observed, that there is no other resemblance between them and Arthur's Oven than the rotundity of form: for those buildings in the northern parts being duns, or Gaelick castles, are rough dry stone edifices, of a circular form, tapering upwards, with an open area or court in the middle. Divers of those structures having been surveyed by Gordon, he tells us, that in the vale of Glenbeg in the county of Inverness, formerly part of Ross-shire, were situated four of the said circular fabricks; two whereof, denominated Castle-chalamine and Castle-chonil, have only their foundations remaining. The third, called Castle-telve, is a rough circular dry stone building, without cement or order in laying the stones: those near the ground are pretty large; but diminishing in size upwards, some of the stones scarcely exceed the thickness of a brick. The only aperture on the outside was a hole in the western side near the foundation; of so small dimensions, that my author was obliged to creep into the fame on his hands and feet. The fabrick consisted of a double wall, with a cavity between, which, being overlaid with large flat stones, not only served as a covering for the lower apartment, but likewise a floor for that above, and a binding whereby the walls are knit together.

The fourth structure, named Castle-troddan, being probably the most entire of the kind in Scotland, please take our author's account thereof as follows. "On the outside were no windows, nor were the materials of this castle any way different from those of the other already described, only the entry on the outside was somewhat larger, but this might be by the falling of the stones from above. The area of this makes a complete circle, and there are doors in the inner wall which face the four cardinal points of the compass: these doors are each eight foot and a half high, and five foot wide, and lead from the cavity between the two walls which run round the whole building: the perpendicular height of this fabrick is exactly thirty-three foot; the thickness of both walls, including the cavity between, no more than twelve foot, and the cavity itself hardly wide enough for two men to walk abreast. The external circumference is one hundred and seventy-eight foot. The whole height of the fabrick is divided into four parts or stories, separated from each other by thin floorings of flat stones, which knit the two walls together, and run quite round the building; and there have been winding stairs of the same flat stones ascending, between wall and wall, up to the top. The undermost partition is somewhat below the surface of the ground, and is the widest: the others grow narrower by degrees, till the walls close at top. Over each door are nine square windows, in a direct line above each other, for the admission of light; and between every row of windows are three others in the uppermost story, rising above a cornice, which projects out from the inner wall, and runs round the fabrick."

By the above accounts of some of the circular buildings which abound in the northern parts of Scotland (of which I shall be more particular elsewhere), it plainly appears they no otherwise resemble Arthur's Oven than in their round form, as aforesaid; and by their having windows in the inner walls, regarding the area or court within, and none without, is demonstrated their having been places of strength, for securing the inhabitants against the attempts of roving plunderers, till assistance came from their friends and neighbours to their relief.

And as to what is said by Buchanan of the stones in the wall of Arthur's Oven being mortified, or let into one another, for the greater security of the building, it is a very great mistake, as I shall in its proper place demonstrate.

Sir Robert Sibbald, without the least reason given for his opinion, declares this edifice to have been erected by the emperor Severus. And Dr. Stukeley thinks it owes its origin to Julius Agricola, by its being sometimes called Julius's hoss, and that it was a temple; which I think is not in the least probable, as I shall presently endeavour to make appear. And Gordon says, "I agree with my friend Dr. Stukeley, that this building was erected by Julius Agricola, the first winter that he was in Scotland; but, I believe, it was never designed for a temple of worship, but was only a facellum or little chapel contiguous to his camp, in which the vexilla or ensigns of the legions were kept. It may perhaps have been also used as a mausoleum, or depository for holding within its hollow basement the ashes of some illustrious Roman, who may have died in that country."

REMARK. It no where appears, that I can learn, that this small circular building was erected by Agricola: and that it was built for a facellum or little chapel contiguous to a camp, or that it was a repository for the ensigns, I think is not in the least probable, for the following reasons. 1. It was not contiguous to a camp; for Camelon, the nearest Roman fortress in that neighbourhood, is about a mile and a half from it. 2. By our author's believing that this fabrick was built with an aperture at top, it could not be a proper conservatory for beautiful and delicate military ensigns, which, by being continually exposed to the inclemencies of the weather, would soon have been rendered useless; which our author seems to have been aware of, by his unluckily telling us, that "great care was taken to preserve the aquilae of the legions, and the signa of the several cohorts, because if they had been always exposed to the weather, without shelter, the images painted upon them, as legionary and company distinctions, would have received damage. These facella were likewise proper to preserve them for lightning, with which when struck it was reckoned an ill omen, portending a defeat:" and a little after, to salve the contradiction, ridiculously imagines, that the cornices within were made to support a canopy or covering, to defend the said ensigns and standards from the weather. This is a notion so wild and trifling, that it makes the Romans guilty of the greatest indiscretion in erecting a stone building, with seemingly no other view than to render it useless, by stuffing it, from within four feet of the floor, with wooden props to support his imaginary canopy! which must have extended through and above the aperture at top, (which was eleven feet and six inches in diameter) otherwise the droppings would have fallen within the house: whereby we see that, even by this preposterous contrivance, the edifice was inclosed above, to the no great applause of the inventor!

But the worst of all is Gordon's saying, perhaps it was a mausoleum: had he given himself the trouble to have inquired into the probability of this surmise, he would have found that the pagan Romans did not, like their Christian descendants, defile their temples or chapels with the putrid carcasses or ashes of the dead; for, by a law of the Twelve Tables, dead bodies were to be burnt, and interred without the city; whereas their temples were all erected within their cities, stations, or camps.

To what has been said concerning Arthur's Oven, I shall add my own opinion, and let it take its chance with the abovementioned; and though I cannot tell who built it, I shall endeavour to point out its use.

This edifice, as already hinted, was of a circular form, and open at top, which, by all that have hitherto wrote thereon, is believed to have been so erected, without observing that there were no coping stones on the upper part of the wall; which, had it been built with an aperture above, there undoubtedly would, not only as a necessary fence against the weather, but to secure and knit together the upper part of the wall, to prevent the stones therein from being loosened by tempestuous winds, which would occasion their falling. But in the upper part of the said wall, instead of being secured by a coping of stones, there was only one half of a common layer remaining: the stones of the other half were fallen down, and carried off; which is a strong presumption that the building at first was not open at top.

Add to this, that as there was a large window over the spacious door-way in the arch or roof of the house, that was sufficient to enlighten the area of this small circular house, without an additional and unnecessary aperture above the said window. Wherefore I am of opinion, that it is not in the least probable there was another opening in the upper part of this edifice, other than the window aforesaid.

Now, as I take the said Arthur's Oven to have been originally close at top, it must, in proportion to the other parts of the building, have had six layers of stones above the half layer aforesaid; so that the edifice must have consisted of thirty-one layers of dry stone ashler in height, and the altitude of the fabrick, including the base, must at first have been about thirty-three feet.

As, by what has been said, I think it does appear that Arthur's Oven was neither a temple, facellum or repository for military ensigns, nor a fortress; I imagine, by the circular form of divers sepulchral monuments I have seen, which are all close at top, with a window in each, it must have been a mausoleum: wherefore, the better to enable the reader to judge in the case before us, I shall, from Wright's Travels, subjoin an account of a mausoleum much resembling our edifice aforesaid.

"We saw the noble monument of Caecilia Metella, the daughter of Q. Creticus, as the inscription, still plain upon it, shews Q. Cretici F. Metella Craffi. It is a rotunda, as several of the ancient mausolea were. One side is much ruined, and there we had an opportunity of observing that the vast stones, whereof it is built, were laid together without mortar, or any other cement. There is a frieze toward the top, adorned with heads of oxen, from which the whole structure is commonly called Capo di bove. There is a fine sarcophagus in the court of the Farnese palace, which they say was brought from hence, and is supposed to have contained this lady's remains. She was wife to the rich Marcus Craffus, who fell in the war against the Persians."

Although the abovementioned mausoleum in a great measure resembles our late circular structure, I am of opinion that, had Wright been more particular in the description, it would probably have been found to be near or of the same dimensions, and manner of construction, with our rotunda, which seems chiefly to have wanted a sarcophagus to demonstrate its having been a sepulchral monument. Besides, our building may be supposed to have been a mausoleum by its having stood by the road-side, leading from the Roman wall at Falkirk to the firth of Forth, which probably was a military way at the erection of our said edifice: for as by the sides of the publick roads were ranged the Roman cemeteries, their sepulchral monuments were erected therein.

Our late fabrick went by two names, viz. that of Julius's hoss, and Arthur's oven: the former it is said to have received from Julius Agricola, the imaginary founder; and the latter from its resembling an oven. But as these appellations have been considered already, that shall suffice, without mentioning certain allegations brought by Mackenzie, (which seem foreign to the purpose) to shew it to have been a temple, from the Gaelick Ardhenan suainhe, signifying a high place, such as the pagans anciently performed their religious duties in.

This memorable and celebrated small rotunda, which by all was deemed the most entire Roman antiquity in Scotland, was, in the year 1742, shamefully pulled down and destroyed by that great enemy to antiquity sir Michael Bruce, the proprietor, to his eternal reproach, who employed the large stones in repairing his mill-dam of Stanners: wherein I observed that the said stones had not been mortified, or let into one another, for the security of the building, as asserted by Buchanan; for the only things remarkable in the said stones are their large dimensions, and a tackle-hole in each, for the convenience of laying them by the help of a pulley.

The destruction of this famous structure enraged the antiquaries to such a degree against the destroyer, that one of them, on beholding the remains thereof in the said mill-dam, wrote the following dialogue concerning the same.

8

Excerpt:
Helinand de Froidmont
from the *Chronicle* of
Helinand de Froidmont,
entry for the year 718

Hoc tempore in Britannia cuidam eremitae monstrata est mirabilis quaedam visio per angelum de sancto Joseph decurione, qui corpus Domini deposuit de cruce; et de catino illo sive paropside, in quo Dominus coenavit cum discipulis suis; de quo ab eadem eremita discripta est historia, quae dicitur de gradali. Gradalis autem sive gradale Gallice dicitur scutella lata, et aliquantulum profunda; in qua pretiosae dapes cum suo jure divitibus solent opponi gradatim, unus morsellus post alium in diversis ordinibus; et dicitur vulgari nomine graalz, quia grata et acceptabilis est in ea comedenti: tum propter continens, quia forte argentea est, vel de alia pretiosa materia; tum propter contentum, id est ordinem multiplicem pretiosarum dapum. Hanc historiam Latine scriptam invenire non potui, sed tantum Gallice scripta habetur a quibusdam proceribus, nec facile, ut aiunt, tota invenire potest. Hanc autem nondum potui ad legendum sedulo ab aliquo impetrare. Quod mox ut potuero, verisimiliora et utiliora succinte transferam in Latinum.

(At this time there was shown to a certain hermit in Britain, through the agency of an angel, a marvelous vision concerning Saint Joseph [of Arimathea], the decurion who took Our Lord's body down from the cross; and concerning this bowl or dish in which Our Lord supped with his Apostles, the history called "Of the Grail" was written down. For the Grail, called "Gradalis" or "Gradale" in French, is a wide, fairly deep serving dish, in which precious foods are ceremoniously presented, one morsel

Patrologiae Cursus Completus, Series Secunda (Latina), vol. 212, ed. J.-P. Migne (Paris, 1855).

Note: Sebastian Evans originally said "platter," "paten," and "dish." See his *High History of the Holy Grail (Perlesvaus)*, Introduction. The Latin is quite prosaic: "deep-dish pie plate," "vegetable bowl," and "serving tray."

at a time, lavishly provided in the varied courses [of a banquet], and the dish moreover is commonly called Grail ["graalz"] because this container gratifies and is welcomed at such a meal, first because this container contains and also probably because
it is either of silver or of some other precious metal, thus, also because of its content,
which is an overwhelming succession of costly delicacies. This history I have not
been able to find in Latin, but so far written in French only, and in the possession
of certain chieftains, and, as they say, not even then in a complete text. That I have
not yet been able to obtain from anyone so that I could sit down and read the whole
thing carefully. As soon as I shall have been able to find such a copy, I will translate
the more likely and more useful passages into Latin.)

9

Chronology

The dates suggested in the following chronology offer current hypotheses, and possibilities indicated by this research, as to the major events between the Roman conquest of Britain and Arthur's lifetime in the Dark Ages. This conjectural flow of events remains subject to modification as knowledge of this scantily documented period in history accumulates.

A. Roman Britain

55 B.C.	First invasion by Julius Caesar of the south of Britain.
A.D. 43	Occupation, by Aulus Plautius, of Britain, thenceforward a Roman province.
60	Boudicca's rebellion and her defeat by the Romans.
78–84	Subjugation of Britain, circumnavigation by Agricola, fortification commenced.
122–23	Fortifications: Hadrian's Wall (Carlisle to Tynemouth); Antonine
139–43	Wall (Firth of Clyde to Firth of Forth, the "Glasgow-Edinburgh Line").
c. 150	Armed rebellion in the north, attacks along Antoinine Wall.
c. 156–157	Reported conversion to Christianity of British King Lucius (Bede).
c. 163	Romans abandon Antonine Wall, fall back, refortify Hadrian's Wall to the south.
c. 180–370	Northern tribes (Picts, Scots, Saxons) launch offensives against Romans.
c. 208	Temporary subjugation of Britain by Severus, as far north as Aberdeen.
212	Declaration by Caracalla: Britons henceforth Roman citizens.
c. 259	Romans administer Britain from France; the opposite shore, or Saxon Shore, now fortified.
286	Roman naval commander Carausius seizes control: Saxon Shore and northern France.

c. 293	Antonine Wall refortified by Carausius (murdered c. 295). The Roman military commanders of Britain designated (a) duke of Britain and (b) count of the Saxon Shore.
c. 297–306	Reconquest of Britain by Constantius Chlorus, died at York.
306–37	Reign of his son Constantine the Great. Building of Constantinople (330), Holy Sepulcher in Jerusalem, other Constantinian and Christian foundations.
314	Attendance by bishops from London and York at Synod of Arles.
347	Attendance by delegates from Britain at Council of Sardica.
367–83	Confederation of Northerners (Scots, Picts, Saxons) launch attacks upon the lines of Roman fortification. Romans, who had maintained 60,000 to 70,000 soldiers in Britain, recoup losses.
395	Administrative reconstruction of the Roman Empire into East (Constantinople) and West (Rome).
397	Death of Saint Martin of Tours and consequent founding of Western monasticism.
c. 396–98	Northerners launching naval offensives across the Firths from Scotland south.
c. 400	Saint Ninian, called Apostle to the Picts, builds Candida Casa, famous Christian monastery and training school, Galloway, Scotland. By this date, withdrawal by the Romans from their second line of forts, or Hadrian's Wall.
406	Successful Germanic invasions of Gaul and Spain, communications cut between Britain and Rome.
410	Sack of Rome by Alaric and the Visigoths. Honorius answers appeal for military assistance from British city states (*civitates*), granting them freedom from Roman rule.

B. The Fifth Century

c. 411	Constantine III, a paternal ancestor of Arthur, slain.
413	The Pelagian heresy in Britain attacked by Orosius.
c. 425–59	Reign in Britain of a native chieftain Vortigern (in British Gwrtheyrn Gwrtheneu).
c. 425–35	Ministry of Saint Patrick in Ireland (d. c. 461).
c. 425–505	Ministry of Saint Illtud in Wales, and his illustrious school. (The saint had once served under King Arthur.)
428	Saxon warships off the east coast of Britain.
429, 49	Saints Germanus and Lupus twice dispatched into Britain to counter the Pelagian heresy.

430	Pope Celestinus sends missionary Palladius into Britain.
431	The Virgin pronounced "Theotocos," Mother of God, at Council of Ephesus.
446	Britons, for the last time, request military aid from Rome.
448–50	Major Anglo-Saxon invasion of Britain commenced in Kent. Their chieftain Hengist reportedly assisting Vortigern against northern allies (Picts, Scots, and Saxons).
450	Anglo-Saxon warships attacking east coast of Britain, reported by Gregory of Tours.
451–52	Attila and the Huns twice invade western Europe. Paris saved by Saint Genevieve.
c. 460–75	Presumed reign in Britain of Ambrosius Aurelianus.
c. 462–547	Ministry of Saint David, patron saint of Wales.
465–95	Reign of King Angus of Munster. Cession of the Isle of Arran as Christian sanctuary.
c. 475	Presumed birth of King Arthur. Presumed reign of Arthur's father, Uther Pendragon.
480–95	Reign in Winchester-Southampton area of King Cerdic of Wessex. Record in *Anglo-Saxon Chronicle*.
481–511	Reign of King Clovis and Queen (Saint) Clothilde of the Franks. Frankish conquest of Gaul. Gaul renamed France.
493–526	Reign of King Theodoric of the Ostrogoths, celebrated in the *Nibelungenlied* as Dietrich.
c. 490–556	Anglo-Saxon victories: Pevensy, Charford, Isle of Wight, Bamborough, Barbury Castle.
c. 490–500	Arthur elected commander (*dux*) by northern British chieftains, launches twelve campaigns, ending with the great victory of Mount Badon (*Mons Badonis*).
c. 500	Saint Gildas born then, presumably at or near Dumbarton, Scotland, the British stronghold on the River Clyde. Born in the same year as a major victory at a Mount Badon (*Mons Badonis*).

C. The Sixth Century

c. 500–42	Period of peace in Arthur's kingdom, following overwhelming victory of Mount Badon.
c. 504, 21	Ordination and elevation of Saint Dubricius, reportedly to have crowned Arthur king. Capital city most often referred to as Arthur's Carlisle, then Scotland.
510	Death of King Domingart, first Irish king of Dalriada, western Scotland.

c. 515–c. 542	Fatal wounding of King Arthur at Camlan, on Hadrian's Wall.
c. 520–51	Reign in North Wales of King Maelgwn Gwynedd, reported to have survived the Battle of Camlan, enemy of Arthur. Gwynedd is one of the possible centers for the composition of the Arthurian literature.
c. 520–50	Victories of the hero Beowulf, who killed the ancient worm (dragon).
527–65	Reign in Byzantium of the emperor Justinian.
531	Comet reported.
c. 540	Saint Gildas' book attests Battle of Mount Badon.
c. 540	Bamborough in Northumbria refortified by its new lord, the Anglian King Ida of Bernicia. The fortress still associated with Lancelot of Arthur's Round Table.
541–94	Outbreaks of bubonic plague, killing, said Procopius, one-third of the human race.
c. 550	Second wave leaves Anglo-Saxons settled east of the Southampton-Edinburgh line.
c. 555	Kingdom of North Wales prospers, Maelgwn Gwynedd's son probably becoming King Brude of the Northern Picts, at Inverness, or at Castle Urquhart.
559–560	King Owain (Rheged) kills King Ida of Bernicia. (This King Owain may be presumed to be the same as Arthur's Round Table knight known in French as Yvain. And Yvain is the putative father of Saint Kentigern, now entombed in Glasgow Cathedral).
565	Ministry of Saint Columba on Iona, isle ceded to him by a king of the Scots or of the Picts.
572–92	Reign of King Urien (Rheged) at Arthur's former chief seat of Carlisle, kingdom of Strathclyde. (A King Urien, claimed Geoffrey of Monmouth, witnessed King Arthur's coronation, after his defeat by Arthur.)
573	Accession of King Rederech or Ridderch Hael at Dumbarton, Strathclyde, near Glasgow. (This may be another Round Table knight, known in French as Erec. The French say he was married in Edinburgh.)
573–76	Ministry of Saint Kentigern in Glasgow.
574	Battle of Arderydd, Arthuret, or Arthur's Head, near Carlisle. Inauguration of King Aidan (d. 603) of Dalriada by Saint Columba. One of King Aidan's sons named Arthur, then an uncommon name.
c. 584	Reported meeting of Saints Kentigern and Columba (commemorative depiction, Church of Saint Columba, Oban, Scotland).

c. 600   Testimony from Scotland as to the great warrior King Arthur in the Scottish heroic poem by Aneirin *Gododdin*, concerning the fabulously brave warriors of the north.

685   Ancient Carlisle still a great city. King Ecgfrith's queen, accompanied by the Anglo-Saxon Saint Cuthbert, tours Carlisle, sees magnificent Roman ruins and fortifications there. (She was awaiting the outcome of the Battle of Nechtansmere, which her husband, the Anglian king of Bamborough, lost to the warriors of the north.)

717–18   The scholar Helinand de Froidmont reports in his chronicle the existence of a much sought and very secret book called *Gradal*. It contained the history of King Arthur, the Holy Grail, and of Avalon.

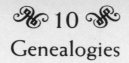

Genealogies

From King Arthur to Colin Mor Campbell, according to three manuscripts (see Appendix 8 to Skene's *Celtic Scotland.*)

MS 1467	Kilbride MS	MacFirbis MS
	Constantine	
Iubui	Ambrosius	Iobhar
Arthur	Arthur	Arthur
Meirbi	Smerbi	Smeirbe
Eirenaia	Feradoig	Feradoigh
Duibne	Duibne	Duibne
Malcolm	Malcolm	Malcolm
Gillespic	Duncan	Duncan
Duncan	Gillespic	Eoghan
Dugald	Dugald	Dugald
Gillespic	Gillespic	Gillespic
Colin	Colin	Colin

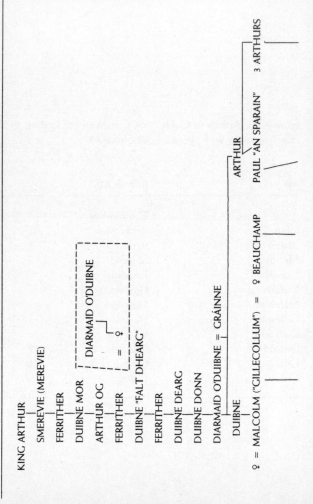

Genealogy of the Campbells

KING ARTHUR

SMEREVIE (MEREVIE)

FERRITHER

DUIBNE MOR

ARTHUR OG

FERRITHER

DUIBNE "FALT DHEARG"

FERRITHER

DUIBNE DEARG

DUIBNE DONN

DIARMAID O'DUIBNE = GRÁINNE

DUIBNE

♀ = MALCOLM ("GILLECOLLUM")   =   ♀ BEAUCHAMP

ARTHUR

PAUL "AN SPARAIN"

3 ARTHURS

DIARMAID O'DUIBNE = ♀

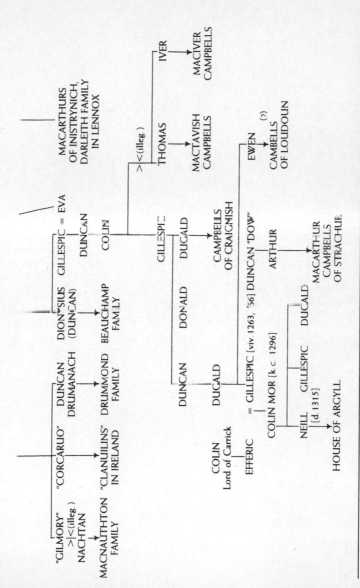

From earliest archives, and see George Crawford's *Peerage of Scotland*, and W. D. H. Sellars "The Earliest Campbells," *Scottish Studies* 17, no. 2 (1973): 109–25. My thanks also to Leslie Campbell.

BIBLIOGRAPHY

Adam, Frank. *The Clans, Septs and Regiments of the Scottish Highland.* Edinburgh, 1918, 1965.

Adam of Domerham. *Historia de rebus gestis Glastoniensibus.* Edited by Thomas Hearne. 2 vols. Oxford, 1727.

Adomnan's Life of Columbia. Edited by A. O. Anderson and M. O. Anderson. Edinburgh, 1961. This work is a prime source for the history of Dalriada and thus, indirectly, of King Arthur.

Ailred. Life of Saint Ninian (vel Ninias). From *Lives of St. Ninian and St. Kentigern,* edited by A. P. Forbes. Edinburgh, 1874. Ailred dates Saint Ninian by the death of Saint Martin, c. 400.

Alanus de Insulis. *Prophetia Anglicana Merlini Ambrosii Britanni.* Frankfurt, 1603, 1908. See p. 22 ff. for the fact that Arthur was known then in Europe, Africa, Asia, Asia Minor, and so on.

Alcock, Leslie. *Arthur's Britain (History and Archaeology,* A.D. *367–634).* London, 1974
———. "By South Cadbury That Is Camelot. . . ." *Antiquity* 41 (1967): 50–53.
———. *Was This Camelot? Excavations at Cadbury Castle, 1966–70.* London and New York, 1972.

Aliscans. Edited by E. Wienbeck, W. Hartnacke, and Paul Rasch. Halle, 1903. One of the best French epics, the title referring to the necropolis Elder (Alder) Fields.

Alliterative Morte Arthure. . . . Edited by John Gardner. Carbondale, Ill., 1971.

Ancient Irish Epic: Táin Bó Cúalnge. Edited by Joseph Dunn. London, 1914. Resemblances here to the adventures of Gawain.

Aneirin. *The Book of Aneirin: Canu Aneirin.* Edited by Ifor Williams. Cardiff, 1938.
———. "The Gododdin." In *The Earliest Welsh Poetry,* edited and translated by Joseph P. Clancy, pp. 33–65. London, 1970. Excellent introduction of 18 pp.

Anglo-Saxon Chronicle. Edited by James Ingram. London, 1912, 1934.
———. Edited by Charles Plummer and John Earle. 2 vols. Oxford, 1892, 1899. Excellent edition; see the bibliographical essay by Dorothy Whitelock.

———. Edited by Benjamin Thorpe. 2 vols. London, 1861. Here 6 MSS (A–F) are printed in vol. 1 and translated by vol 2. Edition superseded by the preceding item.

Annales Cambriae (Harleian MS 3859). Edited by Egerton Phillmore. *Y Cymmrodor* 9 (1888): 141–83.

———. Edited by John ab Ithel Williams. London, 1860. See also Edmond Faral's *Légende arthurienne*, vol 2.

Antonine Itinerary. From *Itineraria Romana*, vol. 1, edited by O. Cuntz. Leipzig, 1929. Here are listed and/or drawn on maps 225 routes in the Roman Empire, including those in Britain, particularly the Carlisle-York-Chester-London-Dover route.

Aratus. *Phaenomena.* Translated by G. R. Mair. London and New York, 1921. A prime scientific work known to medieval authors, such as Geoffrey of Monmouth, who were interested in astrology.

Arnold, Matthew. *On the Study of Celtic Literature.* New York, 1924.

Arthurian Chronicles. Edited by Sir John Rhys. Introduction by Lucy Allen Paton. London and New York, 1912.

Ashbee, Paul. *The Bronze Age Round Barrow in Britain.* London, 1960.

Ashe, Geoffrey. "A Certain Very Ancient Book, Traces of an Arthurian Source in Geoffrey of Monmouth's History." *Speculum*, vol. 56, no. 2 (April 1981): 301–23. Here Ashe amends Sharon Turner's date (437) of Riothamus's defeat by the Visigoths to accord with John Morris's amended date of the 460's, which even so puts Arthur, whom Ashe claims is Riothamus, on the continent fifteen years before he was born. Ashe then returns Riothamus from Brittany to Cadbury, near Glastonbury, for no apparent reason.

———. *Camelot and the Vision of Albion.* New York, 1971. This is not a book about Arthur but a prophetic fantasy drawn from William Blake (1793). Ashe claims Arthur's as a great kingdom similar to Nazi Germany, India, and the "Iroquois confederation." Arthur's was a "Celtic enchanted ground." Arthur is a Titan. Arthur will return from the dead, from his "tomb" in the Glastonbury ruins or from his cave on Cadbury hill where he sleeps surrounded by his treasure. Archaeology has not yet found such a cave. Bibliography of religious, mythological, ideological, and political writings of the twentieth century, which shape the present vision of an Albion, to which King Arthur is then connected.

———. *From Caesar to Arthur.* London, 1960. A book which, without primary evidence or scholarly method, places Arthur at c. 500–550; vs. the Angles at Lincoln (505–10), in the north (510–15), at Mount Badon on the Thames River (517), and at "Camlann" still unidentified. He revives Sharon Turner's theory. See Turner. Ashe here has Arthur born in 475.

———. *The Discovery of King Arthur.* Garden City, 1985. Ashe brings in Geoffrey of Monmouth to assist him in arguing, still without scholarly proof, that Arthur was Riothamus who was defeated in Gaul and who disappeared in c. 470. He also calls in Leslie Alcock's archaeology in Cadbury as support. His dates for Arthur, of 469–70, Ashe now asserts, are the only ones credible. He also openly now claims that all the Arthurian corpus and all the annals of Wales are mere legend. We hear again that Arthur was not named "Arturus," but after a simple Roman infantryman named Artorius and that his name was not Riothamus either, but his title. Illustrated.

————, et al. *The Quest for Arthur's Britain*. London and New York, 1968.

Atkinson, R. J. C. *Stonehenge*. London, 1956.

————. *Stonehenge and Avebury.* . . . London, 1959.

Bain, Robert. *The Clans and Tartans of Scotland*. Glasgow and London, 1938, 1984.

Baltrusaitis, J. *Art sumérien, art roman*. Paris, 1935.

Barber, Richard, ed. *The Arthurian Legends*. Totowa, N.J., 1979. An excellent anthology of 14 excerpts with introduction. Illustrated.

————. *The Figure of Arthur*. Totowa, N.J., 1972. Endorsal of Kemp Malone's 1925 theory of Arthur: that he was the Roman officer L. Artorius Castus, commander of the Sixth Roman Legion at York, A.D. c. 132–35—a theory refuted by Alcock in *Arthur's Britain* and elsewhere.

Barbour, Master John. *The Bruce* (a chronicle of the fifteenth-century, history of Scotland), ed. by Rev. Walter W. Skeat. Edinburgh and London, 1894.

Baring-Gould, Rev. Sabine. *Cliff Castles and Cave Dwellings of Europe*. London, 1911.

————. *Curious Myths of the Middle Ages*. London, Oxford, and Cambridge, 1873. See "The Fortunate Isles," pp. 524–60. Interesting theory on the origin of Protestantism.

————. *Lives of the British Saints*. 16 vols. London, 1914. Denies the existence of Joseph of Arimathea.

————. *Strange Survivals*. London, 1892.

Barrow, G. W. S. *The Kingdom of the Scots*. New York, London, 1973. See especially Part I on the earliest shires of Scotland, and Map 14 (p. 62) for St. Ninians and other *Eccles* names.

Barto, P. S. *Tannhäuser and the Mountain of Venus*. New York, 1916.

Batsford, Henry, and Charles Fry. *The Face of Scotland*. London, 1933.

Bayley, Harold. *Archaic England*. London, 1919.

————. *The Lost Language of Symbolism*. 2 vols. New York, 1912, 1951, 1952. Bayley shows graphics, paper marks, and printers' logos, among which are designs representing, he believed, Camelot, the Grail Castle, and King Arthur's name. Illustrated.

Bede. *Historia ecclesiastica gentis Anglorum*. Edited by Charles Plummer. 2 vols. Oxford, 1896. No mention of King Arthur.

Bede and the Monk of Lindisfarne. *Two Lives of St. Cuthbert*. Edited by Bertram Colgrove. Cambridge, 1940.

Bell, J. H. B., E. F. Bozman, and J. Fairfax-Blakeborough. *British Hills and Mountains*. London, 1940, 1950. Useful for its treatment of Loch Lomond in relation to the route into the Highlands and to the Firth of Clyde.

Béroul. *The Romance of Tristan*. Edited and translated by Alan S. Fredrick. London, 1970, 1978. This old *Tristan* corroborates the geography of King Arthur as endorsed and proposed in this book.

Bertrand, Michel, and Jean Angelini (Jean-Michel Angebert). *The Quest and the Third Reich*. Paris, 1971; New York, 1974.

Bilfinger, Gustav. *Das germanische Julfest*. Stuttgart, 1901. Useful as corroboration of the mythological Arthur re Christmas and Twelfth Night.

Black Book of Carmarthen. Edited by J. Gwenogvryn Evans. Pwllheli, 1906.

Blair, Peter Hunter. *An Introduction to Anglo-Saxon England.* Cambridge, 1956.

———. *Roman Britain and Early England,* 55 B.C.–A.D. 871. London, 1963, 1969, 1975. See especially chapter 7 on religion and chapter 8, "The Age of Invasion" (161 ff.). Appendix A is a table of dates but does not mention Arthur.

Blake, George. *The Heart of Scotland.* London, 1934, 1938, 1951. Helpful concerning the Lord of the Isles.

Boece, Hector. *The History and Chronicles of Scotland.* Translated by John Bellenden. Edinburgh, 1822. Unscientific perhaps, but fascinating history from the Renaissance, widely quoted by Leland (1544) and by modern Arthurian scholars.

Bolton, W. F. *A History of Anglo-Latin Literature,* 597–1066. Princeton, 1967. Pp. 229–93. Bibliography excellent for Gildas, Nennius, Saint Columba, Saint Patrick, and Pelagius.

Bone, James. *Edinburgh Revisited.* Hanslip Fletcher. London, 1913. Illustrated.

Book of Ballymote. Edited by R. Atkinson for the Royal Irish Academy. Dublin, 1887.

Book of Conquests of Ireland (Leabhar Gabhála). Edited by R. A. Stewart Macalister and John MacNeill. Dublin, 1916.

Book of Leinster. Edited by R. Atkinson for the Royal Irish Academy Dublin, 1880.

Book of Llan Dâv, Text of the. Edited by J. Gwenogvryn Evans and Sir John Rhŷs (vel Rhys). Oxford, 1893.

Book of Taliesin, The. Edited by J. Gwenogvryn Evans. Llanbedrog, 1910.

Borlase, William Copeland. *Antiquities of Cornwall.* Oxford, 1754.

———. *Dolmens of Ireland.* 3 vols. London, 1897. Arthur is related to ravens and choughs (2:595).

Boutell, Charles. *Boutell's Heraldry.* London and New York, 1950. Useful in connection with the lion and Lancelot. That lion may be not mythological so much as heraldic and Scottish in his case.

Braun, Hugh. *The English Castle.* Edinburgh, 1936.

Brendan, Saint. *The Voyage of Saint Brendan.* Translated by John J. O'Meara. Dublin, 1976.

Brengle, Richard L. *King Arthur of Britain.* New York, 1964. Unfindable.

Brinkley, Roberta Florence. *Arthurian Legend in the Seventeenth Century.* New York, 1970. Technical and excellent.

Bromwich, Rachel. "Concepts of Arthur." *Studia Celtica* 10/11 (1975–76): 163–81.

———. "The Celtic Literatures." In *Literature in Celtic Countries,* edited by J. E. Caerwyn Williams. Cardiff, 1971.

Brooke, Christopher. "The Archbishops of St. David's, Llandaff, and Caerleon-on-Usk." In *Studies in the Early British Church,* edited by Nora K. Chadwick, pp. 201–42. Attack in depth on Geoffrey of Monmouth.

Brown, A. C. L. *The Origin of the Grail Legend.* Cambridge, 1943.

Brown, Iain G. "Gothicism, ignorance and bad taste: The Destruction of Arthur's O'on," *Antiquity* 40, XL #8 (48), 1974, 283–87. Excellent work; bibliography; Stukeley's drawing reproduced (it is otherwise unfindable).

Brown, P. Hume. *History of Scotland.* Vol. 1. Cambridge, 1911.

Brown, Reginald A. *English Medieval Castles.* London, 1954.

Bruce, J. Collingwood. *Handbook to the Roman Wall.* Edited by Ian A. Richmond. Newcastle upon Tyne, 1863, 1957. Illustrated. Excellent detailed maps of every section of Hadrian's Wall. See in particular no. 12 of Bowness-on-Solway, and for greater detail p. 223; see p. 167 for the "sculptured fragment" from Hadrian's Wall.

Bruce, J. D. *The Evolution of Arthurian Romance from the Beginnings to 1300.* Baltimore and Göttingen, 1923. He also gives a weird etymology for the name *Arthur:* chough or raven.

Brut, or Chronicles of England. Translated by Friedrich W. D. Brie. London, 1906.

Brut (Text of the Bruts). Edited by J. Rhŷs and J. G. Evans. See *The Red Book of Hergest,* vol. 2 (Oxford, 1890).

Buchanan, George. *Rerum Scoticarum Historia.* Translated by William Bond. London, 1722.

Burns, A. R. *The Romans in Britain: An Anthology of Inscriptions.* Oxford, 1932.

Burton, John Hill. *The History of Scotland.* 8 vols. Edinburgh and London, 1873, 1905. The Historiographer Royal for Scotland dismisses Arthur completely: "Here all is fairyland, in which the most sagacious critics have been unable to glean a particle of narrative which can be set apart as well-authenticated fact. The . . . Arthurian story . . . confutes itself by its antagonism to the great conditions of contemporary history" (1:169).

Caesarius of Heisterbach. *The Dialogue on Miracles.* 2 vols. Translated by H. E. Scott and C. C. Swinton Bland. London, 1929.

Caine, Mary. *The Glastonbury Giants.* 1. "From Sagittarius to Taurus." 2. "From Gemini to Scorpio." Glastonbury(?), n.d.

Caradoc (Caradog) of Llancarvan (Llancarfan). *The History of Wales,* ed. by Dr. David Powel, improved by W. Wynne. London, 1697. Original manuscript in Brythonic.

Carman, J. Neale. *A Study of the Pseudo-Map Cycle of Arthurian Romance.* Lawrence, Kans., 1973.

Carrie, John. *Ancient Things in Angus.* Arbroath, 1881. "In the neighborhood of Glamis are three ancient monuments. One in the garden of the manse bears on one side a cross, the figures of two men face to face (one with a hammer in his hand, probably the hammer of Thor), a lion, and a centaur. The reverse side of the stone is much plainer, and is merely adorned with the figures of an eel, a trout, and two circles" (p. 100). Perhaps King Arthur, and not Thor.

Cavendish, Richard. *King Arthur of the Grail: The Arthurian Legends and Their Meaning.* London, 1978.

Chadwick, Nora K. *The Druids.* Cardiff, 1966.

———, ed. *Celt and Saxon: Studies in the Early British Border.* Cambridge, 1963. Valuable work on Nennius, Saint David, and Saint Caradoc of Llancarfan.

———. *Studies in Early British History.* Cambridge, 1954.

———. *Studies in the Early British Church.* Cambridge, 1958. Essays by Chadwick, Kathleen Hughes, Christopher Brooke, and Kenneth H. Jackson.

Chamberlain, H. S. *La Genèse du XIXe siècle.* Paris, 1913.

Chambers, Sir Edmund K. *Arthur of Britain.* Cambridge, 1927; New York, 1964.

Chanson du Chevalier au cygne et de Godefroid de Bouillon, La. Edited by C. Hippeau. 2 vols. Paris, 1874–77.

Charpentier, Louis. *Les Géants et le mystère des origines.* Paris, 1969.

———. *Les Mystères Templiers.* Paris, 1967.

Chevalerie Ogier de Danemarche, La. Edited by J. B. Barrois. 2 vols. Paris, 1842. See also Louis Michel, *Les légendes épiques carolingiennes dans l'oeuvre de Jean d'Outremeuse* (Bruxelles, 1935); no. 4, "Ogier le Danois."

Child, Heather. *Heraldic Design.* London, 1965.

Childe, V. Gordon. *The Most Ancient East: The Oriental Prelude to European Prehistory.* New York, 1929.

Chotzen, T. M. "Emain Ablach, Ynys Avallach, Insula Avallonis, Ile d'Avalon." *Études Celtiques* 4 (1948): 255–74.

Chrétien de Troyes. *Arthurian Romances.* Translated by W. W. Comfort. Edited with an introduction by D. D. R. Owen. London and New York, 1914, 1975.

――――. *Les Romans de Chrétien de Troyes.* Edited by Mario Roques. 5 vols. Paris, 1955.

――――. *Christian von Troyes sämtliche Werke.* Edited by Wendelin Foerster. 5 vols. Halle, 1884–1932. Revised edition by Hermann Brewer. Halle, 1933.

Churchill, Sir Winston S. *A History of the English-Speaking Peoples.* Vol. 1. London, 1956.

Cohen, Gustave. *Chrétien de Troyes et son oeuvre.* Paris, 1931. Cohen notes Chrétien's unexpected and very precise knowledge of British geography as if from personal experience (pp. 89–98). Perhaps Chrétien was raised in Britain, Cohen has theorized.

――――. *Roman courtois au XIIe siècle.* Paris, 1938.

Collingwood, R. G. *The Idea of History.* New York, 1946, 1956, 1966.

Collingwood, R. G., and J. N. L. Myres. *Roman Britain.* Oxford, 1932.

――――. *Roman Britain and the English Settlements.* Oxford, 1963.

Collingwood, William Gershom. *Northumbrian Crosses of the pre-Norman Age.* London, 1927. In the tenth century the Isle of Man still maintained its leadership, dispersing the wheel-crosses it had originated to Cumbria and east across the mainland of Britain. See p. 137 ff. and the Map (Fig. 153). Arthur and Merlin both were depicted inside the Manx or Celtic wheel of time.

Columba, Saint. *Sancti Columbani Opera.* Edited and translated by G. S. M. Walker. Dublin, 1967.

Courtney, M. A. *Cornish Feasts and Folk-lore.* Penzance, 1890.

Coxe, Antony D. Hippisley. *Haunted Britain.* London, 1973.

Crampton, Patrick. *Stonehenge of the Kings.* London, 1967; New York, 1968.

Crawford, George. *The Peerage of Scotland.* Edinburgh, 1716. For Arthur's descendants in Scotland, see "House of Argyll" and "Genealogy of the Campbells."

Crawford, O. G. S. "Arthur and His Battles." *Antiquity* 9 (1935): 277–91.

――――. "King Arthur's Last Battle." *Antiquity* 5 (June 1931): 236–39.

――――. *Topography of Roman Scotland North of the Antonine Wall.* Cambridge, 1949. See in particular the index map, which shows the 17 forts on this wall and the Camelon-Stirling corridor (pp. 11–18). See also the map of the Vale of Menteith (p. 18) for the ancient Fords of Frew.

――――. "Western Sea-ways." In *Custom Is King,* edited by L. H. Dudley Buxton, pp. 181–200. London, 1936.

Cross, Tom P., and Clark H. Slover. *Ancient Irish Tales.* New York, 1936.

Crowl, Philip A. *The Intelligent Traveller's Guide to Britain.* New York, 1983. Chapter II on "Roman Britain" is superb and pp. 92–97 on King Arthur also: "Sub-Roman Britain. 410–550."

Cuchulain of Muirthemne. Translated by Lady Augusta Gregory. Preface by W. B. Yeats. London 1902, 1975.

Cunliffe, Barry. *Guide to the Roman Remains of Bath.* Bath, 1973.

Curle, Alexander Ormiston. *The Treasure of Traprain, a Scottish Hoard of Silver Plate.* Glasgow, 1923. This hoard contained coins from the years 363–423.

Curtayne, A. *Lough Derg: St. Patrick's Purgatory.* London, 1944.

Curtin, Jeremiah. *Hero Tales of Ireland.* London, 1894.

————. *Myths and Folk-Lore of Ireland.* Boston, 1890; London, 1975, 1980; New York, 1975.

Daniel, Glyn Edmund. *The Prehistoric Chamber Tombs of England and Wales.* Cambridge, 1950.

Darby, H. C. *A New Historical Geography of England.* Cambridge, 1973. *Mons Badonicus* is here placed (p. 5) to the west of the Isle of Wight, north of Poole Harbor (a port for Roman galleys), at St. Aldhelm's Head, Isle of Purbeck.

Darrah, John. *The Real Camelot. Paganism and the Arthurian Romances.* London and New York, 1981. Excellent summary of mythological thinking in recent books in English, derivative of Sir J. G. Frazer and R. S. Loomis.

Davidson, D., and H. Aldersmith. *The Great Pyramid.* London, 1941.

Davies, Edward [Rector of Bishopton, County of Glamorgan]. *The Mythology and Rites of the British Druids ascertained by National Documents. . . .* Includes appendix and "Remarks on Ancient British Coins." London, 1809.

Deinert, W. *Ritter und Kosmos im Parzival.* Munich, 1960.

Delisle, L. *La Chronique d'Hélinand.* Paris, 1881. See pp. 141–54.

Didot-Perceval. See *The Romance of Perceval in Prose,* edited and translated by Dell Skeels (Seattle and London, 1966).

Dillon, Myles. *Cycle of the Kings.* London and New York, 1946.

————. *Early Irish Literature.* Chicago, 1948.

Dillon, Myles, and Nora K. Chadwick. *The Celtic Realms.* London, 1967, 1973. Their conclusion: "no satisfactory evidence for a historical Arthur" (p. 72).

Donaldson, Gordon. *Scottish Historical Documents.* Edinburgh, 1970.

Donnelly, Ignatius. *Atlantis: The Antediluvian World.* New York and London, 1882.

Dontenville, Henri. *Mythologie française.* Paris, 1948, 1973.

Driesen, O. *Der Ursprung des Harlekin.* Berlin, 1904. He connects Arthur with the Wild Hunt, or *Maisnee Hellequin.*

Dudley, Donald R., and Graham Webster. *The Roman Conquest of Britain* A.D. 43–57. London, 1965.

Dumézil, Georges. *La Religion des Etrusques.* Paris, 1966.

————. *La Religion romaine archaïque.* Paris, 1966.

————. *Le Problème des Centaures.* Paris, 1929.

————. *Rituels indo-européens à Rome.* Paris, 1954.

Dunn, Joseph. *The Ancient Irish Epic Tale* (translation of the Tain Bo Cualnge). London, 1914.

Duval, Paul-Marie. *Les Dieux de la Gaule.* Paris, 1957.

Eisen, Dr. Gustav(us) A. *The Great Chalice of Antioch* New York, 1933. The brief untechnical account, says Eisen, of his 1923 two-volume edition. He argues that the Antioch Chalice is the Holy Grail.

Ekwall, E. *Concise Oxford Dictionary of English Place-names.* Oxford, 1940.

————. *English River-names.* Oxford, 1928.

Elcock, W. D. *The Romance Languages.* London, 1975.

Elder, Isabel Hill. *Celt, Druid and Culdee.* London, 1973.

Eliade, Mircéa. *Tratado de historia de las religiones.* Madrid, 1954.

Ethérie, journal d'un voyage. Edited and translated by Hélène Pétré. Paris, 1971. This Latin itinerary recounts a trip made c. 400 from western Europe to Egypt, Sinai, Jerusalem, Jericho, Mt. Nebo, and on, thence from the Holy Land via Antioch to Constantinople.

Etienne de Rouen. *Draco Normanicus* in *Chronicles of the Reign of Stephen, Henry II, and Richard I.* 2 vols. Edited by Richard Howlett, London, 1885. See pp. 696–707.

Evans-Wentz, J. D. *The Fairy Faith in Celtic Countries.* London, 1911.

Fairbairn, Neil and Michael Cyprien. *Kingdoms of Arthur.* London, 1983. Illustrated.

Faral, Edmond. *La Légende arthurienne.* 3 vols. Paris, 1929. Primary sources, Arthurian texts included.

Feast of Bricriu (Fled Bricrend). Edited by George Henderson for Irish Texts Society. Vol. 2. London, 1899.

Fenton, M. B. "The Nature of the Source and Manufacture of Scottish Battle-Axes and Axe-Hammers." *Proceedings of the Prehistoric Society* 50, 1984, pp. 217–243. See Professor Fenton's Fig. 1 (p. 219) for the heaviest distribution of axe-hammers such as King Arthur was reputed to have employed, on the Rhinns of Galloway. Such weapons are found mostly between the Roman Walls, in the Arthur country, and many were also found on the Salisbury Crags in Edinburgh.

Fletcher, Robert Huntington. *The Arthurian Material in the Chronicles.* New York, 1966. A renowned work but one that strangely shows little respect for either Britons or Saxons, as on p. 110.

Fleure, H. J. *The Races of England and Wales.* London, 1923. Confirmation and defense of Geoffrey of Monmouth.

Floire et Blancheflor. Edited by E. du Méril. Paris, 1856.

Floris und Blauncheflur. Edited by Emil Hausknecht. Berlin, 1885.

Flutre, Louis-Ferdinand. *Table de noms propres avec toutes leurs variantes figurant dans les romans du Moyen Age.* . . . Paris, 1962.

Fodor's Great Britain. New York, 1979.

Fodor's Scotland. London, 1983. See page 60 for usage in proper names.

Foerster, Wendelin. *Kristian von Troyes; Wörterbuch zu seinem sämtlichen werken.* Halle, 1914.

Foëx, Jean-Albert. *Histoire sous-marine des hommes.* Paris, 1964.

Forbes, Alexander P., ed. and trans. *Lives of Saint Ninian and Saint Kentigerin. Compiled in the Twelfth Century.* Edinburgh, 1874. See lives of Ailred and Jocelyn.

Forbes, J. F. *Giants of Britain.* Birmingham, 1945.

Four Ancient Books of Wales (containing the Cymric Poems attributed to bards of the Sixth Century), ed. William Forbes Skene. 2 vols. Edinburgh, 1868.

Fox, Denton, ed. *Sir Gawain and the Green Knight.* Englewood Cliffs, N.J., 1968. Heinrich Zimmer equates Gawain's death to those of Gilgamesh, Heracles, Theseus and Orpheus. (p. 95 ff.).

Frankfort, Henri. *Kingship and the Gods.* Chicago and London, 1948.

Frankfort, H. and H. A., J. A. Wilson, and Thorkild Jacobsen. *Before Philosophy.* Penguin Books, 1949. Or see *The Intellectual Adventure of Ancient Man* (Chicago, 1946).

Frappier, Jean. *Chrétien de Troyes et le mythe du Graal.* Paris, 1972. The Perceval story viewed as a myth is here recounted in order to lead listeners to the admiration of chivalric virtues. See the bibliographical essays, pp. 1–40.

———. *Etude sur la Mort le Roi Artu.* Paris, 1936.

Frazer, Sir James G. *The Fear of the Dead.* . . . London, 1933–36.

———. *The Golden Bough.* 12 vols. New York, 1935.

———. *A Study in Magic and Religion.* London, 1911, 1913.

Gaster, Theodore H. *Les plus anciens contes de l'humanité.* Paris, 1953.

———. *Thespis.* New York, 1961.

Gautier, Léon. *Les epopées françaises.* 4 vols. Paris, 1878, 1892.

Gelling, Peter, and Hilda Ellis Davidson. *The Chariot of the Sun.* London, 1969.

Gennep, A. van. *Rites de passage.* Paris, 1909.

Geoffrey of Monmouth. *Historia regum Britanniae.* Edited by Acton Griscom and Robert Ellis Jones. London, New York, and Toronto, 1929.

———. *History of the Kings of Britain.* Translated by Sebastian Evans. Introduction by Lucy Allen Paton. Edited by Ernest Rhys. London, 1912, 1944.

———. *Life of Merlin,* or *Vita Merlini.* Edited with introduction, and translated by Basil Clarke. Cardiff, 1973. A most valuable and illuminating scholarly work.

Gerald of Wales [Gerald de Barri, Gerald of Barry, Giraldus Cambrensis]. *The Itinerary through Wales* and *The Description of Wales.* Edited and with introduction by Ernest Rhys and W. Llewelyn Williams. London, New York, c. 1908.

———. *The Journey through Wales. The Description of Wales.* Edited and translated by Lewis Thorpe. London, 1978.

———. *Opera.* Edited by J. S. Brewer, J. F. Dimock, G. F. Warner. 8 vols., London, 1861, 1891. See for the twelfth-century English conquest of Ireland.

———. *Opera,* vol. 6, *Giraldi Cambrensis Opera Itinerarium Cambriae,* edited by James F. Dimock. London, 1868.

Gerbert de Montreuil. "Continuation" de *Perceval.* Edited by Mary Williams. 2 vols. Paris, 1922, 1925.

Gervasius von Tilbury. *Otia Imperialia.* Edited by F. Liebrecht. Hanover, 1856.

Gesta regum Britanniae. Edited by Francisque Michel for the Cambrian Archaeological Assn., Cardiff, 1862. It is one of the numerous verse adaptations of Geoffrey of Monmouth (4923 vv.).

Gibbon, Edward. *The Decline and Fall of the Roman Empire.* (London and New York, 1976). See vol. 3, chapter 28, "The Final Destruction of Paganism . . ."

Gildas. *De excidio et conquestu Britanniae.* Edited by T. Mommsen. Berlin, 1898. See vol. 3, *Cronica minora.*

———. *De excidio et conquestu Britanniae.* Edited by T. Mommsen. In *Monumenta Germaniae Historica, vol. 3.* Berlin, 1898.

———. *The Epistle of Gildas.* Holborne, 1638.

———. *The Epistle of Gildas* ("Vera effigies Gildae"). Holborne, 1638.

———. *The Ruin of Britain and Other Works.* Edited and translated by Michael Winterbottom. London and Chichester, 1978.

Giles, Rev. John A. *Historical Documents concerning the Ancient Britons.* London, 1847. See *Alia Vita Gildae in vol. 1.; and Vita Sancti Gildae* and Nennius in vol. 3.

————, trans. *Six Old English Chronicles.* London, 1900. Contains the Works of Gildas and Nennius.

Gilson, Etienne. "La Mystique de la Grâce dans la Queste del Saint Graal." *Romania* 51 (1925): 321 ff.

Giot, P. R. *Brittany.* London (?), 1960.

Gododdin, the Oldest Scottish Poem. Edited by Kenneth Hurlstone Jackson. Edinburgh, 1969.

Gordon, A. *Itinerarium septentrionale.* London, 1726.

Gottfried von Strassburg and Thomas. *Tristan.* No translator credited. Introduction by A. T. Hatto. London, 1960, 1974.

Grand-Saint-Graal. See *History of the Holy Grail.*

Graves, Robert. *The Greek Myths.* London, 1955.

————. *The White Goddess.* London, 1961, 1962, 1967, 1971.

Gray, Louis Herbert. "Baltic Mythology." In *Mythology of All Races.* Vol. 3. New York, 1964.

Green, R. L. *King Arthur.* Harmondsworth, 1973.

Gregory, Lady Augusta, trans. *Cuchulain of Muirthemne.* Vol. 2. London, 1902.

————. *Gods and Fighting Men.* Vol. 3. London, 1904 . . . 1976.

Grinsell, L. V. *The Archaeology of Wessex.* London, 1958.

Gross, Charles. *A Bibliography of English History to 1485.* Edited by Edgar B. Graves. Oxford, 1975.

Guillaume de Normandie. *Fergus.* Edited by E. Martin Halle, 1872. *Fergus* is a late romance that contains a list of such precise locations in Scotland that G. Paris and G. Cohen associated it with Chrétien de Troyes.

Guillaume de Rennes (?). *Gesta regum Britanniae.* Edited by F. Michel. London, 1862.

Guingamor. *Lais inédits.* Edited by Gaston Paris. *Romania* 8 (1879).

Halliday, W. R. *Indo-European Folk-Tales and Greek Legend.* Cambridge, 1933.

Hanson, Richard P. C. *St. Patrick: His Origins and Career.* Oxford, 1968.

Hapgood, Charles H. *Maps of the Ancient Sea Kings.* New York, 1966, 1979. Chapter VI: "The Ancient Maps of the North," pp. 124–50.

Hardwick, Charles. *Ancient Battlefields in Lancashire.* Manchester, 1882.

Harrison, Jane Ellen. *Mythology.* New York, 1924, 1963.

Hawkes, Jacquetta and Christopher. *Prehistoric Britain.* Cambridge, 1953.

Hawkins, Gerald S. *Splendor in the Sky.* New York, 1961.

————. "Stonehenge Decoded." *Nature,* no. 4904 (October 26, 1963). Reprint. London, 1966.

Heinrich von dem Türlin. *Diu Crone.* Edited by G. H. F. Scholl. Stuttgart, 1852.

Heinzel, Richard. *Über die französischen Gralromane.* Vienna, 1891.

Helinand de Froidmont. "Chronique universelle." In *Patrilogiae,* edited by Jacques Paul Mignes, Cursus Completus, Series Latina, 221 vols. Vol. 212.

Henderson, Isobel. *The Picts.* London, 1967.

Henry of Huntingdon. *Historia Anglorum.* Written ante 1133. Edited by Thomas Arnold. Translated by Thomas Forester. London, 1879.

————. *The Chronicle of Henry of Huntingdon.* London, 1853.

Herm, Gerhard. *The Celts; the people who came out of darkness.* New York, 1975.

Higden, Ranulf. *Polychronicon.* EETS, Original Series no. 166. London, 1926.

Historia Meriadoci and *De Ortu Waluuanii* (Two Arthurian Romances of the XIIIe in Latin Prose). Edited by J. Douglas Bruce. Göttingen and Baltimore, 1913.

History of the Holy Grail. A translation of *Le Grand Saint Graal* made c. 1450 by Henry Lonelich. Edited by Frederick J. Furnivall. London, 1874–78.

Hodgkin, R. H. *A History of the Anglo-Saxons.* 2 vols. Oxford, 1935. Vol. 1, opposite p. 155, has an excellent map of Britain, c. 550, which shows most clearly the Anglo-Saxon penetrations from Lindisfarne in the north past Wight on the Channel coast.

Holmes, Urban Tigner. *Chrétien de Troyes.* New York, 1970.

Homeric Hymns. Edited by W. T. Allen and E. E. Sikes. London, 1904.

Hubner, E. *Inscriptiones britanniae christianae.* Berlin, 1876.

Hughes, Kathleen. *The Church in Early Irish Society.* London and Ithaca, 1966.

———. *Celtic Britain in the Early Middle Ages.* Edited by David Dumville. Woodbridge and Totowa, N.J., 1980.

Hull, Eleanor. *A Textbook of Irish Literature.* Vols. 1 and 2. Dublin, n.d.

———. *The Cuchillin Saga in Irish Literature.* London, 1898.

Huth Merlin. Edited by Gaston Paris and J. Ulrich. Paris, 1886.

Irische Texte. Edited by E. Windisch. Leipzig, 1880.

Irish Sagas. Edited by Myles Dillon. Dublin, 1959.

Irving, J. *Place-names of Dumbartonshire.* Dumbarton, 1928.

Isidore of Seville. *Etymologiae.* Edited by W. M. Lindsay. Oxford, 1911.

Ivimy, John. *The Sphinx and the Megaliths.* London, 1974.

James, M. R. *Two Ancient English Scholars. St. Aldhelm and William of Malmesbury.* Glasgow, 1931.

Jarman, A. O. H. *The Legend of Merlin.* Cardiff, 1960.

Jenkins, Elizabeth. *The Mystery of King Arthur.* London, 1975. A beautiful art book.

Jerphanian, Guillaume de. *Le Calice d'Antioch,* illus. Rome, 1926. Père Guillaume dated the Antioch Chalice at 500, or within King Arthur's lifetime.

Jocelyn of Furness (or Ferns) Abbey [a Cistercian monk of c. 1200 in Lancashire]. *Vita Kentigerni.* Edited by A. P. Forbes. Edinburgh, 1874. Jocelyn's source was Irish ("stilo scotticano dictatum"). See Lives of Saint Ninian and Saint Kentigern.

John of Fordun. *Johannis de Fordun Chronica Gentis Scotorum.* Edited and translated by William F. Skene. 2 vols. Edinburgh, 1871–72.

John of Glastonbury. *Chronica sive historia de rebus Glastoniensibus.* Edited by Thomas Hearne. 2 vols. Oxford, 1726.

Johnson, Stephen. *Later Roman Britain.* New York, 1980. Contains 22 excellent maps, 60 photographs, 20 reconstruction drawings.

Johnstone, P. K. "Domangart and Arthur." *Antiquity* 22 (1948):45–46.

———. "Mount Badon—a topographical clue?" *Antiquity* 20 (1946):159–60. See also a refutation of the above and new support of Glastonbury by Mrs. D. P. Dobson in *Antiquity* 22 (1948):43–45. The "Severn"-versus-"Solway" problem remains unsolved here.

———. "The Date of Camlan." *Antiquity* 24 (1950):44.

————. "The Dual Personality of St. Gildas." *Antiquity* 20 (1946):211–13.

————. "The Victories of Arthur." *Antiquity* 166 (1934):381–82.

Joseph of Arimathie. Edited by W. W. Skeat. EETS no. 44. London, 1871.

Joyce, Patrick Weston. *A Social History of Ancient Ireland.* 2 vols. London, 1903.

————. *Old Celtic Romances*, trans. From the Gaelic. London, 1894. This book should be considered a classic. Its footnotes are also admirable. In the edition of London, 1920, the Irish god Lug is argued to be the same as Manannan, the sea god of the Isle of Man, whose feast day is Midsummer Day, June 24.

Jubainville, H. d'Arbois de. *Le Cycle mythologique irlandais et la mythologie celtique.* Paris, 1884. There is a translation by R. I. Best (Dublin, 1903).

Judson, Harry Pratt. *Caesar's Army.* Boston, 1888. Excellent understanding of artillery, siege tactics, and miles marched by infantry.

Jung, Emma, and Marie-Louise Franz. *The Grail Legend.* Translated by Andrea Dykes. London, 1971. This gives the Freudian interpretation of the legend.

Jackson, Kenneth Hurlstone. "Arthur's Battle of Breguoin." *Antiquity* 23 (1949):48–49.

————. *Language and History in Early Britain.* Edinburgh, 1953. This book is indispensable also for several minor contributions, such as its chronology, collated with the work of R. H. Hodgkin, J. N. L. Myres, and F. M. Stenton, and its dated map "The Anglo-Saxon Occupation of England," which is the best one could find. See pp. 63 and 71.

————. "Nennius and the Twenty-eight Cities of Britain." *Antiquity* 12 (1938):44–55.

————. "Once Again Arthur's Battles." *Modern Philology* 43 (1945):44–57.

————. "The Arthur of History." In *Arthurian Literature of the Middle Ages*, edited by Roger Sherman Loomis. Oxford, 1959. See pp. 8–10, where Arthur as a chieftain of the north is labeled only a "popular notion." Here Jackson locates the battle of Mount Badon improbably in southern England. He admits four authentications of the historical Arthur, however: *Gododdin*, persons named after him, Nennius, and the *Annales Cambriae*.

————. "The Britons in Southern Scotland." *Antiquity* 29 (1955):77–89.

————. *The Oldest Irish Tradition: A Window on the Iron Age.* Cambridge, 1964.

————. "The Sources for the Life of St. Kentigern." In *Studies in the Early British Church*, edited by Nora K. Chadwick, pp. 273–357. Cambridge, 1858. Five sources of Jocelyn's *Life* are diagrammed, p. 342. Linguistic and geographical evidence supports very early origins of the Kentigern material, composed even during the living memory of Saint Kentigern.

James, Edwin Oliver. *The Ancient Gods.* New York, 1960. See the excellent chapters 5, "The Seasonal Festivals" and 6, "The Cult of the Dead." The Arthurian material is much clarified here.

————. *The Cult of the Mother Goddess.* London and New York, 1959.

Kahane, Henry R. *The Krater and the Grail: Hermetic Sources of the Parzival.* Urbana, 1965.

Kempe, Dorothy. "The Legend of the Holy Grail, Its Sources, Character and Development." Essay appended to *The Holy Grail*, ed. Lonelich, EETS, Extra Series, no. 95. London, 1905, 35 pp.

Kemp-Welch, Alice. *Of Six Mediaeval Women.* London, 1913. She finds much to resent in King Arthur's treatment of women; but what she resents are the medieval writers.

Kendrick, Sir Thomas. *Anglo-Saxon Art.* London, 1938.

Ketrick, Paul John. *The Relation of Golacros and Gawane to the Old French Perceval.* Washington, 1931. This is a copy of the author's Ph.D. thesis.

Killip, Margaret. *The Folklore of the Isle of Man.* Illustrated by Norman Sayle. Totowa, N.J., 1976. Original material can be had from the Manx Language Society: *Skeealyn 'sy Ghailck,* translated by Edward Faragher (Castletown, 1973).

Kinvig, R. H. *A History of the Isle of Man.* Liverpool, 1950. Illustrated with maps, charts, and photographs and accompanied by a glossary of the Manx language. There is an excellent illustration of a "Round Table," or ancient condominium, as reconstructed.

Kirk, G. S. *Myth: Its Meaning and Function in Ancient and Other Cultures.* Berkeley and Los Angeles, 1970.

Kittredge, George Lyman. *A Study of Gawain and the Green Knight.* Cambridge, Mass., 1916. Here as in his lectures Professor Kittredge stressed the Celtic sources of the Arthurian material.

————. "Kittredge Anniversary Papers." *American Journal of Philology* VII, no. 176 (1888). See especially p. 239 ff. for his theory of Eochaid Ollathair, as All-Father.

Kneen, J. J. *The Place-names of the Isle of Man.* Douglas, 1925–29.

Knowles, David. *The Monastic Order in England.* Cambridge, 1941.

Kramer, Samuel Noah. *The Sumerians.* Chicago, 1963. There does seem to have been a carryover from the ancient Middle East into the Arthurian material, especially as concerns the worship of Marduk and the life of Gawain.

Lacroix, Paul. *Les Arts au moyen âge.* Paris, 1873.

Laing, Lloyd Robert. *The Archaeology of the Late Celtic Britain and Ireland, c. 400–1200 A.D.* London, 1975. See particularly Appendix B for the excellent chronology of British kings and chiefs.

Lambert de Saint-Omer. *Liber floridus* (medieval encyclopedia). "Miranda Britanniae et Angliae" (Marvels of Britain and of England): "est palatium in Britannia in terra pictorum Arturi militis, arte mirabili et varietate fundatum, in quo factorum bellorumque suis omnium gesta sculpta videntur. Gessit autem bella XII contra Saxones" [there is in Britain a palace, in Pictish territory, of the soldier Arthur, built with marvelous art and diversity, in which highlights of all his deeds and battles are to be seen sculpted. For he fought twelve battles against the Saxons]".

Lancelot, or *Lanzelet.* Edited by W. J. A. Jonckbloet. 2 vols. The Hague, 1846–49.

Lappenberg, J. M. *A History of England under the Anglo-Saxon Kings.* Vol. 1. Translated from the German by Benjamin Thorpe. London, 1845.

Layamon's *Brut,* or Chronicle of Britain. Edited by Sir Frederic Madden. 3 vols. London, 1847; Osnabrück, 1967.

Leahy, A. H. *Heroic Romances of Ireland.* London, 1905; New York, 1974.

Leland, John. *The Itinerary of John Leland the Antiquary.* Edited by Thomas Hearne. 9 vols. Oxford, 1744–45.

Lerner, Gerda. "The Necessity of History and the Professional Historian." *National Forum: The Phi Kappa Phi Journal* 62, no. 3 (Summer 1982): 37–38.

Leslie, S. *Saint Patrick's Purgatory.* London, 1932. This is not the Saint Patrick of King Arthur's day but a later Patrick, of whom Marie de France also wrote.

Lethbridge, T. C. *Gogmagog: The Buried Gods.* London, 1957, 1975.

Levison, Wilhelm. "An Eighth-Century Poem on Ninian." *Antiquity* 14 (1940):280–91. The poet's longest story is that of the wafer, the infant Jesus, and the bread, after the priest has embraced Christ. It is repeated in *Perlesbaus*, as King Arthur worships outside the temple.

Levitt, I. M., and Roy K. Marshall. *Star Maps for Beginners.* New York, 1942, 1974.

Lewis, Charles Bertram. *Classical Mythology and Arthurian Romance.* London, 1932. His conclusions are that (1) Chrétien did not invent his material, (2) the abduction of Queen Guinevere duplicates that of Helen of Troy, and (3) the treatment in poetry of this material is French in origin.

Lewis, Rev. Lionel Smithett. *St. Joseph of Arimathea at Glastonbury.* Cambridge, 1932, 1937.

Lewis, M. J. T. *Temples in Roman Britain.* Cambridge, 1966. William of Malmesbury's *Gesta Pontificum Anglorum* (Deeds of the Anglican Prelates), 3:99, is given here in the original, i.e., his report of a domed temple in the Carlisle area.

Lewis, Timothy, and J. Douglas Bruce. "The Pretended Exhumation of Arthur and Guinevere." *Revue Celtique* 33 (1912):432–51.

Lindsay, Jack. *Arthur and His Time.* London, 1958.

Literature in Celtic Countries. Edited by J. E. Caerwyn Williams. Cardiff, 1971.

Lloyd, John Edward. *A History of Wales.* Vol. 1. London, 1911.

Lockyer, Sir Joseph Norman. *The Dawn of Astronomy.* London, 1894; Cambridge, Mass., 1964.

Loftie, W. J. *Windsor Castle.* London and New York, 1887. Chapter 3 discusses the reign of King Edward III, his pilgrimage to Glastonbury to view King Arthur's bones, and his construction at Windsor, from 52 oak trees, of a Round Table. The famous chronicler Jean Froissart had reported in his Chronicle the belief of the late Middle Ages that King Arthur's chief seat was originally Windsor Castle, which housed the original Round Table.

Logan, James. *The Scottish Gael, or Celtic Manners.* Hartford, n.d. but c. 1830. Excellent social history.

Loomis, Laura Hibbard. *Adventures in the Middle Ages.* New York, 1962.

———. "The Round Table Again." *Modern Language Notes* 44 (1929):511–19.

Loomis, Roger Sherman. *Celtic Myth and Arthurian Romance.* New York, 1926.

———. *Studies in Medieval Literature.* New York, 1970.

———. *The Development of Arthurian Romance.* New York, 1963, 1970.

———. "The Grail." In *From Celtic Myth to Christian Symbol.* New York, 1963.

———. *Wales and the Arthurian Legend.* Cardiff, 1956.

Loomis, Roger Sherman, and Laura Hibbard Loomis. *Arthurian Legends in Medieval Art.* New York, 1938, 1975.

Lot, Ferdinand. *Etude sur le Lancelot en prose.* Paris, 1918.

———, ed. *Nennius et l'Histoire Brittonum.* Paris, 1934. Lot believed in the North British origin of the Nennius compilation and furthermore in the northern locations for King Arthur's twelve battles, including his Mount Badon victory.

Loth, Joseph. *Contributions à l'etude de la Table Ronde.* Paris, 1912.

———. "Des nouvelles théories sur l'origine des romans arthuriens." *Revue Celtique* 13 (1892):475–503.

———. "L'Année celtique." *Revue Celtique* 24 (1903):313–16.

———. *Les Mots latins dans les langues brittoniques.* Paris, 1892.

Lum, Peter. *The Stars in Our Heaven: Myths and Fables.* New York, 1948.

Luttrell, Claude. *The Creation of the First Arthurian Romance.* London, 1974. Luttrell argues that Chrétien invented the story of *Erec et Enide* and was not indebted to Arthurian material that could have existed prior to 1184–86.

Mabinogion, The. See translations: Lady Charlotte Guest, 1838, 1877, 1902; J. M. Edwards, 1900; Gwyn and Thomas Jones, 1949, 1974; Gwyn and Mair Jones, 1974.

Macalister, Robert Alexander Stewart. *Corpus inscriptionum insularum celticarum.* Vol. 2. Dublin, 1949.

———. *The Archaeology of Ireland.* Rev. ed. London, 1949; New York, 1972.

———. *Tara, a Pagan Sanctuary of Ancient Ireland.* London and New York, 1931.

Macaulay, E. J. *The Soul of Cambria.* London, 1931.

McClure, Edmund. *British Place-Names in Their Historical Settings.* London, 1910.

MacCulloch, John Arnott. *Mythology of All Races.* New York, 1918, 1946, 1964. See vol. 3 for "Celtic."

———. *The Religion of the Ancient Celts.* Edinburgh, 1911.

MacDonald, A. *The Place-Names of West Lothian.* Edinburgh, 1941.

MacDonald, William Lloyd. *The Architecture of the Roman Empire.* New Haven, 1965.

MacEwen, Alexander Robertson. *A History of the Church in Scotland.* 2 vols. London and New York, 1915. See vol. 1 for a study of Christian monastic foundations of the fifth century: Carlisle and Saint Ninians, but also Kirkmadrine situated on the Rhinns of Galloway, and between the first two.

McGarry, Mary, ed. *Great Fairy Tales of Ireland.* New York, 1973.

Mackinder, Sir Halford J. *Britain and the British Seas.* Oxford, 1925. Excellent on military history and geography.

MacMullen, Ramsay. *Soldier and Civilian in the Later Roman Empire.* Cambridge, 1963. Figure E shows the floor plan of the palace of the *dux* in Dura on the Euphrates River, which recalls Lambert de Saint-Omer's testimony as to the palace of the *dux* Arthur in Pictland.

MacNeice, Louis. *Astrology.* New York, 1964.

MacNeill, Eoin. *Celtic Ireland.* Dublin, 1921.

McNeill, John T. *The Celtic Churches: A History,* A.D. 200–1200. Chicago and New York, 1974.

MacNeill, Máire. *The Festival of Lughnasa.* Oxford, 1962.

Magnusson, Magnus. *Viking: Hammer of the North.* London and New York, 1976.

Maitland, W. [1693?–1757]. *The History and Antiquities of Scotland: From the Earliest Account of Time to the Death of James the First, Anno 1437,* 2 vols., but see vol. 1. London, 1757.

Major, John. *Historia Majoris Britanniae, tam Angliae quam Scotiae.* Paris, 1521.

Mâle, Emile. *La Fin du paganisme en Gaule.* Paris, 1950.

———. *Religious Art.* New York, 1949.

Malone, Kemp. "Artorius." *Modern Philology* 22 (1925): 367–74. Malone asks the question: Was L. Artorius Castus, an obscure Roman officer, the real King Arthur? And the answer is in the negative. The two do not resemble each other, and the suggestion is insulting. Arthur's name in Latin was Arturus, not Artorius.

Malory, Sir Thomas. *Le Morte d'Arthur.* Edited with an introduction by Norma Lorre Goodrich. New York, 1963.

————. *Le Morte d'Arthur.* Edited with an introduction by Sir John Rhys. 2 vols. London, 1906, 1961, 1976.

Maltwood, Katharine E. *The Enchantments of Britain.* Vancouver, 1944.

————. *Guide to Glastonbury's Temple of the Stars.* London, 1934, 1964. A delightful and very poetical book claiming that earth effigies at Glastonbury represent King Arthur and figures of that material as constellations. King Arthur is Sagittarius, Lancelot is Leo, Gawain is Aries, and so on. Mrs. Maltwood's manuscripts are in Victoria, B.C.

Map, Walter. *De Nugis curialium,* or *Courtiers' Trifles.* Translated by Professor Frederick Tupper and Marbury B. Ogle. New York, 1924. Edited by M. R. James. Oxford, 1914.

Margary, Ivan D. *Roman Roads in Britain.* 2 vols. (London, 1955, 1973). See vol. 2 for roads in the north, in Wales, and in Scotland.

Marie de France. *Espurgatoire Seint Patriz.* Edited by T. Atkinson Jenkins. Philadelphia, 1894.

————. *Lais.* Edited by Karl Warnke. Halle, 1925. Also see the edition of Alfred Ewert of a diplomatic text (Oxford, 1976).

Maritime Itinerary [to the Holy Land]. See *Antonine Itinerary,* edited by O. Cuntz, in *Itineraria Romana,* vol. 1 (Leipzig, 1929).

Markale, Jean. *L'Épopée celtique en Bretagne.* Paris, 1971.

————. *L'Épopée celtique d'Irlande.* Paris, 1971.

Martin, E. *Zur Gralsage.* Strassburg, 1880. Arthur is seen as the Maimed King, p. 31 ff.

Matarasso, Pauline. *The Redemption of Chivalry: A Study of the Queste del Saint Graal.* Geneva, 1979.

Matthews, William. *The Tragedy of Arthur.* Berkeley and Los Angeles, 1960. A study of the *Alliterative Morte Arthure.*

Maynardier, Gustavus Howard. *The Arthur of the English Poets.* Boston and New York, 1907, 1935.

Megaw, Basil. "Norsemen and Native in the Kingdom of the Isles." Illus. *Scottish Studies,* University of Edinburgh, vol. 20 (1976), pp. 1–44. Prof. Megaw is an authority on the Kings of Man.

Menzel, Donald H. *A Field Guide to the Stars and Planets.* Boston, 1964.

Merlin: A Prose Romance. Edited by Henry B. Wheatley. 2 vols. EETS. London, 1899. An excellent edition that lists the places named for King Arthur.

Merlin: Roman en prose du XIIIe siècle. Edited by Gaston Paris and Jacob Ulrich. 2 vols. Paris, 1886.

Merriman, James Douglas. *The Flower of Kings: A Study of the Arthurian Legend in England and between 1485 and 1835.* Lawrence, Kans., 1973.

Meyer, E. H. *Die Mythologie der germanen Miscellanea Hibernica.* Strassburg, 1903. This compilation emphasizes the solar nature of the twelve Round Table Knights, and so on.

Meyer, Kuno. Death Tales from *Selections from Ancient Irish Poetry.* London, 1928.

————. *The Death Tales of the Ulster Heroes.* Dublin, 1906.

Meyer, Paul, ed. "Les enfances Gauvain. *Romania* 39 (1910): 1–32.

Miller, Helen Hill. *Realms of Arthur.* New York, 1969. A careful and readable book emphasizing the Welsh origin of King Arthur. Excellent maps of England in the Dark Ages, locating Camlan at Camelford (Cornwall) and *Mons Badonicus* (Mount Badon) below the Swindon Gap, i.e., at or near Bath, England. Arthur sites in modern Wales are carefully located also.

Millar, Ronald. *Will the Real King Arthur Please Stand Up?* London, 1978. A witty and charming book. Arthur's battle sites believed jokingly to be found in Brittany, France.

Millican, Charles B. *Spenser and the Round Table.* Cambridge, 1932.

Morgan, Mary Louise. *Galahad in English Literature.* Washington, 1932.

Morris, John. *The Age of Arthur.* New York, 1973. See the excellent table of dates.

Morris, Richard, ed. *Legends of the Holy Rood.* London, 1871. Mss. from the British Museum and Bodleian Libraries. See the story of Saint Helena, mother of Constantine, and how she found the Holy Rood in Jerusalem (pp. xxi–xxiv).

Morris, William. *The Defense of Guinevere.* London, 1858.

Morrison, L. *Manx Fairy Tales.* Douglas, 1929.

Mort Artu. Edited by J. Douglas Bruce. Halle, 1911.

Morton, H. V. *In Search of England.* London, 1927, 1960. Illustrated. A beautiful travel book with much material on Glastonbury, Hadrian's Wall, and King Arthur.

Muir, T. S. *East Lothian.* Cambridge, 1915. Excellent folding map after page 52, giving the Pictish place names: Ca(e)rlaverock, Moffat, Laverock (hill), Keith, Traprain (law), Petter, Tantallon (castle), Adder, Calder, Cairndinnis, Tyne, Pencaitland, Aber (lady), Long Niddry, and Tranent.

———. *Linlithgowshire.* Cambridge, 1912. Muir points out that the Battle of Badon Hill can still be thought of as having occurred in Scotland, on Bowden Hill, 5 miles southeast of the royal seat at Linlithgow, thus, adjacent to the Glasgow-Edinburgh corridor. One should add that there is also Bowden Village, on the slope of the Eildon Hills, and that it too is a possibility.

Müller, Friedrich Max. *Chips from a German Workshop.* vol. 2. Paris, 1859; New York, 1897. *Comparative Mythology:* 1856, pp. 1–141.

———. *Essai de mythologie comparée.* Paris, 1859.

Munch, R. A. *Chronicle of Man and the Sudreys.* 2 vols. Douglas, 1874. The Sudreys are the southern islands, held by Norway in the Middle Ages, and including the Isle of Man.

Murray, James A., ed. *The Complaynt of Scotlande.* EETS, Extra Series 17. London, 1872.

———. *The Romance and Prophecies of Thomas of Erceldoune.* EETS. London, 1875.

Myrvyrian Archaiology of Wales. Edited by Owen Jones, Edward Williams, and W. O. Pughe. Denbigh, 1870. There was an earlier edition in 3 vols. (London, 1801–7). Both editions are mentioned for completeness; I have never seen a copy.

Napier, Arthur Sampson. *History of the Holy Rood-tree.* EETS Original Series, # 103. London, 1894.

Nennius. *British History and the Welsh Annals.* Edited by John Morris. London and Totowa, N.J., 1980. There is a reediting of Harleian 3859, which also contains the Welsh Annals (*Annales Cambriae*), as edited (Paris, 1929) by Edmond Faral: *La Légende Arthurienne,* vol. 3, and collated by Mommsen's *Nennius* (Berlin, 1892).

———. *Historia Brittonum,* from *Monumenta Germaniae Historica III.* Berlin, 1898.

————. *Nennius et l'Historia Brittonum.* Edited by F. Lot. Paris, 1934. See also Faral's *La Légende arthurienne,* vol. 1 for the Nennius MS named Chartres, MS fr. 98: *Annales Cambriae, Genealogies of Wales,* and *Mirabilia Britanniae.*

Newell, William Wells. "William of Malmesbury on 'The Antiquity of Glastonbury.' " *PMLA* 18, no. 4 (1903):459–512.

Newstead, Helaine. *Bran the Blessed in Arthurian Romance.* New York, 1939, 1966.

Newton, A. P. *Travel and Travellers of the Middle Ages.* New York, 1930.

Nichols, Marianne. *Man, Myth, and Monument.* New York, 1975.

Niel, Fernand. *Dolmens et Menhirs.* Paris, 1972.

————. *Albigeois et Cathares.* Paris, 1965.

————. *Montségur, la montagne inspirée.* Grenoble, 1967.

————. *The Mysteries of Stonehenge.* Paris, 1974; New York, 1975.

Nilsson, Martin P. *The Mycenaean Origin of Greek Mythology.* Berkeley and Cambridge, 1932.

Nordenskiöld, A. E. *Facsimile Atlas.* Ed. by J. B. Post. Stockholm, 1889; New York, 1973. Two of Ptolemy's maps of ancient Britain (pp. 7 and 11): Boroniae 1462, Argentinae 1513. Both place Geoffrey of Monmouth's "Caledonian Forest" in Scotland.

Notitia Dignitatum, ed. O. Seeck. Berlin, 1876. This record of offices, officials, and their ranks in the Roman Empire; ranks often attributed to Arthur: count of the Saxon Shore *(Comes litoris Saxonici per Britanniam),* and duke of Britain *(Dux Britanniarum).*

Nutt, Alfred T. *Studies on the Legend of the Holy Grail.* New York, 1965.

————. *The Critical Study of Gaelic Literature.* 1902; reprinted New York, 1971.

Nutt, Alfred, and Kuno Meyer. *The Voyage of Bran.* 2 vols. London, 1895–97.

O'Connor, D. *St. Patrick's Purgatory, Lough Derg.* Dublin, 1895.

O'Dell, A. C., et al. "The St. Ninian's Isle Silver Hoard." *Antiquity* 33 (1959):241–68. The excavations here were suggested by the great scholar of Stirling, W. Douglas Simpson, in 1955. The date for the founding of Whithorn is here given as 397, well before the life of King Arthur, then.

O'Donovan, John. *Banquet of Dun na n-Gedh.* Dublin, c. 1841. See the question of the All Father, p. 51, which has suggested to me an etymology for *Arthur:* Ollathair.

————. *Tracts Relating to Ireland.* Dublin, 1841.

Ogier le Danois. For this medieval romance, see the Danish edition: *Olger Danske Kronnike,* illustrated, edited by C. Molbech (Copenhagen, 1842). The Castle of Avalon, where Arthur slumbered for 200 years, is mentioned (pp. 235–36). He is called "King Artus of England."

O'Grady, S. H., ed. and trans. *Silva Gadelica.* 2 vols. London, 1892.

Olrik, A. *The Heroic Legends of Denmark.* Translated by Lee M. Hollander. London and New York, 1919.

Olschki, Leonardo. *The Grail Castle and Its Mysteries.* Translated by J. A. Scott. Los Angeles and Berkeley, 1966.

O'Rahilly, C. *Ireland and Wales.* London, 1924.

O'Rahilly, Thomas F. *Early Irish History and Mythology.* Dublin, 1946.

————. *The Two Patricks: A Lecture on the History of Christianity in Fifth-Century Ireland.* Dublin, 1942, 1957.

Ó Ríordain, Seán P. *Tara. The Monuments on the Hill.* Dublin, 1965.

Ó Ríordain, Seán P., and Glyn Daniel. *New Grange and the Bend of the Boyne.* London, 1965.

Orosius. *Historiarum adversus paganos.* Edited and translated by B. Thorpe. London, 1854. Written c. 418.

Otto, Rudolf. *The Idea of the Holy.* Translated by John W. Harvey. Oxford, 1926.

Owen, D. D. R. *Arthurian Romance.* Edinburgh and London, 1933. Admirable essays from outstanding scholars.

Paien de Maisières. *La Demoiselle à la mule, ou La Mule sanz frain.* Edited by Boleslas Orlowski. Paris, 1911.

Pannekoek, Antoine. *A History of Astronomy.* New York, 1961.

Panofsky, Erwin. *Studies in Iconology.* New York, 1939, 1962. See chapter 3, "Father Time," but Merlin is not mentioned.

Paris, Gaston. *Histoire poétique de Charlemagne.* Paris, 1856. Gaston Paris is admired as a great scholar but also as a man of independent mind.

————. *Mélanges de littérature française au moyen âge.* Paris, 1912. Reprints of early articles on Chrétien de Troyes, where Paris first noticed the uncanny knowledge of British geography in the various romances. He also held strong for Chrétien's probably Celtic origins, noting that his sources were certainly not French.

Patch, H. R. *The Other World.* Cambridge, Mass., 1950; New York, 1970.

Paton, Lucy Allen. "Merlin in Geoffrey of Monmouth." *Modern Philology* 41 (1943): 88–95.

Patrick, Saint. *Libri Sancti Patricii.* Edited and translated by Newport J. D. White. London, 1918.

Pauphilet, Albert. *Etudes sur la Queste del Saint Graal.* Paris, 1921. Here Pauphilet argues that the Grail attributes are the same as God's, its castle a representation on earth of the celestial Jerusalem. Thus, King Arthur's alleged journey to Jerusalem finds another possible interpretation here.

————, ed. *La Queste del saint graal.* Paris, 1923. See the introduction by Pauphilet.

————, ed. *Poètes et romanciers du Moyen Age.* Paris, 1952.

Perceval li Gallois. Edited by Charles Potvin. 6 vols. Mons, 1866–71. This edition contains *Perlesvaus*, Chrétien's *Perceval*, plus his continuators (Pseudo-Wauchier, Wauchier, and Manessier).

Perlesvaus: Le Haut Livre du Graal. Edited by W. A. Nitze and T. A. Jenkins. 2 vols. Chicago, 1932–37; New York, 1972. This immensely valuable critical edition represents textual scholarship at its height.

Perlesvaus. See *The High History of the Holy Graal*, edited and translated by Sebastian Evans, in Everyman's Library, edited by Ernest Rhys (London and New York, n.d. but reprinted under the same English title in 1969).

Pernoud, Régine, ed. *Poésie mediévale française.* Paris, 1947.

Peter de Langtoft's Chronicle, as modified and expanded by Robert Mannyng de Brunne (1288–1338), edited by Furnivall in 1725. See *Chronicle of England* (the Inner Temple MS), EETS (c. 1901), edited by W. E. Mead.

Peutinger Table, The. See *Die Peutingersche Tafel*, edited by K. Miller (Stuttgart, 1916). This is an ancient map of the world, which shows the 16 Roman sites in what is now southeastern England, or the Saxon Shore.

Piankoff, Alexandre. *The Wandering of the Soul.* Edited by Helen Jaquet-Gordon, Bollingen Series XL. 6 (Princeton, 1974). Proof that Irish and Arthurian literature also comes from the much older literature of the Middle East.

Picard, Charles. *Les religions préhelléniques (Crète et Mycènes).* Paris, 1948.

Piggott, Stuart. *Ancient Europe.* Chicago, 1965. Correspondences pointed out between Arthurian literature and that of archaic Greece.

————. *The Druids.* London, 1968. In the series "Ancient People and Places," edited by Dr. Glyn Daniel.

————. "The Sources of Geoffrey of Monmouth." *Antiquity* 15 (1941): 269–86. Brilliant proof and defense of Geoffrey of Monmouth by one of the most eminent historians of our world.

Pindar. *Pythian Odes.* Translated by Sir John Sandys. London and New York, 1927. We have constantly thought of the Grail Castle here in terms of the other, ancient, oracular sites.

Plinval, G. de. "Pelage et le mouvement pelagien." In *Histoire de l'église,* edited by A. Fliche and V. Martin. Paris, 1937. See vol. 4: 79–128 for Pelagius and, thus, for the doctrinal leanings of Uther Pendragon.

Ponsoye, Pierre. *L'Islam et le Graal.* Paris, 1958.

Pourrat, Henri. *Saints de France.* Paris, 1951. Illustrated.

Powell, Thomas G. E. *The Celts.* London, 1958.

Propp, Vladimir Ja. *Morphologie du conte.* Moscow, 1928; Paris, 1970. Study of the fairy tale.

Prose Lancelot. See *Romans de la Table Ronde, Vulgate Version,* etc.

Prose Lancelot ("Death of Arthur" section). See *The Death of King Arthur,* translated by James Cable (London, 1971).

Prose Lancelot ("Quest" section). See *The Quest of the Holy Grail,* translated by P. M. Matarasso (London, 1969).

Ptolemy's Geography: *Claudii Ptolemaei Geographia.* Edited by C. Müller. 2 vols. (Paris, 1883–1901).

Puech, Henri-Charles. *Le Manichéisme.* Paris, 1949.

————. *La Queste du Graal.* Paris, 1965.

Quest of the Holy Grail, The. Translated by Pauline Matarasso from *Queste del Saint Graal,* part of the *Prose Lancelot.* (London, 1969, 1971), introduction and notes.

Rahn, O. *Kreuzzug gegen den Graal.* Fribourg, 1933. Arguing the Albigensian origin of the Grail and of the Grail Castle, situated, then, in southern France, and not in Britain.

Ralph of Coggeshall. *Chronicum Angelicanum.* Edited by J. Stevesson. London, 1875. See Rolls no. 66.

Ravenna Cosmography, The. See *Ravennatis Anonymi Cosmographia,* edited by I. A. Richmond and O. G. S. Crawford, in *Archaeologia* 93 (1949): 1–50. Accurate knowledge of the idea of geography of the ancient peoples.

Ravenscroft, Trevor. *The Spear of Destiny.* New York, 1973. Nazi scholarship and mysticism re the Grail and its initiation ceremonies. See p. 69 ff.

Red Book of Hergest, The. See *Mabinogion,* edited by Lady Charlotte Guest (London, 1877), especially for her notes, such as to the Thirteen Treasures of Britain, among which is the mantle of Arthur, conferring invisibility, as in Hans Christian Andersen's "The Emperor's New Clothes."

Rees, Alwyn and Brinley. *Celtic Heritage.* London, 1961.

Renaut de Beaujeu. *Le Bel inconnu.* Edited by G. P. Williams. Paris, 1929. This is perhaps part of a Gawain cycle.

Rerum britannicarum medii aevi scriptores. [Medieval Writers of British Affairs.] Edited by Rev. Josephus Stevenson. Vols. 1–10. London, 1857–64. The standard chronicles of British history.

Rey, H. A. *The Stars: A New Way to See Them.* Boston, 1952, 1962, 1967, 1970, 1975).

Rhys, Sir John. *Celtic Folklore, Welsh and Manx.* Oxford, 1901.

————. *Celtic Heathendom.* London and Edinburgh, 1888. This book is also sometimes called "The Hibbert Lectures for 1886."

————. *Lectures on the Origins and Growth of Religion.* London, 1892.

————. *Studies in the Arthurian Legend.* London, 1891. 1966.

————. "The Coligny Calendar" [of Gaul]. *Proceedings of the British Academy,* 1909–10, p. 207 ff.

————, ed. Preface and Select Bibliography to *Le Morte d'Arthur,* by Sir Thomas Malory. London, 1906–61.

Rhys, Sir John, and David Brynmor Jones. *The Welsh People.* London, 1900.

Richard of Cirencester. *De situ Britanniae.* In *Six Old English Chronicles,* edited by J. A. Giles p. 419 ff. London, 1900. Note that *De situ Britanniae* is a spurious work, *a fake chronicle, not to be taken seriously.*

Richmond, I. A. *Roman Archaeology and Art.* London, 1969. A most authoritative study of the Romanization and Latinization of Britain.

————, ed. *Roman and Native in North Britain.* London and Edinburgh, 1958.

Rickard, Peter. *Britain in Medieval French Literature: 1100–1500.* Cambridge, 1956. See chapter 3 on the Arthurian material, Geoffrey of Monmouth, and Chrétien de Troyes. Present research corroborates the various positions taken by this scholar, especially his conclusion re Geoffrey of Monmouth: "It is clear . . . that Geoffrey certainly did not invent his heroic conception of Arthur, but rather redeemed him from the relative neglect of previous historians" (p. 75).

Ringbom, L. J. *Graltempel und Paradies.* Stockholm, 1951.

Ritchie, Graham and Anna. *Scotland: Archaeology and Early History.* London, 1981.

Ritchie, Robert L. G. *Chrétien de Troyes and Scotland.* Oxford, 1952.

Rivet, A. L. F., and Colin Smith. *The Place-Names of Roman Britain.* Princeton, 1979.

Roach, W. *Continuations of the Old French Perceval.* Philadelphia, 1949–54.

Robert de Boron. *Le Roman de l'Estoire dou Graal.* Edited by William A. Nitze. Paris, 1927. Or see *Romans de la Table Ronde,* edited by Paulin Paris.

Robinson, J. Armitage. *Two Glastonbury Legends: King Arthur and Joseph of Arimathea.* Cambridge, 1926.

Robinson, James Harvey. "'The Fall of Rome.'" In *The New History,* pp. 154–94. New York, 1912.

Roger of Wendover. *Chronica sive Flores historiarum.* Edited by H. G. Hewlett. 3 vols. London, 1886–89. Roger reports that two monks in the year of 458 found in Jerusalem the head of John the Baptist. Thus, logically, Gawain sought the sword that had beheaded John the Baptist, found it, and presented it to the Grail King.

Roger, Mrs. G. Albert. *The Coronation Stone.* 10th ed. London, 1916.

Rolleston, T. W. *Myths and Legends of the Celtic Race.* London, 1911; Boston, n.d.

Romans de la Table Ronde. Edited and translated by Paulin Paris. 5 vols. Paris, 1868–

77. Paulin Paris, the father of Gaston Paris, was one of the founders of medieval studies and of Arthurian studies.

Roques, Mario. *Le Graal de Chrétien et la Demoiselle du Graal.* Geneva and Lille, 1955.

Roscoe, Thomas. *Wanderings through North Wales.* London, n.d.

Rosenberg, Alfred. *Der Mythus des 20. Jahrhunderts.* Munich, 1930. Again, a part of the Hitler search for the Grail Castle, or myth of the twentieth century.

Ross, Anne. *Pagan Celtic Britain: Studies in Iconography and Tradition.* London and New York, 1967.

"Round Table Again." In *Adventures in the Middle Ages,* p. 86 ff., by Laura Hibbard Loomis. New York, 1962. See bibliography also.

Royal Commission. *An Inventory of the Ancient Monuments on Anglesey.* London, 1937. Such a scholarly and official document eliminates Anglesey as a possible site of the Holy Grail or Grail Castle.

Saint-Graal, Le. Edited by Eugène Hucher. 3 vols. Le Mans and Paris, 1875–78.

St. Vincent, Bory de. *Essai sur les Iles Fortunées et l'Atlantide.* Paris, 1803.

Sakatvala, Beram. *Arthur: Roman Britain's Last Champion.* New York, 1967.

Saxo Grammaticus. *The Danish History.* Translated by Oliver Elton. 2 vols. London, Copenhagen, Stockholm, Berlin, and New York, 1905.

Scherer, Margaret R. *About the Round Table.* New York, 1945. Illustrated.

Schlauch, Margaret. *Romance in Iceland.* Princeton, 1934.

Scott, Sir Walter. *Chivalry; Romance; The Drama.* London, 1834.

———. *Complete Poetical Works.* Edited by Horace E. Scudder. Boston and New York, 1900.

———. *Provincial Antiquities of Scotland.* Edinburgh, 1834.

Scudder, Vida D. *Le Morte Darthur of Sir Thomas Malory: A Study of the Book—Its Sources.* London and New York, 1921.

Sculland, H. H. *Roman Britain: Outpost of the Empire.* London, 1979. See in particular the chronology, pp. 179–81.

Selections from Ancient Irish Poetry. Translated by Kuno Meyer. Edinburgh, 1911.

Sellar, W. D. H. "The Earliest Campbells—Norman, Briton or Gael?" *Scottish Studies* 17, no. 2 (1973): 109–25. One theory traces the Campbells to King Arthur and to the kingdom of Strathclyde, which he ruled, says Sellar.

Severin, Tim. *The Brendan Voyage.* London, 1978. Illustrated.

Severus, Sulpicius (or Sulpitius), c. A.D. 425? *Vita Martini.* Edited and translated with an introduction by Jacques Fontaine. Série des Textes monastiques d'Occident, vol. 133. Paris, 1967. See also the series "Patrologie latine" (Amboise, 1845). It may be possible some day to make a claim for this Sulpicius as the reported tutor of Gawain. The connection between Saint Martin and Saint Ninian of Galloway seems solid.

Seznec, Jean. *The Survival of the Pagan Gods.* Translated by Barbara F. Sessions. Bollingen Series 38. New York, 1953.

Shelley, Henry C. *Untrodden English Ways.* Illustrated by H. C. Colby. Boston, 1910. Chapter 3 notes the equation *Mount Badon* = Bath but does not adopt it.

Simpson, William Douglas. *St. Ninian and the Origins of the Christian Church in Scotland.* Edinburgh and London, 1940. This scholar-librarian finds that archaeology supports his research, which traces St. Ninian's ministry in Scotland from c. 400 to c. 432.

———. *Skye and the Outer Hebrides.* Worcester and London, 1967.

————. *Stirlingshire.* Cambridge County Geographies. Cambridge, 1928. Illustrated. Most helpful on Roman roads in the areas adjacent to the Antonine Wall.

————. *The Historical St. Columba.* Cambridge, 1928.

Singer, Samuel. *Wolfram und der Gral: Neue Parzivalstudien.* Bern, 1939.

Sir Gawain and the Green Knight. Edited by Denton Fox. Englewood Cliffs, N.J., 1968.

"Sir Gawain in Staffordshire." *The London Times,* May 21, 1958, p. 12. In a most ingenious account, the author traces Gawain's journey to the Green Knight's fortress: across the Wirral peninsula, the Dee River, and through North Wales.

Sir Gawayne: A Collection of Ancient Romance Poems . . . Edited by Sir Frederick Madden. Bannatyne Club, 1839.

Sir Perceval of Galles. The Thornton MS. Edited by J. O. Halliwell. London, 1844.

Skene, William Forbes. *Celtic Scotland: A History of Ancient Alban.* Edinburgh, 1887.

————, ed. *Fordun's Chronicle of the Scottish Nation.* Edinburgh, 1873?

————. *Four Ancient Books of Wales.* 2 vols. Edinburgh, 1868. See book 1, p. 297, for "The Death Song of Uthyr Pendragon"—Uther was belted with the rainbow, riding above the storm of battle.

Smeaton, Oliphant. *The Story of Edinburgh.* London, 1905.

Smith, Isobel F. *Windmill Hill and Avebury.* Oxford, 1965.

Snell, F. J. *King Arthur Country.* London, 1926.

Sone von Nansay. Edited by Moritz Goldschmidt. Tübingen, 1899.

Spence, Lewis. *Boadicea.* London, 1937. Illustrated.

————. *The Fairy Tradition in Great Britain.* London, 1948.

————. *The History and Origins of Druidism.* London, 1947; Totowa, N.J., 1976.

————. *The Mysteries of Britain.* 4th ed. Illustrated by Wendy Wood. London, 1945? The books of Lewis Spence are very hard to find. His work on Druidism contains an excellent chapter on Scotland and Saint Columba and a bibliography of 13 pages.

Squire, Charles. *Celtic Myth and Legend.* London, n.d. but probably 1903; Hollywood, 1975.

Steiner, Rudolf. *Le Mystère chrétien et les mystères antiques.* Paris, 1947.

Stenton, Sir Frank Merry. *Anglo-Saxon England.* Oxford, 1961.

Stillingfleet, Edward. *Origines Britannicae.* Oxford, 1842.

Stoker, Robert B. *The Legacy of Arthur's Chester.* London, 1965. Makes a good case for the coronation of King Arthur as at Chester.

Stokes, Whitley, ed. *Irische texte.* Leipzig, 1891.

————. *Three Irish Glossaries.* London, 1862.

Stone, J. F. S. *Wessex before the Celts.* London, 1958.

Strzygowski, Joseph. *L'Ancien art chrétien de Syrie.* Paris, 1936. See the Antioch Chalice on the frontispiece, showing Christ seated, and again opposite p. 88. He argues for the eastern origin of the Antioch Chalice, and he seems to have a well proven case. I do not know that anyone has claimed it as Celtic.

Stuart, John. *The Sculptured Stones of Scotland.* 2 vols. Aberdeen, 1856, 1967. Stones from Whithorn and Kirkmadrine on the Rhinns of Galloway prove the existence of these fifth-century monasteries.

Stuart Knill, Ian. *The Pedigree of Arthur.* Devon, 1972.

Stukeley, Rev. Dr. William. *An Account of a Roman Temple and other antiquities near Graham's Dike in Scotland.* London, 1720.

————. *Itinerarium curiosum.* London, 1776.

————. *Stonehenge, a British Temple restored to the British Druids and Avebury.* Parts 1 and 2. London, 1740. Works and drawings of Stukeley may be seen at Avebury.

Sulpicius, or Sulpicius. See Severus.

Taliesin (Taliessin). *The Poems of Taliesin.* Edited and annotated by Sir Ifor Williams. Dublin, 1975. The introduction and notes are in English.

————. *The Poems of Taliesin.* Translated by J. E. Caerwyn Williams. Dublin, 1967.

————. "Hanes Taliesin." See Giles's *Six Old English Chronicles.* Appendix 2, p. 501 ff.

Tatlock, John Strong Perry. *Legendary History of Britain: Geoffrey of Monmouth's Historia Regum Britanniae and Its Early Vernacular Versions.* Berkeley, 1950.

Taylor, Henry Osborn. *The Classical Heritage of the Middle Ages.* New York, 1901, 1911, 1925. A handy reference book for names and rapid identification of authors and texts.

Taylor, Rev. Isaac. *Words and Places. . . .* London, 1885. He suggested that the name Arthur came perhaps from the Celtic *ard* = high.

Tennyson, Alfred Lord. *Idylls of the King.* Illustrated by Gustave Doré. London, 1859–85. A first edition in the Denison Library, Scripps College, Claremont, Calif.

Thom, Alexander. *Megalithic Sites in Britain.* London, 1967.

Thomas, Charles. *Britain and Ireland in Early Christian Times: A.D. 400–800.* London, 1971. See pp. 38–42 for a discussion of *Mons Badonicus,* which the author incorrectly says "present opinion" places in Dorset, at Badbury Rings.

Thomas, Nicholas. *A Guide to Prehistoric England.* London, 1960. Excellent maps of the Glastonbury area.

Thomas of Britain and Brother Robert. *The Romance of Tristram and Ysolt.* Edited and translated by Roger Sherman Loomis. New York, 1967.

Thompson, E. A. "Zosimus on the End of Roman Britain." *Antiquity* 30 (1956): 163–67. Zosimus is the Greek historian, born c. 365, whose history covers the years 407–25. He speaks of Constantine who left Britain in 407; and then there was a rebellion.

Thompson, Stith. *Motif-index of Folk-literature.* Bloomington, Ind., 1932–36.

Thorpe, Benjamin. *Anglo-Saxon Chronicle.* 2 vols. London, 1861.

Thurneysen, R. *Irische Helden- und Königsagen.* Halle, 1921.

Todd, Malcolm. *The Northern Barbarians.* London, 1975.

Togail Bruidne De Derga (The Destruction of Da Derga's Hostel). Edited by Whitley Stokes. Paris, 1902.

Toland, J. *History of the Druids.* London, 1726.

Tolkien, J. R. R., and E. V. Gordon, eds. *Sir Gawain and the Green Knight.* Oxford, 1968.

Tompkins, Peter. *Secrets of the Great Pyramids.* New York, 1971.

Toynbee, Jocelyn M. C. *Art in Roman Britain.* London, 1962, 1963.

Trevelyan, M. *Folklore and Folk-Stories of Wales.* London, 1909.

Trioedd Ynys Prydein (The Welsh Triads). Edited and translated with commentary and introduction by Rachel Bromwich. Cardiff, 1961, 1979.

Tristan and Iseut, The Romance Of. Edited by Joseph Bédier and translated by Hilaire Belloc and Paul Rosenfeld. New York, 1965.

Tristan and Isolt, The Romance of. Translated by Norman B. Spector. Foreword by Eugène Vinaver. Evanston, Ill., 1973.

Turner, Sharon. *The History of the Anglo-Saxons.* Vol. I. Paris, 1840. Turner notes under the year 437 that Riothamus, a British chieftain in Brittany, led 12,000

Britons vs. the Visigoths, according to Sidonius Apollinaris, III, 9. Turner asks if Riothamus could have been Arthur. See John Morris, *The Age of Arthur* (pp. 90, 251, 256); he changes the date.

Two Old French Gawain Romances. Edited by R. C. Johnston and D. D. R. Owen. Edinburgh, 1972.

Tyler, F. C. *The Geometrical Arrangement of Ancient Sites.* London, 1939.

Uden, Grant. *Dictionary of Chivalry.* London, 1968. Excellent for names and descriptions of weapons and siege machinery.

Van Gennep, A. "Rites de passage." In *Religions, et moeurs et légendes.* 5 vols. (Paris, 1908–21).

Varley, Rev. Telford. *Winchester.* Illustrated by Wilfrid Ball. London, 1910. This informed work uncovered no evidence of King Arthur's presence in Winchester, but Varley was "grateful" to Geoffrey of Monmouth for his assertions to that effect.

Varro, M. Terentius. *Res rusticae.* Edited and translated by W. D. Harper and H. B. Ash. Cambridge and London, 1954.

Vernant, J.-P. *Mythe et pensée chez les Grecs.* Paris, 1965.

Vian, Francis. *La Guerre des géants.* Paris, 1952.

Villemarqué, Viscount Hersart de la. *Myrrdhinn ou l'enchanteur Merlin, son histoire, ses oeuvres, son influences.* Paris, 1867.

―――. *Romans de la Table Ronde et les contes des anciens Bretons.* Paris, 1842. This antiquarian-scholar has been repudiated, especially his anthology of Arthurian pieces. His work began appearing in the *Revue de Paris* in 1841. Thus, he was a true precursor of medieval studies.

Vinaver, Eugène. *Malory.* Oxford, 1929.

Vincent de Beauvais. *Speculum historiale.* See *triplex,* lib. 23, cap. 147. Vincent reports on Helinandus and his Graal report, as translated in the appendix.

Vita Gildae, as attributed to Caradoc of Llancarvan. Edited by T. Mommsen. Berlin, 1894.

Vulgate Version of the Arthurian Romances. Edited by Heinrich Oskar Sommer. 8 vols. Washington, 1908–16.

Wace. *Le Roman de Brut.* Edited by Le Roux de Lincy. 2 vols. Rouen, 1836.

Wace and Layamon. *Arthurian Chronicles.* Translated by Eugene Mason and edited by Gwyn Jones. London, 1912, 1977.

Wacher, John S. *Roman Britain.* London, 1978. Wacher speaks of King Arthur as a "shadowy figure" (p. 267).

―――. *The Towns of Roman Britain.* Berkeley and Los Angeles, 1974. See p. 406 et passim for Carlisle.

Waddell, L. A. *Phoenician Origin of Britons, Scots, and Anglo-Saxons.* London, 1924. Supporting material in defense of Geoffrey of Monmouth.

Wade Evans, Arthur. *Welsh Christian Origins.* Oxford, 1934.

Wainwright, F. T. *The Problem of the Picts.* Edinburgh, 1955.

Warner, Rev. R., F. A. S. *History of the Abbey of Glastonbury.* London, 1826.

Watkins, Alfred. *The Old Straight Track: British Trackways.* London, 1920, 1922.

Watson, William J. *The History of the Celtic Place-Names of Scotland.* Edinburgh, 1926.

Weigall, Arthur. *Wanderings in Roman Britain.* London, 1926, 1938.

Wells, H. G. *Outline of History.* Vol. 1. New York, 1920, 1961.

Wentz, W. Y. E. *Fairy-Faith in Celtic Countries.* Oxford, 1911.

West, G. D. French Arthurian Verse Romances, 1150–1300: An Index of Proper Names. Toronto, 1969.

Weston, Jessie L. From Ritual to Romance. Cambridge, 1920.

——. Lancelot. London, 1901.

——. Legend of Sir Perceval. 2 vols. London, 1906–9.

——. The Quest of the Holy Grail. London, 1913.

Wheeler, Sir Robert Eric Mortimer. Maiden Castle, Dorset. Oxford, 1943.

Whitehead, Alfred North. Religion in the Making. The Lowell Lectures. New York, 1926.

Whitelock, D. English Historical Documents, c. 500–1042. Cambridge, 1954.

William of Malmesbury. De antiquitate Glastoniensis ecclesiae. 1129–39. Quoted extensively by Edmond Faral in vol. 2 of La Légende arthurienne, p. 452 ff.

——. De gestis regum anglorum. Edited by William Stubbs. London, 1887. Written c. 1120; second recession made in 1127; third and fourth recensions made in 1135 and 1140. Translated as Chronicle of the Kings of England by J. A. Giles (London, 1911).

Williams, Charles, and C. S. Lewis. Arthurian Torso. London, New York, and Toronto, 1948.

Williams, Sir Ifor. "Mommsen and the Vatican Nennius." Bulletin of the Board of Celtic Studies 11 (1944):43–48.

Windisch, Ernst. Concise Irish Grammar. Translated by Norman Moore. Cambridge, 1882.

Winstanley, Lillian. "Science and the Celtic Tradition." The Welsh Outlook 4 (1917):237–39. An early corroboration and defense of the historical material in Geoffrey of Monmouth.

Winter, William. Over the Border. New York, 1911. Twenty-three illustrations, many of important sites in the Arthur country of Scotland.

Wolfram von Eschenbach. Parzival. Edited by Karl Lachman. Berlin and Leipzig, 1926.

——. Parzival. Edited and translated by A. T. Hatto. London, 1980.

——. Parzival. Edited and translated by Helen M. Mustard and Charles E. Passage. New York, 1961.

Wood, Eric S. Collins Field Guide to Archaeology in Britain. London and Glasgow, 1963.

Woodland, W. Lloyd. The Story of Winchester. London, 1932.

Wood-Martin, W. G. Traces of Elder Faiths in Ireland. London, 1902 or 1903. One copy in the British Museum, London.

Wright, J. K. Geographical Lore in the Time of the Crusades. New York, 1925. Knowledge of two hemispheres explains why King Arthur was called "king of the antipodes" in the twelfth century. Theory explained: reversal of the seasons.

Young, Ella. Unpublished material bequeathed to Scripps College, re Irish Fire Festivals. Denison Library. Women's Collection.

Zachrisson, Robert Eugen. Romans, Kelts and Saxons in Early Britain. Uppsala, 1927.

Zarnecki, George. Art in the Medieval World. New York, 1975.

Zatzikhoven, Ulrich von. Lanzelet. Edited by K. A. Hahn. Frankfurt, 1845.

Zimmer, Heinrich. Nennius Vindicatus. Berlin, 1893. See also "Nennius Retractus," Revue Celtique, no. 15, p. 174 ff.

Zumthor, Paul. Merlin le Prophète. Lausanne, 1943.

INDEX